Alberto Cavalli

The Master's Touch

Essential elements of artisanal excellence

with Giuditta Comerci *and* Giovanna Marchello

foreword by Stefano Micelli

Marsilio

Authors
Alberto Cavalli
with Giuditta Comerci *and* Giovanna Marchello

A project of
Cologni Foundation for the Métiers d'Art

Coordination
Alessandra de Nitto

in collaboration with
Federica Cavriana
Francesca Sammartino

Original edition: *Il valore del mestiere. Elementi per una valutazione dell'eccellenza artigiana*, by Marsilio Editori s.p.a. in Venice (October 2014)

The English edition was made possible thanks to the generous support of the Michelangelo Foundation for Creativity and Craftsmanship.

Translation
Alphaville

Editor
Christina Grisewood

Unless an English source is referenced in the footnote, all translations of quotations are our own.

First published: May 2017
ISBN 978-88-317-2434-0
www.marsilioeditori.it

Cover photo
Parchment rosette by Elena Dal Cortivo (Milan, 2000), replica of the decorative soundboard rosette on the Gilbert Desruisseaux harpsichord 1678–1679 (Cité de la Musique-Philarmonie de Paris). Photo © Emanuele Zamponi

Design by InEdita servizi editoriali, Milan

TABLE OF CONTENTS

11 Preface
by Barbara Geary Truan

15 Foreword
by Stefano Micelli

THE MASTER'S TOUCH

19 1. From an idea to its realization: artisanal work and Italian excellence
by Alberto Cavalli

- 19 1.1. The role of the artistic crafts in Italy's manufacturing pre-eminence
- 29 1.2. The artistic crafts and the truthfulness of the hand
- 33 1.3. The artistic crafts today: talent and method
- 36 1.4. Recognition: a way out of the economic and vocational crisis
- 41 1.5. The artistic crafts as cultural deposits and methodological paradigms

45 2. Legal aspects: attributions, competent bodies and comparisons
by Alberto Cavalli, Giuditta Comerci, Giovanna Marchello

- 45 2.1. National legislation, regional jurisdiction and production specifications
- 58 2.2. Legislation governing the artistic crafts in Italy, France, Germany, the United Kingdom and Japan
  - 61 2.2.1. Artisans and artisanal activities: legislation and definitions
  - 63 2.2.2. Fields in which artisans and craft enterprises can operate: directories, rolls and registers
  - 65 2.2.3. Territorial jurisdiction and prerogatives of national and regional bodies

68 2.2.4. The titles of "Master Craftsperson" and "Maître d'art"
70 2.2.5. Intangible Cultural Heritage, Living National Treasures and Living Heritage Companies
74 2.2.6. Can craft enterprises be classified as "cultural and creative industries"?
75 2.3. The criteria for assessing excellence

77 3. Craft excellence: reflections on definitions
by Alberto Cavalli, Giuditta Comerci, Giovanna Marchello
77 3.1. An evolutionary paradigm for a dynamic definition
82 3.2. A qualitative assessment of the criteria
89 3.3. Defining the concept: terms used to describe craft excellence
89 3.3.1. Authenticity
98 3.3.2. Competence
104 3.3.3. Craftsmanship
111 3.3.4. Creativity
118 3.3.5. Innovation
125 3.3.6. Interpretation
131 3.3.7. Originality
141 3.3.8. Talent
147 3.3.9. Territory
155 3.3.10. Tradition
160 3.3.11. Training

169 4. Perceptions of the artistic crafts in Italy: a quantitative survey
by Alberto Cavalli
169 4.1. Sample and questionnaire design
175 4.2. Survey findings
180 4.3. Future scenarios

183 5. Master artisans in Milan and Lombardy
by Alberto Cavalli, interviews by Giovanna Marchello
183 5.1 The notable features of the artistic crafts of Milan and Lombardy: authenticity and beauty
185 5.2. Between cultural industries and design: a quintessentially Lombard vocation
189 5.3. Crafts and creators: interviews with Lombard masters
193 5.3.1. Carlo Andreacchio, master tailor
201 5.3.2. Renata Casartelli, lacemaker and promoter of Cantù lacemaking
209 5.3.3. Caterina Crepax, paper artist
217 5.3.4. Elena Dal Cortivo, violin-maker specializing in parchment rosettes
223 5.3.5. Pierluigi Ghianda, cabinetmaker
231 5.3.6. Pino Grasso, embroidery

239 5.3.7. Eugenio Monti Colla, marionette theatre director
249 5.3.8. Gio Batta Morassi, violin-maker
257 5.3.9. Alessandro Rametta and Andrea Capriotti, metal sculptors
265 5.3.10. Lorenzo Rossi, violin-maker
273 5.3.11. Gabriella Sacchi, ceramicist
281 5.3.12. Filippo Villa, jeweller
287 5.4. Master matrix
289 5.5. Intangible heritage and the artistic crafts

293 6. Assessing excellence: working tools
by Alberto Cavalli, Giuditta Comerci, Giovanna Marchello
293 6.1. Annotated summary of the overall findings
297 6.2. Proposal for an assessment matrix and rating system
302 6.3. Applicability of the matrix

305 Conclusions: protect, promote, progress
by Franco Cologni

EPILOGUE

315 Expanding the vision of excellence
by Alberto Cavalli, interviews by Giovanna Marchello
319 1. Ludovic Avenel, cabinetmaker
327 2. José Luis Bazán, leather craftsman
335 3. Sophie Beale, milliner
343 4. Marc-Jens Biegel, jeweller
351 5. Elke Dannenberg, porcelain decorator
359 6. Ulrike Dederer, violin-maker
367 7. Gérard Desquand, metal engraver
375 8. Philippe Dufour, independent watchmaker
383 9. Keith Levett, ceremonial and livery tailor
391 10. Dinis Pereira, wool felt embroiderer

399 BIBLIOGRAPHY

411 Acknowledgements

413 Photo credits

Those who fall in love with practice without science are like a sailor who enters a ship without a helm or a compass, and who never can be certain whither he is going.

LEONARDO DA VINCI, *The Book of Painting*

PREFACE

The idea of craftsmanship is in vogue. For years now the word "crafted" seems to appear on products of all kinds – from the cardboard sleeve that fits around a take-away coffee cup, to soap or even pickles – as an indication of quality and authenticity. This is not entirely a bad thing, even if in some cases marketing professionals could be taken to task for a lack of imagination or stretching the truth.

It's not entirely a bad thing because this phenomenon speaks to a real need, conscious or not, to reassert a human element into the post-industrial, increasingly mechanized, technological era that is upon us. In a world where machines seem to be gaining the upper hand, somewhere the pendulum swings and we find ourselves returning to our own hands and remembering how important they are. We find ourselves searching for connections to what is human, to our creative selves, to one another. And it is precisely these vital connections that are embodied in craftsmanship.

Still, as with all things fashionable, there are dangers inherent in craftsmanship's growing popularity: a danger that words become meaningless, or that the beautiful appears banal, or that we are unable to distinguish true from false when it comes to artisanal work.

In its own very precise way, *The Master's Touch* seeks to establish a line of defence in the face of such dangers. The book you hold in your hands, a translation from the original Italian, began with a question and an aspiration. The question: what does excellence in craftsmanship look like? The aspiration: to lay the groundwork of a common language and set of criteria that can be used to distinguish the work of master artisans.

It was natural to focus on Italy. A bastion of high-quality craftsmanship, Italy is recognized the world over for products that are original, durable and exquisite. And for decades, the Made in Italy imprimatur has been growing into what is now a differentiating label for Italian exports. Through careful and systematic research and analysis and in-depth interviews with the finest masters, the authors – like sculptors themselves uncovering shapes in the marble – teased out key ideas in the form of a select terminology: authenticity, competence, craftsmanship, creativity, innovation, interpretation, originality, talent, territory, tradition, training.

Like the very best artisans, the authors published their findings in a spirit of building, inviting discussion and dialogue with a view to refining and perfecting these ideas. They were especially interested in forging a language and way of evaluating craftsmanship which could transcend national boundaries.

In keeping with this spirit, the English edition expands on the original work and the epilogue features ten additional in-depth interviews with master artisans in countries outside Italy. These interviews, which took place in France, Germany, Portugal, Spain, Switzerland, and the UK, allowed for the further testing of the terms in another language across six different cultures and proved them to be both robust and meaningful.

The English translation of *Il valore del mestiere*, the original Italian title of this book, was one of the first projects that the Michelangelo Foundation for Creativity and Craftsmanship undertook. Founded in 2015 by South African business luminary Johann Rupert and Italian entrepreneur, author and cultural authority Franco Cologni, the Foundation is an international, non-profit institution set up to defend the creation of cultural, social and economic value as embodied in master craftsmanship at the very highest levels.

For the Foundation, defining excellence in craftsmanship is important because these definitions allow for the assignment of value and a way of determining – ultimately, in the case of the Foundation, in order to celebrate – which artisans are true masters. They also allow for the showcasing of master artisans and an articulation of a "gold standard" for craftsmanship, one that can inspire all artisans and attract new generations to this realm. This is especially critical in light of the important amount of time and dedication required to become a master artisan. If the very best craftsmanship remains undefined and unrecognized, what would motivate someone to pursue what is a long and sometimes painstaking path?

Building a common language for excellence in craftsmanship also allows people to cross borders: borders that arise naturally due to a diversity of countries and languages, borders associated with the wide-ranging expertise in the various sectors of craftsmanship, and even the borders that separate activities or labels assigned to what constitutes doing or making versus thinking or imagining. As our globalized, interconnected world today so clearly throws into relief, crossing borders is what moves people forward. So building a common language is also a way to usher in the future of craftsmanship.

We hope this book will stimulate an ongoing, vibrant conversation among those interested in the matters explored here. We also hope it will inform, encourage and inspire all artisans everywhere and that it will serve as a concrete testimony to the deep value and ongoing need for their good work.

BARBARA GEARY TRUAN
Secretary General
The Michelangelo Foundation for Creativity and Craftsmanship

Geneva, March 2017

STEFANO MICELLI

FOREWORD

In recent years, the debate surrounding the relevance of craftsmanship to the contemporary world has become increasingly lively and intense. Moreover, growing attention from a variety of sources has been focused on artisanal know-how as an integral component of the entire concept of "Made in Italy" production. Economists, sociologists and design experts have contributed to devising a radically new and forward-looking framework, encompassing a wealth of practices and knowledge that continue to underpin the value of quality Italian products, from fashion and design to engineering and the food industry. In short, craftsmanship is back in the spotlight and once again rightly considered an essential ingredient for Italian businesses to compete on the global stage.

It is worth recalling that the debate has been fuelled in recent years by the rapid change in the general economic climate. The downturn that has plagued Italy since 2008 has led people to think "outside the box" in relation to work. An entire generation has struggled to find a steady, rewarding job, and this has prompted everyone (and especially younger people) to take a fresh look at the concept of employment. Occupations that had long been considered of lesser importance or even doomed to extinction have been reinvigorated, acquiring a new-found appeal, "contaminated" as they often are by digital natives, who see their potential through fresh eyes in a profoundly altered economic environment.

Alberto Cavalli's book is timely, being the first to endeavour to consolidate and summarize the different viewpoints that have proliferated in this period of upheaval. After years of proposals and attempts to revamp the whole "Made in Italy" sector, and artisanal production in particular, it was important to try to reconstruct the findings that had emerged at the national and international levels by reviewing the wide range of contributions on the issue. Cavalli deserves further credit since, in compiling this study, he has tackled head-on some very challenging issues, including the notion of craft excellence.

The question of craft excellence has been dealt with on numerous occasions from both the academic and the legislative perspectives. However, in the light of the debates that have arisen in recent years, it was important to address this topic once more, in order to set out up-to-date assessment methods and to revisit the legislative tools available to national and regional executive bodies. In general, defining excellence is no easy task and is in itself a slippery slope. The word *eccellenza* – excellence – is often abused in the Italian language and has been applied to a variety of institutions and programmes whose chosen paths or projects are not, in truth, necessarily perceived by the market to be either unique or worthy of the term.

The work undertaken by the Cologni Foundation for the Métiers d'Art may surprise even the sceptics. The study has examined an abundance of theoretical material and a wide variety of empirical evidence. Indeed, this book analyses and presents a set of quantitative data alongside a series of interviews with leading artisans from Lombardy and Milan. The masters interviewed represent every facet of quality craftsmanship, from cabinetmaking and fashion to ceramics and violin-making. Their accounts lend significant substance to themes that may otherwise appear elusive: when asked to elaborate on key words, such as "craftsmanship", "authenticity", "competence", "creativity" and "originality", the masters explored their meaning in their respective spheres of expertise, providing references and examples that give life and added depth to the academic narrative.

Similarly, the proposed method for assessing and ranking artisanal skills constitutes a successful marriage of rigour and practicality. By way of conclusion, Cavalli and his working group offer an operating tool, the assessment matrix, that can measure and substantiate that which is judged to be craft excellence. The same themes and categories that the authors used to gather empirical data become the parameters on which the process for assessing quality craftsmanship is built. This method is of particular value as it provides the grounds for awarding the title of "Master" in the traditional sense of the term. The approach is of great utility today in both legal and cultural terms. On the one hand, it enables us to adapt our legislation to be more in line with that of other countries (take, for example, the title of "Maître d'art" awarded in France or that of "Living National Treasure" in Japan). On the other hand, it has finally given us recourse to a reliable procedure for recognizing, in an appropriate manner, the commitment, dedication and hard work of so many artisans in recent years.

THE MASTER'S TOUCH

ALBERTO CAVALLI

1.

FROM AN IDEA TO ITS REALIZATION: ARTISANAL WORK AND ITALIAN EXCELLENCE

1.1. THE ROLE OF THE ARTISTIC CRAFTS IN ITALY'S MANUFACTURING PRE-EMINENCE

> It is not cement or wood or stone or iron or glass that is the most durable material. In construction, the material that stands the test of time is art.
>
> GIO PONTI, Italian architect and designer

In his Bauhaus Manifesto of 1919, Walter Gropius wrote: "Architects, sculptors, painters – we all must return to craftsmanship! For there is no such thing as 'art by profession'. There is no essential difference between the artist and the artisan. The artist is an exalted artisan."

The artist is an exalted artisan. Or, rather, the artist and the artisan are two sides of the same coin, working together in harmony to achieve a level of excellence that manifests itself in difference, uniqueness and competitive advantage. Any study of Italy's current artisanal excellence that aims to provide an accurate portrayal of the know-how that represents the country's true cultural wealth[1] needs to take into account the intellectual, cultural, technical and artistic origins of that excellence. Nor can it overlook the economic relevance of this domain: "[F]our million small businesses and eight million self-employed workers constitute Italy's entrepreneurial heritage. But if all these people, toiling from morning till night in their workshops, share a

[1] See Franco Cologni, "Introduzione", in Paolo Colombo, Alberto Cavalli and Gioachino Lanotte (eds), *Mestieri d'arte e Made in Italy: Giacimenti culturali da riscoprire* (Venice: Marsilio, 2009), pp. 7–10.

feeling that they are working 'against' the system, there is an issue that needs to be addressed".[2]

Despite the economic crisis, and despite the Italian artistic craft sector's severe and longstanding inability to promote itself,[3] the country's extensive and interconnected network of master artisans provides a solid foundation on which a successful economy based on ideas, commitment, experimentation and tradition can be built.

However, ensuring the emergence of a new generation of artist-artisans, capable of turning their talent and creativity into a profession, is and will remain a pressing concern. Therein lies the key to Italy's economic development, for the country's vocation to produce export goods is "deep-seated and stems from the conditions of a fixed physical environment".[4] Also vital to the economy is the web of small businesses through which "Italy has been able to affirm its excellence", and which maintains a firm belief in the "notion of artistic excellence. Because this is what we need: genuine masters of their craft, people who, like all masters, also know how to teach and pass on a constantly evolving *savoir-faire* that can make a tangible, visible and desirable 'difference'".[5]

To foster a new generation of master artisans is thus to ensure a future for Italian quality, a quality that "resides in the workshop *savoir-faire* that consciously underpins all the fields in which our country excels, from the nautical industry to fashion, from design to textiles, and from footwear to woodwork and glassware".[6] It is an excellence rooted in Italy's great and longstanding traditions and is connected to the world of fine crafts: for centuries, Venice, Florence, Milan, not to mention Lucca, Genoa, Naples and Palermo, produced crafts of such artistic and celebrated quality that they were sought after by courts the world over. To this day, Italian craftsmanship can still steer this very challenging market towards the acknowledgement of special, authentic, legitimate and often unique products, at all times made to the highest professional standards, that is, *a regola d'arte* (according to the rules of the art).

All this goes to prove that the "culture of a product crafted *a regola d'arte*, with well-honed skills and creative invention, is by no means centred on the simple and trite replication of an unrepeatable past".[7] This undisputed capacity to revive a centuries-old tradition in

[2] See Dario Di Vico, *Piccoli: La pancia del Paese* (Venice: Marsilio, 2010), pp. 8–9.

[3] *Ibid.*, p. 7.

[4] See Giuseppe Medici, "Editoriale", in *Affari esteri*, No. 1 (January 1969), www.affari-esteri.it/medici.html.

[5] See Franco Cologni, "La scuola dello stile", *AD*, No. 342 (November 2009), pp. 112–114, especially 114.

[6] *Ibid.*

[7] See Lorenzo Ornaghi, "Prefazione", in Paolo Colombo (ed.), *A regola d'arte: Attualità e*

a contemporary key is accompanied today by new prospects linked to distribution systems and specific business sectors: "[T]he artistic crafts – always the same yet always different – are changing. And far from striving merely to survive in the jungle of modern professions, the artistic crafts are quite possibly leading a most adventurous vanguard, steadily heading towards a place where tomorrow's craftsperson will be able to combine, as never before, manual skill and intellectual innovation".[8] The artisans of the future will function as creators, as suppliers, as salespeople, and as links in a network that unites not only a product with a customer but also a territory with a "story".

While the importance of the artistic crafts within the realm of "Made in Italy" excellence is gaining recognition,[9] full awareness of its impact is still far from being achieved. As Italian architect, designer and prominent applied art expert Ugo La Pietra has said,

> The public most often comes in contact with the artistic crafts at street markets [...]. This kind of crafts, however, is often overly ornate and excessive, of a sort that is, with a few exceptions, mostly viewed by official culture as kitsch (or, to put it baldly, bad taste). There is also a more refined artisanal production that reproduces styles and models from the past [...]. Those practising the artistic crafts have always held themselves apart from these spheres, distinguished by their ability to renew the language defining what we shall call "Artistic Crafts of Excellence", fashioned by individual creators and expressed in a contemporary language, yet without trespassing into the world of art.
>
> To these categories must be added those artisans (carvers, inlayers, engravers, etc.) working for medium-sized firms (especially in the furniture and fashion industries) who handmake components that are eventually assembled, as well as artisans whose work is integral to industrial production, who craft the moulds and models (in wax, plaster, wood, etc.) used in serial production. Another category (and perhaps the most refined of all) comprises artisans working on one-off assignments, such as custom-made furnishings (for both private and public spaces). This last category has recently expanded to include artisans producing limited edition objects commissioned by designers (artist editions).
>
> [...] Within such diversified categories, it is difficult to outline a strategy for development and valorization: each category is a world of its own, with its specific set of creative, productive and commercial rules and principles.[10]

prospettive dei mestieri d'arte in Lombardia e Canton Ticino (Milan: Vita & Pensiero, 2005), pp. 7–9, especially 9.

[8] See Paolo Colombo, "Stabili confini e mutevoli frontiere", in Colombo (ed.), *A regola d'arte*, pp. 11–30, especially 14.

[9] See, for example, Dario Di Vico, "Le scuole d'arte e i mestieri da salvare", *Corriere della Sera* (6 April 2010), p. 3, and Colombo, "Stabili confini e mutevoli frontiere", p. 15.

[10] See Ugo La Pietra, "Dov'è l'Artigianato?", *Artigianato tra Arte e Design*, No. 75 (September–November 2009), p. 6.

Italy's artisanal professions are thus both diverse and well defined, as are the positions they occupy within the country's production system.

Many artisans today, as La Pietra reminds us, still own their shops and sell their goods directly to the consumer. Their workshops are often strategically located in streets laden with history, and the toponymy of Italy's city centres is frequently linked to the "trades" that were once practised there. Hidden away in these streets are what one might call "survivor workshops", still selling unique pieces, made by hand or using highly specialized manual techniques; these little-known establishments are often perceived as relics of a bygone era, yet they have the potential to become extremely attractive and indeed successful modern-day destinations for customers and experts in search of exclusive, original and authentic items. A new approach to cultural and responsible tourism could therefore involve promoting these destinations, highlighting traditions and an expertise not found anywhere else, replete with memory and meaning on a par with artistic heritage but also in tune with today's changing marketplace.[11]

But that is not all. A master craftsperson is also a professional working in his or her own atelier, supplying high-quality products, representing an economic reality of high added value for all the categories that fall under the "Made in Italy" umbrella, a sector that has always been passionate about personalized creations: "The success of Gucci, which [...] went from bankruptcy in 1994 to its recent worth of over nine billion dollars, is founded on two rather simple but essential elements. The first is innovative design [...]. The second [...] has always been at our fingertips – right here in our own back yard – and consists of our incredible culture of quality, a culture that enables us to deliver a truly special product. [...] This cultural strength is something unquestionably unique to Italy and holds a real and perceived value even abroad."[12] From fashion to design, from the nautical industry to mechanics, the crafts sector – as we are about to illustrate – builds, complements or effectively produces components or parts essential to the perfect accomplishment of the final product.[13]

Lastly, there are the highly prestigious firms, whose central figure is the artistic director, around whom the whole organization very often revolves.

[11] A hope expressed, for instance, by Silvia Venturini Fendi, creative director at Fendi, president of AltaRoma and promoter of *The Whispered Directory of Craftsmanship: A Contemporary Guide to the Italian Handmaking Ability*, Vols I and II (Milan: Mondadori Electa, December 2010 and September 2011 respectively).

[12] See Domenico de Sole, "Gucci e i mestieri d'arte", in Fondazione delle Arti e dei Mestieri (ed.), *L'intelligenza della mano* (Milan: Vita e Pensiero, 2000), pp. 47–51, especially 49.

[13] See Colombo, Cavalli and Lanotte (eds), *Mestieri d'arte e Made in Italy*.

Whether tailors or decorators, tyre-tread engravers or wood inlayers, today's master artisans cannot be considered merely as a specialized workforce. Rather, they should be looked upon as a precious reserve of knowledge and ideas essential to the development of Italy's high-end production system. As Martin Roth, former Director of London's Victoria and Albert Museum, said in an interview with the Russian newspaper *Vedomosti*: "The luxury goods sector relies on craftsmanship and artisanal know-how: take, for instance, the deluxe car industry, where so much of the detail is still made by hand. But if you are too conservative, you lose sight of what it means to have these skills, of how to apply them in real life. New artisanal profiles should be considered."[14]

The emergence of new profiles, new professions and specific new sectors has given rise to unexpected new artistic crafts, unimagined only a few years ago: "[E]ven along unbeaten, tortuous and sometimes invisible tracks, the artistic crafts of the past have proved capable over the decades of reinventing themselves, rising successfully to the challenges posed by changing processes and techniques and gaining a vital economic role even in the context of the post-industrial society".[15]

Eloquent examples of this gradual evolution of the artistic crafts can be found in restoration, a field encompassing not only the conservation and protection of Italy's rich cultural heritage, but also the preservation of works of contemporary art and design. Indeed, the latter are often made of perishable or cutting-edge materials that are difficult to restore. But not impossible: in Italy, there are specialized workshops where the most advanced technologies combine with a tradition-rich know-how, mindful of the artworks' "soul" and thus ensuring a sensitive and respectful approach to the task in hand.

The artistic crafts thus seem to occupy a rightful place at the very heart of the "Made in Italy" concept, shaping and enlivening a creative and cultural production process keenly focused on uniqueness, innovation and quality.

A fresh approach, one that accords well with recent international studies carried out in this field, might involve revising the classic definition of crafts (the Italian term *artigianato* has a very broad and inclusive meaning, which says more about the size of the business than the techniques or the quality of the finished product) to focus more on the different relationships that the master artisan is able to develop with the world of production. But first of all we must reflect briefly on the typical

[14] See Alberto Cavalli, "Ручное управление", in *Vedomosti Pyatnitsa*, No. 41 (273), (21 October 2011), p. 4.

[15] See Colombo, "Stabili confini e mutevoli frontiere", p. 14.

characteristics of artisanal work, ones that are shared by all those who feel they belong in this domain, namely: "[A]n autonomy that translates into entrepreneurship; an aptitude for dialogue and relationship-building that favours the development of tailor-made products; [and] a capacity to reinvent tradition in a way that transforms cultural production".[16]

The role, the function and the value of artisanal work thus belong to a macro-area characterized by entrepreneurship, the capacity to create customized products, and a contemporary interpretation of tradition. Within this macro-area there are specific niches and sectors where the talent and skills of the artist-artisan become yardsticks and the source of genuine and authentic cultural products. And while it is true that these master artisans number little more than a few hundred,[17] it is also true that their example and their capacity to perfectly blend tradition with the spirit of the times provides an important touchstone for all those artisans who have chosen instead to devote themselves to a single segment of the production process, specializing in crafts of perhaps a less artistic nature, but nonetheless bearing the stamp of personalization, independence and perfect adherence to the customer's wishes.

As New York Times journalist and Pulitzer Prize-winner Thomas L. Friedman wrote,

> average is officially over. Being average just won't earn you what it used to. It can't when so many more employers have so much more access to so much more above average cheap foreign labor, cheap robotics, cheap software, cheap automation and cheap genius. Therefore, everyone needs to find their extra – their unique value contribution that makes them stand out in whatever is their field of employment. *Average is over.*[18]

"Average is over" means that, to gain a competitive edge, there is a need to develop something more, based not only on a knowledge economy or on a workforce devoted to mass production, but also on a genuine capacity to continually reinvent one's professional skills so as to be able to follow, meet or even foresee the market's needs.

Master craftspeople often naturally possess this capacity, their trade having always been inseparable from a production process that involves personal creativity, and in which communication with designers, clients, distributors, colleagues and other stakeholders is essential to the elaboration of new solutions.

[16] See Stefano Micelli, *Futuro artigiano* (Venice: Marsilio, 2011), p. 98.

[17] *Ibid.*, p. 97.

[18] See Thomas L. Friedman, "Average Is Over", *The New York Times* (24 January 2012), www.nytimes.com/2012/01/25/opinion/friedman-average-is-over.html.

Ca' Foscari University professor and economist Stefano Micelli made an interesting distinction between three types of artisans, which he divided into "translators", "creatives" and "adapters".[19]

The "translators" are those artisans who are capable of infusing a project with all the care, design awareness, culture and passion[20] that are key to transforming an industrial designer's or fashion designer's sketch into an excellent final product. Model-makers, for instance, do not merely execute a concept, they *interpret* it. Their expertise relates not only to the "physical execution of a drawing, but also to ensuring that these shapes are meaningful for people's lives and that they will be compatible with complex production processes".[21]

As the Italian art critic, painter and philosopher Gillo Dorfles affirms: "[T]oday [...] we are finally witnessing the return of a greater balance between the upholders of standardized design processes and those who still believe that, for man and for the artist, working by hand is not only possible, but indeed desirable".[22]

The fame and prestige of the "Made in Italy" mark also (and rightly) derives from the high quality of even its series-produced goods – a quality that in many cases is directly attributable to the artisans behind them, such as the aforementioned model-makers.

For their part, the "creatives" are the great masters descended from the Renaissance tradition: perfectly adhering to the rules of their artistic discipline, they very often create highly recognizable one-off pieces that convey a sense of community and local identity born of a culture rooted in centuries of purchases, designs and products, often successfully conceived in the face of prejudices and custom. The culture of the Renaissance "workshop", seeped in experimentation and innovation, is still the cornerstone of the success of the "Made in Italy" sector, adapted and handed down by the great masters of the past, for whom the workshop is a laboratory not only for techniques but also, first and foremost, for ideas.

Indeed, in their Manifesto, sociologists Francesco Morace and Giovanni Lanzone assert that to overcome the country's modest economic growth and cultural stagnation, Italy must "bring back to the fore the culture of doing, the experience of the arts and crafts, [and] the concept of the workshop apprenticeship, endowing manual skills with a new dignity and prestige and combining technological innovation and

[19] The distinction is Micelli's and described by him in *Futuro artigiano*, pp. 104–148.

[20] *Ibid.*, p. 108.

[21] *Ibid.*, p. 109.

[22] See Gillo Dorfles, "Finalmente è pace tra design e artigianato", *Mestieri d'Arte*, No. 1 (June 2010), p. 16.

traditional artisanship. In so doing, it should draw inspiration from the Renaissance, with its capacity to integrate knowledge, progress and learning".[23]

The revival of manual activity, which is attracting not only increasing attention but also demand, attests to the newfound need among people today to leave a direct mark on the objects they come into contact with or indeed produce. The Renaissance workshop, a melting pot of art and techniques, is currently experiencing a comeback as an emblem of the true excellence of Italian manufacturing, synonymous with a unique and recognizable style encompassing fashion design, design, stringed instruments, glassware, embroidery and goldwork, not forgetting textiles, floriculture, entertainment, restoration, nautical products and much more.

These are the artistic crafts that generate products of excellence and international renown, exported worldwide thanks to the passion and creativity that artist-artisans still put into their fusion of materials, history and art. These are the workshops that keep the Italian manufacturing system alive, that successfully combine flexibility in the production process with creative intelligence, marketing awareness and a more human touch, creating a virtuous cycle between workshops, design studios and businesses.

Lastly, there are the artisans that Micelli termed "adapters", those who contribute to the life of an object after it has been cut loose by its creator: if it is true that luxury is that which is made to last and can be repaired, as they like to remind us at Hermès, it can also be said that "personalization of a product by means of artisanal work is not a prerogative of luxury goods".[24] Therefore, concludes Micelli, "it might be interesting to envision [...] ways we could promote a new work pattern between industry and crafts in order to bridge the gap that separates global industrial production and the design flair of our artisanal laboratories".[25] To be a master artisan today means, therefore, to take account of a multifaceted reality, often, it must be said, sharing only a similar methodological approach, namely: a lengthy learning process, workshop training, business skills and autonomy, as well as vision, innovation and mastery of traditional techniques. But do artistic craft workshops akin to those that over the centuries have produced some of the world's most beautiful artefacts, such as Cellini's salt cellar or Stradivari violins, still exist?

[23] See "Manifesto", in Francesco Morace and Giovanni Lanzone, *Verità e bellezza: Una scommessa per il futuro dell'Italia* (Milan: Nomos, 2010), pp. 112–113, especially 112.

[24] Micelli, *Futuro artigiano*, p. 137.

[25] *Ibid.*, p. 148.

The answer to this question can be found in the most profound meaning of the expression "Made in Italy". For "Made in Italy" does not refer merely to the place where the item was manufactured; it has a much loftier and broader significance, recalling not just the act of making but also the know-how behind the making, namely the ability to blend technique and creativity, precision and talent. It is a gift that has been enriching Italy for centuries and does so to this day, finding expression in a host of different activities that can be described both as "artisanal", in light of the know-how and technical expertise they require, and as "artistic", owing to the creativity and experimentation they involve.

We cannot talk about the Cremonese art of making stringed instruments, for instance, without acknowledging the extraordinary legacy of Amati, Stradivari and Guarneri del Gesù. But giving due recognition to the past should not blind us to the fact that to this day master artisans are still building superb instruments within a realm that attracts students and enthusiasts of every nationality, while the triennial "Antonio Stradivari" violin-making competition is a rite of passage for every budding master in this field.[26] The mark made by Amati, Stradivari and Guarneri "goes beyond the direct line: musicians have been endorsing the excellence of their instruments for over five centuries, and countless artisans from all over the world choose to follow, partially or entirely, in their footsteps. Many contemporary instruments bear a clear echo of their work, paying meaningful, immediate and daily homage to the classical Cremonese school and to the genius of its masters".[27] And, today, some 155 workshops in Cremona and its surroundings – veritable "urban woodlands" where wood is transformed into musical instruments – are the places where "the ritual of work and effort, of silent dialogue with the materials that have a life of their own and that therefore eloquently respond to the incisive questions posed by the tools and the hands"[28] is celebrated every day.

A master artisan's contribution to contemporary society involves not only the creation of an object, but also the transmission of a method, of an attention to quality and innovation, and of a hands-on approach that is still capable of making the difference. As Jean-Michel Delisle, former president of the Institut National des Métiers d'Art, so aptly puts it:

[26] See, for example, Renato Meucci, *Strumentaio: Il costruttore di strumenti musicali nella tradizione occidentale* (Venice: Marsilio, 2008).

[27] See Virginia Villa, "'L'arte di far instrumenti'. Liutai a Cremona tra XVI e XIX secolo", in Virginia Villa (ed.), *Costruttori di armonie: La liuteria dalla materia al gesto* (Venice: Marsilio, 2012), published in conjunction with the exhibition of the same name, held at the Milan Auditorium Fondazione Cariplo (5 December 2012–5 May 2013), pp. 24–27, especially 26.

[28] See Alberto Cavalli, "Artefici di bellezza autentica", in Villa (ed.), *Costruttori di armonie*, pp. 52–53.

"[F]or their vitality and authenticity, and for the enduring qualities of their products, these professions are more crucial than ever for the stability of our territories, for our quality of life and for job creation [...]. The artistic crafts [...] represent hope for a whole generation of upcoming entrepreneurs, artisans and creators who want to forge a new path towards economic and social development".[29]

Traditional artisanal activities, such as those that still uphold the name of Murano for glasswork, Cremona for stringed instruments, Milan for fashion, Naples for tailoring, Turin for cars, Modena for engines, Vicenza for goldwork, Valenza Po for jewellery, Como for silk, several Italian regions (Tuscany, Liguria, Campania, Veneto and Marche) for nautical products, and so on – although admittedly some of these areas are experiencing a period of crisis – are now joined by a new breed of artisanal activities.

Contemporary artisans in fact have their roots in and reinterpret ancient traditions, endeavouring to give form to the demands and expectations of a changing and fast-moving society, while constantly pursuing new ways to marry state-of-the-art technologies with tradition and innovation.

The excellence of Italian manufacturing is still based on a workshop mindset that values creativity, manual skill, expertise and curiosity. The requisite qualities of a master artisan are in fact intelligence, patience, exceptional artistic flair and a firm determination to learn and create. Today's artist-artisans are irreplaceable professional partners not only for industrial designers, but also for fashion designers, who could not achieve international fame and success without the aid of tailors, model-makers, *premières mains*, embroiderers and visual merchandisers. Theatre directors could not bring their visions to life without stage and costume designers; the key players in the luxury goods industry could not possibly meet the needs of their extremely demanding clientele if they did not work side by side with the great artisans specializing in the creation of shoes, leather goods, jewellery, timepieces, perfumes and goldwork, not to mention those working in the nautical and mechanical industries.

These master artisans, who are becoming increasingly rare and are highly sought after and valued, are the embodiment of a person who can "think, imagine, mentally elaborate, develop, model, cut, sew, conduct, interpret and adapt. In other words, they are capable of creation".[30] The products of Italy's "manual intelligence" are much in demand and

[29] See Jean-Michel Delisle, "Giornate Europee, i mestieri d'arte entrano in scena", *Mestieri d'Arte & Design*, No. 7 (April 2013), p. 16.

[30] See Gianluca Tenti, "La bottega delle meraviglie ci salverà", *Mestieri d'Arte & Design*, No. 7 (April 2013), p. 5.

internationally admired. They represent an extraordinary cultural as well as economic resource, an established and valued excellence that relies on quality and efficiency, but also on passion and a willingness to accommodate technology, contemporary tastes and research. This is why we must make sure that these "living treasures", as the greatest master artisans are called in Japan, pass on their know-how to a new generation of masters who can embrace tradition, reinvigorate it and carry it forwards to the future.

Very few areas in Europe can boast an array of activities, professions and traditions as rich and as vital as Italy's. Such variety and richness require not only a nomenclature, but also, first and foremost, a proper cultural framework. To reiterate our earlier point, master artisans must not be looked upon merely as a skilled workforce, but as the originators of our much-celebrated excellence.

That excellence must now be revitalized, reclaimed and rediscovered, both in terms of production and distribution and in terms of training and communication.

1.2. THE ARTISTIC CRAFTS AND THE TRUTHFULNESS OF THE HAND

As Carlalberto Corneliani, founder of the eponymous menswear firm established in Mantua in the 1950s, rightly points out: "[F]ashion has always been a symbol of social elevation. One of Isabella d'Este's gowns could cost as much as a ship. That is why clothes were considered part of a family's patrimony and included in inheritances. It is hardly surprising, therefore, that clothing [in Italy] is seen more as an art form than merely as something to wear".[31]

Clothing as an art form represents an extremely delicate balance between function and design, between the tangible and the intangible expressions of a culture[32] that is quintessentially Italian. While Italy's manufacturing prowess encompasses creation, transformation and production at every level, we must keep in mind that in today's globalized world, the country can and must meet the demand for beauty above all by offering a culturally significant product that remains both pleasing in its style and uncompromising in its quality but that does not cost considerably more than that of its foreign competitors.

[31] See Antonio Mancinelli, "L'eleganza del cuore", in Antonio Mancinelli, Flaminio Gualdoni and Omar Calabrese (eds), *Corneliani* (Bologna: FMR, 2008), pp. 12–25, especially 25.

[32] See Marco Pedroni and Lucia Ruggerone, "La moda nelle discipline sociali", in Paola Bertola and Giovanni Conti (eds), *La moda e il design: Il trasferimento di conoscenza a servizio dell'innovazione* (Milan: POLI.design, 2007), pp. 14–50, especially 15.

A reflection on the essential characteristics of this kind of product must acknowledge the role of those high-end crafts that possess "the strength to create, the will to undertake a challenge, the speed, the ideas, and the passion for the task".[33] Can we continue to extol the virtues of the artistic crafts in an era where the spotlight is resolutely turned towards aspects of a more ephemeral kind? Fashion, some might argue, is by its very nature ephemeral, since it is transitory, elusive, ever-shifting. A clothing style becomes "fashionable" when enough people adopt it. Conversely, when those same people move on to the next trend, that style goes "out of fashion". Fashion's imperative, therefore, is to have a built-in obsolescence, inducing in people the constant urge to buy new clothing in the latest style.[34]

But fashion's ephemeral nature must not, or at least should not, blind us to the fact that this industry is a beacon of research, endeavour, care for detail and personal expression: Italian fashion is a shining example of the successful fusion of art and craft.

The risk of decline, oblivion or, indeed, extinction is anything but remote for more than one of fashion's so-called "artistic crafts", a sector that tends to idolize its master artisans but then swiftly forgets or sidelines them, where they languish in the shadow of the great designers' dazzling careers.[35] Yet, we must include artisans among those that Christian Lacroix defines as the "timeless masters", whose expertise "stems from their eternal youth. Their territory, which was in danger of turning into an elephants' graveyard, is gradually reawakening thanks to the passionate yet respectful kisses of young artisan princes and princesses who have sensed that tomorrow belongs to the hand as much if not more than to the machine".[36]

And if tomorrow does belong to the hand, it is now more important than ever to return this "hand" to centre stage. As the French art historian Henri Focillon reminds us:

> Have we banished from our reflections, as we might banish artisans with a purely mechanical skill, those masters who with exquisite and faultless patience have evoked more concentrated dreams from choice materials and in refined forms? Is the hand of the engraver, the goldsmith, the illuminator, and the lacquerer merely an adroit and complacent servant broken into the practice of

[33] Bertola and Conti (eds), *La moda e il design*, p. 192.

[34] See Teri Agins, *The End of Fashion: How Marketing Changed the Clothing Business Forever* (New York: Harper, 1999), p. 7.

[35] See Paolo Colombo, Alberto Cavalli and Emanuela Mora, *Artefici di bellezza: Mestieri d'arte nella moda italiana* (Venice: Marsilio, 2013).

[36] See Christian Lacroix, "Préface", in Amandine Maziers and Johanna de Tessières (eds), *L'oeil et la main: Les artisans de la haute couture* (Paris: Editions du Collectionneur, 2005), pp. 4–5.

fine work? Is what we call perfection, then, the virtue of a slave? Working in the smallest scope, sure of itself and of its direction, such a hand has already become a prodigy, because it subjects the enormous scale of man and of the world to the dimensions of the microcosm. It is no mere device for reducing something. The discipline of restricted size is less important to it than its own capacity for action and truth.[37]

The word "truth" comes up time and again when examining the relationship between the artistic crafts and the modern manufacturing world. That is because today more than ever the pursuit of authenticity, and therefore of originality and trustworthiness, is considered to be a prerequisite for every luxury object.

The gesture of the artisan's hand conveys a truthfulness that emanates from the material and its transformation and from its creation through the interpretation of a design that becomes a personal expression of talent.

The truthfulness of the hand, and by extension of the materials and the shapes that emerge from it, is essential to the appeal of Italy's finest production, in which the designer's flair is – discretely, quietly, but no less stringently – complemented by the artisan's skill.

Knowledge and intelligence (in the sense of the Latin *intelligere*, to listen and to realize, or to understand) are becoming the distinctive attributes of a work that tends to be anonymous and repetitive. And from this "intelligence", from this deep understanding and instinctive grasp of a product's "meaning", derives that perpetual search for improvement that leads to "achievement", that is, the accomplishment of an objective that requires a combination of knowledge, application, intuition and know-how.[38]

No such achievement would be possible without a dialogue between the person who designs an object and the person who brings that design to life, between the person who feels the spirit of the times and the person who interprets the materials, fashioning them into extraordinary shapes: "Craftsmanship is the one principle through which these brands encapsulate their unique skills within their offering. [...] Craftsmanship is generally a choice, not the lack of one."[39]

Premium crafts must be a choice, a conscious choice – one that, although often undervalued, is shared by all the leading exponents

[37] See Henri Focillon, *The Life of Forms in Art,* 2nd English edition, enlarged (New York: Wittenborn, Schultz, 1948), p. 77.

[38] See Manfredi Ricca and Rebecca Robins, *Meta-luxury: Brands and the Culture of Excellence* (New York: Palgrave Macmillan, 2012), p. 9.

[39] *Ibid.*, p. 44.

of Italian-made excellence. They recognize that at its roots is a hard-working, often scarcely visible, social, cultural and economic entity which falls under the broader category of "artistic crafts" and which infuses Italy's products with a soul, a distinctiveness and a sensual desirability that make them unique. The artistic crafts are thus crucial to the creation of one-of-a-kind or limited-edition objects. Such objects cannot be replaced or exchanged with others that do not share the same creative and productive origins; they radiate an unmistakable intrinsic as well as symbolic and emotional value, the tangible manifestation of those human qualities – talent, inventiveness, skill and masterly interpretation – that make them distinct.[40]

And while it is true that what is beautiful by its nature stands out from the rest,[41] it is also true that Italian manufacturing has often made "beauty" its defining and almost objective criterion, constantly nurturing it through stylistic research alongside artisans' exquisite handiwork.

To foster a better understanding of the contribution made daily by master artisans to the excellence of Italian fashion, we need, however, to adopt a two-pronged approach: one is, of course, to highlight the value of our best creations; the other is to endeavour to avoid falling into the pattern of considering fashion, design and the creation of high-end goods more generally as an artistic discipline and therefore alien to the notions of distribution and production.

Art without the support of the finest techniques would be voiceless for, as Focillon put it:

> [A]rt begins with transmutation and continues with metamorphosis. It is not man's language for communicating with God; it is the perpetual renewal of Creation. Art is the invention of materials as well as the invention of forms. It develops its own physical laws and its own mineralogy. It plunges its hands into the entrails of things to shape them to its own pleasure. First of all art is both artisan and alchemist.[42]

The artisan is an alchemist or, as Walter Gropius would say, the artist is an exalted artisan. Raising this awareness begets the competence, which then becomes excellence. And that calls for a reflection on the economic relevance of this world.

[40] *Ibid.*, p. 47.

[41] As affirmed, for instance, in Hannah Arendt, *Rahel Varnhagen, The Life of a Jewess* (Baltimore: Johns Hopkins University Press, 1997), pp. 88–89.

[42] See Focillon, *The Life of Forms in Art*, p. 71.

1.3. THE ARTISTIC CRAFTS TODAY: TALENT AND METHOD

The source of the much-celebrated but somehow little-studied Italian "excellence" can therefore be traced to the skill, the artistry and the talent intrinsic to the artistic crafts – virtues whose role is not confined to the repetition of outmoded gestures or the replication of antique styles. Quite the reverse, they are essential factors of economic growth, a process that, as Chris Anderson, former editor-in-chief of the US magazine *Wired*, declared, could be led by a new generation of "cottage industries", spanning high-tech and crafts and offering innovative, highly personalized, small-scale products.[43]

Today's master artisans on the one hand fit into the "classic" definition of craftsperson, marked by workshop training, a perhaps informally acquired artistic culture, an ongoing dialogue with customers and designers, and a perfect mastery of the materials and the techniques. On the other hand, they also conform to a more "social" notion of artisan, such as the one described by sociologist Richard Sennett, who sees manual work carried out to the highest professional standards as sharing a variety of characteristics, such as the pursuit of quality, the desire to push creative and technological boundaries, and a deep bond with its roots. These are the elements that, combined, lead to the qualification of a product as "excellent", or indeed "authentic", namely "the fruit not just of an artisanal but also of a 'moral' excellence, born of the recognition of the importance of the bond between a product and its place of origin, including respect for environmental norms – a set of ethical rules crucial in the training of a master artisan and vital to a product's aesthetic outcome".[44]

Workmanship and territory are thus fundamental, as are inspiration and the ability to develop a design through hands-on practice that is always accompanied by thought and experimentation – "technical, interpretive and practical [qualities] that combine with motivation and meaningfulness to determine a product's excellence".[45]

The dividing line between crafts, as described and regulated by Italian law, and the work of master artisans is often hard to discern. The adjective "artistic", as used in the Decree of the President of the Republic No. 288 of 25 May 2001, which lists the artisanal activities related to artistic work, is flexible enough to cover activities and professions that are continually evolving, but not quite precise enough

[43] As reported by Micelli in *Futuro artigiano*, p. 39.

[44] See Franco Cologni and Alberto Cavalli, "Dall'etica all'estetica", *AD*, No. 366 (November 2011).

[45] *Ibid.*

to differentiate between amateurish output and perfectly made crafts fashioned with precious materials using rare techniques – the fruit of creativity and inspiration, a deep connection with their origins, and a close dialogue with customers and designers. Those are the crafts that represent the true competitive advantage in an economic system that has made flexibility and quality of execution the key ingredients of its success.

The International Charter of Artistic Craftsmanship defines works of artistic craftsmanship as:

a) creations, production and works of high aesthetic value, whether inspired by forms, models, decoration, styles and techniques that are traditional or historical, or the result of individual creative development and of personal and artistic forms of expression;

b) works which are mainly carried out using manual techniques, at [a] highly professional technical level, using equipment, but excluding wholly mass-produced works; separate mechanized or automatic work stages are allowed, using innovative techniques and high-technology instruments.

c) [...] works of restoration, designed to conserve, consolidate, or restore works of art, or objects [belonging to the] architectural, archaeological, ethnographic, bibliographic or archival heritage.[46]

This definition, integrating the principles set forth in the Italian Constitution and European Union directives in the field of artistic craftsmanship, is further complemented by the aforementioned set of value-based, cultural and social benchmarks that in the Charter are broken down as follows:

1) Economic value. As well as a cultural heritage, artistic craftsmanship is a key economic and productive resource: a widespread productive network, made up of small companies, workshops and SMI's that are deeply rooted in their local territory, and which constitute a not inconsiderable part of economic value created by the manufacturing sectors.

2) Cultural value. Artistic craftsmanship is a unique cultural heritage and expression of society throughout the ages. Craft businesses are the fruit of an age-old artistic and productive tradition. They are repositories of material and immaterial knowledge, rooted in their local territory. They are also bearers of "universal" cultural values, with their emphasis on design, on the project and

[46] International Charter of Artistic Craftsmanship, issued in 2010 by Ateliers d'Art de France, Confartigianato Imprese, the Confederazione nazionale dell'artigianato e della piccola e media impresa (CAN) and the Kyoto Traditional Arts and Crafts Sponsorship Foundation, and subsequently endorsed by several other partners, Definitions, para. 2, http://wcc-europe.org/sites/default/files/The_International_Charter_of_Artistic_Craftmanship_1.pdf.

on history, and contaminations between other, very different cultural sectors are frequent.

3) Social value. Artistic craftsmanship also contains a "social value", created through interaction with the economy and society of its local area, the community and the surrounding environment. In fact, artistic craftsmanship always has deep roots in the local territory, is integrated into the culture and influences local society. The question of transmission of craft skills should be considered in the light of the above: because, as well as safeguarding traditions and skills, such transmission is essential to protect the social structure of local areas. Craft working is a widespread type of occupation that supports the local economy and small-scale production. It creates jobs, social stability and potential future development. Many areas have age-old productive realities, which risk extinction for lack of generational handover. Artistic craftsmanship is also the primary motor of sustainable economic development in underdeveloped or depressed areas.[47]

These economic, cultural and social values are based on an expertise that can be hard to pass on via a formal school education, but is nonetheless worthy of being safeguarded and protected. At the same time, this is a kind of production that does not want to and can no longer be considered "art" owing to the object's functionality and the working process in which master artisans fully immerse themselves, to the point where life and work often merge into one.

A serious reassessment and communication of the value of the artistic crafts, highlighting their role in Italy's culture, economy and society, is therefore of particular importance in the redefinition of an economic system in perpetual search of identity and characterized by a saturated market that is nonetheless appreciative of the "beautiful and well-made" crafts for which the country is famous.

Such reassessment must go hand in hand with a constant drive to provide education, training and guidance for upcoming generations so that they can familiarize themselves with the contemporary and traditional artistic crafts.

The loss of know-how is a social, economic and cultural loss. And in many sectors this loss is already a looming threat. And while many have voiced support for preserving this precious heritage, we need to put in place the conditions conducive to this long-talked-of "third Renaissance".

[47] See *ibid.* Values, paras 1–3.

1.4. RECOGNITION: A WAY OUT OF THE ECONOMIC AND VOCATIONAL CRISIS [48]

The description of today's master craftsperson as an "artist-artisan" is surely one of the most apt. Falling midway between artist and craftsperson, artist-artisans are professionals who express their talents through processes, techniques, materials and tools dedicated to the creation of one-off or limited-edition objects.[49]

But artist-artisans are more than that: their work lies at the very core of the entire Italian production system. From tiny workshops to larger studios and major companies, Italy's artisanal know-how – be it in the creation of one-of-a-kind artefacts, the production of made-to-measure items or the flawless interpretation of a designer's vision – gives the country a distinct structural and competitive edge.

When we talk of "territory" as the fundamental cultural and economic resource that determines the output of master craftspeople, we are also referring to the "industrial districts".[50] These are networks of generally small and medium-sized enterprises (SMEs), operating in the same area and in a specific sector, benefiting in most cases from the involvement of local institutions – notably universities, research centres and polytechnics – ideally working directly with or in support of the local industry. An industrial district, in other words, is proof of the capacity of local entrepreneurial and institutional (political and technical) systems to promote the competitiveness and long-term development of an area.

These "concentrations" of businesses came into being mainly during the 1970s and 80s on the basis of boundaries defined over the course of centuries, and grew in efficiency and productivity in subsequent decades. The territorial element is manifested in an infrastructure that has a very high economic, social and substantive value arising from the factors that contributed to a district's creation, and successfully underpinned by a forward-thinking and flexible approach to meeting the ever-shifting demands of the global market.

If the artistic crafts are indeed an expression of a territory, in most cases it would be unthinkable to remove these activities from their birthplace (which would imply parting them from their *genius loci*). Yet it has often been lamented that Italy's production system is too fragmented, and many small firms and individual businesses still suffer from isolation. Therefore, establishing a system that preserves the artisan's (or the entrepreneur's) autonomy and independence while promoting a more

[48] This section was written in collaboration with Giuditta Comerci.

[49] See Federica Vacca, *Design sul* filo *della tradizione* (Bologna: Pitagora editrice, 2013), p. 139.

[50] Hereinafter referred to simply as "districts".

efficient pooling of limited resources (such as investment in research and infrastructure) would go a long way towards improving the districts' logistical, economic and cultural performance. This is especially true in light of globalization: far-reaching distribution chains are one of the factors that inspired the district model and, with international competition growing ever more intense, should in fact be an incentive to develop these areas further and restructure the "networks".

The creation of a super-network connecting businesses from different districts is one of the constructive and long-term solutions to the current crisis suggested by many economic and industrial researchers, entrepreneurs and master artisans. The output of master artisans, whenever it forms part of a production chain and even if it is modest or tends towards limited series, should be integrated into such a network. This model of entrepreneurial cooperation is duly being promoted and sponsored through the joint initiatives of several institutions, including the Fondazione Symbola per le Qualità Italiane (Symbola Foundation for Italian Quality), Confartigianato Imprese (Confederation of Crafts and SMEs), Confindustria (General Confederation of Italian Industry), Federazione Distretti Italiani (Italian District Federation), Unioncamere (National Union of Chambers of Commerce), Censis (Centre for Social Studies), Bank of Italy, Fondazione Edison, Istat (National Institute for Statistics) and Intesa Sanpaolo bank.[51]

While master artisans hold their independence dear, a challenging and competitive context such as the present one necessitates the creation of a connected system. No small and lovingly tended garden – to borrow one of Voltaire's favourite metaphors – can be left to languish on the sidelines, cut off from the world's economic and cultural flows. For they represent a fertile opportunity for Italy to recover the splendour and pre-eminence that, during the early part the second millennium, made the country, in the words of French historian Fernand Braudel, one of the most extraordinary displays of intelligence on the face of the earth.[52]

There is no shortage of candidates to take this initiative forward. Notable among these is the Italian District Federation, whose mission is to foster relations between its different constituents, helping to match needs and skills. Founded in 1994, the Federation serves as a focal point for the many national districts, working closely with universities, financial

[51] This partnership led to the creation of the National Observatory of Italian Districts in 2009. The institution's mission includes providing, in a timely manner, clear and reliable data on the evolution of Italy's district system. Its reports documenting the state and vitality of the districts and the difficulties facing them are an important resource in this respect. The fourth report was issued on 21 March 2013.

[52] See Fernand Braudel, *Le Modèle italien* (Paris: Flammarion, 2008).

institutions and banks. One of its achievements has been the injection of specific competences into single districts, to make available the latest innovative financial solutions that are best suited to the development of research projects and the introduction of new technologies.[53]

The interrelationship between know-how, creativity and enterprise – a formula that has always set the "Made in Italy" mark apart and that has been the subject of sociological and small business policy studies in the United States – perfectly encapsulates the country's greatest productive strength, and highlights the historical debt that Italian entrepreneurship owes to the peninsula's age of greatest splendour: the Renaissance. This precious heritage has endowed the country with a unique sense of beauty and aesthetics, superior technical quality, limitless creativity, and mastery.

The Renaissance workshop has become once again the paradigm of the finest Italian production, one that epitomizes its manufacturing quality through its ability to infuse competence, local know-how, creativity and innovation into different contexts and sectors.

Italy's small and medium-sized enterprises have drawn the nutrients for their development from the build-up of knowledge over time. Even prior to the celebrated union with design, the importance of these enterprises has always resided in that skilled artisanal know-how capable of accomplishing great work with limited tools or in that sheer love of producing something of the highest quality, which is ultimately an expression of self-love, respect for one's work and a desire to make something worthy for the community. For years, nay, decades in these territories this culture of "making things well" has been enriched by an experiential knowledge and practical intelligence passed down from one generation to the next, and by the specialization of production chains. [...] This is the story of the thousand mayors who, along with the Chambers of Commerce, gave these small enterprises their first means to become competitive, the story of the rural and artisans' banks which, knowing their clients, gave businesses the loans they needed to turn an idea into a reality. Italy might not have venture-capital structures, but it can count on a network of small and medium-sized banks that have protected the country from the invasion of "junk finance".[54]

[53] "Among the Italian District Federation's other noteworthy initiatives are those supporting the testing of innovative models of district networks. The Federation was, for instance, behind the creation of the 'Ultra-district', bringing together the agricultural, fishing and food-producing districts of San Daniele del Friuli, Nocera Inferiore-Gragnano, Mazara del Vallo and Vulture to jointly promote their 'Made in Italy' products. A cooperation project has also been launched between Verona's fashion district and Puglia's textile districts for the supply of semi-finished materials to the 145 members of the Verona Fashion Consortium." See Antonio Ricciardi, "Le PMI localizzate nei Distretti industriali: vantaggi competitivi, evoluzione organizzativa, prospettive future", *Quaderni di ricerca sull'artigianato, Rivista di Economia, Cultura e Ricerca dell'Associazione Artigiani e Piccole Imprese Mestre CGIA*, No. 54 (May 2010), note 14, p. 142.

[54] See Emilio Genovesi, "Officina Italia", in Giovanni Lanzone and Francesco Morace (eds), *Il talento dell'impresa: L'impronta rinascimentale in dieci aziende italiane* (Milan: Nomos, 2010), p. 214.

It is not just the broader dimensional aspect of the Italian company, but first and foremost its origins and, in consequence, its cultural and functional structure and means of passing on knowledge that have defined its trajectory, its strengths and weaknesses. Its limited size, which has shaped its identity, and its technical specialization also entail downsides arising from weak political power, high risk and scarce capital to invest in relevant areas of research, innovatory restructuring, internationalization, brand communication, and management. This is the reason mergers in the small business sector have been found to be unworkable and are consequently very rare. The system of networks has instead proved to be the most effective and appropriate solution, successfully conveying a message of unity and strength while preserving the individuality of each component.

And this is precisely why the further development of the districts and the creation of a "super-network", backed by an effective communication strategy, targeted research and innovation, are the best ways to steer Italy out of the doldrums precipitated by the 2007–2008 global financial crisis.

In this respect, Francesco Morace invites us to consider the crisis as an opportunity to enact change to bring about stronger and more lasting growth:

> In a crisis, the eye of the storm can produce a miracle: it can offer a new perspective, allowing for a more holistic vision of the world and a deeper reflection on the meaning of our existence – the basis for a new Renaissance. […] The eye of the storm helps us see with new eyes, and we are seeking to concretize this vision with the people and the businesses that have made clear that they want to be part of this adventure. In Italy, that adventure involves using our talents and qualities to give renewed impetus to the "Made in Italy" sector. Further afield, it means searching out other renaissances elsewhere in the world, from Silicon Valley's green energy to Indian microcredit schemes, from the social power of Web 2.0 that helped propel Obama to the White House, to the cultural festivals that can revitalize a city. […] The renewed emphasis on *substance*, understood as the pursuit of a tangible quality, is at the root of a phenomenon that places manual skill, and therefore the very essence of crafts, at its centre. This approach has gathered momentum over the last few years, and is manifested mainly in the array of objects, those everyday neo-artisanal items (without disregarding a connection with series production). From fashion to design, all the way to expressions of a more artistic nature, competence and technical skill have become the drivers and soul of creativity, giving life to "industrial products" that are nonetheless original, surprising and pleasing to the eye.[55]

[55] See Francesco Morace, "La sfida e il senso della nuova impresa italiana: Dalla evocazione alla vocazione", in Lanzone and Morace (eds), *Il talento dell'impresa*, p. 227.

Within the world of the artistic crafts, quality is rightly considered the key ingredient of success, to which many companies in recent years have aspired in revamping their production processes and which has been the object of research and innovation. With this in mind, this publication has made it its mission to shed an empirical and historical light on that elusive notion of "excellence".

The district system has proved effective in supporting and facilitating research and knowledge-sharing among the companies forming part of it. Coexisting in the same territory certainly favours the immediate exchange of a know-how that can only be learnt through repetition, as practitioners of the artistic crafts well know.

Within a network system, the mindset and problem-solving abilities of a master artisan can translate into a surprising capacity for resource mobilization, the coordination and repositioning of skills, and the selection of new energies and technical or creative expertise. In other words, they can play a role at the level both of a single product and of a company's overall functioning in ways that larger-scale enterprises are unable to do. The true lesson that artisans still have to teach is their way of assessing size, potential and material in order to devise solutions to real problems, drawing on Italy's resources, cultural wealth and idiosyncrasies. To accommodate small and medium-sized enterprises that cannot or do not want to grow, we must develop an economic, social, financial (bank loans) and production policy that can make the most of these resources, supporting them in developing their potential and overcoming their deficiencies.

The world of artistic craftsmanship is certainly one where independence plays a key role in ensuring that artisans have the creative and practical freedom to "do well to feel well". But independence does not, or should not, imply isolation; on the contrary, the history of the country and of its economic development (of which the districts are a noteworthy manifestation) has always put the individual and the community at its centre.

A perceptive, receptive, cultured and participative community naturally leads more smoothly to the development of that "territorial authenticity" that makes the difference. It moreover provides a cultural, economic, logistical and institutional framework in which the master craftsperson can feel completely at home in a system that is devoted not to mass production but to the pursuit of quality.

Our analyses carried out in the course of this research into the characteristics and definitions of the artistic crafts indicate the need for more complete and specific legislation in this domain. The definitions provided by the 2001 presidential decree, not unlike many of the regional production specifications, tend to lack precise assessment criteria. How do you identify the "high artistic value" of a creation? At what point can you say that the link with tradition has been broken? Is the use of a material characteristic of an area enough to make a product "typical"? How far can you push innovation before an artefact ceases to be just that? What level of mechanical intervention is allowed for a product still to be considered hand-made?

The answers to such questions will provide the basis for determining what constitutes craft excellence.

1.5. THE ARTISTIC CRAFTS AS CULTURAL DEPOSITS AND METHODOLOGICAL PARADIGMS[56]

Having gifted hands, inventiveness, flair and ability is all very well. But you also need courage, study and, of course, knowledge. You need that whole set of competences that can turn natural talents into powerful tools. What you need, in a word, is *method*.[57]

Method is the ability to reproduce excellence by following the path of tradition, while constantly reinventing it by means of creativity and interpretation. These are the distinguishing attributes of a master craftsperson, which need to be channelled into a "method" that can be passed on only by means of workshop training – a practice that the district and network structures could happily turn into a production system that in and of itself would ensure quality as well as attention to aesthetics and substance.

Workshops and ateliers can teach us important lessons – ways of doing things that may apply to fields outside the sphere of the artistic crafts and that could be of use even to non-artisans. The daily effort artisans consistently put into transforming materials, according to their craft's specific "rulebook", into things of exquisite beauty and singular character can surely inspire new ideas and good practices.

Indeed, those "rulebooks" should be prized also for the precious information they can impart for a society that, as Ugo La Pietra reminds us, is seeking to "duly acknowledge the true value of artisanal culture by undertaking a profound overhaul of the educational and regulatory framework".[58] This transformation is taking place in consultation with

[56] This section was written in collaboration with Giuditta Comerci.

[57] See Sergio Givone, "Socrate e il calzolaio", in Stefania Ricci (ed.), *Il calzolaio prodigioso: Fiabe e leggende di scarpe e calzolai* (Milan: Skira, 2013), published in conjunction with the exhibition of the same name held at the Museo Salvatore Ferragamo, Florence, 19 April 2013–31 March 2014, pp. 65–69, especially 66.

[58] See Ugo La Pietra, "In difesa di una vera cultura del fare", in *Mestieri d'Arte*, No. 1 (June 2010), p. 12.

the design sector, which "is endeavouring to develop its productivity in relation to its own realities [...] and is looking closely at all kinds of small-scale production in which a high level of excellence is attainable through the use of new materials and, most importantly, through adherence to the values embodied in the finest craftsmanship".[59]

The goal is therefore to define a quintessentially Italian *modus operandi*, from which can be derived a methodology that will serve as a set of obligatory criteria to be used in assessing the level of competence or craftsmanship necessary to achieve the highest possible quality.

Step by step, every effort must be made to preserve the artistic crafts from marginalization, an eventuality that could doom them to invisibility or to becoming mere curiosities better suited to a marketing scenario than to a culture of *savoir-faire*. To this end, it is crucial to come up with a relatively objective definition of "excellence", setting out the ideal features of a master craftsperson's methods and practices and backed up by a truly effective and efficient "network", founded on a strong sense of shared identity and informed by a major cultural shift in the way we view artisanship.

Identity and culture are part of the essence of an artefact. Fashioned by the hands of a master artisan, such objects are the fruit of a dynamic balance between virtuoso skill, function and aesthetics.[60] All of this should be placed in a context – be it urban or district – in which the master artisan plays a central role and enjoys a recognition that is currently often lacking.

Effectively communicating these specificities, determined through as objective an analysis as possible, would help master artisans to cast off the cloak of invisibility, afford them the recognition that could inspire new generations to follow in their footsteps, and enhance the level of social prestige that these highest of manual professions deserve. This is especially true in Italy, a country whose land yields no rare raw materials, but which retains an exceptional and unique wealth of knowledge and competence. Italy may not have oil, uranium or gold deposits, but

its cultural patrimony is as vast as the ocean. It is home to priceless artworks and centuries-old traditions and trades that have not been wiped out by modernity but, quite the reverse, have been revitalized by advances in technology and design. A people's wisdom can only grow out of a specific territory, which is in turn an essential value in itself – a value that must be protected, rediscovered and appreciated no less than gold or oil. For a territory is the mother of that

[59] *Ibid.*

[60] See Howard S. Becker, *Art Worlds* (Berkeley and Los Angeles: University of California Press, 1982), p. 275.

sapere (knowledge) and that *sapore* (flavour) that have always embodied a community's identity. Indeed, these two Italian words come from the Latin verb *sàpere*, meaning both "to know" and "to taste of something". It is a flavour that enriches and preserves; it is a wisdom that retains a uniquely human and specific quality, passed down not only by mouth but also by hand, and is thus elevated to a shared and eminently marketable heritage. To consider the territory as a priceless asset, therefore, leads to the awareness that turning the spotlight on culture, arts and crafts does not impoverish anyone, but rather creates a virtuous cycle of knowledge that enriches us all.[61]

That uniqueness, that singularity, that distinctiveness with which only a master craftsperson can imbue an object is deeply linked to the concept of "Made in Italy" excellence and to the cultural significance of this expression. But we must find an appropriate way to communicate this "difference", not only by giving master artisans back the central role that they deserve, but also by rediscovering those methodological paradigms that can provide a holistic and up-to-date image of the "Made in Italy" sector. Seeking to establish an objective assessment of excellence can prove to be an effective communication tool, bearing in mind that, given its complexity, the artistic crafts system, as stated above, "cannot be reduced to a few basic, finite and simplified components, nor can the transmission process be reduced to a mere matter of 'pure meanings' and 'objective messages' [...] Passing on know-how does not mean transferring blocks of information, nor does it mean creating something out of nothing. It is somewhere in between, a way station [...] on the path of a knowledge that is in constant evolution".[62]

Certainly, attempting to attach a mathematical formula to artisanal excellence would be misguided. Rather, we should try to define as clearly as possible the attributes that an "excellent" artisanal product must possess. This means communicating the uniqueness and beauty of the object itself, contributing to an awareness and acknowledgement of that which is "well-made beauty".[63] Such an exercise would serve a dual concrete purpose: that of improving the creators' visibility and that of presenting their method as a set of rules, practices, knowledge and experiences essential to the attainment of the "character" that is the main ingredient of "Made in Italy" excellence.

[61] See Cologni, "Prefazione", p. 7.

[62] See Pascal Mathiot, *Passaggi singolari: Saggio sulla trasmissione dei saperi* (Milan: Vita e Pensiero, 2003), p. 100.

[63] An expression attributed to Mario Boselli, former President of the National Chamber of Italian Fashion.

ALBERTO CAVALLI - GIUDITTA COMERCI - GIOVANNA MARCHELLO

2.

LEGAL ASPECTS: ATTRIBUTIONS, COMPETENT BODIES AND COMPARISONS[1]

2.1. NATIONAL LEGISLATION, REGIONAL JURISDICTION AND PRODUCTION SPECIFICATIONS

A broad survey of the rules and regulations governing craftsmanship, in particular traditional, typical and innovative artistic crafts, will enable us not only to gain a better idea of the extent of existing protection for this sector in Italy, but also to see where the gaps are, assess the political weight of the sector in general on account of its social and economic importance, and gauge the impact, if any, of the protection to date.

Italian legislation pertaining to the traditional and artistic crafts is fixed at different levels. At the national level, it consists of certain guiding principles, which have been left to the regional authorities to clarify and implement through specific legislation. Attention at this level has thus focused on the wording of Framework Law No. 443 of 8 August 1985 for the Crafts and Trades Sector and on Presidential Decree No. 288 of 25 May 2001, entitled "Regulation concerning the identification of the artistic and traditional craft trades, as well as of the made-to-measure garment manufacturing sector". At the regional level, it involves the reception of European and national directives and, accordingly, the enactment of legislation by the regional authorities to give them tangible effect, on the basis of the prerogative conferred on them under revised Section V of the Italian Constitution.[2]

This is not the place for a detailed commentary on the wording of

[1] Section 2.1 was written by Giuditta Comerci; section 2.2 was written by Giovanna Marchello; section 2.3 was written by Alberto Cavalli.

[2] See Article 117 of the Italian Constitution.

national laws. For the sake of brevity and to make it easier to understand what follows, it is sufficient to recall that according to the Framework Law for the Crafts and Trades Sector, the regional authorities are required to adopt measures to protect and develop crafts and trades and to promote artisanal production in all its forms, be they typical, artistic or traditional. This includes, in particular, "facilitating access to credit, technical assistance, applied research, professional training, membership of economic associations, the establishment of craft districts, and export concessions" (Article 1). The Framework Law then provides definitions of "craftsperson" and "craft business" (Articles 2 and 3), sets the limits of a craft business in terms of size (Article 4), establishes a professional register (Article 5) and provides for the possibility of joining consortia, companies and craft associations (Article 6). It furthermore affirms the need to set up Provincial Craft Committees (CPAs) (Article 10) and Regional Craft Committees (CRAs) (Article 11) and entrusts them with the tasks of keeping the registers, checking that businesses are correctly constituted, ensuring the sector is adequately protected and maintaining records of regional statistics.

The regional authorities have taken their cue from this overarching regulation of the sector and its governing bodies. In addition to determining more precisely, through regional instruments, the manner in which those bodies should be established, they have the important function of identifying which crafts and trades are active in their areas, establishing which of these merit specific legislation, compiling the identifying characteristics of each branch of the sector and laying down the methods, specificities and controls that accompany them. Such measures, where implemented properly, have certainly had a favourable impact on the quality of products and provided safeguards for those businesses that follow the rules of authentic artisanal production. At the same time, we felt it necessary to draw attention to all those branches that play a key role in local production and even in the global marketplace, yet are still not covered by any regulations other than those laid down by their own cooperatives.

The regional provisions that articulate and regulate the ethical, commercial and production requirements for artisanal products that are typical of an area and reflect its history are known as *disciplinari* (specifications). Their aim is to provide precise guidelines for those involved in producing artistic crafts of outstanding quality. The specifications are linked to the attribution of regional labels for artistic craftsmanship, where they exist, with slight variations in wording from one region to another. This labelling system was originally devised as a guarantee that an artisanal product met certain standards of excellence. Above all, however, it aims to ensure that artisanal workshops or enterprises are run according to set criteria relating to processes, aesthetics and ethics.[3]

Identifying the characteristics of artistic craftsmanship that meets the highest standards should be the main thrust of the above-mentioned "specifications". Indeed, we must seek to provide as detailed a description as possible of the materials used for a given artisanal trade, including the production and/or decorating techniques, and the tools that can be used, partially or exclusively, for the production method to be considered true to the tradition of its place of origin.

Despite the regional variations and inevitable differences in production techniques, all the specifications have the aim of laying down certain characteristics that apply in relation to the artistic crafts. An examination of the legal texts reveals that certain concepts recur and, although described in slightly differing terms, there are some key words that tend to crop up consistently.

The table (pages 50 and 51) summarizes these terms as indicated in the specifications (or with slight variations). The frequency with which they recur is indicative of how some of the terms in particular were considered to be crucial by regional legislators in defining artistic craftsmanship or artistic and traditional products of excellence.

When comparing the different specifications, therefore, it becomes evident that some terms come up more frequently than others:

– Tradition (looking back to, following in the footsteps of)/typicality/historical culture
– Artistic/artistry
– Innovation (research, design, experimentation, elements of novelty)
– Quality
– Link with new generations
– Manual skill (predominant or the ability to manage semi-finished goods)
– Uniqueness (or limited series)/optimum quantity
– Specific processes and/or materials
– Link with the territory/identifiable geographic area

Other terms that recur, though with less frequency, include:

[3] This concept is well explained, for example, in Article 3 of Calabria's Regional Law 15/2002 on artistic craftsmanship: "The Regional Council [...] has identified [...] those artistic production processes worthy of the mark of origin, and also defines the aesthetic, product and processing characteristics to be followed by companies and groups of companies that intend to market their products with the mark of origin provided for by Article 2." See Regional Law No. 15 of 15 March 2002, Regulations for the protection, restoration and promotion of the artistic and typical crafts of Calabria (*Norme sulla tutela, il recupero e la promozione dell'artigianato artistico e tipico della Calabria*), Article 3(2).

excellence (with reference to the craftsmanship and/or the product), technical excellence, modernization, training, continuity and aesthetic/taste (both as characteristics and/or requirements).

It should be noted that regional legislators are certainly supportive of the need to ensure the traceability of certain characteristics so that a quality artisanal product may be categorized as such, but they do not impose restrictions on some of those characteristics or define the characteristics of others, and make absolutely no reference to yet other characteristics that are nonetheless important.

Craftsmanship is often described as being "of quality" or "of excellence", without specifying by what criteria those judgements have been reached. Innovation in the form of research and experimentation, "without disrupting the links with tradition",[4] is billed as an essential attribute, but no limits have been set in either case that would make it clear if tradition has indeed been disrupted. A product's link with the territory is explained in terms of the recognizability of local characteristics, production techniques and/or aesthetic culture or more generally "historical culture", but without defining what is meant by this term when applied to an object.

There are two possible extremes when defining the link with tradition: to restrict it simply to the use of traditional techniques and time-honoured models, limiting the creativity of present-day master artisans, who may not wish just to make faithful copies; or to legitimize the idea that, to create a product based on tradition, it is sufficient to apply just one element that evokes this, the link being reinforced with every additional element.

The specifications thus provide a useful basis for the qualification of artistic craftsmanship, whether traditional or innovative, but also highlight the pressing need for in-depth definitions of the identified key words, or "concept-terms" as we will call them, and for unambiguous standards to be applied to all areas of artistic production, which can then be used as the criteria for distinguishing, as objectively as possible, different levels of quality.

When considering, below, each of the terms found in the regional specifications, we felt it appropriate to specify the meaning that the legislator has given to those that come up most frequently. A deeper analysis of these concept-terms, when used in reference to the artistic crafts, will be dealt with in the next chapter.

[4] Piedmont Region, *Disciplinare dei Metalli* (Specifications for Metal). As for Sardinia's specifications, the products have innovative value when "they communicate a stylistic choice and/or express the individual language of their creator, while retaining their relationship with the Sardinian culture". This statement holds true also for some of Lombardy's specifications.

– Tradition (looking back to/following in the footsteps of)/typicality/ historical culture

In the specifications, the terms "typical" and "traditional" are often written as one or used interchangeably.[5] However, some regional authorities (Piedmont, in particular) make a distinction between traditional crafts and typical crafts by recognizing their individual origins: the former term has a historical dimension and is connected with a manufacturing culture that has been clearly established over time and handed down through the generations; the latter has a geographical dimension, "typical" implying "local" and associated with technical and production methods that are attributable to a specific territory.

In fact, the link with the territory is relevant, although in different ways, to both terms. Throughout the evolution of a particular tradition, it is almost always connected to a geographical area and is a strong reflection of its people, culture and history. Traditional and typical can therefore be joined in many different ways or can be inextricably linked: the meaning of each needs to be contextualized so that master craftspeople can formally determine into which of the two categories their work falls. It is therefore appropriate to inscribe the use of these terms in the general framework of "historical culture", another key term that came up regularly in the documents reviewed, always with reference to the "traditional" or "typical" spheres.

– Artistic/artistry

The attribute "artistic" is strongly associated with craft in all the legislative documents, but what it actually means can only be deduced. In almost all the texts, artistic craftsmanship is defined using certain parameters of excellence: they are unequivocal in requiring perfect workmanship and one-off or small-series production. Many specifications add the necessity for particular attention to be paid to the aesthetic-formal value, as well as to the materials, techniques, finish and decoration.[6] Some refer to artistic production that has a specific end use, thereby providing a partial indication of the sector to which it might apply: "Production […] must comply with and/or be inspired

[5] In Calabria's specifications, for example, "typical and traditional products" are defined as "identifiable by their traditional and typical production methods, through the use of materials and production techniques linked to the traditions of their places of origin and local culture, in compliance with the types of production previously described".

[6] See, for example, Calabria Region, *Disciplinari della Ceramica, Vetro, Tessile* (Specifications for Ceramics, Glass and Textiles): "Production that falls under the heading of artistic craftsmanship must be characterized by the quality of its workmanship, with particular attention given to the aesthetic-formal value, as well as to the materials, techniques, finish and decoration." Lazio, Liguria, Lombardy, Piedmont and Umbria have similar stipulations.

Recurring terms in Italian regional specifications

REGION	Material	Tradition/typicality	Artistic	Masterfully made	Historical culture	Innovation	Quality
BASILICATA	Wrought iron, wood	x	x		x	x	x
CALABRIA	Ceramics, iron, wood, gold, glass	x	x		x	x	x
	Textiles	x	x		x	x	x
LAZIO	Processing of metals, wood, jewellery and precious metals, terracotta and ceramics from Viterbo	x	x		x	x	x
LIGURIA	Slate from Valfontanabuona	x	x		x		x
	Ceramics	x	x		x	x	x
	Chocolate	x	x		x	x	x
	Floral compositions	x	x		x	x	x
	Damasks and other textiles from Lorsica, filigree, chairs, velvet, glass	x	x		x	x	x
	Wrought iron and other ornamental materials	x	x		x	x	x
LOMBARDY	Textile fibers, gelato and related products, wood, common metals, precious metals, bread-making	x	x		x	x	x
MARCHE	Liccetto weaving, textile fibers	x			x	x	x
	Precious metals	x	x		x	x	x
MOLISE	Ceramics and terracotta products, wood, common metals, precious metals, processing of hardstone, stone and similar materials	x			x	x	x
PIEDMONT	Dairy products, chocolate, sweets, nougat	x	x			x	x
	Ceramics, conservation and restoration of buildings, leather and upholstery, decoration on various products, wood, common metals, wood restoration, book printing/binding/restoration, photography, drawing reproduction, musical instruments, weaving; tapestry, embroidery and clothing, glass, other typical and traditional crafts	x	x		x	x	x
	Bread-making, spirits, liqueurs, beer, blended coffee, fresh pasta; fresh pastries and biscuits, gelato	x	x			x	x
	Precious metals, hardstone and associated processes	x	x		x	x	x
SARDINIA	Artisanal ceramics	x	x	x		x	x
	Knives, wrought iron, artisanal inlay, artisanal wickerwork	x		x		x	
	Artisanal filigree	x			x	x	x
	Artisanal fabrics and weaving techniques	x		x		x	x

Excellence	Updating	Training/professional qualifications	Link with new generations	Continuity	Peculiarity	Aesthetics/palatability	Manual skill	Uniqueness/Optimum quantity	Technical excellence	Innovative and autonomous formal value	Specific processes and/or materials	Link with the territory	Recognizable category	Sophistication and creativity	Safety	Taste/smell	Experience and responsibility	Customer's taste	Professional ethics
x	x		x	x		x	x	x	x		x	x							x
x						x	x	x	x		x	x							
x						x	x	x	x		x	x		x					
x	x	x	x	x	x	x	x	x	x		x	x							
							x				x	x					x		
				x		x	x	x			x	x					x		
x		x		x		x	x	x	x		x	x		x			x		
x		x		x		x	x	x	x		x	x		x					
x				x		x	x	x	x		x	x							
x		x		x		x	x	x	x		x	x		x				x	
x	x	x	x	x	x	x	x	x	x	x	x	x	x						
							x	x			x	x	x	x					
		x					x	x			x	x	x	x					
	x		x				x	x			x	x							
x	x	x	x				x	x			x	x			x				
	x	x	x				x	x			x	x							
x	x	x	x				x	x			x	x			x				
	x	x	x				x	x			x	x							x
							x	x			x	x							
							x	x			x	x							
							x	x			x	x							
x							x	x			x	x							

by models, shapes, styles and decoration that are historically recognized artistic expressions";[7] or "[t]here exists a production of particular artistic value: sculpture. These are unique, hand-made pieces of great merit that are inspired by local or religious values or are otherwise groundbreaking and modern".[8]

Only some regional authorities, such as Lazio, Lombardy and Piedmont, provide more specific directives, notably: "The term 'artistic' can be defined as the creation of an object or a product whose use is dictated by aesthetic requirements, that is technically excellent and that has formal individual and innovative value. In other words, in its stylistic choice and/or as an expression of its creator's originality and expertise, it is either an example of perfect workmanship using traditional methods or involves, at an experimental level, new production processes."[9] In this last definition, the text attempts to introduce a reference to the art world and a master craftsperson's need for self-expression. However, the most common truth about artistic artisanal production remains the link between the object and the art world generally, which refers implicitly to its content and values.

– *Innovation (research, design, experimentation, elements of novelty)*

The clearest definition of the term "innovation" is found in the production specifications of Lazio and Lombardy, which similarly state: "The creation of an article or a product can be defined as innovative when, to a greater or lesser extent, it introduces modifications in the choice and use of the raw materials (processed according to specific methods), in the article's aesthetic and functional features, in the criteria and/or in the systems used to create it, and represents in itself elements of novelty with respect to the past."[10] This definition provides quite a comprehensive understanding of the term, but detailed criteria setting the scope of its application are missing: how far, for example, can the boundaries be pushed for the sake of novelty?

In other specifications, the conditions for innovation focus on the objectives of functionality or on the necessity for research or design, or are limited to the use of technology in the production process. They all encourage innovation when it can "lend particular artistic or other

[7] All the specifications of Sardinia and Liguria and some of the specifications of Piedmont.

[8] Calabria Region, *Disciplinare del Legno* (Specifications for Wood).

[9] Lazio Region, *Disciplinari di produzione delle lavorazioni artigianali artistiche* (Specifications for Artistic Artisanal Production).

[10] Lazio Region, *Disciplinare della Ceramica* (Specifications for Ceramics). The same applies to all of Lazio's other manufacturing specifications.

added value to the final product",[11] as well as when there is "a desire to explore and experiment with new creative systems and new production models that help to overcome outdated distinctions between art, design and craftsmanship".[12] In one, apparently isolated case, the use of technology is permitted, provided that it "satisfies the requirements of the design and enhances performance and durability".[13]

– *Quality*

The first time this term appears in many of the specifications – which in turn are derived from regional legislation – is in the titles. For example, the word figures in the title of Section VI, Article 26 of Piedmont's Regional Law No. 27/97 ("Artigianato artistico e tipico di qualità"), and the corresponding specifications mention quality as an intrinsic element of artistic craftsmanship. Whether an object is classified as traditional, typical or innovative, quality implies a certain standard of workmanship: "Production that falls under the heading 'artistic craftsmanship' must be characterized by the quality of its workmanship, with attention given to the aesthetic-formal value, as well as to the materials, techniques, finish and decoration."[14]

Similarly, other regions such as Lombardy specify that artistic crafts in general must display "characteristics of quality, meaning that they must possess particular aesthetic, design and technical features that convey the professional excellence of the individuals who have created them".

Even if the aesthetic parameters that determine the quality of a product are somewhat shaky, there are very few doubts as to the relevance of the material execution, which, defined under the various headings – aesthetics, design, production techniques, finishing and decoration – must be inspired by certain standards of perfection.

– *Link with new generations*

Some regions, such as Piedmont, place the link with new generations among the key characteristics of the artistic crafts; in other words, one that allows them to be recognized as such is "the concrete opportunities they afford for training and learning".[15] The same goes for Lombardy (in the preamble to the specifications) and for Lazio: among the characteristics

[11] Calabria Region, *Disciplinari del Vetro e del Ferro* (Specifications for Glass and Ironwork).

[12] Piedmont Region, *Disciplinare dell'Oro* (Specifications for Gold).

[13] Piedmont Region, *Disciplinare del Legno* (Specifications for Wood), Art. 5.1 and, similarly, *Disciplinare della Ceramica* (Specifications for Ceramics), Art. 7.1.

[14] Piedmont Region, *Disciplinari manifatturieri* (Manufacturing Specifications).

[15] *Ibid.*, Art. 1, "Cultural courses" (*Percorsi culturali*).

of the artistic crafts listed is the "link with new generations, which is necessary for the continuity and the vitality of an artisanal business, to be understood as the readiness to offer concrete opportunities for apprenticeship, specialist training, and jobs for the young".

This is without doubt a founding element of the artistic crafts: it goes back to the "Renaissance workshop", which remains to this day a reference for master artisans in their work, because it is still, in every sense, the only viable model. Modern-day artisanal workshops and companies safeguard the continuity of their craft or business through on-the-job training for young apprentices. The traditions, research, capacity for innovation and development methods established in the realm of the artistic crafts can continue to live on in the years to come through the immediate transmission of content, values, techniques, management strategies, and workplace and business organization.

The specifications do not clearly state that master craftspeople must teach their craft, but the regional legislation on craftsmanship in general defines the parameters for the attribution of a label of excellence and the resulting possibility for the designated master to become a fully recognized "teacher".

– Manual skill (predominant or the ability to process semi-finished goods)

Liguria's specifications state that "manual work must make up the highest percentage in all products and production processes".[16] Indeed, all the regional authorities require that the products be made predominantly by hand. Lombardy's regional authority, in the preambles to all its specifications, stresses that this is an essential characteristic of any "hand-made" item: "The terms 'hand-made/hand-produced' in this context are synonymous and should be understood as being the outcome of activities carried out by hand, or with the aid of machines and tools, as specified in Article 3 of the present Production Specifications." Article 3 reiterates the preliminary concept regarding the fact that "high quality" manual skill is predominant, and not accessorial, in hand-made production, including when machinery is used.

A further note on this matter can be found in the preamble to Calabria's Specifications for Wood: "The manual skill of a craftsperson in carving, engraving and decoration is manifested in the considerable differences of style and individual forms of expression." This basic and well-founded motivation refers to the ability of the master craftsperson to imprint, through manual skill, stylistic and qualitative traits on a given material, in addition to personal and authorial touches that bridge

[16] Liguria Region, *Disciplinare del Ferro* (Specifications for Iron), Art. 4.4.

the divide between craft and art. Herein lies the connection between the concepts "hand-made" and "of quality" that are briefly referred to in Lombardy's above-mentioned specifications. In addition, it explains why Calabria requires a high percentage of manual input also in the processing of semi-finished goods, when traditional crafts are involved.[17]

Piedmontese legislation goes into this aspect in greater detail. After returning to the above concepts, the Specifications for Metal, in the section relating to manual skill and technology, indicate that:

> Manual skill is the distinguishing feature that allows a differentiation between an artisanal and an industrial enterprise: it is thus essential during the processing phases not only that manual skill be involved, but also that it be a determinant of the quality of the final product. [...] Machinery and technological tools may serve a supporting role in high craftsmanship production, not only when their use is necessary for the personal safety of the workers, but also when the product entails initial or intermediate steps in which the use of machinery (even when technologically advanced and cutting-edge) can accelerate certain processes without deviating into mass production and without altering the original, traditional processing systems.[18]

According to the legislator, in this case manual skill determines the quality of the final product but also the excellence of the work, because they are both linked to the skills of the master craftsperson. The specifications further stipulate the necessary conditions for and limits to the use of machinery, without specifying at which point production can be deemed to have become serial or when traditional processing systems have been altered.

– *Uniqueness (or limited series)/optimum quantity*

As we have seen, the concept of manual skill is directly linked to small series production, or even more specifically to the idea of uniqueness, which underlines the artistic side of the matter. The term "uniqueness" is closely related to concepts such as "unrepeatability and inimitability" (Liguria), "artistry" (Lombardy and Piedmont) and "manual skill and professionalism" (Lombardy and Piedmont). In all its specifications, Calabria excludes the notion of serial production, deeming it incompatible with all those elements that define artistic crafts of excellence.

This insistence on one-off or small-series production is a natural

[17] Calabria Region, *Disciplinare del Legno* (Specifications for Wood), Art. 5.2.
[18] Piedmont Region, *Disciplinare dei Metalli* (Specifications for Metal), Art. 5.

consequence of the characteristics of the type of production analysed so far: the requirement for work to be carried out mainly by hand and to a certain standard of perfection, with a cultural and stylistic "imprinting" characterized by good taste and uniqueness, qualities incompatible with the high volumes of industrial schedules. This is uncontroversial and confirmed by Article 1 of all of Lombardy's specifications which, in differentiating between artistic, traditional, typical and innovative crafts, underlines the necessity for an artefact to be "a single specimen or made in a limited number".

It should be noted, however, that no indication is given of what constitutes "a limited number", especially in relation to the distinction between the output of master craftspeople – featuring characteristics and numbers very similar to those of art works – and that of companies involved in artisanal production.

– *Specific processes and/or materials*

The regional authorities have few doubts about the significance of the use of specific processes and materials in relation to artistic craftsmanship, and in all cases and for all materials, they connect them with the continuity of tradition and the basis for applying the adjective "typical" to a product.

Calabria's specifications for the production of gold items provide that: "Traditional and typical production means that products are obtained using materials and processing techniques linked to the traditions of their places of origin and local culture and comply with the types of production previously described."[19]

The specifications of other regions similarly state that, together with other factors, the use of certain materials (often explicitly mentioned) denotes traditional artisanal production.

Reference to raw materials is also made in the definitions concerning innovative artistic craftsmanship: innovation can, in fact, relate also to the raw materials used, which may be totally new or mixed with traditional ones. In this respect, Article 5 of all of Lombardy's manufacturing specifications (apart from those governing precious metals) is devoted to the definition of raw materials: "In order to provide a more accurate definition, we feel it appropriate to distinguish between the raw materials used to create objects or products emanating from quality traditional and typical artistic craftsmanship, and those used to create innovative objects/products of quality." In the first case, the distinction is linked to the use of traditional materials, which the specifications also

[19] Calabria Region, *Disciplinare dell'Oro* (Specifications for Gold), Art. 1.1.

require; in the second case, any type of material is permitted if it does not pose a threat to health and "is suitable to create [an object] designed in compliance with the laws in force". This leaves considerable leeway in terms of innovation and research, posing no limits other than those deriving from the malleability of the material itself.

– *Link with the territory/identifiable geographic area*

According to many specifications, the connection of an object with its place of origin is based on the fact that production of that object is linked to a certain area, a condition that some regions (Calabria, Liguria and Sardinia) explicitly impose for the awarding of the regional label of excellence. Moreover, the articles in the legal texts that refer to a specific area are the same that define "typical" and "traditional" artisanal production.

The manufacturing specifications of Molise state: "Artistic and traditional products must be realized according to historically traditional methods and criteria that allow results that can be easily appreciated and recognized." In this case, the legislator has tied the area of origin to the historical traditions with regard to production methods and materials used, and where "appreciable" and "recognizable" are both assessment criteria. Piedmont and Lombardy use the same criteria, although they provide further detail on the potential of "recognizability": "Typical means creations that contain one or more technical and formal characteristics that are specific to and over time have become common to other creations in the same category and made in the same geographic area, in such a way that an object is recognizable for its very own and constant characteristics and its origin can be identified."[20] Article 1 of the specifications, relating to "cultural developments", adds a definition of the reference to tradition and territory, "to be understood as the capacity acquired by a specific culture, not only in material terms, that belongs to a certain sector and area".

Thus, the presence of geographical elements that are specific to a certain production category gives an object its recognizability. When, however, the connection with an area is defined as the "capacity acquired by a specific culture", the wording is open to different interpretations depending on the area, leading to potential controversy over a decision as to whether or not an object has been created using traditional methods. When it is a condition for obtaining the regional label of excellence, it becomes essential and urgent to provide more elements and tools with which to identify such products.

[20] Piedmont Region, in the preamble to all manufacturing specifications.

2.2. LEGISLATION GOVERNING THE ARTISTIC CRAFTS IN ITALY, FRANCE, GERMANY, THE UNITED KINGDOM AND JAPAN

As we have seen, Italy has established a set of rules and standards not only to delineate or regulate craft activity itself, but also, in individual areas and with reference to specific sectors, to define, protect and promote a certain level of "excellence". The term is defined according to the above-mentioned criteria, which come up fairly frequently in the legal provisions adopted by the competent regional authorities.

Italy's membership of the European Union (EU), however, makes it necessary to look more closely at similar legal provisions elsewhere and, more generally, at the role played by craft businesses in the continent's socio-economic development. Artisanal activities are, in fact, "theoretically not easy to categorize among the 'small enterprises' or other forms of self-employment, and are apparently difficult to 'standardize' at European level. Indeed, the historical and cultural characteristics and regulatory requirements of each of the EU member States mean that this type of enterprise can have vastly differing national connotations".[21]

While it is difficult to harmonize the classification of artisanal activity across Europe, it is equally complicated to understand the way in which the different member States assess excellence within the boundaries of national artistic crafts. It is certainly possible, however, to make a comparison between them, based on the assumption that "the culture of the artistic crafts in Europe is shared across language and geographic boundaries: in fact, the divisions and distinctive features make them even more precious and allow structural peculiarities to emerge, proclaiming to the world that the greatness of a message continues to be determined by creative passion. And it maintains its power over time".[22]

In order to better identify, as objectively as possible, excellence in the Italian craft sector, we believe that a comparison between the legislation of Italy and that of other countries pertaining to artisanship and the artistic crafts would enable us to develop a matrix that is more cross-cutting and consequently more appropriate for the goals of this study.

Three European countries (France, Germany, the United Kingdom) were selected for this comparison, along with Japan, a nation with a cultural heritage that is very distant from ours, yet, as we will see,

[21] See Angelo Michelsons (ed.), *L'artigianato in Europa e in Italia* (Turin: Osservatorio dell'Artigianato della Regione Piemonte, 2003), p. 6.

[22] Franco Cologni, "La mente creativa, la mano intelligente: il 'codice' Cellini", in Paolo Colombo (ed.), *La Grande Europa dei mestieri d'arte: L'artigianato artistico d'eccellenza nei Paesi dell'Unione Europea* (Milan: Vita e Pensiero, 2007), pp. 11–15, especially 15.

very sensitive to the topic of safeguarding traditional craftsmanship of excellence. France, Germany and the United Kingdom were selected for the importance that the skilled crafts and trades sector occupies from a cultural, economic and social standpoint, as well as for their centuries-old traditions and the high levels of creativity, competence, innovation, artistic expression, mastery and know-how that have put and kept them in the global limelight.

France, Germany and the United Kingdom provide a more homogeneous comparison with Italy also from a historical perspective, owing to the network of cultural and commercial exchanges that have flourished over the centuries, the variety of traditional crafts that were developed and practised in each country, their artistic and cultural heritage, their industrial and technological development, their economic importance within Europe and the EU, and their population sizes. Historical elements (both in a prospective sense and regarding more contemporary politics), political and economic developments aimed at sustaining small businesses, and the presence or absence of incentives and protective measures may have contributed significantly to the differences in each country's legislative approach to the crafts and trades sector.[23]

However, it should be kept in mind that, as member States of the EU, they are also united by its legislation (albeit within the limits mentioned above). International agreements, meanwhile, provide further inspiration and reference points, creating a bridge and an opportunity to draw comparisons with Japan, which we chose to include in this study in order to provide a different viewpoint from that of Europe. The Empire of the Rising Sun has a very ancient artistic and cultural history; similarly to the nations of Europe, it has had to deal with the difficult issue of protecting and maintaining both its tangible and intangible cultural heritage, including traditional crafts, in a highly industrialized and technologically advanced context. Like France, Germany, Italy and the United Kingdom, Japan is contending with a large population that is ageing rapidly due to a falling birthrate, and is facing significant social problems which it must solve for the sake of the future development of its economy.

The different cultural, historical and political approaches of the countries included in the study have led to very different outcomes. With the sole exception of the United Kingdom, each has developed laws, standards, regulations, codes and acts recognizing and regulating the specific productive, financial and cultural aspects of the skilled crafts and trades sector.

[23] See Michelsons, *L'artigianato in Europa e in Italia*, pp. 20–21.

In Italy, France, Germany and Japan there are specific laws in place governing traditional crafts and trades. The following sources have provided elements of comparison for this study:

Italy:
– *Legge-Quadro per l'Artigianato* (Framework Law for the Crafts and Trades Sector) No. 443 of 8 August 1985;[24]
– Presidential Decree No. 288 of 25 May 2001, Regulation concerning the identification of artistic and traditional craft industries, as well as of the made-to-measure garment manufacturing sector;[25]
– Consolidated Act for Apprenticeships, Legislative Decree No. 167 of 14 September 2011.[26]

France:
– *Code de l'Artisanat* (Trades and Crafts Code), developed from the 1950s onwards;[27]
– Law No. 96-603 of 5 July 1996 relative to the development and promotion of trades and crafts;[28]
– Decree No. 98-247 of 2 April 1998 relative to artisanal qualifications and the trade directory;[29]
– Decree of 21 December 2003 establishing the list of craft trades;[30]
– Decree No. 2006-595 of 23 May 2006 relative to the establishment of the label of "Living Heritage Company";[31]
– Decree of 26 May 2006 relative to the procedure for granting the label of "Living Heritage Company";[32]

[24] Legge-Quadro per l'artigianato, Legge 8 agosto 1985, n. 443, www.normattiva.it/uri-res/N2Ls?urn:nir:stato:legge:1985;443.

[25] Decreto del Presidente della Repubblica 25 maggio 2001, n. 288, Regolamento concernente l'individuazione dei settori delle lavorazioni artistiche e tradizionali, nonché dell'abbigliamento su misura, www.normattiva.it/uri-res/N2Ls?urn:nir:stato:Decreto.del.presidente.della.repubblica:2001-5-25;288.

[26] Testo unico dell'apprendistato, Decreto Legislativo 14 settembre 2011, n. 167, www.normattiva.it/uri-res/N2Ls?urn:nir:stato:decreto.legislativo:2011-09-14;167.

[27] Code de l'artisanat, Version consolidée du 7 août 2016, www.legifrance.gouv.fr/affichCode.do?cidTexte=LEGITEXT000006075116.

[28] Loi n° 96-603 du 5 juillet 1996 relative au développement et à la promotion du commerce et de l'artisanat, www.legifrance.gouv.fr/affichTexte.do?cidTexte=JORFTEXT000000193678.

[29] Décret n°98-247 du 2 avril 1998 relatif à la qualification artisanale et au répertoire des métiers, www.legifrance.gouv.fr/affichTexte.do;jsessionid=3BEF27CD0444BF1F02BA62962BEBCD73.tpdjo12v_1?cidTexte=JORFTEXT000000571009&dateTexte=20090202.

[30] Arrêté du 12 décembre 2003 fixant la liste des métiers de l'artisanat d'art, www.legifrance.gouv.fr/affichTexte.do?cidTexte=JORFTEXT000000610273.

[31] Décret n°2006-595 du 23 mai 2006 relatif à l'attribution du label "entreprise du patrimoine vivant", www.legifrance.gouv.fr/affichTexte.do?cidTexte=JORFTEXT000000607662.

[32] Arrêté du 26 mai 2006 relatif à la procédure d'attribution du label "entreprise du patrimoine vivant", www.legifrance.gouv.fr/affichTexte.do?cidTexte=JORFTEXT000000607920.

– The title of *Maître d'art* created in 1994 by the Ministry of Culture and Communication.

Germany:
– *Handwerksordnung* (Trade and Crafts Code), developed from the 1950s onwards.[33]

Japan:
– *Densan Act* (Law for the Promotion of Traditional Craft Industries) No. 57 of 25 May 1974;
– Law of 30 May 1950 for the Protection of Cultural Heritage;
– The title of "Master Craftsman";
– The title of "Living National Treasure".

In the United Kingdom, the regulation of craft businesses is based on general provisions regarding enterprise, training and employment.[34] However, the home of the arts and crafts movement has an efficient, well-developed system of national associations that coordinate and promote activities, provide training and professional certifications, and generally contribute, at a centralized level, to the protection of both traditional and modern craft businesses in the country.

2.2.1. Artisans and artisanal activities: legislation and definitions

In Italy, the 1985 Framework Law for the Crafts and Trades Sector defines and regulates the legal person of the artisan-entrepreneur and the craft enterprise. However, the law does not define the artisan's attributes, nor does it specify if or which skills are necessary in order to practise the profession; it is thus assumed that artisans who decide to set up their own company have already acquired all the skills required to run the business. According to this law, an artisan-entrepreneur personally owns and professionally runs the company and "is mainly involved in the production process, also using manual methods".

France's *Code de l'Artisanat* states that a "compagnon" is a skilled worker employed in a craft business who possesses a professional qualification attested to either by a certificate of "skilled craft worker" obtained after an apprenticeship or by the exercise of a trade for a long period of time. According to the Decree relative to artisanal qualifications

[33] Gesetz zur Ordnung des Handwerks, 17 September 1953, www.gesetze-im-internet.de/bundesrecht/hwo/gesamt.pdf.

[34] Source: Heritage Crafts Association (HCA), http://heritagecrafts.org.uk/.

and the trade directory, the qualification of artisan is awarded by the president of each regional chamber of trades and crafts to anyone who has obtained a professional certificate or a licence following a vocational course or to anyone who has worked in the trade at a comparable level for at least six years. The qualification of artisan can also be granted to anyone who possesses a certificate of professional competence. A decree of the relevant Ministry establishes for each trade the list of approved or connected diplomas and titles.

According to Germany's Trades and Crafts Code, in order to set up a craft business it is necessary to obtain the professional qualification of *Handwerksmeister* (master craftsperson) by passing the *Meisterprüfung* examination. The Code also specifies the occupations that fall within the definition of "skilled crafts". Although originally the *Meisterprüfung* was compulsory for self-employed craftspeople, since 2004 this obligation applies only to activities for which precautions are necessary to protect public health.

In our survey, we have looked at a Japanese law that focuses exclusively on traditional craft industries.[35] Of the five nations studied, in fact, Japan is the only one to have a specific law covering the country's most traditional crafts. The competent bodies establish the standards that characterize each traditional craft, which is defined with regard firstly to the product and secondly to the production methods used. The law specifies that "the article must be used mainly in everyday life; the article must be primarily manufactured by hand; the article must be manufactured using traditional techniques; the materials should be mainly those which have been traditionally employed; the industry must be of a regional nature".[36]

According to Italy's Framework Law of 1985, a craft enterprise is involved in the production of goods, services or semi-finished goods, and the majority of partners participate personally in the production process, to which they contribute even their manual work. An artisan-entrepreneur is a person who "is primarily involved" in all phases of the production process, including the manual ones. The Framework Law establishes the principle whereby in a craft business "the work performed has a prominent effect on the capital value", thus restricting the firm's legal form. It also sets the limits on the size of craft businesses,

[35] Information provided by the Public Relations Office of the Ministry of Economy, Trade and Industry (METI).

[36] See https://kogeijapan.com/locale/en_US/Aboutdensan/. The METI also specifies that the term "traditional" refers to a craft or trade that has been practised for at least a century; "regional" implies that it involves at least 10 craft companies or 30 artisans producing specific items in a given region or area.

distinguishing between, among other things, those that do not engage in serial production, those that have a semi-automated production process, and those that manufacture artistic or traditional articles and made-to-measure clothing.

Article 19 of France's 1996 Law relative to the development and promotion of trades and crafts provides that a craft business may employ no more than ten people (although this limit may be exceeded, for example if the owner has the qualification of Master Craftsperson), but places no restrictions on the legal form. It further states that artisans "must exercise, primarily or secondarily, an independent activity in the production, transformation, repair or supply of services related to a list of artisanal products that is established by Decree of the Council of State".

In Germany, the law limits neither the number of employees nor the company's legal form.

2.2.2. Fields in which artisans and craft enterprises can operate: directories, rolls and registers

In Italy, an artisan-entrepreneur can be involved in the production of any type of goods or services. The 2001 Regulation concerning the identification of artistic and traditional craft industries as well as of the made-to-measure garment manufacturing sector identifies the specific professions involved. The Ministry of Labour and Social Policy is promoting the compilation of a "Directory of Professions". To date, however, Italy has no official, codified list of craft trades and related macro activities. No qualification is required to carry out an artisanal trade in Italy, nor is it necessary to be included in a professional roll or register (although a diploma or qualification is compulsory to undertake certain professions). According to the 1985 Framework Law, it is obligatory for the company to be entered in the Provincial Register of Craft Enterprises (*Albo Provinciale delle Imprese Artigiane*) managed by the local chamber of commerce. Registration is necessary for the purposes of taxation and social security, not for exercising the profession itself.

In France, on the other hand, the company must be entered in the National Register of Artisans. The 1998 Decree relative to artisanal qualifications and the trade directory[37] lists all the sectors of craft industries. The 2003 Decree establishing the list of craft trades deals specifically with artistic crafts and provides a detailed list of those

[37] The Decree was consolidated in July 2013.

covered: floral art; theatrical arts; popular arts and traditions; graphic arts; mechanical arts, games and toys; fashion jewellery, jewellery, goldsmithery and watchmaking; wood; leather; decorations; the construction of musical instruments; lighting; metal; occupations linked with architecture; fashion; stone; cabinetmaking; ceramics; textiles; and glass. Even in France it is necessary to obtain a qualification in order to practice specific professions.[38]

In Germany, skilled craft occupations are identified and listed in the Trades and Crafts Code: building and interior finishes; electrical and metalworking; woodcrafts and plastic; clothing, textiles and leather; food; health and body care, as well as chemicals and cleaning products; and graphic design. Registration is not mandatory. The national confederations of skilled crafts "represent the specific specialist interests of a trade or group of trades. They also fulfil the function of employers' organizations, e.g. they negotiate wage rates. [...] Self-employed craftsmen can form a 'guild' at local level. Membership is voluntary. Various guilds combine to form 'Local Councils of Skilled Crafts'. Regional confederations exist at federal state level. The 48 confederations of guilds nationwide and eight other professional associations acting as cooperation partners together form the German Association of Skilled Crafts Confederations".[39]

Japan identifies the "macro" areas covering the various traditional crafts: woven textiles; dyed textiles; ceramics and porcelain; lacquerware; woodcraft; bamboo craftwork; metalworking products; household Buddhist altars and fittings; paper; writing tools; stonework; dolls; semi-precious stone craftwork; industrial arts materials and tools; and other crafts.[40] In addition, "items that are not craft products themselves, but which are indispensable for the production of Traditional Craft Products are categorized as Traditional Craft Tools and Materials designated by the Ministry of Economy, Trade and Industry (METI), and are promoted in the same way as Traditional Craft Products".[41] These activities are carried out by the Association for the Promotion of Traditional Craft Industries, an agency of METI. Under the guidance of national and regional authorities, it also actively encourages the transmission of traditional craft trades to the younger generations.[42]

[38] See law No. 96-603 of 5 July 1996 relative to the development and promotion of trades and crafts.

[39] See www.zdh.de/eno/organisation/.

[40] See http://kogeijapan.com/locale/en_US/list/.

[41] See http://kougeihin.jp.e.oo.hp.transer.com/association/.

[42] One of the several agencies within METI deals with small and medium-sized enterprises; see www.chusho.meti.go.jp/sme_english/index.html.

The United Kingdom does not have specific laws for artistic crafts, but there are institutions and bodies responsible for the development, promotion, protection, census and registration of craft industries, including traditional ones. The Crafts Council is a registered charity which was granted a Royal Charter in 1982 to "advance and encourage the creation and conservation of works of fine craftsmanship and to foster, promote and increase the interest of the public in the works of fine craftsmen and the accessibility of those works to the public in England and Wales".[43] Moreover, the Crafts Council "works to raise the profile of contemporary craft through critical debate and by building an evidence base demonstrating the nature and value of craft. It supports makers' professional development, builds the market for contemporary craft by running fairs and promoting export, and works to encourage participation and learning, promoting opportunities for interaction and informal engagement with craft". It also possesses one of the most extensive collections of contemporary artefacts, which it lends to museums and art galleries. The Craft Council is also engaged in the census of craftspeople in the United Kingdom through the National Directory of Makers. The activities of the Crafts Council are supported using public funding by Arts Council England.

The Heritage Crafts Association (of which the Prince of Wales is president) "is the advocacy body for traditional heritage crafts. Working in partnership with Government and key agencies, it provides a focus for craftspeople, groups, societies and guilds [...] to support and promote heritage crafts as a fundamental part of [the United Kingdom's] living heritage".[44] The Guild of Master Craftsmen is the national association that brings together more than 400 crafts, trades and professions to safeguard the interests of artisans and consumers alike.[45]

2.2.3. Territorial jurisdiction and prerogatives of national and regional bodies

Italy's Framework Law for the Crafts and Trades Sector delegates to the regional authorities responsibility for: establishing their own legal provisions relating to craft industries; adopting specific measures to protect and develop the sector; and enhancing the status of artisanal production in all its manifestations, be they typical, artistic

[43] See www.craftscouncil.org.uk.
[44] See www.heritagecrafts.org.uk.
[45] See www.guildmc.com.

or traditional. Such provisions and measures must cover, in particular, areas such as access to credit, technical assistance, applied research, vocational training, creation of trade associations, creation of artisanal clusters, export concessions and administrative functions. The regional authorities are furthermore charged with promoting and coordinating business and refresher courses.

France's Trades and Crafts Code provides that the Regional Chambers of Trades and Crafts (*Chambres de Métiers et de l'Artisanat de Région*) are the bodies representing the general interests of the craft industry within their constituencies. The Network of Chambers of Trades and Crafts is made up of the Permanent Assembly of Trades and Crafts and the Regional and Departmental Chambers, which are public institutions placed under the protection of the State and which contribute to the economic development of businesses registered in the Trade Directory, in the general interests of the craft sector. The first two chapters of the Code are entirely dedicated to laying down the rules and functioning of the Chambers. The Permanent Assembly formulates the Network's national strategy, sets and ensures compliance with operating standards, and oversees its national projects. It is interesting to note that, although jurisdiction over these matters, similarly to Italy, is delegated to the regional authorities and departments, a centralized body of control and coordination is provided for and governed by national law. It is also significant that the members of the Chambers, whether regional or departmental, perform their duties free of charge and claim only an allowance and expenses falling under the budget of the Ministry of Trades and Crafts, which also fixes the upper limit of these expenses.

The responsibilities of the Regional Chambers of Trades and Crafts include:

a) maintaining the Trade Directory;

b) defining the qualification of "craftsperson" and "artistic craftsperson", awarding the title of *Maître artisan* in accordance with the relevant conditions set down by the Code;

c) organizing apprenticeships in the trades and crafts sector;

d) fostering career development both of business owners and employees in the sector;

e) contributing to the growth of the sector by creating new opportunities or developing existing ones, for example through the organization of trade shows;

f) improving the profitability of businesses, the quality of products and services, and production and marketing techniques and methods, by encouraging cooperation among businesses and the creation of common services;

g) creating systems of mutual support or helping to make such systems work;

h) carrying out studies that might be useful or of interest to the trades and crafts sector, and issuing notices on matters falling within their remit;

i) contributing to the prevention and resolution of difficulties faced by craft businesses, in collaboration with State financial services, social security agencies and any moral, public or private persons concerned;

l) initiating and coordinating actions to promote the artistic trades and crafts at regional level;

m) defining the positions and coordinating the actions of the Departmental Chambers within their jurisdiction in order to contribute to regional economic development;

n) participating in the development of initial and further vocational training;

o) providing support and guidance in the development of craft firms' global outreach and the export of their products, in coordination with the French agency for international business development;

p) acting as the competent authorities for the vocational qualifications required for the exercise of relevant professional activities.

These responsibilities come under the administrative and financial control of the regional prefect, and the budget must be drawn up in the manner prescribed by the competent Ministry and approved by the National Assembly.

In Germany, the German Confederation of Skilled Crafts (*Zentralverband des Deutschen Handwerks – ZDH*) rests on two pillars: the Chambers of Skilled Crafts (*Handwerkskammern*) and the National Confederations of Skilled Crafts (*Zentralfachverbände*): "The Chambers are non-profit organizations under public law, with compulsory membership for all skilled craft enterprises. The chambers offer a wide spectrum of services ranging from advice on technical, financial and legal matters to consultancy on vocational training. They keep the Crafts Register and are responsible for holding examinations. As self-governing business entities, they also represent the interests of the crafts sector in their district vis-à-vis the political institutions and the public administration. This task is taken over at federal state level by a state's working group of chambers or the state skilled crafts sector representatives. The 53 chambers of skilled crafts are confederated at national level in the German Confederation of Chambers of Skilled Crafts (*Deutschen Handwerkskammertag* DHKT)."[46]

[46] See www.zdh.de/en/organisation/.

2.2.4. The titles of "Master Craftsperson" and "Maître d'art"

In Italy, the title of Master Artisan (*Maestro Artigiano*) is instituted at regional and provincial levels. Since the regional and provincial authorities can establish the criteria and purpose of this qualification independently, there is no standardized regulation. The fields in which these authorities concentrate their activities may also vary considerably, ranging from artisanal professions (such as carpenter or beautician) to the artistic crafts in the true sense of the term. In Tuscany, for instance, the qualification of *Maestro Artigiano* is issued by the Chamber of Commerce, subject to the judgement of the Regional Committee for Crafts and Trades (*Commissione Regionale per l'Artigianato*). The candidate must have worked for a certain length of time (at least ten years) in the trade, have certain professional skills (proven by awards, certificates or diplomas, as well as by samples of their work or even by a specific and recognized expertise and competence) and an aptitude for teaching their trade.[47]

The Autonomous Province of Trento introduced the title of *Maestro Artigiano* "to promote the transmission of know-how, so that the know-how and skills of an artisan do not remain inaccessible to others. [...] The title serves two functions: it is firstly a recognition of excellence and secondly a training tool". It is awarded based on a public notice that "prescribes the entry requirements for the training courses, subdivided into those relating to professional experience and those relating to technical, professional and entrepreneurial skills, assessed according to candidates' existing know-how and relevant professional skills at the time of submitting their application to receive the title, and which thus constitute the 'entry level'".[48]

In the Province of Trieste, "the title of *Maestro Artigiano* is awarded by the Provincial Committee for the Crafts and Trades (*Commissione Provinciale per l'Artigianato*) at the request either of the owner of a craft business or one of the partners, provided that this person is personally involved in the company's activities, or at the proposal of a craft organization or Chamber of Commerce. The awarding of the title gives its holder the right to create training workshops and to the registration of the title in the Directory. The title of *Maestro Artigiano* must be expressly mentioned on the registration certificate and may be incorporated in the company name, sign or trademark".[49]

[47] See www.fi.camcom.gov.it/maestro_artigiano.asp?ln=&idtema=1&page=informazioni&index=1&idtemacat=1&idcategoria=1889.

[48] See www.provincia.tn.it.

[49] See www.ts.camcom.it/uffici/nome=Albo+Imprese+Artigiane&id_po=10&id_ufficio=20.

For the Autonomous Province of Bolzano, “the diploma of *Maestro Artigiano* is awarded only after the passing of the relevant qualification exam [...], which consists of four parts: company management, vocational pedagogy, professional theory and professional practice”.[50]

France’s Regional Chambers of Trades and Crafts award the title of *Maître artisan* pursuant to the provisions of Decree No. 98-247 of 2 April 1998 relative to artisanal qualifications and the trade directory. The title is conferred by the president of the competent regional chamber to persons holding a licence to practise the trade for which the applicant initially obtained a licence and with two years’ professional experience. It can also be awarded to a person who has exercised a profession without possessing a licence, through a special commission which verifies that they have the necessary management expertise and psychopedagogical knowledge, which must be equivalent to that of a person holding the licence of *Maître*.

The competent Ministry establishes by decree which diplomas and titles are approved for each trade. Furthermore, the title of *Maître artisan* can be awarded by a regional commission to anyone who has been listed in a trade directory for at least ten years and who, in the absence of a diploma, has a specific *savoir-faire*. Applications must be submitted together with any qualifications, awards and certificates. The commission takes its decision within three months.

In Germany, the title of *Handwerksmeister* is the highest professional qualification in the crafts and “authorizes the person to manage an enterprise and to train apprentices. Skilled workers and master craftsmen can select from a wide variety of options for further training. [...] In many *Länder*, the master craftsman qualification opens the door to studies in a polytechnic or university”.[51]

In Japan, the Association for the Promotion of Traditional Craft Industries, founded in 1975 following the passing of the Act on the Promotion of Traditional Craft Industries (Densan Act) of 1974, may award the title of “Master of Traditional Crafts”.[52] The title of “Contemporary Master Craftsman” (or “Master Craftsman of Modern Times”), on the other hand, is awarded each year by the Ministry of Health, Labour and Welfare to craftspeople who display outstanding skills and who have distinguished themselves in their professional lives.

In the United Kingdom, the title of “Master Craftsman” has been awarded for centuries and dates back to the era of the great guilds. It

[50] See www.provincia.bz.it/it/default.asp.

[51] See www.zdh.de/eno/vocational-education-and-training/.

[52] See http://kougeihin.jp.e.oo.hp.transer.com/association/.

is no longer awarded officially, except through the guilds themselves. To join the Guild of Master Craftsmen, prospective members must prove that they have earned the right to be called Masters through high standards of workmanship and customer service. Once their request to become a member of the Guild has been accepted, they undertake to maintain the aims and objectives of the Guild, on penalty of expulsion.[53]

In Italy, the title of *Maestro d'Arte* was formerly conferred on students who successfully achieved their diploma at art colleges (*istituti d'arte*),[54] which became "artistic high schools" (*licei artistici*) in the recent reform of the secondary school system. In France, meanwhile, the Ministry of Culture and Communication, inspired by Japan's recognition of its "Living National Treasures", created the title of *Maître d'art* in 1994.[55] The title is awarded each year by the Ministry "to professionals who have outstanding *savoir-faire* and who practise a rare skilled craft, in a similar way to Japan's Living National Treasures".[56] Since 2012, the Ministry of Culture and Communication has entrusted the Institut National des Métiers d'Art (INMA) with the management of the *Maîtres d'art-elèves* training scheme, which exists only in France and inextricably links the title of *Maître* with the imparting of knowledge and know-how. In fact, in order to obtain this title, which is for life, the *Maître* must undertake to transmit his or her *savoir-faire* to a pupil, who in turn undertakes to receive exceptional teaching, developing a project together with the *Maître*. The apprenticeship may last up to three years, for which the *Maître d'art* receives a grant of 16,000 euro per year from the INMA, by mandate of the Ministry.

2.2.5. Intangible Cultural Heritage, Living National Treasures and Living Heritage Companies

The master artisan's workshop can therefore be described as a "living heritage company", a wellspring of know-how, technique and aesthetic sense, characterized by the ability to interpret the customer's precise wishes, the ingeniousness to find solutions to manufacturing problems, and the flexibility in design and production: a set of attributes that can and must be kept alive and handed down to subsequent generations. It is therefore worth recalling the definitions provided in the 2003 UNESCO Convention for the Safeguarding of the Intangible Cultural Heritage:

[53] See www.guildmc.com/about/aims-and-objectives.aspx.

[54] Legislative Decree No. 297 of 16 April 1994.

[55] See www.institut-metiersdart.org/. The directory of *Maîtres d'art* can be consulted on the website of the Association des Maîtres d'Art: www.maitresdart.com./en/home.html.

[56] See www.institut-metiersdart.org/action-ministere-culture/maitres-d-art/titre-maitre-d-art.

1. The "intangible cultural heritage" means the practices, representations, expressions, knowledge, skills – as well as the instruments, objects, artefacts and cultural spaces associated therewith – that communities, groups and, in some cases, individuals recognize as part of their cultural heritage. This intangible cultural heritage, transmitted from generation to generation, is constantly recreated by communities and groups in response to their environment, their interaction with nature and their history, and provides them with a sense of identity and continuity, thus promoting respect for cultural diversity and human creativity. For the purposes of this Convention, consideration will be given solely to such intangible cultural heritage as is compatible with existing international human rights instruments, as well as with the requirements of mutual respect among communities, groups and individuals, and of sustainable development.

2. The "intangible cultural heritage", as defined in paragraph 1 above, is manifested inter alia in the following domains:

a) oral traditions and expressions, including language as a vehicle of the intangible cultural heritage;
b) performing arts;
c) social practices, rituals and festive events;
d) knowledge and practices concerning nature and the universe;
e) traditional craftsmanship.

3. "Safeguarding" means measures aimed at ensuring the viability of the intangible cultural heritage, including the identification, documentation, research, preservation, protection, promotion, enhancement, transmission, particularly through formal and non-formal education, as well as the revitalization of the various aspects of such heritage.[57]

It is interesting to note that paragraph 2 of the Convention expressly mentions traditional craftsmanship.

In Italy, the regional authorities of Sicily and Lombardy were the first to set up, in line with UNESCO recommendations, a local register of intangible heritage (*Registro delle Eredità Immateriali*), subdivided into different areas of application. Lombardy has articulated these according to five sectors of skilled crafts, setting up a "Register of Craft Knowledge dedicated to working techniques and agricultural and artisanal skills connected, among other things, to the production of both durable and ephemeral articles, foodstuffs, stockbreeding, hunting and fishing, etc.".[58]

Similarly, Sicily has created "the Book of Skills (*Libro dei Saperi*), which will encompass the techniques, raw materials and manufacturing

[57] Convention for the Safeguarding of the Intangible Cultural Heritage, Paris, 17 October 2003, Article 2, www.unesco.org/culture/ich/en/convention.

[58] See www.aess.regione.lombardia.it/reil/?page_id=2.

processes involved in particular products that are related to a community's history and typical traditions (for example, artistic crafts, textiles, specific artefacts or goods, food and wine products, etc.)".[59]

There are still no specific laws in place for the preservation of Italy's intangible cultural heritage, although an attempt was made to implement the directives of the UNESCO Convention via the Legislative Decree No. 62 of 26 March 2008.[60] However, the Decree did not entirely resolve the issue, as the international convention was not followed up by a specific national law.

In sum, with the partial exception of stringed instrument production in Cremona, Italy lacks national-scale, centralized and exhaustive legislation to protect, preserve and promote the valuable intangible heritage of its artisanal know-how. This is all the more regrettable in a country whose most prized and recognizable asset – sought-after and imitated the world over – is based on the distinguishing national characteristics that are represented by the "Made in Italy" label.

In Japan, the title of "Living National Treasure" (the popular term for "Preserver of Important Intangible Cultural Properties"), which inspired the title of *Maître d'art* in France, is awarded by the Ministry of Education, Culture, Sports, Science and Technology (MEXT) through its Agency for Cultural Affairs.[61] The designation Living National Treasure (in Japanese, *Ningen Kokuho*) is conferred on those who, individually or collectively, have attained the highest levels of mastery in the fields of traditional drama, music and applied arts. The government provides each such "Preserver" with an annual grant of 2 million yen.

This initiative falls within the purview of Japan's Law for the Protection of Cultural Property of 30 May 1950.[62] According to Article 2, the term "cultural property" covers both tangible and intangible assets that are of significant historical or artistic value to Japan, including: monuments, sites, applied arts, antique documents; arts and skills employed in drama, music, applied arts and other intangible cultural products; manners and customs related to food, clothing and housing, religious faith, folk entertainment; and shell mounds, ancient tombs and historical palaces, fortresses, castles and other ancient sites. Japan drafted this law, which also provides guidelines for the protection,

[59] See www.Regione.sicilia.it/beniculturali/dirbenicult/info/news/rei/index.html.

[60] Decreto Legislativo 26 marzo 2008, n. 62, "Ulteriori disposizione integrative e correttive del decreto legislativo 22 gennaio 2004, n. 42, in relazione ai beni culturali", www.parlamento.it/parlam/leggi/deleghe/08062dl.htm.

[61] See www.mext.go.jp/english/a08 and www.bunka.go.jp/english/.

[62] Law No. 214 of 30 May 1950, www.unesco.org/culture/natlaws/media/pdf/japan/japan_lawprotectionculturalproperty_engtof.pdf.

preservation and transmission of the Intangible Cultural Heritage, including the artistic crafts, more than 50 years before the adoption of the UNESCO Convention.

The UNESCO Convention was ratified by France and Japan in 2004, Italy in 2007 and Germany in 2013, while the British Government has yet to make its position known. In ratifying the Convention, Italy left it to the regional and provincial – as opposed to national – authorities to adopt the necessary implementing measures.

Still on the topic of "Intangible Cultural Heritage", in 2005 France enacted a law introducing the *Entreprise du Patrimoine Vivant* (Living Heritage Company or EPV) label[63] and followed it up a year later with a decree defining the awarding procedure.[64] The purpose of creating the label was to enrich and enhance the country's economic, historical, cultural and artistic heritage, and above all the *savoir-faire* of French craft enterprises. The label is awarded by the Ministries for Small and Medium-Sized Enterprises, for Commerce and for Crafts. To qualify, a company must possess at least one criterion from each of three sets of standards. The first set requires ownership of a specific economic heritage (*patrimoine économique spécifique*), which includes: rare equipment, tools, machinery, designs or technical documentation; intellectual property rights for products, services or production equipment; and a significant customer network.

The second set of standards relates to the mastering of rare skills that draw on traditional or technically advanced techniques: an acknowledged and unquestionable know-how that is either exclusive or shared with a restricted number of companies; know-how that is not accessible through standard training channels, and that can only be taught within the company itself; and the presence of one or more staff members who have acquired a particularly fine level of expertise requiring years of training, possibly accompanied by prestigious awards.

The third set concerns the age and reputation of the company, and includes: having been founded in its current location over 50 years before, or whose premises have an objective historical or architectural value; the production is carried out exclusively within the area in which it was founded; and the company possesses a name or trademark with a reputation, in particular because it was awarded national distinctions or has been

[63] Loi n° 2005-882 du 2 août 2005 en faveur des petites et moyennes entreprises (Law on Small and Medium-Sized Enterprises of 2 August 2005), Article 23, www.patrimoine-vivant.com/en/a-state-label. For more details, see www.patrimoine-vivant.com/en.

[64] Décret n° 2006-595 du 23 mai 2006 relatif à l'attribution du label "entreprise du patrimoine vivant" (Decree on the award of the EPV label of 23 May 2006), www.legifrance.gouv.fr/affichTexte.do?cidTexte=JORFTEXT000000607662.

referred to in trade publications, or because it operates on property that forms part of the country's protected heritage or on objects or furniture that are stamped or that perpetuate a certain style of French art.

In 2012, a similar bill was put before the Italian Senate.[65]

2.2.6. Can craft enterprises be classified as "cultural and creative industries"?

According to the Heritage Crafts Association, in the United Kingdom craft enterprises and the artistic crafts are classified as Cultural and Creative Industries, but there is currently an interesting debate on the appropriateness of this classification. In addition to promoting the UNESCO Convention for the Safeguarding of the Intangible Cultural Heritage, both the Crafts Council, which supports contemporary crafts with public funding by Arts Council England, and the Heritage Crafts Association, which sponsors traditional crafts, have been instrumental in opposing the elimination of craft businesses from the definition of Creative and Cultural Industries. Their action followed the report published in April 2013 by the Department for Culture, Media and Sport, which did not contain any figures relating to the weight of craft businesses within the framework of the creative industries, either in terms of turnover or of employment. This triggered a protest involving petitions and lobbying of the government, which subsequently confirmed on its website that "the definition of creative industries will remain the same and continue to include crafts".[66]

The European Commission appears to be moving along the same lines. Its strategic plan to boost growth and employment in the cultural and creative industries – presented in September 2012 – includes promoting the key role of the cultural and creative sectors in the economic and social development of member States and in enhancing the image of the EU as a whole.[67] However, at present the definition of the cultural and creative industries seems to be overly broad, encompassing "architecture, artistic crafts, cultural heritage, design, festivals, film and television, music, performing and visual arts, archives and libraries, publishing and radio".[68]

[65] Disegno di Legge, Norme per l'istituzione e la disciplina del marchio "impresa del patrimonio vivente" (Rules for the creation and regulation of the "Living Heritage Company" label), 22 March 2013, www.senato.it/japp/bgt/showdoc/17/DDLPReS/699535/index.html?part=ddlpres_ddlpre%2051-articolato_articolato1.

[66] See Giovanna Marchello, "Firmly in the saddle", *Arts & Crafts & Design*, No. 4 (April 2014), pp. 50–55, especially 52. See also www.gov.uk/government/consultations/classifying-and-measuring-the-creative-industries-consultation-on-proposed-changes.

[67] See http://europa.eu/rapid/press-release_IP-12-1012_en.htm.

[68] See http://europa.eu/rapid/press-release_IP-12-1012_en.htm.

Promoting the artistic crafts as a potentially powerful driving force for both the economy and tourism – which might prompt a reassessment of the concept of "creative production", placing it alongside authentic *local* excellence – is a truly fascinating and groundbreaking prospect. The same notion has been endorsed and popularized by Richard Sennett, who placed the *homo artifex* at the centre of a creative and operational model in which skills are developed thanks also to the productive relationship between the identification and resolution of problems.[69]

According to Sennett, the secret of excellence lies in the passion for doing one's work in the best way possible. Any master craftsperson is all too familiar with this secret, which, as we have seen, could be used as a methodological and paradigmatic element in assessing the excellence of an artistic craft.

A lively debate is also taking place in Italy on the role of the cultural and creative industries, although to date there is still no "official" register. While this is not the place to discuss this unfortunate state of affairs, it is still important to underline the attention paid by European lawmakers to the sector, and to understand how the "cultural" parameters of authenticity, creativity and connection to the territory are of relevance in devising a matrix for the assessment of artisanal excellence, at least at a "local" level.

2.3. THE CRITERIA FOR ASSESSING EXCELLENCE

From the above review of Italian legislation, the comparison with the assessment criteria of other countries where the artistic crafts play a significant economic and cultural role, and recognition of the importance the EU attaches to "cultural production" in its broadest sense, we have been able to identify a number of key criteria or "concept-terms" by which "excellence" can be defined:

– authenticity, non-manipulation, respect for the materials;
– competence, expertise, complete familiarity with the materials and the techniques;
– craftsmanship, mastery;
– creativity, inventiveness, imagination, vision;
– innovation, taste, the ability to find new and effective solutions;
– interpretation, subjective (not mechanical) execution of the project;
– originality, distinctiveness, uniqueness;

[69] See Richard Sennett, *The Craftsman* (New Haven: Yale University Press, 2009).

– territory, expression of the culture of the place, of a specific territory;
– tradition, continuity, longstanding experience;
– transmission, training, extended apprenticeship.

To these criteria should be added talent, understood as an innate gift that grows with experience, as a vocation and as a strong motivation that drives an individual from an early age. Talent, nurtured through repetition and practice, is a key ingredient in achieving a level of "excellence" that includes all of the above-listed criteria.

Our next steps will be to conduct a detailed examination of the meaning of each concept-term when used in relation to the world of the artistic crafts and to gauge its relevance through a peer review and the opinions of experts and critics.

The next chapter is therefore devoted to providing as specific and as objective an understanding of each concept-term as possible.

ALBERTO CAVALLI - GIUDITTA COMERCI - GIOVANNA MARCHELLO

3.
CRAFT EXCELLENCE: REFLECTIONS ON DEFINITIONS[1]

3.1. AN EVOLUTIONARY PARADIGM FOR A DYNAMIC DEFINITION

In sooth I had not been so courteous
While I was living, for the great desire
Of excellence, on which my heart was bent.[2]

So says Oderisi da Gubbio in Dante's *Purgatory*, Canto XI, which is dedicated to the sins of the proud. The connection Dante makes between pride and excellence is borrowed from Thomas Aquinas, who in his *Summa Theologiae* states that "superbia dicitur esse amor propriae excellentiae, in quantum ex amore causatur inordinata praesumptio alios superandi".[3] Excellence as an excess of self-love, which leads to a disordered and uncontrollable desire to outdo others, is certainly a vice to be stigmatized and not an element of objective perfection. The distinction must therefore be sought in terms of the "inordinate presumption" of which Thomas Aquinas speaks. When "excellence" is used to describe an unseemly ostentation, it suggests something that is at once morally and objectively disproportionate, inappropriate and anything but beautiful.[4] However, when it is the issue of a genuine cultural process that involves a perpetual quest to achieve the utmost

[1] Sections 3.1 and 3.2 were written by Alberto Cavalli, sections 3.3.2, 3.3.3, 3.3.4, 3.3.5, 3.3.6, 3.3.8, 3.3.9, 3.3.10 and 3.3.11 by Giuditta Comerci, and sections 3.3.1 and 3.3.7 by Giovanna Marchello.

[2] Dante Alighieri, *The Divine Comedy: Purgatory*, Vol. II, Canto XI, translated by Henry Wadsworth Longfellow (London: George Routledge & Sons, 1867), https://en.wikisource.org/wiki/The_Divine_Comedy/Purgatorio/Canto_XI.

[3] "[P]ride is said to be 'love of one's own excellence', inasmuch as love makes a man presume inordinately on his superiority over others", translation from www.logicmuseum.com/wiki/Authors/Thomas_Aquinas/Summa_Theologiae/Part_IIb/Q162.

[4] See Umberto Eco (ed.), *History of Beauty* (New York: Rizzoli, 2004), p. 61.

possible through the application of knowledge and intuition, know-how and creativity, the word takes on a highly positive meaning.[5]

The term "excellence" has often been overused and misused in recent years, at times even as a mere marketing ploy. It is important to remember that

> from its very etymology, the word excellence has a vertical thrust: it denotes an objective ascent and evokes a rising above the average and the masses. Sublimely outstanding, or *eccelso* in Italian, refers to something of the highest possible order, while excellent, or *eccellente* in Italian, refers to something that is the best that can be found. "Excellence" has also become a key word to describe Italian companies, organizations or institutions that function and function well, including certain hospitals and universities, famous museums, magnificent parks, fashion icons, renowned designers, and those businesses that bring an unquestionable style, quality and beauty to the world that can only originate in a country like ours; "excellence" is now something to aim for. But, as often occurs with key words, it also risks being gradually devalued – many are called but few are chosen. This is why we must have a very clear idea of what we really mean by "excellence" and why we must have recourse to specific assessment criteria. We need therefore to ask ourselves what the real roots are that bring sap, nourishment and life to the excellent branches of industry, crafts and agriculture, and Italian creations in general. No longer can we justify mediocrity.[6]

The online Oxford Dictionary defines "excellence" as the "quality of being outstanding or extremely good" and "to excel" as "to be exceptionally good at or proficient in an activity or subject".[7] In the field of the artistic crafts, as we saw in the previous chapter, various regions of Italy and several other countries have identified and codified certain criteria for defining, as objectively as possible, an "excellence" that is a real and authentic expression of values and cultures and that enables superlative artistic and artisanal products to be clearly distinguished. Using this work as a basis, we felt it important to establish a precise, albeit multifaceted, definition of this "excellence", a composite term that is rich in nuances, each of which we will analyse in detail in relation to the world of the most authentic artistic crafts.

This process is all the more urgent because endowing the term "excellence" with a precise meaning allows us to objectively assess whether the criteria that determine excellence, or at least near-excellence,

[5] See Manfredi Ricca and Rebecca Robins, *Meta-luxury: Brands and the Culture of Excellence* (New York: Palgrave Macmillan, 2012), p. 53.

[6] Franco Cologni, "La scuola dello stile", *AD*, No. 342 (November 2009), p. 112.

[7] See online Oxford Dictionary, https://en.oxforddictionaries.com/.

are present in a given situation. This constitutes a linguistic exploration that is at the same time an analysis of reality, if it is true that "[t]he name, in the realm of language, has as its sole purpose and its incomparably high meaning that it is the innermost nature of language itself. [...] Only through the linguistic being of things can [man] get beyond himself and attain knowledge of [those things] – in the name".[8]

In our search for the true meaning of "excellence" in relation to the artistic crafts, we started with the facts as objectively noted by legislators, and invited scholars, experts and leading figures from the craft world to reflect on the topic. These interviews, extracted below, are pertinent to an understanding of the dynamic relationship between the term "excellence" and its various components, each with its own import, function and consequence.

Later in this chapter, the meaning of each concept-term is discussed in reference to the artistic crafts, with a view to generating a matrix that can be used to assess, as objectively as possible, craft excellence. According to Ugo La Pietra, excellence can be seen as "the utmost in design and the utmost in factual value",[9] as design and execution, therefore, but also as a capacity for mediation between the very rich tradition of Italian style and the necessary prefiguration of future tastes and needs. These are very important factors in determining the desired excellence and in rebuilding a perspective in not only economic but also social and philosophical terms.

As Stefano Micelli asserts, "the word 'excellence' applied to the artistic crafts suggests a 'conflict of interests'. On the one hand, it explicitly evokes the predominance of practices rooted in the tradition of a specific profession; on the other, it hints at a subjectivity that is able to freely reinterpret those same practices in an original way. Excellence is a characteristic of those who naturally incorporate both aspects: fully at ease with traditional practices, they demonstrate their expressive aptitude by transforming their craft into a tool and never an end in itself".[10]

Craft as a tool is thus the expression of a capacity that is nurtured by characteristics that determine excellence, characteristics that may well be heterogeneous but are nonetheless always brought together by the centrality of the human hand and mind. Anty Pansera, historian of applied arts, former president of the Higher Institute for Artistic

[8] Walter Benjamin, "On Language as Such and on the Language of Man", *Selected Writings. Volume I: 1913–1926*, edited by Marcus Bullock and Michael W. Jennings (Cambridge, Mass.: The Belknap Press of Harvard University Press, 1996), p. 65.

[9] Interview with Ugo La Pietra, April 2012.

[10] Interview with Stefano Micelli, May 2012.

Industries of Faenza (ISIA) and currently president of the D-come Design Association for the promotion of female creativity in design, points out that:

> The term "excellence", when referring to the artistic crafts, means different things to different people. Awareness of the past but also of the present certainly plays its part. And the value placed on the artistic crafts frequently leads many to look more to the past than to the present, where the shoddiness of certain goods – especially those intended for the tourist market – displays a linguistic repetitiveness that very often, though not always, coexists with a "no longer knowing-how-to", as it were.[11]

The aforementioned characteristics go hand in hand with a strong emphasis on perfection and on respect for techniques, materials and traditions. As Jean-Michel Delisle, former president of the Institut National des Métiers d'Art (INMA),[12] succinctly puts it: "I think that it's important to consider these two words: perfection and respect. Perfection of the gesture, of the hand, of the detail. Respect for the client, respect for the material that you work with, respect for the time, and respect for the tradition, the history and the culture that the artisan represents. This is excellence."[13]

Respect for history and culture, tradition and innovation, beauty and functionality is what leads to distinctiveness. These attributes require an extraordinary balance of form and gestures, actions and materials. Leonardo Ferragamo, CEO of the luxury goods conglomerate Palazzo Feroni Finanziaria, expresses this concept thus: "The difficult balance between a pleasing form and performance is a key element: beauty would not be authentic if it were not accompanied by an absolutely perfect functionality. [...] [A] luxury product does not fear the passage of time. Time is a friend, an ally."[14]

Time as a crucial factor in attaining excellence would lead one to infer that achieving this goal is the result of an extensive and often demanding process. Mariapia Garavaglia, president of the non-profit Manlio e Maria Letizia Germozzi Foundation (the cultural arm of Confartigianato Imprese, Italy's Confederation of Craft Trades) and

[11] Interview with Anty Pansera, May 2013.

[12] The Institut National des Métiers d'Art (National Craft Institute or INMA) is a French institution responsible for promoting, protecting and overseeing traditional and contemporary crafts. The Institute awards prizes and organizes initiatives and exhibitions of international importance, including the annual Journées européennes des métiers d'art. See www.institut-metiersdart.org/.

[13] Interview with Jean-Michel Delisle, May 2012.

[14] Interview with Leonardo Ferragamo, October 2012.

signatory of the bill of 17 July 2012 that instituted the title of "Impresa del Patrimonio Vivente" ("Living Heritage Enterprise"), certainly agrees with this view: "I think that the term excellence, as its etymology suggests, should be used to indicate a level that is difficult to attain in terms of perfection of form, precision of process, and judgement; it therefore implies not only a product but also a process, which leads additionally to an almost shared appreciation and recognition."[15]

Cesare Fumagalli, secretary-general of Confartigianato Imprese, similarly places as much emphasis on the process as on the product: "The term 'excellence', when applied to the artistic crafts, clearly indicates the highest qualitative level. This definition has been expressed in practical terms in a variety of ways in many regions, the first of which was Piedmont, where the Eccellenza Artigiana (Artisanal Excellence) mark of quality was created. But it is clear that even the most painstakingly detailed guidelines cannot cover every possible attribute; the highest level of quality may well depend on various factors, including, but not limited to, historical roots, innovation, creativity, consummate proficiency and dexterity, and the uniqueness of the item. We must also bear in mind that other attributes might be thought relevant in the future. If the concept of excellence in relation to the artistic crafts cannot be contained within a definition, we can at least delineate its perimeter by indicating some parameters."[16]

The indication, analysis and definition of these parameters are the objects of the following sections, which set out to examine each criterion individually in relation to the artistic crafts. The eleven criteria or "concept-terms" that will be thus analysed – derived from a comparative analysis of the main legal and regulatory documents emanating from different regional bodies in Italy – are: *authenticity, competence, craftsmanship* (to be understood as mastery), *creativity*, *innovation*, *interpretation*, *originality*, *talent*, *territory, tradition* and *training*.

These concept-terms provide the framework for an ideal "assessment matrix", which, to be fully effective, nonetheless encompasses yet other notions, notably the connection between each characteristic and the world of the artistic crafts and an idea of the priority each one should take in assessing artisanal excellence. Those notions are addressed below.

[15] Interview with Mariapia Garavaglia, April 2013.
[16] Interview with Cesare Fumagalli, April 2013.

3.2. A QUALITATIVE ASSESSMENT OF THE CRITERIA

And what if doing were thinking? And what if it were speaking? And what if it were being? And what if an artisan's every creative act was driven by a desire to tangibly capture the exuberance of life, to express their innermost selves and experience joy as the object's shape emerges through a constant dialogue with the material?[17]

Making as thinking – or rather, thinking through making – is what connects the creative act and the creator's awareness. The Institut National des Métiers d'Art organized a two-day meeting on this theme, held at the Institut National d'Histoire de l'Art in Paris in February 2013, with the aim of clarifying and further exploring the historical and semantic development of the artistic crafts. It brought together curators, historians, economists, experts and public officials from a number of countries to exchange views on ways to promote the artistic crafts, including a review of the current definition. The common thread raised by the participants was the (sometimes intimate) bond between doing and thinking, between the creative act and its intellectual inflections, between the culture of "craft" and its correlative objective. The role of the artistic crafts in the economic and social life of countries such as France, Italy and the United Kingdom is back centre stage, thanks to the search for and recognition of an "excellence" that, as we have seen, affords a real competitive advantage at the global level.

Focusing on the words that define this domain, which lies at the crossroads between culture and economics and whose practices are tied to a more harmonious way of life, prompts us to engage in a multilayered reflection not only on how the artistic crafts are understood, but also on how to represent them. To do this, we must transcend the friction between hand and spirit, to quote Hugues Jacquet, author of *L'intelligence de la main*,[18] and recognize the social role of the artistic crafts as it has been structured and has evolved from the "traditional" society to a society "in the process of postmodern emersion".[19]

The economic potential of this role is still largely unrecognized, although it is closely linked to the "excellence" that the Italian economy

[17] *Les métiers d'art à mots découverts*: *Quelle est la place des métiers d'art dans notre société d'un point de vue historique, socio-économique et prospectif?*, Programme of the Journées d'études internationales, organized by the Institut National des Métiers d'Art and Les Arts Décoratifs, Paris, 14–15 February 2013, p. 2.

[18] From Hugues Jacquet's speech at the international meeting *Les métiers d'art à mots découverts*, Paris, 14–15 February 2013.

[19] From an interview with Michelle Bergadaà of the University of Geneva during the international meeting *Les métiers d'art à mots découverts*, Paris, 14–15 February 2013.

relies on for sustenance and to differentiate itself. That difference derives from the excellent definition of every detail or, put another way, from the care for and culture of the well-made, of the "craft" that grows into an expression of competence and wisdom. The artistic nature of a craft is thus synonymous with excellence only when, as explained above, certain characteristics are present, its relevance dependent on the perpetual capacity to attain perfection, to overcome obstacles and to become part of a "value system" that, according to Harvard anthropologist Michael Herzfeld, is crucial in giving meaning to a product.[20] This perspective overturns and demolishes that "polite racism" (the term is Herzfeld's) that craftspeople, considered more as skilled labour than as excellent creators, have been subjected to for decades. When the divide between art and craft is also a social and economic divide, the value system of the artistic crafts is profoundly misunderstood, negating its past and present validity.

As we have already said, excellence does not come from nowhere but is described as "continuous". In the words of Ettore Bocchia, executive chef at the Villa Serbelloni in Bellagio (on Lake Como) and founder of Italian molecular cuisine: "Behind the word excellence lie a deep knowledge and skill that allow a thought to be formulated, turning it into a solid constant, a product that is in itself a guarantee and a promise kept."[21] Elisabetta Canali, communication director of the family-run fashion house Canali, internationally renowned for the quality of its Italian-made men's suits, also talks of "promises kept": "The territory's DNA is, for me, a vital component of our product's identity. Our artisans' roots and history, along with their sartorial skills, singularity and love of their work, are deeply embedded in the Italian identity, which springs from the land and a predisposition for beauty. Luxury is a promise that the artistic crafts help to keep."[22]

According to Franco Cologni, founder and president of the Cologni Foundation for the Métiers d'Art and co-founder of the Michelangelo Foundation for Creativity and Craftsmanship, the desire to own a beautiful object arises from the perception of an excellence "that not only signifies luxury or exclusivity, but primarily authenticity".[23] It is also important to stress the ability to mediate between tradition and stylistic renewal, between respect for the past and a contemporary vision. In the Hermès philosophy, the details are necessarily entrusted

[20] See Michael Herzfeld, *L'artigianato come modello degli atteggiamenti sociali* (Craft as a model of social attitudes), Talk given at the University of Milan-Bicocca, 13 February 2013.

[21] Interview with Ettore Bocchia, April 2012.

[22] Interview with Elisabetta Canali, May 2013.

[23] Franco Cologni, "Revers", *Monsieur*, No. 95 (February 2011), p. 142.

to expert artisans, skilful interpreters of a timeless style: "The emotions that each Hermès object conveys derive from the hands of the artisans who constantly interpret the designers' vision, transforming it into beautiful objects", says menswear designer Véronique Nichanian. "The dialogue with the artisan is vital to achieving the perfect result. I love working closely with master artisans, studying new ways of treating leather, seeing what can be done with a fabric [...]. The meeting of our imagination and their hands is a game in which everyone wins, in which everyone is energized and enriched."[24]

However, even if the characteristics required to identify excellence are strongly underpinned by the idea evoked by the product's beauty, we remain firmly convinced that, in the words of Ettore Bocchia, "if there were an absolutely objective way of assessing excellence, we would not define it as such: so the emotional factor makes the difference". In his view, "true art is attained by way of a gesture, which may even be prolonged in time, communicating the self and touching on aspects that are not simply objective – a perfect balance of imperfection, where synaesthesia and emotion converge".

This view is closely linked to the poetry of making, as well as to passion and a sturdy work ethic. However, it complements rather than replaces the need for an approach based on objective criteria. The criteria are not exclusively Italian, of course, but they seem to be particularly at home in Italy's fertile contexts, which must nonetheless be constantly explored to stimulate their potential. "There are doubtless myriad superlative artisanal skills in every part of the world. The concept of 'hand-made' can also be perceived as utopian, as an ideological hypothesis", says Italian designer and architect Alessandro Mendini. "'Handmade' is even mandatory as far as hypertechnological products are concerned. The materials and techniques of the 'artistically made' are infinite, but the losses that the contemporary world inflicts on the great craft traditions are just as infinite. Today 'there's no time', but these thirteen objects [created for the exhibition *Arts & Crafts & Design. Time according to Alessandro Mendini and his artisans*] mean to 'have time'. The fact that they have been 'manufactured', quite literally 'hand made', is intended as a demonstration of this. In our case they show that effort translated into an artefact that is an end in itself, regardless of its objective, is beautiful. And that there are spaces teeming with possibility in the intermediate areas between art, craft and design, beyond their institutional enclosures."[25]

[24] Interview with Véronique Nichanian, January 2012.

[25] Interview with Alessandro Mendini, November 2012.

The cross-fertilization of art, craft and design indicates the exact path along which the artistic crafts of excellence are being productively channelled, where techniques, tools and knowledge are not only different means to an end but also fundamental creative possibilities for the very essence of the invention of things. As Giuseppe Furlanis, consultant to Italy's Ministry of Education, Universities and Research, says: "Craft provides the most fertile ground for the formal and typological innovation of products, making it for the designer a privileged space for research."[26] According to this view, the master artisan's most striking attribute is the ability to "interpret" the design, and thus transform an idea into an absolutely perfect object.

This ideal, which brings together practical and creative know-how, is the expression of an entirely modern and very contemporary aspiration at a time when artisanal know-how seems threatened on all sides. "Efforts are currently focused on reconnecting art and production through the rediscovery of aesthetic values and the reassertion of the role of the artist as designer (industrial design)", says Gisella Capponi, director of the Istituto Superiore per la Conservazione ed il Restauro (Higher Institute for Conservation and Restauration or ISCR) in Rome. "A demonstration of this trend is the founding of vocational schools in the very early 20th century to train designers, technician-managers, master artisans and specialist workers. At the end of the First World War, Walter Gropius founded the Bauhaus in Weimar with the aim of training a class of industrial artist-designers. But these initiatives were driven by a constant need to safeguard a culture or a sort of 'aesthetic experience' that was historically linked to craft skills and that cannot be dissipated by industrial technicism."[27]

These exchanges between art, craft and design have, over the years, enabled the Italian production system to develop objects that have "borne witness to our history, marked our identity", as Furlanis puts it. It is a trend that is leading to an excellence – both formal and ethical – that it appears important to test, now, through the deployment of progressive assessment criteria. According to Anty Pansera, these should include "the quality of the artefact, linguistic innovation, and a significant and updated typological review of the product". She adds: "Excellence today must combine the know-how of tradition with the

[26] Giuseppe Furlanis, "Design e artigianato", in Maria Pilar Lebole (ed.), *L'Arte del Fare e il Fare Arte: Lezioni, approfondimenti e confronti sull'artigianato artistico fra tradizione e innovazione* (Florence: Edifir, 2004), pp. 9–19, especially 10.

[27] Interview with Gisella Capponi, Lidia Rissotto, former director of the ISCR's Scuola di Alta Formazione e Studio, and Anna Maria Falcone, director of the ISCR's Laboratori di Restauro, November 2012.

modernity of an expressive grammar and syntax able to intercept new typologies. I think, therefore, that artisan-artists may be defined as 'excellent' when, strengthened by an understanding and awareness of their own know-how, they are able to face the complexities of our time and create objects that are able to attract attention and engage the user (or buyer) thanks to a topicality that is not merely formal."

Ugo La Pietra also points to the importance of a "syntax of the contemporary" in assessing "craft excellence", and this is why it is perhaps easier to distinguish and define this excellence "in works that hark back to the past, where we can identify and measure the design's role in recreating an object from the past in its philological entirety and where, by comparing it with the original object, we can assess the manual and factual ability that has gone into its making. It is more difficult to objectively define excellence in new, contemporary works, where the determining factors are mainly the product's originality, factuality, and ability to serve as a model that other authors want to replicate".

Stefano Micelli underlines the difficulty of establishing an objective assessment method based, to the extent possible, on measurable criteria: "Peers are able to judge technical competence. In a vibrant, healthy community, people recognize common values and are also normally able to articulate these from a quantitative standpoint according to analytical and graduated criteria. It is less likely that members of a community be able to gauge the excellence of subjective expression, which belongs to the world of art. Within the artistic context, judgement is more elusive. Notably, those called on to give their opinion in the second instance belong to a different community from the first. A positive assessment in both contexts could in itself be seen as an indication of excellence."

The delicate balance between art and craft thus comes back into play, no longer as the clear (and now surpassed) distinction between a visionary and sophisticated approach and a more modest aptitude for the transformation of material, but as a fundamental working method for devising a modern view of the artistic crafts that determines the absolute and indisputable quality from which "excellence" must derive its sustenance. It is a method that, to paraphrase the former French Minister for Culture and Communication Christine Albanel, is perpetuated and regenerated every day in studios, workshops and, consequently, in industries as well, but only if "we promote, recognize, love and value artisanal *savoir-faire*".[28]

The experts interviewed for this study frequently stressed the importance of the "recognizability" of a product when talking about

[28] See Franco Cologni, "Revers", *Monsieur*, No. 78 (June 2009), p. 194.

the future of the artistic crafts in Italy. For, it is only by fostering a real awareness of the hard work, passion and culture that a master craftsperson puts into the creation of an object that we will be able to give this sector the prominence it deserves, thus making the product more desirable and inspiring new generations to follow this vocation. As Micelli goes on to say, "the master craftspeople of the future will tend to free themselves from their traditional links with territory in the strict sense (for example, the districts) and from any other constraint that does not derive from their own skill and invention. The challenge for these new artisans is to give their craftsmanship a contemporary edge. This will require a great deal of courage (not least in entrepreneurial terms) and a considerable propensity for new forms of expression (fashion, design, art, communication)". And as Jean-Michel Delisle sees it, tomorrow's master artisans "will have a personal philosophy that enables them to escape from the hysterical pace of the world. They will also have to be teachers so as to be able to share their culture, their passion".

It is therefore important to know how to innovate, but also how to transmit one's know-how over time. We must reconnect the ability to reflect and teach (albeit through the rather particular medium of the "workshop") with the skills and in-depth knowledge that derive from tradition. But tradition must serve as a cultural reserve and not as a constraint. For Mariapia Garavaglia, "the master craftsperson of the future will be an artisan by profession and master of techniques and knowledge, but also an 'artist' who uses the hand to express an identity, thanks to the distinctive nature of a work which is unique even when it is reproduced or reproducible, because it is the fruit of authentic and personal creativity".

That creativity must never be self-indulgent, but rather in tune with the different materials, with the changing times and with the wealth of possibilities offered by design. According to Stefano Micelli, the "excellent" craftsperson of tomorrow will therefore be able to combine practical skills with "relational" attributes, such as "an ability to listen to the customer, a willingness to communicate with designers and artists, and a receptiveness to technological innovation. The artist-artisan must demonstrate openness and continuity – in other words, the typical traits of a master".

Two important points emerge from the views expressed by the peers and experts. The first is that at the heart of Italian excellence lies an approach that is more akin to that of a Renaissance workshop. In other words, both the making and, more importantly, the culture of making are nourished by creativity, *savoir-faire*, beauty and intuition. The second is that protection and promotion of the Made in Italy mark of excellence necessarily require recognition of the fact that, in the Bel

Paese, the artistic crafts are still equated with culture and know-how and that their many professional facets enrich each of the sectors in which the Made in Italy label is synonymous the world over with perfection, prestige, research and elegance. Awareness signifies choice: knowing which artisanal professions nourish Italy's productive system is the basis on which to direct one's career, to manage excellent craftsmanship and to understand how to open up to the future without discarding the important lessons of the past.

Asking ourselves how to assess the cultural, economic and productive excellence that seems to be Italy's unique, stand-out feature – wonderfully inimitable but also extremely fragile and perhaps even under threat – is possibly crucial. This is because assessing excellence means not only bestowing dignity, recognition and status on those who genuinely deserve it, but also providing anyone still developing, in a transitional phase or in training with a credible and successful model to emulate in their quest for achievement. The key ingredient of that model is the human hand, whose intelligence not even the passage of time can call into question.

Drawing on their knowledge of the historical and cultural value of the artistic crafts, the experts consulted for this study gave their views on the characteristics they deemed most apt in distinguishing craft excellence from other kinds of production, however worthy of merit. Their starting point was the list of criteria outlined above, which itself was the result of a careful analysis of national and local laws, directives and regulations designed to define, identify, promote and protect the artistic crafts.

The experts contacted included historians, economists, institutional representatives, architects, designers, artisans and businesspeople. They were asked to go through the list of criteria and rank them. An analysis of the outcome of this exercise is vital in order to gauge the relative importance of each category as it is defined by national and local laws, directives and regulations.

"Tradition" and "territory" are two criteria that were judged to be of primary importance in determining excellence, in that they are objectively identifiable and easily verifiable. However, in this context we have used them always in a dynamic sense, or as a cultural crucible where know-how and beauty (layers of which have been added over the centuries) blend with "inventiveness", "creativity" and "innovation".

In its own way, the next criterion that emerged – "competence" – unites and connects tradition and territory. A competent person in this context is someone who is familiar with tradition and consciously plays an active role in their own territory or region. They are able to seize new trends and interpret them in their own way.

Next in the list come "authenticity" and "originality". These two criteria are closely linked to the legal protection of artisanal products and express a different aspect of the territory and of the intuition that guides the artisan's hand.

If "talent" is considered important but not all that fundamental, it is perhaps because craftsmanship, although closely associated with inspiration and vocation, is still perceived to reveal its secrets only gradually, through steady and regular application in the workshop. This is why "craftsmanship" seems to take precedence over "training", even though the latter is more easily and objectively verifiable. This also goes some way to explaining why craft is no longer seen as a predestined goal, but as a consciously chosen career path that has drawn the individual from an early age and that, over the years, gradually unveils its power through the training of the hand, the mind and the heart to achieve the excellence that is its natural destination.

The experts' responses, although crucial for understanding the relative importance of each category, would not, however, be sufficient to give a complete idea of the relationship between craft excellence and the Italian economic, productive and cultural system. It was thus necessary to go beyond this circle of experts to find out to what extent the Italian public is aware of and appreciates the artistic crafts, and which characteristics are regarded as relevant in determining excellence in the craft professions. Chapter 4 details the outcomes of a quantitative study undertaken to this end in June 2012 by the sociologist Enrico Finzi on behalf of the Cologni Foundation for the Métiers d'Art.

3.3. DEFINING THE CONCEPT: TERMS USED TO DESCRIBE CRAFT EXCELLENCE

3.3.1. Authenticity

> Some writers confuse authenticity, which they ought always to aim at, with originality, which they should never bother about.
>
> W.H. AUDEN, *Aphorisms on Writing*

What is authentic is true, not false, not forged, and can be proved to be so. The word derives from the late Latin *authenticus,* which in turn originated from the Greek *authentes* meaning "author; one acting on one's own authority". Since its origins, "authentic" has implied a binding and essential connection between a work and its author. By extension, an authentic work is in fact a work of art or literature "that surely belongs to the author to whom it is attributed, and is not an imitation or a fake".[29] Authentic is also something that corresponds to reality, to a truth "that excludes all possibility of contradiction; true, genuine, sincere, convincing".[30]

The first acceptation of "authenticity", which is also the most common and straightforward, is therefore related to the necessity of tracing a work back to its author, and of ascertaining its parentage beyond any doubt. This requisite derives from two main factors: the first is the correct attribution of the artistic and economic value of a work to the person who possesses the skills to produce it; the second is to be able to connect the work, through the acknowledgement of its creator, to a context, an experience, as the expression of individual and/or historical, artistic and social values.

This initial reflection on the need to recognize the authenticity of a work helps us understand how the bond between author and object has implications that are not tied exclusively to the artist, but also to the universe that revolves around the artist and the value – the *pretium*, in other words – that ensues from this relationship. This concept is particularly relevant in the discourse on artistic crafts, because the coexistence of different features (a condition that, as we have seen so far, is necessary and has a variety of subjective, objective and contextual ramifications) summarizes, in the notion of an object's authenticity, everything that an artistic craft is and should be.

The combination of features intrinsic to creation (contextual circumstances together with those related to the maker) bestows on the artisan the responsibility of producing unique and original objects that must also be universally recognizable. That recognizability implies not only the mere generic and formal identity of the object's production – a violin in the shape of a violin, a vase in the shape of a vase, wine made from grapes – but also the specific identity expected of an artisanal object: an identity that encapsulates all those qualities of craftsmanship, competence, creativity, tradition, territory and originality that are peculiar to this kind of manufacturing. As the art critic Giovanni Urbani remarked in relation to works of art, "authenticity [...] ensures that the aesthetic sentiment has an objective and rationally verifiable content, which can be proved and certified at all times on the basis of factual

[29] See Giovanni Treccani, *Dizionario Enciclopedico Italiano* (Rome: Istituto Poligrafico dello Stato, 1970), s.v. "autentico".

[30] See Giacomo Devoto and Gian Carlo Oli, *Il dizionario della lingua italiana* (Florence: Le Monnier, 2011) , s.v. "autentico", and Salvatore Battaglia, *Grande Dizionario della lingua italiana* (Turin: UTET, 2004), s.v. "autentico". Authenticity is defined in the online Oxford Dictionary as "of undisputed origin and not a copy; genuine" and "made or done in a traditional or original way, or in a way that faithfully resembles an original".

certainties, such as those that can be obtained from scientific analysis, documentary evidence, etc.".[31]

Authenticity in the strictest sense (i.e. that which is genuine, not fake) goes hand in hand with a broader understanding of the concept, embracing what stems from a culture and a tradition and is made with materials and techniques that comply with certain specifications that have been developed and perfected over the centuries in a given territory. Thus the parameters that underpin a product's authenticity are related not only to its genuineness but also to its true source. This is why individual nations and multilateral institutions, including UNESCO, put such effort into the identification, promotion, conservation and protection of humanity's tangible and intangible cultural treasures.

A definition of authenticity based on objective parameters, similarly to what we are undertaking here with regard to the artistic crafts, was proposed by the 1964 Venice Charter[32] and adopted the following year by the International Council on Monuments and Sites (ICOMOS). The Charter constitutes a pragmatic and impartial approach to the identification and conservation of the world heritage, providing practical reference criteria without being fettered by philosophical and ideological conceptions (which nonetheless deeply permeate it) that would remain open to interpretation.

The Charter served as a reference point for the 1994 Nara Conference[33] and was later integrated into the 2003 UNESCO Convention for the Safeguarding of the Intangible Cultural Heritage, which eventually led to the creation of the system for the identification, promotion and preservation of the so-called "Living Human Treasures". Article 1 of the Charter states that a historic monument reflects "evidence of a particular civilization, a significant development or a historic event".[34] Article 3 further states that the "intention in conserving and restoring monuments is to safeguard them no less as works of art than as historical evidence".[35]

This last objective is pursued by respecting the monument's original destination, conserving the traditional environment in which it is located, and preserving the original volumes, colours and proportions, because

[31] Giovanni Urbani, *Intorno al restauro* (Milan: Skira, 2000).

[32] International Charter for the Conservation and Restoration of Monuments and Sites (The Venice Charter), adopted at the Second International Congress of Architects and Specialists of Historic Buildings, 25–31 May 1964, www.icomos.org/charters/venice_e.pdf.

[33] Nara Conference on Authenticity, organized by the Japanese Agency for Cultural Affairs, in cooperation with UNESCO, the International Centre for the Study of the Preservation and Restoration of Cultural Property (ICCROM) and ICOMOS, Nara, Japan, 1–6 November 1994.

[34] Venice Charter, Article 1.

[35] *Ibid.* Article 3.

> [a] monument is inseparable from the history to which it bears witness (Article 7) […] The process of restoration is a highly specialized operation. Its aim is to preserve and reveal the aesthetic and historic value of the monument and is based on respect for original material and authentic documents. (Article 9) […] Replacements of missing parts must integrate harmoniously with the whole, but at the same time must be distinguishable from the original so that restoration does not falsify the artistic or historic evidence (Article 12).[36]

It is thus clear that the principle of authenticity can also express a notion of "non-manipulation" and respect for materials, history, tradition, culture and society.

The Nara Document on Authenticity, one of the outcomes of the Nara Conference, also affirms:

> In a world that is increasingly subject to the forces of globalization and homogenization, and in a world in which the search for cultural identity is sometimes pursued through aggressive nationalism and the suppression of the cultures of minorities, the essential contribution made by the consideration of authenticity in conservation practice is to clarify and illuminate the collective memory of humanity.[37]

Authenticity is therefore the ultimate reference point for cultural heritage, which, as we have seen, is by definition pre-existent and the source of all things, even when time and history make it hard to identify the passages and the connections:

> Conservation of cultural heritage in all its forms and historical periods is rooted in the values attributed to the heritage. Our ability to understand these values depends, in part, on the degree to which information sources about these values may be understood as credible or truthful. Knowledge and understanding of these sources of information, in relation to original and subsequent characteristics of the cultural heritage, and their meaning, is a requisite basis for assessing all aspects of authenticity.[38]

The sources of information, according to the Nara Document, can be "physical, oral, written or figurative, which make it possible to know the nature, specificities, meaning and history of the cultural heritage.[39] […] The use of these sources permits elaboration of the specific artistic,

[36] *Ibid.* Articles 7, 9 and 12.
[37] Nara Document on Authenticity, 1994, para. 4, whc.unesco.org/document/9379.
[38] *Ibid.*, para. 9.
[39] *Ibid.* Definitions

historic, social, and scientific dimensions of the cultural heritage being examined".[40] Depending on the nature of the cultural heritage, its cultural context and evolution through time, the parameters of authenticity should also be sought in "form and design, materials and substance, use and function, traditions and techniques, location and setting, and spirit and feeling, and other internal and external factors".[41]

Furthermore, the Convention for the Safeguarding of the Intangible Cultural Heritage defines the "intangible cultural heritage" as

> the practices, representations, expressions, knowledge, skills – as well as the instruments, objects, artefacts and cultural spaces associated therewith – that communities, groups and, in some cases, individuals recognize as part of their cultural heritage. This intangible cultural heritage, transmitted from generation to generation, is constantly recreated by communities and groups in response to their environment, their interaction with nature and their history, and provides them with a sense of identity and continuity, thus promoting respect for cultural diversity and human creativity.[42]

UNESCO recognizes as part of the intangible cultural heritage: oral traditions and expressions, including language as a vehicle of the intangible cultural heritage; performing arts; social practices, rituals and festive events; knowledge and practices concerning nature and the universe; and traditional craftsmanship.[43]

Within this context, UNESCO has instituted the "Living Human Treasures" programme, stating in the introduction to its guidelines for the establishment of such systems that "one of the most effective ways to achieve the sustainable safeguarding of the intangible cultural heritage would be to guarantee that the bearers of that heritage continue to further develop their knowledge and skills and transmit them to younger generations".[44] UNESCO prompts Member States to establish national systems to identify, give official recognition to and encourage the bearers of intangible cultural heritage in order "to preserve the knowledge and skills necessary for the performing, enactment or re-creation of intangible cultural heritage elements with high historical, artistic or cultural value".[45] The epigraph chosen by UNESCO to introduce the guidelines is a quote from Igor Stravinsky's *Poetics of Music* (1952): "A

[40] *Ibid.*, para. 13.

[41] *Ibid.*

[42] Convention for the Safeguarding of the Intangible Cultural Heritage, 2003, Article 2(1), www.unesco.org/culture/ich/en/convention.

[43] *Ibid.* Article 2(2).

[44] UNESCO, Guidelines for the Establishment of National "Living Human Treasures" Systems, updated 2002, p. 2, www.unesco.org/culture/ich/doc/src/00031-EN.pdf.

[45] *Ibid.*

true tradition is not the witness of a remote past; it is a living force that enlivens and nourishes the present. Far from a mere repetition of what has gone before, a tradition is an on-going reality. It can be considered as family property, a heritage one receives on the condition that it be allowed to fructify before its transmission to future generations."[46]

The primary objective of the programme is to conserve and transmit the knowledge and skills of the Living Human Treasures, and at its root, as the Nara Document makes clear, is a firm commitment to the concept of authenticity in the sense of recognizability and attribution. Italy has the largest number of UNESCO world heritage sites (51 at October 2016).[47] Yet, notwithstanding its immense cultural history and tradition, the country can currently lay claim to just seven examples of officially recognized intangible cultural heritage: Sicilian puppet theatre (*opera dei Pupi*); Sardinian pastoral songs (*canto a tenore*); traditional violin craftsmanship in Cremona; the Mediterranean diet; celebrations of big shoulder-borne processional structures (*macchine a spalla*); Pantelleria's traditional agricultural practice of cultivating head-trained bush vines (*vite ad alberello*); and falconry.[48] Italy has yet to identify and give official recognition to a living human treasure.

Japan, meanwhile, enacted a specific law for the protection of the country's artistic treasures as far back as 1929 and, following the adoption in 1950 of the Law for the Protection of Cultural Properties, established the title of "Holder of an Important Intangible Cultural Property" for those masters who practise traditional crafts and performing arts, demonstrating that artistic techniques and skills are considered as much a part of the country's heritage as ancient monuments and artefacts.[49]

Italy, in fact, has a wealth of "living treasures", individuals who, while not officially recognized as such, represent the country's finest production. Indeed, the competence, spirit and know-how of Italian artisans are a perfect antidote to the vagaries of the financial markets and the recipe for the survival of the national economy in a world where globalization and delocalization have become synonymous with mass production without soul, quality or history.

In recent years, the great luxury brands have been the first to realize that their communication strategies could not focus on quality, elegance, exclusivity and excellence alone, but had also to reflect their "heritage", that is to say the values "denoting a traditional brand or product

[46] *Ibid.*
[47] The full list can be found at http://whc.unesco.org/en/statesparties/it.
[48] See www.unesco.org/culture/ich/en/lists.
[49] See www.unesco.org/culture/ich/doc/src/00177-EN.pdf.

regarded as emblematic of fine craftsmanship":[50] in a word, authenticity.

Following the global financial crisis of 2008, there was a marked shift in consumer trends in the "mass luxury" sector: people started to look for articles with a label (a "signature") that was a promise not only of exclusivity, but also of the product's utmost quality and authenticity.[51]

While the concepts of "signature" and "authenticity" are inextricably bound, the existence of a signature, although relevant, is not decisive in determining the authenticity of a product. As Gisella Capponi reminds us:

> The assessment of the authenticity of a work of art is not limited to the presence of the artist's signature, or to its distinction from an imitation or a fake. Every artwork is the result of a complex series of inseparable facts: from the historical context within a particular epoch or culture to the character of a specific artistic personality.[52]

Capponi goes on to say that:

> The two concepts of originality and creativity are well exemplified by Argan in his seminal work on the history of art criticism. Argan points out that if we were to observe the famous sculpted salt cellar that Benvenuto Cellini made for Francis I merely from an analytical perspective, it would necessarily fall into the category of furnishing, then into the subcategory of tableware, and eventually into the sub-subcategory of salt cellars; in terms of technique, it would fall into the category of semi-enamelled gold sculptures. In other words, this object would belong to the same category of countless similar objects if the artist's creativity and originality had not redeemed it from the humble *niveau* of everyday item, transforming it into a masterpiece capable of defining "the development of sculpture or, in a broader sense, the Florentine Mannerist artistic culture" from that moment onwards.[53]

According to the art historian and critic Michele Cordaro, the possibility of judging an artwork thus

> derives from the ability to broaden the field of relations, encompassing all those phenomena specifically inhering in its creation, as well as those relations or those non-specific references that, sometimes implicitly, are relevant in the origin and the determination of an artwork.[54]

[50] See www.oxforddictionaries.com/definition/english/heritage.

[51] See Stefano Micelli, *Futuro artigiano* (Venice: Marsilio, 2011), p. 69.

[52] Interview with Gisella Capponi, November 2012.

[53] *Ibid.* referring to Giulio Carlo Argan, "La storia dell'arte", *Storia dell'arte*, No. 1–2 (1969): pp. 5–36, especially 18.

[54] Michele Cordaro, "La storia dell'arte nella concezione di Argan", in *Annali dell'Associazione Bianchi Bandinelli* (founded by Giulio Carlo Argan), No. 12 (Rome: Graffiti, 2002).

Even a product's provenance may, in itself, represent a guarantee of quality, originality and authenticity, and have significant economic value and considerable impact on the market. As early as 1891, the Madrid Agreement for the Repression of False or Deceptive Indications of Source on Goods was adopted at the international level; Italy ratified it in 1967 following the adoption of the 1958 Lisbon Agreement for the Protection of Appellations of Origin and their International Registration (implemented in Italy by Law No. 676 of 4 July 1967 and Legislative Decree No. 656 of 26 February 1968). It was only in 1994, following the multilateral trade negotiations of the Uruguay Round (1986–1994), that the countries party to the World Trade Organization,[55] including the European Union (EU), signed the Marrakesh Agreement on Rules of Origin (adopted with European Council Decision No. 94/800/EC).

In particular, the Marrakesh Agreement states that "rules of origin should provide for the country to be determined as the origin of a particular good to be either the country where the good has been wholly obtained or, when more than one country is concerned in the production of the good, the country where the last substantial transformation has been carried out".[56] On the basis of this Agreement, WTO members must ensure the transparency of the rules of origin, without creating "restrictive, distorting, or disruptive effects on international trade; [...] rules of origin should be administrable in a consistent, uniform, impartial, and reasonable manner"[57] and be based on "a positive standard"[58] (i.e. the rules must define what confers origin, not its opposite).

The European Union Council Regulations (EEC) No. 2081/92 and (EC) No. 510/2006 identify and protect the "geographical indications" and the "designations of origin" for agricultural products and foodstuffs (in compliance with the Lisbon Agreement) via the registration mechanism, explicitly acknowledging that:

> When a food product becomes well-known outside its area of origin, it may find itself competing in the marketplace with imitation products making use of the same name. This unfair competition not only undermines the efforts made by the producer or manufacturer to acquire the good name in the first place, it leaves consumers confused as to which product is genuine and which is a copy. [...] Registration will mean that these products are protected at Community

[55] The World Trade Organization (WTO) replaced the General Agreement on Tariffs and Trade (GATT) and was instituted during those same negotiations.

[56] Lisbon Agreement for the Protection of Appellations of Origin and their International Registration, 31 October 1958, Article 9(b), http://eur-lex.europa.eu/legal-content/EN/TXT/HTML/?uri=CELEX:21994A1223(12)&from=IT.

[57] *Ibid.* Articles 2(c) and 9(e).

[58] *Ibid.* Article 9(g).

level against competition from imitations and misleading products. This protection is exactly the same as would derive from an industrial property right such as a patent or trademark. In other words, once a geographical indication or designation of origin is registered, only producers in a designated area who comply with strict production rules set out in the product specification may use that name.[59]

Unlike the designation of origin, the "Made in" denomination remains unregulated, and is the subject of much debate. Within the EU, the main reference on this matter is the Community Customs Code, Article 24 of which, in accordance with the Lisbon Agreement, states: "Goods whose production involved more than one country shall be deemed to originate in the country where they underwent their last, substantial, economically justified processing or working in an undertaking equipped for that purpose and resulting in the manufacture of a new product or representing an important stage of manufacture."[60] The "Made in" denomination therefore has to do with the regulation of the exchange of goods within and outside the EU, while the regulation of product labels (food and non-food) is mainly related to transparency and to consumer protection, rather than to the protection and promotion of the history, traditions and cultural heritage of their place of origin, the only exceptions being the PGI (Protected Geographical Indication) and PDO (Protected Designation of Origin).[61]

In the absence of specific legislation that may serve as a reference point also for the assessment of "authenticity" in the output of master craftspeople, we need to define how and to what extent an artisanal product should be "authentic". To do so, we must consider an artisanal

[59] See Press Release IP/96/153, "Commission adopts draft decision protecting the designations of various agricultural and food products", 6 March 1996, http://europa.eu/rapid/press-release_IP-96-492_en.htm.

[60] Council Regulation (EEC) No. 2913/92 of 12 October 1992 establishing the Community Customs Code, http://eur-lex.europa.eu/LexUriServ/LexUriServ.do?uri=CELEX:31992R2913:en:HTML.

[61] Italy, which has clearly every interest in protecting and supporting the "Made in Italy" denomination, has unilaterally tried to introduce changes, through the Reguzzoni-Versace Law No. 55 of 8 April 2010, in the regulations governing the commercialization of textile products, leather goods and footwear. The Law's declared purpose was to provide consumers with all due information on the manufacturing process, establishing a labelling system that guarantees the traceability of textile products, leather goods and footwear, i.e. the main products of the Italian fashion industry. However, the Law was never implemented because the European Commission declared its illegitimacy on formal and substantial grounds. It is nevertheless apparent that, however arbitrary, this Law aims to establish a more rigorous protection of the "Made in Italy" label, affirming that this denomination can be used (as per Article 4) "only for finished products resulting from processing phases […] that were carried out mainly within the national territory and in particular if at least two of the processing phases […] have been carried out within the same territory and that there be verifiable traceability for all other phases".

product within the entire production chain: for a final product (be it a piece of jewellery, a dress, a hat or a violin) to be authentic, all the elements that compose it, including those entrusted to a master artisan, must also be authentic. Indeed, to achieve authenticity, the master artisan must operate in a specified and predetermined place, in a certain way and with specific materials and tools.

Although most people can perceive the value of a designation of origin or of a "Made in" label, there is still much to be done to provide consumers with the necessary tools to understand, assess and appreciate the craft and skill of master artisans.

The authenticity of an artisanal product therefore manifests itself *within the production chain* and can be traced to a few key factors:

– the quality by which a product is *not imitable*, in that it draws on and expresses the *tradition of a district, local craft knowledge or a cultural heritage*;

– *it is the outcome of a creative effort*, it eschews imitation and mass production and, even when concerning the making of products that are not unique but serialized, it retains its *character of uniqueness and authenticity in the techniques, in the processes, in the use of materials and in its aesthetic sensibility*.

3.3.2. Competence

Competenza, or "competence" in English, is defined by both the Zingarelli and Devoto-Oli dictionaries as the ability to find one's bearings in certain situations or to carry out a specific activity.[62] As such, it requires an in-depth knowledge of the activity concerned, coupled with experience gained over a long period and an effortlessness in performing the activity that is the mark of the maker's proficiency and skill. If applied to our own field of inquiry, it is clear that each prerequisite determines specific properties of both the craft and the artisan, and acquires value in its own right.

Someone who has the necessary training to carry out a specific activity or task is considered "competent". In the field of artistic craftsmanship, this training takes place through hands-on experience and over a certain period. Knowledge is a fundamental requirement for an artisan to comprehend the particularities of their chosen craft and is primarily acquired through training courses or workshop apprenticeships. That

[62] See Nicola Zingarelli, *Vocabolario della lingua italiana* (Bologna: Zanichelli, 2010) and Giacomo Devoto and Gian Carlo Oli, *Vocabolario della lingua italiana* (Florence: Le Monnier, 2011), s.v. "competenza".

knowledge is therefore necessarily a blend of theory and practice: the artisans must be familiar with the models, shapes and designs that are typical of the product being created, just as they must know how to recreate, design and propose a version of the product that expresses both a tradition and, through certain distinctive traits, the maker's own development.

In the mid-17th century, Jean-Baptiste Colbert, French minister of finance under King Louis XIV, fully understood the importance of having artisans with the necessary "competence" and skills to work on the artistic and luxury objects produced at the Manufactures he founded under the aegis of the Crown. Indeed, tapestries, porcelain, arms and crystalware were created at the Royal Manufactures, and then exported throughout Europe as symbols of a French power that was artistic as well as political. This would have been unthinkable without the contribution of those highly skilled artisans, who were often "poached" from other countries where their craft had been practised for centuries. This was the case, for instance, with the master glassworkers of Murano, whose invitation to work in France sparked a serious diplomatic incident. The Venetian Republic had begun protecting its production methods as early as 1271 by imposing a ban on the importation of glass from abroad and prohibiting the entry of foreign glassworkers into its territory. Moreover, a decree of the Republic prohibited Venetian glassblowers from working in kilns outside Venice to avoid any risk of others learning their techniques.

Colbert was frequently accused of going too far in favouring, protecting and promoting "craft work" over the agricultural labour that was the lifeblood of the vast majority of the French population. In reality, the innovations introduced to the French economic system by Colbert had reverberations that went well beyond those relating simply to domestic demand:

> The state manufactures set up by Colbert were designed precisely to meet and profit from the demand of fashion; they also were set up through a state system regulating production. The new arrangement helped to transfer both cultural and economic power from independent artisans and city guilds to the state, making fashion a political tool for empowering the central government. The new manufactures (royal or state-sanctioned) being developed under Colbert produced consumer goods that were both designed for the marketplace and distinctively French. They were neither traditional wares derived from regional cultures nor slavish copies of fashionable objects found elsewhere, but rather ones made according to directives from the state.[63]

[63] Chandra Mukerji, *Territorial Ambitions and the Gardens of Versailles* (Cambridge: Cambridge University Press, 1997), p. 103.

For merchants it was entirely different. In Colbert's view, a five-year apprenticeship followed by a *compagnage* of a further five years made it too difficult to enter the job market.[64] The expertise of the artisans who worked at the Royal Manufactures was, on the other hand, mostly and necessarily gained on the job and over time. This way of passing on skills is also highlighted by the authors of the *Encyclopédie*, who placed a very high value not only on the apprenticeship itself but also on the judgement a master craftsperson can give to a pupil.[65]

The knowledge required to gain "competence" thus involves both theoretical learning (of the names of the materials and equipment needed for production, the intrinsic properties of the raw materials, and the work processes used) and its practical application. Through repetition and experimentation, the theory becomes engrained in the mind, allowing the learner to understand the most common options available and to experience the most remote variations. In her essay on the historical success of Italian craftsmanship during the Renaissance, sociologist Linda Gobbi describes the essential requirements of the artistic crafts, which, still today, demand complex, multidisciplinary skills: someone specializing in a craft will also have to face moments in which "the slow pace of maturation must go hand in hand with timeliness, which does not imply acceleration or speed, but the ability to be responsive in a changing and complex situation".[66]

The dissemination of knowledge was a fundamental feature of the culture associated with the "Renaissance workshop", which is often used to describe the interpretive, practical and creative skills of the Italian masters. This can be likened to the importance placed today on the dissemination of "knowware", which is the in-built knowledge that comes with practice and experience. However,

[64] "They are so rigorous in many great Cities of your Kingdom, that they will not receive Tradesmen among them; which is an abuse *Your Majesty* ought not to suffer; for it keeps many from applying themselves to Trade, who perhaps would thrive better, than those that are in it. What necessity is there of serving an Apprenticeship to a Master? It may perhaps be necessary for Handicrafts-men and Artificers, because no body should venture upon a Trade which they do not understand; but for others, why must they lose their time, or why must they be hinder'd from following a Trade they have learn'd in Foreign Countries, or because they cannot shew a Certificate that they serv'd an Apprenticeship?", Gatien Courtilz de Sandras and Jean-Baptiste Colbert, *The political testament of M. Jean Baptist Colbert, minister and Secretary of State wherein is contain'd all that hath pass'd under the reign of Lewis the XIV unto the year 1684: with remarks upon the government of the kingdom of France*, translated from French by William Granville (London: Printed for R. Bentley, 1695), Chapter 15, p. 319.

[65] Denis Diderot (ed.), *Encyclopédie, ou Dictionnaire raisonné des sciences, des arts et des métiers* (Paris: Chez Briasson, 1765), Vol. 20, pp. 911–915, s.v. "Maitrises".

[66] Linda Gobbi, "L'Impronta Rinascimentale dalla prima persona singolare alla prima persona plurale", in Giovanni Lanzone and Francesco Morace (eds), *Il talento dell'impresa* (Milan: Nomos, 2010), p. 22.

> [t]he idea of weaving a *knowware*, that is to say, a space-time of community-based icons designed through shared and diversified learning practices in hybrid (virtual and real) networking practices embraces research on the anthropology of digital networks wherein work, learning and innovation co-exist in a state of play. "Communities of practice" (after Wenger's approach to knowledge management in organizations) can only be grasped through "composite concepts" such as "learning-in-working", which represent "the fluid evolution of learning through practice".[67]

Once again, therefore, focusing only on the elements of "symbolic analysis" is not sufficient for anyone seeking to ascertain the criteria for assessing competence: knowledge, which is a crucial component of competence, is acquired and must be obtained via a serious and structured hands-on approach, which has always characterized the learning and working methods of any master artisan. Therein lies the awareness that only "the profound maturation of skills makes it possible to react promptly later, because it ensures a level of expertise and knowledge that allows one to deal with the unforeseen".[68] The concept of competence thus

> involves various aspects, from the ability to deal with complex problems to the ability to weigh up, choose and take actions, including in areas bordering one's own area of expertise, and to the ability to relate to others. For this reason, the knowledge needed to be competent cannot be acquired only through school or other kinds of academic learning. [...] To be able to gain a foothold in the market and stay there, in fact, depends more and more often on one's professional skills and the ability to respond to unexpected situations.[69]

Expertise, proficiency and skill are all terms still closely associated with competence, at least to the same extent as experience. Indeed, experience consists in knowledge that is acquired through direct application or mere observation, while practice implies exercising a certain activity, which leads to direct learning and the command of a certain task. As Gobbi points out, the limits placed on the use of machinery in artisanal production take into consideration, among other things, that any detachment from the material and the activity is a lost

[67] Gilson Schwartz, *Iconomics: Challenges for Theory and Policy* (São Paulo: City of Knowledge Research Group, Dept. of Film, Radio and TV, School of Communication and Arts, University of São Paulo, Brazil, 2009), p. 58.

[68] Gobbi, "L'Impronta Rinascimentale", p. 22.

[69] Anna Maria Ajello and Saul Meghnagi (eds), *La competenza tra flessibilità e specializzazione: Il lavoro in contesti sociali e produttivi diversi* (Milan: Franco Angeli, 1998).

opportunity for learning, which is "stolen" as it were by the machines and used by these for their own improvement.[70]

The Zingarelli dictionary, meanwhile, observes with regard to the different meanings of the term "esperienza"[71] that expertise is a higher level of mastery, which necessarily also implies experience, practice and personal ability. Expertise thus falls within the concept of competence as an excellent ability that characterizes a high level of know-how, which itself is a blend of knowledge of the craft, mastery of the material and the techniques, and technical skill. In other words, it implies a superior ability coupled with style, applied with greater ease and confidence than normal when carrying out a certain task.[72]

Returning to the initial definition of competence, let us recall that other aspect, the "ability to find one's bearings". In this sense, more generally, it refers to the ability to deal with the structural, ethical and formal difficulties involved in the everyday management of a craft firm and with the progressive development of artisanal products. The artistic crafts have a close relationship with reality, driven as they are by a range of factors, such as innovative materials and techniques, feedback from what are often niche markets, consumer needs, changes in taste, economic survival, transmission of knowledge, and research. A master artisan has to deal constantly with different situations from which to draw new stimuli and inspiration, and must always come up with considered, responsible decisions. The notion of responsibility in particular can be considered inherent to the concept of competence. Leaving aside for a moment the legal meaning of the term, which also implies the management of a company, making complex choices has consequences for which one is responsible and which require further action: this is the ability to find one's bearings.

Knowledge becomes a key element of the new assessment paradigm with regard to the "quality" of work, as underlined by Enzo Rullani, professor of industrial economics at the University of Venice:

> I propose measuring this distance [between the classic concept of work and anything new] along the following three axes:
>
> – knowledge, which considers work as an intelligent strength and the know-how to generate value;

[70] Richard Sennett makes a similar point: "Thanks to the revolution in micro-computing, however, modern machinery is not static, through feedback loops machines can learn from their experience. Yet machinery is misused when it deprives people themselves from learning through repetition." See Richard Sennett, *The Craftsman* (New Haven: Yale University Press, 2008), pp. 38–39.

[71] See Zingarelli, *Vocabolario della lingua italiana*, s.v. "esperienza".

[72] See Devoto and Oli, *Vocabolario della lingua italiana*, s.v. "bravura".

> – power, which sees work as a self-regulator that responds to itself and not only to an external authority;
>
> – risk, in other words the fact that the results of the work fall, at least partly, upon the worker.
>
> […] The three dimensions of the map are all related, in the sense that knowledge, power and risk are all connected with the work performed: a person who claims intelligence and power in their work – in other words the discretionary use of intelligence – can hardly escape the risks arising from the outcome of their work. If, however, the cognitive and decisional functions are delegated to others (the company owner or manager), the risk will also be transferred: the physiology of the system demands that the risk is assumed by those with knowledge and those who make the decisions.[73]

Applied to the artistic crafts, similar competences are closely intertwined and can be acquired through practical experience and the critical acknowledgment of the place of one's activity, its limits and its potential. In essence, it is a *savoir-faire* that could be extended to the entire concept of artistic craftsmanship and that has always been typical of Italy's manufacturing industry.[74]

Lastly, many manufacturing specifications in force throughout Italy now stipulate a minimum training/apprenticeship period, as well as continuity of work, without which an artisan cannot be registered with the *Albo Regionale delle Imprese Artigiane* (Regional Directory of Craft Firms), a sure sign that the acquisition of experience, in the various meanings given above, is becoming a more and more objective requisite for artisanal mastery.

The notion of "excellence", which is tightly bound up with an idea of competence that is not merely an expression of *savoir-faire* but also of design capacity, goes hand in hand with technical mastery. But, as Richard Sennett reminds us, this "is founded on skill developed to a high degree. By one commonly used measure, about ten thousand hours of experience are required to produce a master carpenter or musician. Various studies show that as skill progresses, it becomes more problem-attuned".[75]

Time is thus paramount in determining a level of competence, which transcends and enhances talent (seen as a gift) and is structured in a *savoir-faire* which starts with talent and turns into the ability to design, to create, to produce and, as described by Stefano Micelli, to interpret. The time factor combines the "slow pace of maturation"

[73] Enzo Rullani, "Dopo Taylor: il nuovo rapporto tra conoscenza e produzione", in Andrea Ranieri (ed.), *Il sapere e il lavoro* (Milan: Franco Angeli, 2008), p. 25.

[74] Gobbi, "L'Impronta Rinascimentale", p. 22.

[75] Sennett, *The Craftsman*, p. 20.

with, as Linda Gobbi put it, a timely response to a complex and ever-changing situation: "Normally this quality, which is difficult to teach or even just to describe, belongs to the Italian *genius loci*, and in particular to small and medium-sized enterprises that make up the vital fabric of our country. Patience that is transformed into timeliness. Without this mental agility, an artisan cannot make that leap of quality needed to compete in the global marketplace."[76] Once again, Richard Sennett summarizes the meaning of a superior level of mastery, where technique is no longer a mere mechanical activity: "[P]eople can feel fully and think deeply what they are doing once they do it well. It is at the level of mastery, I will show, that ethical problems of craft appear".[77]

Competence in reference to the artistic crafts can thus be summed up as a quality composed of different, connected aspects:

– *knowledge*: acquired at school or in a workshop, relating to materials and techniques, brought to life by constant interaction with other players in the system, and inseparable from knowledge of standards and regulations;

– *experience*: gained directly on the job, accrued over an extended period and always called into question by new projects;

– *expertise*: a superior level of mastery implying highly developed personal skills;

– *responsibility*: referring to the management side of the work and to an awareness of the project that requires the ability to find one's bearings and react promptly;

– *excellence*: understood as outstanding design, interpretation and execution of the project;

– *innovation*: the ability to express oneself with authority with regard to progressive changes in or hybridization of established techniques.

3.3.3. Craftsmanship

> A lack of practical know-how is no longer a status symbol for a modern intellectual, but rather a sign of passive subjection, of an enduring servitude, of a never recovered freedom.
>
> CESARE DE MICHELIS[78]

[76] Gobbi, "L'Impronta Rinascimentale", p. 22.

[77] Sennett, *The Craftsman*, p. 20.

[78] Cesare De Michelis, "Dopo la modernità, l'emozionante ricerca della regola del Talento", in *La regola del talento: Mestieri d'arte e Scuole italiane di eccellenza* (Venice: Marsilio, 2014), pp. 21–23, especially 23.

Giorgio Vasari, in the Preface to his *Lives* (first published in 1550), describes the act of creation, both in the sense of universal creation and artistic creation:

> [T]he first model whence there issued the first image of man was a lump of clay, and not without reason, seeing that the Divine Architect of time and of nature, being Himself most perfect, wished to show in the imperfection of the material the way to add and to take away; in the same manner wherein the good sculptors and painters are wont to work, who, adding and taking away in their models, bring their imperfect sketches to that final perfection which they desire.[79]

The perfect object is achieved by manipulating material, through addition and subtraction, leading to the full execution of an idea, of that vision the master artisan has of an as yet shapeless mass, akin to the vision the Creator had of the earth before the introduction of time and nature. In other words, contemporary craftsmanship is an ongoing dialogue between material and action, between design and its flawless translation into an outstanding product.

The International Charter of Artistic Craftsmanship defines works of artistic craftsmanship as those that are "mainly carried out using manual techniques, at a highly professional technical level, using equipment, but excluding wholly mass-produced works; separate mechanized or automatic work stages are allowed, using innovative techniques and high-technology instruments".[80] From this we can deduce a number of other characteristics pertaining to artistic craftsmanship which need to be considered individually.

Manipulation leads to knowledge of the material through touch: it is undisputed that humans learn through the senses and from experience. It is also true, however, that the mind continues to elaborate every acquired notion, comparing it with all the previously assimilated information; in this way, thought stimulates further learning and experimentation.

The transposition of this principle into the definition of "craftsmanship" sets the limits on the use and misuse of machines, but the finer details that are encapsulated in this concept are expressed and developed according to different parameters. The use of machines is allowed and even to be

[79] Giorgio Vasari, *Lives of the Most Eminent Painters, Sculptors and Architects,* translated by Gaston du C. de Vere (New York: Modern Library, 2006), p. xxxviii, www.gutenberg.org/files/25326/25326-h/25326-h.htm.

[80] International Charter of Artistic Craftsmanship, Definitions, para. 2(b), www.artex.firenze.it/sites/default/files/contenuti/Rete%20Internaz%20Artig/international_charter_of_artistic_craftmanship.pdf.

encouraged when it concerns specific production phases, provided that the machines are at the service of mental and manual intelligence.

The core of the concept of craftsmanship lies in understanding that it is not an abstract principle, nor does it serve a mere commercial function in identifying the greater or lesser value of a product: the artisan's manual skill is what determines an object's highest commercial value.

Craftsmanship is, therefore, not about a preconception connected to an *a priori* assessment of a product's possible positive outcome, but the result of a millenary experience that has led humanity to the realization of its intellectual supremacy and manual intelligence. Richard Sennett reflects on this aspect in these terms:

> The issue – I want to stress – is more complicated than hand *versus* machine. Modern computer programs can indeed learn from their experience in an expanding fashion, because algorithms are rewritten through data feedback. The problem, as Victor Weisskopf says, is that people may let the machines do this learning, the person serving as a passive witness to and consumer of expanding competence, not participating in it. This is why Renzo Piano, the designer of very complicated objects, returns in a circular fashion to drawing them roughly by hand. Abuses of CAD illustrate how, when the head and the hand are separate, it is the head that suffers.[81]

The link between head and hand is effectively carried over into the definition of the work and knowledge of a master craftsperson, illustrating very concretely the importance of a perpetual dialogue between design and possible ways to execute it and establishing the real and multifaceted complexity of artisanal work and the necessary validity of an all-inclusive view of production. The "translation" of a design through the creation of a three-dimensional prototype is in fact a key stage in an object's passage from concept to reality.

Giving tangible form to an object helps to define the end result, inspiring further ideas and improvements. Designers can literally hold their intuition in their hands and gauge how it feels and the rightness of its proportions, gleaning suggestions from the "model-makers", who know the material inside out – its distinctive features, its consistency, its malleability and every detail of its shape.

In this instance, the master artisans put their skill and knowledge at the service of somebody else's idea, seemingly abdicating their role in the creative design process that is so important in the artistic crafts.

[81] Sennett, *The Craftsman*, p. 44.

But because the final product is a synthesis of a range of fundamental skills and knowledge, the master artisan's contribution is nonetheless essential, not only for the product to take shape but also for it to become a multilayered and complete reality. That reality is made up of an appreciable and original aesthetic identity as a counterpoint to the object's functionality and efficacy: qualities that have to be found in its components as well. In other words, the object must become what it is supposed to become, that is, the *unicum* or unique specimen that the designer could not fully visualize and that the master artisan had not envisioned.

Mauro Ferraresi, an expert in the sociology of consumption, writes that "one of the main sources of pride a work can elicit is, in fact, the comprehensive execution of a task that, pictured in the mind as a whole, is brought to a perfect conclusion".[82] We are therefore talking about a rendition of a design that entails all the competences of the master artisan, including that of adapting an idea to a manufacturing reality and a brand identity: creativity is therefore not cast aside or ignored, but directed towards artistic interpretation.

The manual skill involved in artistic craftsmanship is not confined simply to the act of the hands working on the material: the quality and level of professionalism must be high, if not excellent. The perfection that Vasari attributed equally to artists and the divine Creator can also be applied to a more mundane treatment of the subject and a commercial appraisal of the aesthetic and execution qualities of a modern, contemporary product. To put it succinctly, the object created by a master craftsperson must be the outcome of perfect workmanship.

D'Alembert understood this clearly by observing the manual activities illustrated in his *Encyclopédie*, so much so that he specified it in general terms for the mechanical arts in the Preliminary Discourse, stating: "It is workmanship that makes the artisan, and it is not in books at all that one can learn to work by hand."[83] The learning curve – that is, the speed at which an artisan can learn and therefore become a virtuoso in the techniques involved in making a product – is affected by the subjective gift of talent, which is what makes a professional artisan unique.

Two hundred and fifty years later, and from a perspective diametrically

[82] Ampelio Bucci, Vanni Codeluppi and Mauro Ferraresi, *Il Made in Italy: Natura, settori e problemi* (Rome: Carocci, 2011), p. 141.

[83] Jean Baptiste Le Rond D'Alembert, "Preliminary Discourse", *The Encyclopedia of Diderot & d'Alembert Collaborative Translation Project*, translated by Richard N. Schwab and Walter E. Rex (Ann Arbor: Michigan Publishing, University of Michigan Library, 2009), http://hdl.handle.net/2027/spo.did2222.0001.083. Originally published as "Discours préliminaire", *Encyclopédie ou Dictionnaire raisonné des sciences, des arts et des métiers*, Vol. 1, pp. i-xlv (Paris, 1751).

opposed to D'Alembert's, Jonathan Ive, Apple's Chief Design Officer, perfectly backed up the French philosopher's statement when he explained that it is "very hard to learn about materials academically, by reading about them or watching videos about them; the only way you truly understand a material is by making things with it".[84] The issue still revolves around the possibility of drawing something on a computer and then asking the software to make the material visible by means of "rendering", a process that excludes the designer from coming into contact with the material and marks a significant and dangerous split between the form and the material from which it will be made.

Gucci, which the international brand consultancy company Interbrand ranks among the top Italian brands for value creation, creativity and trendsetting, regularly markets its products based on their artisanal origins, as attested by its 2011 "Forever Now" campaign celebrating the fashion house's 90th anniversary. The Florentine label is well acquainted with today's meaning of the intelligence of the hand, a crucial aspect in a business producing high-end leather goods and textiles, where the intuition and experience of artisans, and their deep knowledge of the materials when working on a prototype, constitute a competitive advantage. This view was shared and amplified by Gucci's former creative director Frida Giannini, who established a direct and constructive dialogue with the company's artisans, who were seen as one of the brand's key assets:

> When in Casellina – where our production processes start and where we select and test the leather – I speak directly with the artisans, discussing my ideas and the innovations I would like to introduce. I must say that occasionally they do look a bit worried, and sometimes they just tell me that no, that cannot be done. But in the end we always get the best possible result, which is a positive development compared to the past.[85]

Another area where the artisan's global perspective and comprehensive technical, artistic and, above all, design skills become a point of strength is the so-called "self-production" sector. According to Ugo La Pietra, "self-production is often defined as a practice somewhere between art and design". More specifically, however, this term indicates "not only

[84] Rain Noe, "Core 77 speaks with Jonathan Ive on the design of the iPhone4: Material Matters", *Core 77*, 25 June 2010, www.core77.com/posts/16817/core77-speaks-with-jonathan-ive-on-the-design-of-the-iphone-4-material-matters-16817.

[85] See Alberto Cavalli, "Il mestiere d'arte, alla radice dell'eccellenza della moda italiana", in Paolo Colombo, Alberto Cavalli and Emanuela Mora (eds), *Artefici di bellezza: Mestieri d'arte nella moda italiana* (Venice: Marsilio, 2013), pp. 13–35, especially 23.

the actual capacity to *make* an object (something that the artisan-artist knew, and still knows, how to do) but also to design, market and sell their own work".[86] These are the creatives who are passionate about giving tangible shape to their ideas through manual execution. Self-production therefore implies a strong creative streak, as well as proficiency in all the phases of the production process and in the techniques required to work with the chosen materials, which, unlike those of a traditional master artisan, can be of a variety of kinds, each depending on specific production techniques and skills.

In this respect, there is a notable trend, reminiscent of Renaissance practice, among artists throughout Europe: the quintessentially Italian apprenticeship. "Italy has become the favoured destination for many of these new creatives with a passion for 'making'", says Micelli. "Some enrol in schools, others look for on-the-job experience in firms or workshops."[87] That's not all, however. As La Pietra states, "[t]here is an ever-growing number of respected artisans turning (though not without difficulty) to self-production, inventing new objects, inventing new technical processes and uses of materials, and inventing new ways to sell and communicate". Self-production thus becomes "a combination of activities encompassing self-organization of design, of construction/production, of promotion and of distribution".[88]

Effective and sophisticated techniques and their highly skilled application constitute another essential feature of craftsmanship. In *Art Worlds,* Howard Saul Becker formalizes function, bravura and beauty as aesthetic parameters of artistic craftsmanship. About the virtuoso technique of a master artisan, he asserts: "Most crafts are difficult, requiring years to master the physical skills and mental disciplines of a first-class practitioner. An expert, having mastered the skills, has great control over the craft's materials, can do anything with them, can work with speed and agility, and can do with ease things that ordinary, less expert craftsmen find difficult or impossible."[89]

Fine craftsmanship – be it in the field of traditional or contemporary crafts, with or without the aid of machines – is thus based on a know-how that delivers an excellent, indeed perfect, result, a job well done, carried out to the highest professional standards – *a regola d'arte* – and properly thought-out, designed and communicated.

[86] Ugo La Pietra, "Auto-produzione (da non confondersi con autopromozione)", *Mestieri d'Arte & Design*, No. 5 (April 2011), pp. 46–50, especially 50.

[87] Micelli, *Futuro artigiano*, pp. 125ff.

[88] La Pietra, "Auto-produzione", p. 50.

[89] Howard S. Becker, *Art Worlds* (Berkeley and Los Angeles: University of California Press, 1982), p. 275.

The adjective "artisanal" is often used to denote high quality; more often, though, it refers (especially in relation to foodstuffs and drinks) to the genuineness of a product or compliance with traditional techniques. In Italian, however, *artigianale* or "artisanal" can also have a pejorative sense, suggesting slapdash or shoddy workmanship. The kind of excellence that can be expected of a master artisan is the one that derives from the perception of their artistic skill and dexterity, thus becoming an elevated and exemplary goal. In Micelli's words, "[t]o express the strong link between craftsmanship and execution of the highest professional standard, in Italian we have such expressions as 'maestro d'arte' or 'maestria artigiana', which indicate a complete mastery of artisanal techniques and knowledge and imply an unwavering commitment to personal and professional improvement".[90]

This is what Micelli believes should be the general social and economic understanding of the expression "quality craftsmanship", without forgetting the relationship between the anthropological essence of first-class artisanal know-how – which Sennett describes in his book, *The Craftsman* – and the commercial and industrial spheres. Indeed, these spheres could embrace that essence without distorting it, or, rather, could transform it into a cornerstone of production, as Gucci has done. Micelli further points out that emphasis on one-off or limited-edition pieces can be counterproductive and tie down many artisans who might otherwise better fulfil their potential within an innovative and large-scale production chain. "Why not imagine, at least in some cases, the work of a creative artisan as a proposition (or a prototype) for a mass-produced item? [...] When the relationship between the artisan and industry is based on the correct management of intellectual property and on a fair division of the economic benefits, there can be space for shared growth."[91]

A shared purpose could in fact beneficially increase the personalization of industrial production, a notion that is more common to artisanal practices and conjures up many related values, such as reliability, communication, and dialogue with the clientele, all of which contribute to making an individualized and therefore more desirable product. This would certainly lead to a more complex production process, but it is something that currently seems to be eliciting an ever-increasing interest from manufacturers and consumers in their common quest for an object that is not unique in the sense of a limited edition but in its response to the particular needs of the people who own and/or use it,

[90] Micelli, *Futuro artigiano*, p. 23.
[91] *Ibid.*, pp. 129–131.

achieved via excellent production, premium materials and a design that is as functional as it is beautiful.

To sum up, we could say that *craftsmanship is the natural and specific aspect of a product made by a master artisan*. The definition of craftsmanship thus necessarily encompasses the following characteristics:

– *predominance of manual work* in the execution of a product, while allowing for the use of machines if it is subordinated to the maker's intellectual and sensorial skills and it involves technological research in the treatment of the materials;

– consideration and implementation of *the master artisan's entire knowledge set regarding the materials' intrinsic characteristics, potential and limits* in terms of their treatment and sophistication;

– use of production techniques designed to achieve the perfection and excellence that is expected of a product *made according to the highest professional standards* (*a regola d'arte*);

– *in relation to industrial production, compliance with the above-mentioned characteristics by*: referring back constantly to the master artisan's initial proposals and suggestions; endowing the prototype with the distinctive features of an artisanal product (proper handling of the materials, predominance of manual work, correct matching of the materials with the design requirements, execution *a regola d'arte*, personalization of the product based on ongoing communication with the client); and translating into and retaining all these aspects throughout the serial production phase.

3.3.4. *Creativity*

Creativity is conventionally defined as a person's capacity to invent and above all to come up with new ideas.[92] In this sense, creativity seems to have much in common with such concepts as originality, imagination, intuition and innovation, as opposed to mere reproduction or slavish imitation. When the term is applied to the manufacture of artistic goods, however, we need to be even more specific. Indeed, "creativity" manifests in several ways, not only in terms of invention or the creation of something completely new, but also in how a product relates to tradition and the overall production environment, the amount of creative freedom the maker enjoys, the production methods used, and the product's intrinsic and artistic value. In short, the term "creativity" in relation to the artistic crafts is used to describe a personal ability to

[92] See Zingarelli, *Vocabolario della lingua italiana*, and Devoto and Oli, *Vocabolario della lingua italiana*, s.v. "creatività".

devise unexpected, innovative and compelling solutions, while imbuing them with the values inherent in the working method and the finished product. Lastly, creativity in relation to the artistic crafts encompasses the essential notion of interpretation.

The word "creativity" has its origins in the founding act *par excellence*: the creation of the universe out of nothing but an idea that God conceived and made a reality. Creative, in the sense of "exclusive to the creator", is also used to describe the actions of Plato's Demiurge ("craftsman"), who brings supreme order to the primal chaos, thus "creating" a meaningful system. In both cases, the term implies an action that leads to the completion of something, starting from an ideal and tangible position that does not necessarily presuppose the end result in its minute detail.

For centuries, the creative gesture was wrapped in an otherworldly aura: it was inspired by the Muses or was a gift of God in the form of *ingenium* (talent), bestowed as a token of gratitude for a service to mankind. In its artistic declinations – those connected with the reproduction and interpretation of nature, with its signs and symbols – the creative gesture has retained that strong aura of mystery and indebtedness to the divine.[93] Athena, the goddess of wisdom and patron of the city of Athens, was also the goddess of feminine arts and crafts; Apollo, the god of the sun and harmony, also represented the liberal arts, poetry, painting, sculpture, music – anything that comes from creativity and the human gesture and that is intended to create beauty.

It would thus appear that true beauty can be found where the gifts of Athena, namely dexterity and superlative manual skill, combine with the gifts of Apollo, namely sophisticated artistic creativity. According to the philosopher François Cheng: "We can objectively observe that, in fact, our sense of the sacred, of the divine, does not come from simply witnessing the truth, that is to say, something that carries out its function, that operates smoothly. It comes much more from witnessing beauty, that is, something that is striking for its enigmatic splendour, that dazzles and enthralls."[94] That sense of sacredness and that sense of beauty, which are intimately connected, find a *tertium comparationis* in the creative gesture that unites them, making it possible to reveal one through the human (and thus not only artistic but also artisanal) fulfilment of the other.

[93] See Marco Pedroni, "La questione della creatività: Un'introduzione", in Marco Pedroni and Paolo Volonté (eds), *La Creatività nelle professioni*, Atti del convegno, Bolzano, 14 February 2007 (Bolzano: Bozen-Bolzano University Press, 2007), pp. 5ff.

[94] François Cheng, *The Way of Beauty: Five Meditations for Spiritual Transformation* (Rochester: Inner Traditions, 2009), p. 22.

In the Renaissance, while art and artisanship began to be perceived, used and understood as different terms, there was nevertheless recognition of the obvious relationship between mastery and creativity and divine inspiration. To underline the greatness of Michelangelo, for example, Vasari likened him to the supreme Artificer when he wrote: "And indeed we can affirm with certainty that those do in no way err who call him divine, seeing that he has within his own self embraced the three arts most worthy of praise and most ingenious that are to be found among mortal men, and that with these, after the manner of a God, he can give us infinite delight."[95]

The association between divine creativity and human intuition is a leitmotif in all historical analyses of art in all its forms, including the applied arts, even if in those cases that "visible divinity" (in the words of French poet and art critic Théophile Gautier) that is richly celebrated by disciplines such as music, painting, theatre and sculpture is less evident. In his treatise, "On the Most Ancient Wisdom of the Italians", however, Giambattista Vico, considered to be one of the fathers of aesthetics and the philosophy of complexity, writes:

> The Latin word *mens* means the same as our *pensiero* [mind]. *Mens* was also said "to be given to" or "placed in" human beings "by the gods". It is fitting therefore that the authors of these phrases should have thought that ideas are created and awakened in men's spirits by God. [...] For since the mind manifests itself in thinking, and God thinks in me, I know my own mind in God.[96]

For Vico, therefore, progress is always based on "ingenuity", in the sense of "the faculty proper to knowing [...] whereby man is capable of observing things and of imitating them".[97] Observing, and thus recognizing; imitating, and thus reproducing.

The authors of the *Encyclopédie*[98] were also cognizant of the need to valorize creative ingenuity in order to bring about real progress in history, attributing to Nature the origin of human faculties and the principles that inspire them, and agreeing that genius and ingenuity are innate faculties.

In his general considerations on the mechanical arts, Diderot

[95] Vasari, *Lives of the Most Eminent Painters, Sculptors and Architects*, p. xxxiv.

[96] Giambattista Vico, *Selected Writings*, edited and translated by Leon Pompa (Cambridge: Cambridge University Press, 1982), p. 66.

[97] *Ibid.*, p. 73.

[98] Denis Diderot (ed.), *Encyclopédie, ou Dictionnaire raisonné des sciences, des arts et des métiers*.

attributed the greatest value of the Manufactures – which, thanks to Colbert, became a driving force for France's economy – to the quality of the raw materials and the speed and perfection of workmanship brought about by the division of labour. He nonetheless added that: "It is also true that when a great number of workers are assembled, taste and workmanship necessarily improve because there will be some who are able to reflect, put facts together, and discover the only way to surpass their fellow workers: they must economize on materials, make better use of time, or excel in inventiveness. This they can do by introducing either a new machine or a more practical process."[99] Man-made innovations to work processes that can be considered the result of human ingenuity and "genius" are evident in the understanding of the world and in the tangibility of mechanical art. Beauty is a system of associations that are regulated yet still dependent on the creative power of the individual who, through art, can read things that nature may represent but does not always reveal.

In the 20th century, the idea that only a select few possess the ability to "create" lost traction in many ways. Moreover, the very concept of art as a relationship between mimesis and catharsis, typical of the standards of beauty inherited from Greek tradition and filtered by Western experience, began to break down. As François Cheng puts it: "Through a sort of generalized expressionism, artistic creation, following the example of literature, which had experienced an earlier awakening, meant to come to terms with the entire reality of living beings and the entire human imagination. No longer aimed exclusively at beauty, except on the level of style, it willingly resorted to the most extreme ruptures and distortions".[100]

In the world of the applied arts, the search for a functionality that is strictly linked to a concept of "beauty", still based on the classical criteria of harmony, symmetry, research, perfection and creativity, makes an abstract and expressionist interpretation of artistic inspiration seem less drastic. Essentially, master craftspeople still interpret the creative process in the manner implied by Vico with regard to the development of techniques based on ingenuity; although they follow the spirit and trend of the moment, they do not betray the functionality and originality that determine the specific nature of their craft.

In this context, creativity can also be defined as the "interpretation and translation" of a pre-proposed idea, such as that described by Micelli. In his book *Futuro artigiano*, he dedicates a paragraph to

[99] Diderot, *The Encyclopedia of Diderot & d'Alembert*, s.v. "Art".
[100] Cheng, *The Way of Beauty*, beginning of "Fifth Meditation".

"artisan-translators", as we saw in chapter 1, which also addresses the issue of artisanal creativity in "serial" production. Pointing to the many successful examples of the prototype-maker Giovanni Sacchi, Micelli traces the often long and difficult process of defining a product, from its initial design to the creation of a prototype. This process takes place in a continuous dialogue between designer and artisan, in other words between the creative needs of the former and the panoply of skills of the latter, which must come together to allow artistic intuition to bear fruit.

Master artisans are similarly called upon to apply their creative potential and specific skills to industrial production. This normally occurs when an artistic craft product completes or contains an industrial product, where the origin of a prototype "is linked to a brief that the marketing director of a brand submits to the supplier, and has to follow broadly established stylistic standards, in line with a market segment and a certain pattern of use. In short, anything but an expression of pure art".[101]

From the mystery of creativity we come to the genius of the creative act using time-tested methods, which leads to the development of a certain shape, form or structure without undermining its function. Today's master artisans often no longer attribute their creative impetus to a spark of divine intelligence but to inspirations and interpretations that allow them to establish a personal style.

If we look at the different layers that make up the definition of "creativity", we can identify several constant elements that are useful for "dissecting" the term from a master artisan's point of view.

Giuseppe Gandolfi, an expert in occupational psychology and the psychology of organizations, associates creativity with human potential, summarizing it as the ability to see new connections, come up with unusual ideas and intuitions, and break away from traditional patterns of thought.[102] To generate new ideas, it is essential but not sufficient to gather and analyse information. He defines creativity concretely as "the ability to supply suitable responses to new situations and new responses to situations that have already been dealt with", adding that "to be creative, a person has to know how to form meaningful associations between unusual or unlikely ideas".[103] With regard to the specific content of creative ability, this certainly involves a combination of existing notions, acquired through tradition, and the breaking away from such notions (Domenico De Masi defines this as a synthesis of

[101] Micelli, *Futuro artigiano*, p. 129.

[102] See Giuseppe Gandolfi, *Sviluppare il potenziale nelle professioni, nel lavoro, nello studio, nello sport… Approcci, metodi, applicazioni* (Milan: Franco Angeli, 2009), pp. 96ff.

[103] *Ibid.*

apparently dichotomous aspects: fantasy and reality, a straight line and a curved line, *thesis* and *metis*[104]).

Using very similar terms, the Italian philosopher and writer Emilio Garroni defines creativity in a more bluntly philosophical manner, also rejecting the Romantic myth of pure spirituality and endowing the term with a clearly objective meaning. According to him, the hand of a master must always seek a balance between creative, innovative and visionary abilities and the rules of the specific art.[105]

The juxtaposition of seemingly contradictory concepts – rules and freedom, standards and imagination – is thus the primary essence of creativity. And the artistic crafts, which rely on a system of traditional rules, are in fact historically linked to the creation of unique products that combine rigour with exceptionality and technical and aesthetic innovation.

We must therefore consider that, within the realm of artistic manufacture, creativity plays a fundamental role in the overall success of an artisanal product as it simultaneously instils legitimacy and exceptionality. Legitimacy defines the production, anchors it to an excellence perfected over time, and ties it to the best of that residual *savoir-faire* that has survived in spite of technical developments and changing tastes. Exceptionality is the lifeblood of material and formal experimentation, is aimed at satisfying the immediate desires of a product's creator as well as of its end user, and adds another element to those rules of excellence that become a residual heritage, essential to the evolution of the history of manufacturing art. This predetermined and regulated goal must, however, always be exceeded.

Swiss psychologist and philosopher Jean Piaget specifies the notion of creativity and institutionalizes it as the "internal engine of structural transformations" that characterize "man's process of appropriating reality, his construction of cognitive structures that are more and more elaborate, to the extent that they each represent a 'more powerful' system (in a logical sense) than the preceding structure",[106] hence a construction of knowledge that is systematic, gradual, effective and continuous.

In this regard, two terms come up frequently in connection with the adjective "creative": originality and taste.

The possibility of creating something new presupposes knowledge of everything that has come before and everything that is required to achieve it. Verrocchio could not have transmitted his own genius to

[104] See Domenico De Masi, *Il futuro del lavoro* (Milan: Rizzoli, 2003).
[105] See Emilio Garroni, *Creatività* (Macerata: Quodlibet, 2010).
[106] *Ibid.*, p. 96.

Leonardo, for example, but he was certainly able to convey that knowing how to mix pigments to make a fresco was of prime importance, as important as the idea for the fresco itself.

As Linda Gobbi points out, the divergence between artists and artisans has been clearly delineated since the Renaissance. That divergence has waxed and waned considerably over time, and accounts for the different ways in which artisans have been considered socially and economically: "Artisans are outward thinking, propelled towards their community; artists are inward thinking, driven towards themselves. In the material culture of the Renaissance, in order to sell the most diverse products, it became more and more important to indicate the name of the maker."[107] It was during the Renaissance that artisanal products began to express an aesthetic awareness, a sense of wonder that their makers wanted to arouse in their customers and for which they desired to be acknowledged and rewarded, while conserving the basic utility of their products within the community. "Benvenuto Cellini is proof incarnate, breaking away from the standards with his famous salt cellar made for King Francis I of France and setting himself up as an artist recognizing only Michelangelo as his Master."[108]

The distance of the master artisan from the "standards" shows how creativity brings together emotional and cognitive elements of personality, making it necessary to define the substance of "creativity" in even more complex terms. The factors that make a product excellent, a craftsperson a master and a craft a *savoir-faire* that becomes a discipline in its own right all fall within the purview of the "possibility of experience" that is given to each of us but that only a few seize and build on to the extent that, for them, it becomes a raw material on a par with the other materials used. We can certainly believe that this condition belongs to the subjective sphere of the maker – to the personality and the talent that complement the concept of creativity.

To summarize the above, we can say that creativity is a faculty that master artisans possess and are able to develop and demonstrate in their creations. It is a complex concept that:

– *requires specific knowledge* of everything that relates concretely to the manufacturing sector concerned, from materials to design techniques, from the study of proportions to the study of colours and their reaction to light and technical processes, from elements of tradition to cutting-edge research – the knowledge of traditions and techniques as a source

[107] Renata Borgato, Ferruccio Capelli and Andrea Ceriani, *Nuovo Rinascimento: Idee per la formazione* (Milan: Franco Angeli, 2010), pp. 9–10.

[108] Gobbi, "L'Impronta Rinascimentale", p. 19.

of elements that creative masters will know how to put together in an original way;

– *combines rules with vision and standards with imagination*, using these rules as an essential trajectory on which to create new and efficient vehicles of expression; a system of dynamic balances between fixity and invention, rules and solutions that the master craftspeople, through the use of their hands, reinvents time and again;

– *evidences a personal dimension of the creator,* without neglecting the requirements of the product and, consequently, of the customer, as well as the capacity to transform a design or indeed a sketch into a perfect, contemporary, functional product, just as the designer envisaged it, without resorting to slavish imitation and while remaining unfazed by difficulties; in sum, a perfect interpretation of a design, sketch or customer's idea and of the material's characteristics;

– *weaves together all the residual value of tradition and an artistic vision of the here and now* that is mediated by the creator's flair and gaze, and is thus both a vision and a talent in taking the elements available to all of us and putting them together in an expert way that only a truly creative individual knows how, to bring about something original, legitimate and exceptional.

3.3.5. Innovation

It may seem oddly contradictory to place the terms "tradition" and "innovation" in the same list of fundamental elements needed to define the excellence of artistic craftsmanship. Craftsmanship is still commonly associated with an exclusively manual type of work undertaken using old, traditional methods in a small workshop frozen in time. "Innovation", meanwhile, makes us think immediately of modern technology or of something totally original, new, never seen before. However, Zingarelli's Italian dictionary makes the meaning of "innovation" clear, giving as the sole definition: "a modification that involves elements of novelty".[109] To innovate thus implies a dual, simultaneous action: to modify something that already exists and to add elements of novelty.

The entire field of artistic crafts is particularly affected by the possibility, if not the need, for change and development. As Ermete Realacci, president of the Fondazione Symbola per le Qualità Italiane (Symbola Foundation for Italian Quality), writes: "Today more than ever, cultural production and the quest for quality and beauty must converge with innovation, research and the new frontier of the green economy.

[109] See Zingarelli, *Vocabolario della lingua italiana*, s.v. "innovazione".

This convergence is increasingly strengthening the new concept of 'Made in Italy', and is happening to a much greater extent than is visible to the political sphere in many areas and districts throughout Italy."[110]

The point made by Realacci underlines the necessity for the "Made in Italy" label to bring its long-standing knowledge of aesthetic standards, high-end production and the territorial and historical specificities of a product to bear in boosting the development of such areas as techniques, design, materials and technological research.

This aspect impacts on high-end artistic craftsmanship in different, sometimes sensitive ways. Indeed, we need to:

– *restore the link with territory and tradition*. In certain sectors, these links are tightly bound up with the product's identity, for example food and wine products bearing the DOC (Controlled Designation of Origin) or IGP (Protected Geographical Indication) labels, indicating that parmesan cheese is "reggiano" and cherry tomatoes are "vesuviano", or with the specific nature of the materials and workmanship, such as blown glass that is naturally associated with Murano or paper with Amalfi. In these cases, substantial, formal or structural changes may be introduced, which may be acknowledged as novelties but must not alter the product's identity;

– *preserve the essential characteristics of a product*, while bringing it in line with current, albeit constantly evolving, needs and tastes. Those characteristics might concern, among others: raw materials, shape, production techniques and functionality.

With regard to the artistic crafts, one of the main interpretations of the term "innovation" relates to production techniques, in particular to cutting-edge technology that facilitates work, accuracy and design while maintaining the high standard of quality that is the mark of excellent craftsmanship. This inevitably leads to a discussion of the concept of *techne*, or what was referred to as *savoir-faire* until the late 18th century and is now associated with technical and manual skills.

The gesture of the hand is clear and irreplaceable; the basic characteristics of original production persist, evidencing its deep historical and territorial roots. What research can achieve is to broaden the possibilities open to a master craftsperson, from the design phase to the actual act of creation. Alongside the classic procedures that constitute the core identity of goldsmiths, glassmakers, restorers and watchmakers, to name but a few, there is a wealth of technological tools

[110] Ermete Realacci, "Premessa", in *L'Italia che verrà: Industria culturale, made in Italy e territori*, I Quaderni di Symbola, 2011, p. 6, www.symbola.net/assets/files/Ricerca%20Industrie%20culturali_1326723510.pdf.

enabling master artisans to express their skills to the full and thus widen their scope.

Today, pupils at training college come into direct contact with the raw materials and their basic characteristics, as well as with cutting-edge design and three-dimensional drawing techniques, the chemical and physical treatment of materials for unprecedented uses, new possibilities of transformation, and new interpretations of the materials used and consequently of the final product.

There are numerous examples not only of where technology and artisanal know-how have successfully combined, but also where this fusion has broadened the outlook and creative potential of the craft world in terms of both design and production. From the point of view of artistic craftsmanship, the two aspects are inseparable.

The process of merging manual skill and technology is complex and not always straightforward. Innovation is the fruit of technical research and intuition – one, in fact, may lead to the other, and the invention of a product is triggered the first time a certain technology is used. True innovation occurs, however, when it is actually feasible to produce an invention, and it satisfies (or creates new) parameters in terms of style, functionality, cost, market demand, taste and ethical values, both formal and substantial. The Italian philosopher Giangiorgio Pasqualotto points out: "As is well known, in the 20th century the avant-gardes spurred innovation to such a degree that novelties came about not yearly, but daily. These even risked disappearing into insignificance, given that the search for novelty can in itself lead – and in some cases did lead – to self-dissolution."[111]

The Osservatorio sulle Arti Applicate nel Mobile (Observatory of Applied Arts in Furniture), which is directly managed by the Aldo Morelato Foundation, created to express and promote a practical culture able to "restore the connection between historic memories and contemporary proposals",[112] has from the outset been looking into the difficult relationship between traditional artistic craftsmanship and contemporary innovation. It has been doing so as part of the Observatory's flagship *Il mobile significante* (The Significant Furniture) project, focusing on furniture and interior design. During the 2008 International Days of Study, in particular, experts representing different professional skills came together to discuss the relationship between, on the one hand, artistic craftsmanship, design and creation and,

[111] Giangiorgio Pasqualotto, "Avanguardia e tradizione tra Oriente e Occidente", in Luigi Bonotto, Roberto Melchiori and Tiziano Santi (eds), *Fatticità dell'arte: Il fare artistico tra etica e tecnica* (Rome: Derive Approdi, 2001), pp. 45ff.

[112] See www.fondazionealdomorelato.org.

on the other hand, the needs that information technology and other technological tools have now imposed on our daily lives, in which these products are expected to serve a purpose and enhance our living spaces.

Silvana Annicchiarico, director of the Triennale Design Museum in Milan, described the complexity of the problem, recalling once again the interconnection between intuition and finished product: "[I]nnovations never depend solely on a particularly ingenious technical solution that a single designer is able to give to a problem. [...] [I]n other words, there is always a binding element behind the creation of objects and their social acceptance. Innovation is never only a case of engineering or technical skills but is created when technology is combined with other factors".[113] Economic, functional, formal and institutional factors all contribute to the conception of a product, while the master craftsperson translates this into reality through a qualified and specific *savoir-faire*.

Annicchiarico emphasizes, however, that combining local characteristics and innovation can be problematic. Above all, she believes that one of the main factors to bear in mind for this development to be successful is the globalized setting in which crafts can be produced and displayed, together with the now necessary universal appeal. "These local characteristics are important and should be defended. But it is not on these models that we can build our future. Today, each place is crossed by many streams which eternally mix and remix in time and space. These places should become part of the Web."[114]

Without a doubt, the local-global aspect is one of the greatest challenges that master craftspeople currently face. However, when an artisanal product is distinguished and defined by territory and tradition, these elements endow it with an authentic and desirable added value for a market that seeks and appreciates quality. It is a question of social values, a sense of living life to the full and of consciously dwelling, which more than ever prevails over the desire for brand names or coordinated products. As Ettore Mocchetti, project designer and editor-in-chief of the Italian edition of the design magazine *AD*, explains: "Today, the buyers' universe is no longer layered according to wealth, but consists of 'islands', some big some small, which sometimes – but not always – interact and overlap in terms of culture, behaviour and expectations. On the other hand, different technologies make it possible to produce objects in limited series with only minimal differences in production costs. The effect of this evolution is the trend to personalize objects

[113] Comments made by Silvana Annicchiarico during the seminar *Il mobile significante. Gli oggetti d'arredo e la strumentazione telematica. Giornate Internazionali di Studio 2008* (Santarcangelo di Romagna: Maggioli Editore, 2008), pp. 31ff.

[114] *Ibid.*

and purchases: nowadays, a significant proportion of consumers buy (or, rather, are going back to buying) things that reflect them (or their tastes) and not those that identify them (status and social class). They buy according to the emotions and story conveyed by an object rather than just its shape and function."[115] Certified quality rather than serial production and unrestricted individuality rather than passive standardization are thus the salient characteristics of the craft market.

Innovation is already perceived, both by master craftspeople and by those companies dedicated to combining industrial production with artisanal uniqueness, as a specific kind of investment in technical research and game-changing strategies tied to the product and production processes. In an article published in the quarterly *Quaderni di ricerca sull'artigianato*, Luigia Campagna and Attilio Pasetto, senior economists at the Unicredit Group, summarized the findings of a survey carried out among manufacturing companies in Europe over the three-year period from 2007 to 2009. The research was conducted for the EFIGE (European firms in a global economy) project, in which Unicredit participated along with six other international research institutes. It confirmed the vitality of small Italian enterprises and their capacity to compete internationally, in reference to the way these enterprises produce "value", thanks mainly to their great craft skills:

> Despite the economic downturn, business investment remained constant even during the difficult three-year period of 2007–2009. Small Italian enterprises were no exception, even if they appear to have invested less in comparison with the average of the seven countries studied. [...] As regards innovation strategies, the survey shows that Italian enterprises are more prone to innovation than the other countries surveyed [Austria, France, Germany, Hungary, Spain and the United Kingdom]: 66.4% of companies in Italy declared they had introduced at least one form of technological innovation, compared with the average of 64.4% in the seven countries as a whole. Although this propensity for innovation increases with company size, the percentage recorded by large enterprises is in line with the average of the seven countries, while it is above average for small and medium-sized enterprises.[116]

The survey also showed that there was greater investment in product innovation than in process innovation. In terms of innovative strategies, patent applications and the registration of trademarks and of industrial

[115] Comments made by Ettore Mocchetti during the seminar *Il mobile significante*, pp. 74ff.

[116] Luigia Mirella Campagna and Attilio Pasetto, "Artigianato e piccole imprese: Strategie di innovazione e di esportazione nel mercato globale", *Quaderni di ricerca sull'artigianato: Rivista di Economia, Cultura e Ricerca sociale dell'Associazione Artigiani e Piccole Imprese Mestre CGIA*, No. 58 (Second quarter, 2011), pp. 99ff.

designs and copyrights played a not insignificant role. In many respects, the seeds of change are already visible in various district companies. Indeed, there is a growing trend among these companies to adopt an integrated model of innovation that focuses both on the product and on investment strategies in intangible elements such as management organization, customer relations, marketing, communication and internationalization aimed at continuously enhancing the products' added value.

There is yet another way in which master craftspeople have already knowingly interpreted the term "innovation", making it a factor of success and breathing new life into their work, and that is *collaboration*. This involves a "coming together" in a broad sense, referred to as *an aggregation of dimensions* or *a synergy of knowledge and skills*.

The EFIGE survey demonstrates that the meagre amount of aid available from public bodies in the form of financial and fiscal incentives is pushing small enterprises to "'form networks' to increase their critical mass and exert greater power on the market. From this point of view, these aggregations seem to be the most effective means of overcoming any dimensional limitations and thus of sharing the high fixed costs associated with high-quality, highly innovative products".[117]

But there is more to it. As we have already seen, bringing together experts in design, scientific research or cutting-edge machinery can lead and has already led to the expansion of the creative space of many manufacturing companies that started out as artisanal workshops and small-scale production establishments. These companies have expanded their production without compromising in the slightest on the quality and style that are inherent to their nature and identity.

The ability to "form networks", to maintain lively relations with other manufacturing branches, and to remain alert and open to stimuli from unforeseen production or research sources, are attributes that have distinguished the most authentic master craftspeople since the Renaissance.

The skills, capacities and *intuitus personae* that have always belonged to master artisans, together with their ability to remain true to themselves and to their specific sphere of craftsmanship over time and to live in their own social and temporal dimension, have contributed significantly to the success of present-day manufacturing companies. However, owing to its specificities (in contrast to the business-oriented management approach that exists in similar criteria), the craft sector must, as we have seen, have direct contact with every aspect of the creative process –

[117] *Ibid.*

from concept to design and from choice of materials to execution and prototype testing – in order to produce an artistic work epitomizing shared skills and mastery. It is not possible to establish standards of expertise that can be applied equally to different types of artistic craftsmanship or different regions; each has its own criteria for design and specific territorial acknowledgements that nonetheless have the shared goals of producing high-quality objects that reflect an authentic and personal expression of their culture and values and of investing in research.

Linda Gobbi aptly sums up this concept: "The different phases that have marked the growth of the companies and the entrepreneurs that we have visited are very often extremely casual, and show an ability to seize the moment and to interpret external conditions: this ability is acquiring more and more importance for companies, and is replacing the rigid, linear programming that has characterized management over the last 20 years, an approach deeply permeated by a typically Anglo-Saxon scientistic vision. Today, we need creativity mixed with common sense and nourished by research, reliability, freedom, technology and culture."[118]

Promoting an artisanal know-how and philosophy as a company's heritage and as a strategic value of innovation processes is increasingly proving to be an effective strategy for the Italian manufacturing system to remain competitive internationally. Creative skills, excellent workmanship, familiarity with the materials and the techniques used to transform them, the accumulated knowledge of the arts that has been handed down through the ages, and the ability to apply that knowledge to the present day by combining all the particularities of high-quality craftsmanship are the key elements behind the innovation rationale of successful companies. There are a growing number of small craft firms that, individually or in collaboration with large companies, are producing excellent items of international fame, on which the success and competitiveness of an entire regional production system depends.

In conclusion, we can say that innovation – that is, the inclination and the ability to find novel, effective ways of doing things – can be assessed by analysing the following factors:

– the ability to *modify something that already exists* by adding elements of novelty;

– familiarity with the materials and techniques, and *investment in technical research and innovative strategies* relating to the product and production processes;

[118] Gobbi, "L'Impronta Rinascimentale", p. 21.

– the *fertile dialogue between technology and artisanal know-how* aimed at obtaining new and original shapes, styles, functions and aesthetics, also in response to changing needs dictated by tastes, market demands, costs and ethical values;

– the aggregation of dimensions or *synergy of knowledge and skills* ("forming networks"), also across different spheres and thus beyond the specific field of one's own craft or trade.

3.3.6. Interpretation

> The main difference between a Beethoven symphony and the sonnets of Shakespeare is that, although the words, as written in the book, are a notation of Shakespeare's thoughts – in the same way that the score is nothing but a notation of what Beethoven imagined – the difference is that the thoughts existed in Shakespeare's mind and in the reader's mind. But in the Beethoven symphonies, there is the added element of actually bringing these sounds into the world: in other words, the sounds of the Fifth Symphony do not exist in the score.[119]

With this wonderful literary comparison, conductor Daniel Barenboim explains the essence of the intermediation that an interpreter introduces between the score and the audience, that is, between what to some may look like an incomprehensible jumble of ink marks on a sheet of paper and the idea in the composer's mind, the human and artistic values it expresses and the emotions the composer felt when conceiving it.

To understand the essence of artistic intermediation and how it translates into and is embodied in the work of a master artisan, we must first look at the matter from a juridico-philosophical point of view, such as that put forward by the Italian jurist and philosopher Emilio Betti. He wrote: "Art is not creation, but a discovery that often surprises even the artists, who find themselves confronted by a beauty that exceeds anything they had envisioned."[120]

A genius is someone who is able to comprehend universal values and translate them into tangible form in whatever way a personal sensitivity allows, rendering the invisible visible, awakening the spirit and "making the inexistent" – that is, the values – "exist" in the reality of the external world. As Betti goes on to say: "The fact that, when contemplating a work of art or a poem, anyone with a modicum of sensitivity can evoke

[119] Daniel Barenboim and Edward W. Said, *Parallels and Paradoxes: Explorations in Music and Society* (London: Bloomsbury, 2004), p. 30.

[120] Emilio Betti, *Teoria generale della interpretazione* (Milan: Giuffrè, 1990), pp. 25ff.

that work's artistic or poetic value as if it were a product of their own generation, signifies that that work's deepest roots and origins do not lie in a single individual (*ipse solus*), but rather in a shared way of thinking (*forma mentis*) that can be found in the genius of humanity that lives and breathes in every one of us."[121]

Those universal values that enable human beings to recognize something as enduring and unchanging despite the effects of time, fashion and the most fleeting of trends, are for Betti anchored in a collective mindset, existing in an essentially shared ethos deployed throughout history in the form of the genius of humankind. Hence, if this is the dimension where truth and authenticity reside, what the artist's interpretation conveys is an understanding of how the universal and the enduring are immanent dimensions, alive and occurring in the ever-changing present. And, *mutatis mutandis*, it can be said that the master artisan also operates within these dimensions.

This is especially true for a master artisan who is practising a trade in an area – the artistic crafts – that is inseparable from its local and historical dimensions, and who is therefore expected not only to reconcile those values that anyone might recognize as such (and are thus "universal"), but also to capture and give tangible form to other specific sensitivities. Those are the sensitivities that bind the master artisan to a given territory and to a technical and artistic tradition that finds expression in the materials chosen, in the techniques used, in the aesthetics achieved, in the *genius loci* and, of course, in the creativity of the person who came up with the original concept for the product that the master artisan transforms into reality.

> Because if it is true that the product must always express universal values, it is also true that these values must be knowingly interpreted according to the whole panoply of cultures that forms the wondrous, multifaceted "customer" universe, a universe whose identities, sensitivities and specificities we must, moreover, understand and appreciate.[122]

Having thus highlighted the importance of the proactive role of the "customer" in the world of the artistic crafts, Franco Cologni goes on to say:

> To do this, we need to marry material conditions and intangible values. Among the former I would include demographic changes and generational

[121] *Ibid.*
[122] Interview with Franco Cologni, April 2012.

cycles, while among the latter I would rank not only customs and traditions, but also local cultures as expressed by territorial values, civilizations and religions. Only through a conscious union of these factors can that "authentic" relationship with the customer be wrought, setting in motion all the other responses, from magic to sixth sense.[123]

For this reason, Cologni proposes that we reappropriate the term "patronage" from the Renaissance period, when it denoted the actions of a wealthy noble elite who commissioned works of art from the best master artisans of the time.

It was a commission from the D'Estes family that first gave Cellini the idea for his famous salt cellar, and renewed impetus from the French king Francis I that inspired the artist to develop the final design and realize it. Cellini was certainly up to the task, and in fact delivered an exquisite artefact that was so stunning that, unlike so many other objects of its kind once they fell out of fashionable favour, it was never melted down. Cellini's salt cellar is an extraordinary example of an artistic craft demonstrating breathtaking expertise and mastery. As an object it paved the way for the style that developed in Fontainebleau and successfully translated and mirrored its patronage and its epoch's entire aesthetic and literary vision, reproducing its symbols, its beloved myths and its fundamental values, indelibly identifying with them while also acquiring the status of timeless masterpiece.

Today, 500 years on from Cellini's fervid and active creativity, there is still a valid case to be made for a direct relationship between master artisan and patron. A patron may well, in fact, be a source of specific elements for the artisan to translate and the repository of inspiring values. It would be rather pointless, explains Cologni,

to devise a "global" approach to customers, because customers are in fact individuals, single identities: if we want the transmission of the values of craftsmanship to be effective, we need to base our customer approach on empathy. Let's say it once more: we need to respond to the globalization of the market by the personalization of products and services, but above all by a personalized approach to the customer. Federico Fellini said that every language interprets the world differently: and it is precisely these "languages" that we must learn, or learn again, today – those that make us speak the language of culture, emotions and know-how.[124]

[123] *Ibid.*
[124] *Ibid.*

It is no coincidence that this concept also translates into responsibility and, consequently, into the notion of a successful "translation". As Umberto Eco explains:

> When a message is put in a bottle [...] – that is, when a message is issued not for a single recipient but for a community of readers – the author knows that message will not be interpreted according to his intentions but according to a complex web of interactions which also involves the readers, together with their understanding of their language as social heritage. By social heritage I do not mean only a given language as a system of grammatical rules, but also as the entire encyclopedia that has come into being through the use of that language, meaning the cultural conventions that that language has produced and the history of the preceding interpretations of many texts, including the one the reader is reading in this moment.[125]

This means that master artisans, through that aspect of their work that is more closely connected to art, introduce into their "text" echoes of a specific patronage, as well as reflections of a broader taste, two ingredients that are part of a collective language and the constituents of a complex and well-developed social communication code. An artwork eloquently expresses the personal genius of its maker, reflecting values the customer can relate to and complying with a generally accepted idea of beauty. All this certainly fits with the notion of "interpretation" as a mediation between what a community possesses and what an artist is capable of translating and revealing in a perfect work.

The master artisan is therefore an *interpreter* of reality, of the immanent and universal sphere, but also an *intermediator*, a *negotiator*, someone who institutes value, or *pretium* in Latin, as the etymology of the word *inter-preter* suggests.[126] In its definition of "interprete", the Devoto-Oli Italian dictionary adds that an interpreter is a person who not only "translates" but also "understands", by turning an occurrence or a document into "intelligible and practical terms".[127]

The bond between reality and its artistic interpretation, on the one hand, and an authentic territorial entity, consisting of technical, material and aesthetic traditions that are "interpreted" or "translated" into a work by a master craftsperson, on the other hand, is intrinsic to the very notion of design execution, as Fabio Fabbrizzi, lecturer in architectural design at the University of Florence, underlines:

[125] Umberto Eco, *I limiti dell'interpretazione* (Milan: Bompiani, 1990), p. 110 (our translation).

[126] See Carlo Battisti and Giovanni Alessio, *Dizionario etimologico italiano* (Florence: Barbèra, 1975), s.v. "interpretazione".

[127] See Devoto and Oli, *Vocabolario della lingua italiana*, s.v. "interprete".

The concept of tradition is inextricably bound up with the equally complex concept of interpretation. Interpretation can be understood as a mediated and filtered actualization of themes, figures, spaces and connections plumbed from the depths, and which the body and structure of the city unveil only after a careful and constructive reading.[128]

There is, however, another aspect of interpretation we must consider, and that happens when a master artisan works with a designer, who is a different, special kind of patron. Executing an idea, turning a designer's vision into reality, is another form of "interpretation and translation", where the artisan serves as a bridge between another artist (the designer) and the end user.

Master artisans are likewise called upon to express their own creative potential and specific skills when the patron in question is industrial production.

But how *do* master artisans express their creativity in such cases? The object (be it a prototype or an element that is integral to an industrial product) comes into being thanks to the master artisan's "translation" of the design and the combination of different skills essential to the definition of that product. In this framework, artisans express all their know-how in that personal interpretation of the proposed elements or indications, which leads directly to the creation of a *unicum*: the union of ideas and skills coming from two different sources. This process highlights the need, in the realization of a design, for someone to have a comprehensive overview of all the product's distinctive characteristics. Master artisans are the only ones who can envision the project as a whole, and it is in this capacity that they are completely creative. It is the master artisan who makes the marriage between design inspiration, execution and brand identity possible. Where creativity seemed to be diminishing, it is in fact alive and present in the form of artistic interpretation.

This circumstance is, for instance, one of the liveliest aspects of the work undertaken at Pino Grasso's haute couture embroidery atelier, as we will see later. "The impulse we are referring to is complex", he explains. "We have to get into the designers' heads and know their tastes intimately in order to create embroideries that correspond to their concept."[129]

So, we are brought back once more to the concept of interpretation as a creative act: interpreting means "extracting", rendering comprehensible what might at first seem obscure. The way this "extraction" is carried

[128] Fabio Fabbrizzi, *Opere e progetti di scuola fiorentina, 1928–2008* (Florence: Alinea, 2008), p. 25.

[129] Interview with Pino Grasso by the Cologni Foundation, www.fondazionecologni.it/it/interviste/ar/pino-grasso.

out is in itself original and personal, especially when it involves all the master artisan's knowledge, experience and ability to fashion the material so as to give shape to an idea.

This continuous process of "capturing and adapting" is where we learn about beauty, social and professional commitment, and the pursuit of quality, the very essence of artistic craftsmanship. Betti's words once again sum up and clarify this concept: "Artworks and poetry, which start out as an unexpected discovery and revelation for their authors, teach others how to grasp an idea and sense of style and help them build up a personal repository of insights, images and ideas."[130]

We must also keep in mind that, besides relating to independent workshops and small enterprises, this kind of artisanal work also permeates much of the "Made in Italy" output in general. As Micelli reminds us:

> It is artisanal skills that enable large fashion and luxury goods groups to produce the clothing, bags and accessories of outstanding quality for the international market. It is the artisanal skills of the model-makers that allow the exponents of the so-called Italian Style to convert their sketches into the prototypes and first series on which their brands can base their industrial production, even in faraway countries.[131]

The main concepts contained in the term "interpretation" in the work of a master artisan, who is never a simple executor but always a skilful interpreter, can be summed up as follows:

– the realization, through production, of a work that *interprets* the traditional, historical and local nature of the artistic crafts, "*transporting*" *them into the present day* to respond to the sensitivities and needs of contemporary patrons;

– the manifestation of the *creator*'s *personal import*, without neglecting the requirements of the manufacturing category in question or of the patrons; the *translation of the desires* of one's clientele, serving thus not only as executors but also as someone capable of transforming those needs into something beautiful, useful, personal and original – a work of artistic craftsmanship;

– the fulfilment, in the professional relationship with the designer, of the role of *creative model, or prototype-maker*, able to translate a sketch, or indeed a design, into a contemporary, functional product while deferring to the designer's taste and without resorting to mere imitation;

[130] Betti, *Teoria generale della interpretazione*, p. 44.
[131] Micelli, *Futuro artigiano*, p. 45.

the perfect interpretation of a drawing, of a vision, of a patron's idea, and of a material's intrinsic features and their translation into something real and tangible.

3.3.7. Originality

The great Catalan architect Antoni Gaudí considered originality a "return to the origins": for him, the word referred mainly to something inherent to the beginning, *ab origine*, and that has existed ever since. But the term "originality" has other connotations, too.

Originality can also be described as the quality of being novel and different, both features that make an object or a person stand out amongst the rest. This interpretation is particularly apt for poets and writers, whose understanding of originality in artistic work was summed up by Herman Melville, when he said that "it is better to fail in originality than to succeed in imitation", or by Edith Wharton, who asserted that "true originality consists not in a new manner but in a new vision". Voltaire noticed the underlying paradox, ironically observing that "originality is nothing but judicious imitation".

In seeking a definition of originality to suit the world of the artistic crafts, we can include all the aforementioned meanings, on the basis that a multiplicity of connotations does not necessarily mean that one invalidates the other, but rather that each one reflects a different yet valid angle from which to assess artisanal work. Therefore, what is original derives from a certain and recognizable "origin" (be it a territory, a school or a workshop); it is the manifestation of the author's new and certainly creative perspective (in our case, the master craftsperson who, through the use of a specific technique, is the original interpreter of a design); and it is not counterfeited.

According to the *Dizionario Enciclopedico Italiano*, something original is "that which is made by the hand of the author (or crafted, dictated or directed by the author), as opposed to a copy, a reproduction or an imitation".[132] Examples of things that are original (in the strictest sense of the word), as opposed to those that are not, include: a manuscript versus a printed book; a text in its original language versus its translation; a document versus its photocopy; an artefact versus its reproduction; the sitter versus the portrait; the place of origin of a product as a guarantee of quality and tradition versus an imitation; the prototype of a garment versus serial production; the master track of an audio or video recording versus its copies. So, going back to Gaudí, it is plausible and legitimate to

[132] See Treccani, *Dizionario Enciclopedico Italiano*, s.v. "originale".

reaffirm that "the original" (noun) indicates the matrix, the model, the archetype, the prototype, while "original" (adjective) pertains to what is authentic, genuine. But what if the author makes an original copy, a copy that contains and retains the two opposite notions of "copy" and "original"? What would "original" mean in this case? It is important to keep this point in mind as we go further into our analysis.

While something original has existed from the beginning and did not exist before, it is also something "that does not depend on and is not inspired or suggested by other examples or models, that does not resemble any similar works, and that therefore has a sense of novelty, its own distinct character".[133] Artists are original, therefore, when "they are not inspired by other people's ideas and models, but rather draw new ideas and motifs from their own imagination".[134] So now we can see clearly the meaning of originality put forward by Melville and Wharton: what is original is new, personal, distinctive, innovative, unique, peculiar, independent and different. Originality is a quality that is closely related to such concepts as inventiveness and creativity and goes so far as to encompass a certain degree of exaggeration or even eccentricity.

Originality, in sum, is a complex construction of concepts and connotations. As we have seen, the very definition of this term reflects multiple meanings. In particular, the Devoto-Oli Italian dictionary defines it as something "pertinent to a first, single and rigorously personal operational moment, excluding any 'reproduction', especially in the form of a 'copy', 'version' or even 'variation'".[135]

Battaglia's *Grande dizionario della lingua italiana* goes into further detail, defining originality as "the ability to find new ways and obtain positive results in a specific field, in particular those pertaining to art, literature, intellectual disciplines or research, without imitating others".[136] Originality connotes "the innovative nature of an activity, of a product". It is therefore characterized by "considerable independence from tradition or from a model, and by a marked uniqueness and novelty",[137] but it is also something "that goes back to its origins, and that is therefore closely connected to its nature, constitution and character".[138] Originality is about "expressing individuality and personality", as well as reflecting the "typical or national character of a population".[139]

[133] *Ibid.*
[134] *Ibid.*
[135] See Devoto and Oli, *Vocabolario della lingua italiana*, s.v. "originalità".
[136] See Battaglia, *Grande dizionario della lingua italiana*, s.v. "originalità".
[137] See Devoto and Oli, *Vocabolario della lingua italiana,* s.v. "originalità".
[138] *Ibid.*
[139] See Battaglia, *Grande Dizionario della lingua italiana*, s.v. "originalità".

The Devoto-Oli dictionary provides yet another important criterion in understanding originality not as mere eccentricity, but rather as the authentic value inherent to the character and nature of the action. Indeed, it defines originality as "a valuable peculiarity or novelty".[140] The adjective "valuable" highlights the positive connotation of this concept.

In an attempt to summarize the "construction of meaning" that we have outlined so far around the word "originality", we can say that something original is the start, the beginning: it is a creative thought and/or act, a technique or an invention that over time becomes established in tradition. The element of novelty – which may initially be seen as so distant from the norm as to suggest a certain degree of excess – retrospectively takes on a different connotation, becoming instead a cornerstone of a *modus operandi* or a means of defining and delimiting a personal approach that is always directed towards innovation and research yet never departs from the "origin" of the creative act, in other words from what we can define as the "legitimacy" of the creation.

An examination of this perspective and its application (albeit brief) to the world of the applied arts may help in formulating as objective a definition of originality as possible in relation to the artistic crafts. In his *Lives*, Giorgio Vasari once again introduced an important concept. Allowing for the partiality of his personal historical perspective, he explains: "I know very well that it must needs be that at some time and from some one man there came the beginning. [...] For since, of the works that are the life and the glory of the craftsmen, the first and step by step the second and the third were lost by reason of time, that consumes all things, and since, for lack of writers at that time, they could not, at least in that way, become known to posterity, their craftsmen as well came to be forgotten."[141]

In order for the creative act to be handed down and spread, the technique – the "craft", that is – must be kept alive and imparted. The human hand must repeat the same gesture an infinite number of times, endlessly perfecting it, to ensure the due development of knowledge, experience, technique and individual style.

As briefly touched upon above, the artistic and literary debate on tradition and originality (going back to the origins versus novelty and wondrous eccentricity) has always been very animated, with temporary and partial victories on both sides. While, on the one hand, novelty, individuality and personality are certainly characteristics of an "original"

[140] See Devoto and Oli, *Vocabolario della lingua italiana*, s.v. "originalità".

[141] Vasari, *Lives of the Most Eminent Painters, Sculptors and Architects*, p. xliii.

work, on the other hand, artists must always relate to a tradition, to history and to their craft. Originality is, in fact, a delicate balance between innovation and tradition – nothing new in that. But it also implies taking a risk, as much for those who seek it as for those who frown on it. At the point where risk and balance meet, we must search for the *tertium comparationis* that still defines the work of master artisans, who are original both in the application of centuries-old techniques and in the creation of artefacts, objects or products displaying creativity, formal perfection and artistic flair, yet without indulging in extravagance, without forgetting the link with their origins and without eschewing research and contemporary inspiration.

Originality is therefore a vision that allows artists to express themselves in a new way, while staying true to a tradition and to time-honoured – and therefore shared – techniques and stylistic features, which can perhaps be ascribed to broader concepts such as those of art, literature and craft.

In this respect, we can turn to an enlightening reflection by American architect Frank Lloyd Wright, who in his book, *A Testament*, revealed how much his work owed to William Blake's notion that "exuberance is Beauty":

> Beauty always is the consequence of utter fullness of nature in expression: expression intrinsic. Excess never to be mistaken for exuberance; excess being always vulgar. He who knows the difference between excess and exuberance is aware of the nature of the poetic principle, and not likely to impoverish, or be impoverished, by his work [...]. The more a design is creative revelation of intrinsic nature, whatever the medium or form of expression, the better.
>
> "Creative", then, implies exuberance. It is not only true expression but true interpretation, as a whole, of the significance, truth and force of Nature, raised to the fullest power by the poet. That design revealing truth of inner being most abundantly is best design. Design that lasts longest; remembered by mankind with greatest profit and pride.
>
> Art formalized, empty of this innate significance, is the cliché.[142]

Wright further clarified his point by remarking that art is never a repetition.[143]

For a reflection more directly relevant to today's master artisan, however, it is probably best to look at the fashion industry. Indeed, fashion, more than any other sector, provides the perfect example of a combination of originality and tradition, achieving a balance that has

[142] Frank Lloyd Wright, *A Testament* (New York: Horizon Press, 1957), Part One.
[143] *Ibid.*

seen this discipline on the front line and victorious in the battle against time. Fashion is the most popular – although not always the most affordable – expression of originality in the sense of novelty, character and distinctiveness. It is, as German sociologist Georg Simmel reminds us, a system yielding profound cultural meanings.[144] Fashion brings together creativity and know-how, because to make a clothing item, a bag or a shoe, you need artisans with knowledge and a command of ancient techniques that are still indispensable today. This is especially true of the "luxury" fashion sector, in which originality and exclusivity, uniqueness and style, design and function blend seamlessly. A luxury fashion item is a status symbol, signalling that the owner is a member of an exclusive circle that wants to stand out (distinctiveness being another of originality's facets) and be recognized (by wearing original products that are authentic, and therefore respectable).

In her introduction to the Italian version of Honoré de Balzac's 1830 *Treatise on Elegant Living*, Tiziana Goruppi reminds us that fashion "stems from the ideal of an individualistic statement and is, by definition, self-normative, for it is associated with the transformation of the existent [...]. However, fashion responds to a dual request, for the pursuit of novelty goes hand in hand with a need for conformity, in the sense of rapid adaptation to novelty. In short, fashion is based on the rapid oscillation between old and new, developing two opposing and conflicting actions: imitation and creation".[145] Balzac also made a distinction between the "phenomenon of fashion and elegance in itself", and therefore, in the light of what was outlined above in relation to the arts, the famous French novelist and observer of society did not always ascribe a positive meaning to originality. He nonetheless saw clothing as "an effective and reliable key to the interpretation of history [...], the front line where the objective meaning perfectly overlaps with the symbolic one".[146]

Fashion and originality make excellent bedfellows, for fashion is constantly evolving and changing in parallel with the history of humankind, naturally following and sometimes even contributing to the great changes happening in our society. But whenever the "original" side of fashion is too tightly bound up with a sense of "uniqueness", the criterion of originality is only partially represented: in today's clothing industry, be it fast fashion or couture, the "one-of-a-kind" item is a

[144] See Georg Simmel, "Fashion", *The American Journal of Sociology*, Vol. 62, No. 6 (May 1957), pp. 541–58, originally published in *International Quarterly*, No. X (October 1904), pp. 130–55.

[145] Tiziana Goruppi, "Introduzione", in Honoré de Balzac, *Trattato della vita elegante* (Pisa: ETS, 1998).

[146] *Ibid.*

rarity. No matter how luxurious, original and distinctive, fashion targets a relatively large market, and what is "bespoke" is mostly intended as a personalized, limited edition, customized piece, but no less original or distinctive for that.

It is also true that, specifically in the field of fashion, originality (also in the sense of authenticity) is an important value from an economic and legal point of view: today, original, branded products – as opposed to imitation or counterfeit (i.e. non-original) copies – address a market that has grown exponentially over the last 20 years. In the so-called "luxury" sector, originality is something to aspire to, a goal for millions of consumers ready to pay good money for an "original" item as a way to access something once available only to the elite. Fashion therefore still retains that notion of originality that in 1770 prompted John Adams (diplomat at Versailles and later second president of the newborn United States of America) to write that Queen Marie Antoinette's clothing was "everything art and wealth could make it".[147] And at the same time, fashion keeps relying on originality, even when clothes become a widespread product, distributed in every corner of the planet.

The battle between "original" and counterfeit fashion reflects the importance of this principle in the safeguarding of a production and distribution system that, in Italy especially, employs millions of people. As Dana Thomas stated in her 2008 book on the topic: "Today, luxury brand items are collected like baseball cards, displayed like artwork, brandished like iconography."[148] Since "luxury tycoons have shifted the focus from what the product *is* to what the product *represents*",[149] even consumers have followed in their footsteps and "don't buy luxury branded items for what they *are*, but for what they *represent*. And good fakes – the kind that can pass for real – now represent socially the same thing as real".[150]

Fashion is thus an important channel for gaining a fully rounded understanding of the concept of originality, both as "creative inspiration" and as tradition, expertise, craftsmanship and authenticity. It is through fashion that we can clearly grasp how originality can be defined even via its opposites, imitation and counterfeit. This gives us the opportunity to ascertain whether legally there can exist a definition of and therefore a safeguard for the originality of products made by master craftspeople. Artists, authors and inventors, for their part, are able to "exploit" their

[147] See Dana Thomas, *Deluxe: How Luxury Lost Its Luster* (London: Penguin Books, 2008), p. 22.

[148] *Ibid.*, p. 41.

[149] *Ibid.*

[150] *Ibid.*, p. 280.

creations and inventions commercially, while being protected against violations by third parties that might imitate, copy or even counterfeit them. As Ciro Fontana writes, "the right to repress counterfeit constitutes a crucial component of the protection of original intellectual work".[151]

It is important to stress that artisanal and industrial products, however excellent, do not automatically qualify as "intellectual property". In Italy, artisanal products are protected by copyright only if they are "artistic works" (Law No. 633 of 22 April 1941 and Articles 2575–2583 of the Italian Civil Code), while industrial products are "intellectual property" when they can be categorized as industrial inventions, utility models, designer objects or brands, or fall under the description of Protected Geographical Indication or Protected Designation of Origin, as provided by the Industrial Property Code (Legislative Decree No. 30 of 10 February 2005 and Articles 2569–2574 and 2584–2594 of the Italian Civil Code). The Italian Civil and Penal Codes and international treaties include specific regulations for the protection of brands, patents, designs, models and designations of origin to prevent and repress counterfeiting, piracy and copying. Protection is provided in those cases where counterfeiting may mislead the customer as to the product's origin, provenance or quality, an occurrence that may discredit and cause severe economic losses to single authors, artists and firms and, in some cases, even to an entire nation, as in the case of the counterfeit "Made in Italy" label. Therefore, with respect to counterfeiting in its broad sense, originality is clearly and univocally defined and can be understood as being synonymous with "authenticity".

While the argument for placing artisanal work within the field of the arts calls for an analysis that cannot be fully accomplished in this publication, it is certainly important to establish the characteristics that products emanating from the artistic crafts must possess in order to attain the status of intellectual work and therefore be automatically protected by copyright. Similarly, we need to define the requirements for these products to be registered and hence entitled to protection under the Industrial Property Code.[152]

In his treatise on copyright, jurist Mario Are observes that:

> An artisanal product and a work of figurative art share the same exterior characteristic consisting in the requisite physical existence of the object. Notwithstanding, it is commonly agreed that the artisanal product is worthy of

[151] Ciro Fontana, *L'attività creatrice come oggetto del diritto di autore* (Bergamo: Bolis, 1953), p. 34.

[152] Codice della proprietà industriale, Decreto legislativo 10 febbraio 2005, n. 30, www.wipo.int/wipolex/en/text.jsp?file_id=229339.

no protection whatsoever, for it boasts no element of creativity. Others consider these products subject to the protection reserved for patented designs. [...] The fact that this kind of work might result in the creation of a shape that can be considered to be either a work of art or a patented design is an accidental event foreign to pure and simple artisanal work, and entails a different kind of activity (of a creative kind) that must be protected in the same way as all other activities fulfilling the same objective conditions.[153]

Under Article 2575 of the Italian Civil Code, referring to Article 1 of Law No. 633 of 22 April 1941, protection is accorded to intellectual works of a creative character belonging to science, literature, music, figurative art, architecture, theatre or cinematography, no matter the style or form of expression. In the preface to his treatise, Are makes a distinction between "aesthetic creation" and "technical creation". This distinction can be useful because a significant proportion of artisanal production surely falls into the first category without being confined solely to the second. The first category (aesthetic creation) in fact encompasses "intellectual productions that are not devoid of utility and purpose [...], but that find utility and purpose in the intellectual sphere, therein fulfilling a need for beauty, taste and knowledge of a few or many individuals". By contrast, the second category (technical creation) aims "at the accomplishment of given effects in the outer reality and not at the mere fulfilment of intellectual needs".[154] To illustrate this distinction, Are gives the example of a statue, as opposed to a pillar, holding up an architrave: "The physical object must in itself be viewed as a load-bearing element of the construction, while the form it is given retains, in its abstract quality, the artistic and ornamental autonomy that fulfils its function in the intellectual field."[155] This example helps clarify the "value judgement" aspect for assessing a work not on its subjective "beauty" and/or "utility", but rather "on the work's or the product's objective position in relation to the pre-existing common intellectual heritage, regardless of its beauty or ugliness, its usefulness or harmfulness. Practically, you will thus have a simple assessment of creativity".[156]

The difficulty clearly resides in the fact that every human aesthetic creation stems from a "pre-existing cultural heritage". This is a fundamental point that is also relevant to the notion of authenticity. The form of expression through which the work is manifested "is the general

[153] Mario Are, *L'oggetto del diritto di autore* (Milan: Giuffrè, 1963), pp. 470–476.
[154] *Ibid.*, pp. 23–24.
[155] *Ibid.*
[156] *Ibid.*, p. 28.

prerequisite for every artistic production, but does not complete the range of ways in which a work can relate to the pre-existing cultural heritage".[157] It is also true that even for "works whose derivation from pre-existing productions is evident [...], the law explicitly recognizes the protection of that element of novelty that is within them, considering these works as 'elaborations' on a par with 'original' works".[158] Mario Are concludes that "the legal expression 'intellectual creative work' cannot be understood as 'creativity' in an absolute sense but only as an individual's 'contribution' to the pre-existing cultural heritage".[159]

A definition of "originality" can thus emerge from a new and certainly creative way of looking at the role of the author. "Every creation as such is by definition the result of an action of its author",[160] but a jurist – unlike a philosopher – is bound to "necessary factual ascertainment"[161] of the requirements of the law. Because the law does not define the formal and essential requisites but only refers to "creative character", jurists and judges must turn to legal doctrine for a more precise delineation. The concepts most often referred to in treatises are "creativity", "novelty" and "originality". According to jurist Vittorio M. De Sanctis:

> Novelty and creativity cannot be confused with originality, which is not an essential attribute of intellectual creation and which, moreover, is not even a requisite for protection under patent legislation. [...] The concept of originality is improperly used as synonymous with creativity, in the sense of authenticity or novelty. [...] Conversely, the concept of originality is fully valid and correctly used in legal terminology [for example when] it is used in comparing one work with another. Therefore, there are autonomous works (original works) and derivative works and, in that sense, the creative elaborations are by definition non-original works. The protection of these works is effectively based on a creative relationship that overlaps [...] with other relationships; therefore we can say that the author-elaborator adds a personal and recognizable touch to the work, making it worthy of protection (while the work in itself cannot be said to be original). [...] When a production does not manifest personality, even to the slightest degree, there is no creation. [...] The work's individuality does not change with time, because this would imply an autonomous development. On the contrary, it is the authors who evolve with regard to their work, owing to the continuous and incessant progress of each individual's creative and intellectual development.[162]

[157] *Ibid.*, p. 39.
[158] *Ibid.*, pp. 42–43.
[159] *Ibid.*
[160] *Ibid.*, p. 52.
[161] *Ibid.*, pp. 26–27.
[162] Vittorio M. De Sanctis, *Il carattere creativo delle opere dell'ingegno* (Milan: Giuffrè, 1971), pp. 25–27 and 41–44.

Mario Are also makes a distinction between "subjective originality" and "objective originality": the former relates in some ways to the concept of "authenticity", where originality is the distinctive feature that subsequent copies (even those made by the same author) don't possess, and also the direct link between the work and its author, and therefore synonymous with *personality* and *individuality*. "Objective originality", meanwhile, is defined as "the particular aspect of a work that makes it different from all other works for its intrinsic characteristics".[163] Every work therefore possesses subjective originality, represented by the direct relationship with its author, but its objective originality can be ascertained and verified only in relation to the works that came before it. He further remarks:

> When "creativity" is construed as "novelty", in as much as it possesses a given minimum value of newness, clearly everything that is "creative" is also "new". Yet, not everything that is new is also always "creative". [...] When originality is understood as a work's ability to distinguish itself from previous productions, it is clear that, since the distinctive elements are essentially "new elements", the concept of "originality" corresponds to "novelty", but not always to "creativity". When, instead, "originality" is attributed that same minimum value ascribed to "creative character", "originality" will correspond to this "creative character". In this case, however, not all that is "new" will be "original". [...] "Creativity" and "originality" can correspond but do not necessarily coincide; they are in fact concerned with two different facets that pertain to a work of art and its creation as a whole. "Creativity" is identified through a specific aspect of "objective novelty", that is, through the existence of a new contribution characterized by that minimum value that makes the work eligible for protection. "Originality", on the other hand, is the work's ability, in corresponding amounts, to distinguish itself from other productions, due to the "creativity" of the elements of which it is composed. "Originality" will thus be an effect that, as such, will be distinct from the cause (creative character) from which it originates.[164]

In our case, however, we must deal with an additional difficulty arising from the fact that master craftspeople often work by commission. The modern-day manifestation of this relationship occurs when companies commission a master artisan to make a product based on a concept developed by a fashion or industrial designer. The designer determines the shape, volume, proportions, colours, materials and overall effect, and then entrusts the master artisan with the actual realization of the concept, relying on that person's specific competencies to bring the idea

[163] Are, *L'oggetto del diritto di autore*, pp. 60–61.
[164] *Ibid.*, pp. 62–63.

to fruition. In these circumstances, which are quite common in industrial production (in which the first prototype that serves as a model for serial production, especially in the luxury goods sector, is often hand-made by an artisan), the intellectual and industrial property belongs to the company and not to the person who made the item, no matter how much creativity and original interpretation they might have put into it.

It is interesting to note that in this context the "originality" factor is doubled, for on top of the designer's "original" idea, master artisans add their own "original interpretation": drawing on tradition, expertise and years of developing a personal style, the artisan is the one – the *only* one! – who can interpret and give form and substance to the designer's idea, by using materials and techniques in combination with a personal dose of creativity, invention and originality. This is why it is often hard to attribute to a work of a master artisan all the prerogatives usually ascribed to an "artist", understood in the strictest sense of the word (although even an artist often works by commission or for a patron), for they in fact play the role of subordinates (a goldsmith making jewellery designed by a great jeweller, a model-maker giving shape and volume to the creation of a great fashion designer, a prototype-maker creating a model for an industrial designer, to give just a few examples).

In conclusion, originality in the context of the artistic crafts, is:

– the ability to take risks, using creativity to develop *something distinct from anything that has been done before*;

– the ability to use materials and working procedures *in new and different ways*, while respecting tradition;

– the *ability to interpret,* in innovative ways, the creativity of a third party;

– synonymous with curiosity, implying the *pursuit of alternative points of view* that can be found even outside one's familiar sphere of activity;

– also determined by *an object's specific provenance*, in the sense of a product made in a territory characterized by specific traditions, by the hands of a master artisan who has assimilated the theory, practice and cultural and aesthetic essence of that territory.

3.3.8. Talent

Cesare De Michelis, professor at Padua University and founder of the Marsilio Editori Publishing house, writes:

> Talent is at once a measuring weight that tilts the scales towards the side on which it sits and, in metaphorical terms, anything – money, firstly – that defines the primacy of one part over the other. Talent is therefore a measure that becomes a value the moment we dispense with numerical measures and

look for measures of a different kind. Talent and value have thus transmigrated from the solid ground of quantity to the more impalpable ones of ethics and aesthetics, involving impulses such as desire and force of ambition. Whether quantitative or qualitative, talent is the foundation on which rankings that are also meritocratic are based, rankings that are able to attribute a value to an invention, to highlight the aptitude for *doing* that is the cornerstone of every artisanal production, that depends on the use of one's own hands and only on the use of machines if they are operated in person, imaginatively and sensitively. All the trades that have been wiped out by industrial machinery belong to the realm of craftsmanship; machines have replaced human work with standardized objects that are always identical to the prototype. Modernity has asserted itself by celebrating the triumph of the copy.[165]

From this perspective, talent is a basic trait, that of practical aptitude, which is essential to high-quality crafts; it is a personal feature that cannot be taught but can be spotted with certainty, for it is one of the ingredients of success.

The Zingarelli dictionary defines talent as "ingenuity, skill, inclination".[166] It is the propensity to carry out a certain activity with the added value of being able to do it well, to the highest standard. So, one thing of which we can be sure from the start is that talent is personal: it is an inclination, a predisposition to do something well, with ease.

Isabella Medicina and Silvia Mazzucotelli Salice – experts, respectively, in the analysis of public policies on education and training and in sociology and communication in the cultural industries – carried out a major socioeconomic study on the artistic crafts in Milan. The interviews with artist-artisans they conducted show clearly that talent is seen as a gift, a quality that can fall into a young apprentice's lap regardless of merit, constituting a precious opportunity that can be seized or not.[167] As in any artistic field, an inborn familiarity with a creative practice provides an individual with the chance to fulfil a natural potential, but the elements that make a difference in the achievement of excellence are dedication, drive and sheer hard work.

Similarly, Mazzucotelli and Medicina drew the following conclusions from their interview with Alessandro Grassi, a world-renowned specialist in stained-glass windows: "Talent is not a fixed asset, but rather a predisposition, an ability that must be exercised with sacrifice and dedication. [...] Talent is, therefore, similar to a vocation, which can certainly manifest itself at a young age, but that needs to be nurtured.

[165] De Michelis, "Dopo la modernità", pp. 21–23.

[166] See Zingarelli, *Vocabolario della lingua italiana*, s.v. "talento".

[167] Silvia Mazzucotelli Salice and Isabella Medicina, *Maestri del fare: Indagine socio-economica sulla domanda di mestieri d'arte a Milano* (Venice: Marsilio, 2012), p. 75.

Only through practice can talented young individuals learn how to channel their aptitude and control their creative force."[168]

The productive and cultural vitality of a country is measured according to the efficiency of the different levels of its creative, cultural, technical and scientific industries. In a globalized world where that efficiency is constantly challenged by international competition, the impetus to develop the potential of individuals and social groups becomes as crucial as the imperative of quality.

America's quest for an objective measure of talent using IQ tests has undoubtedly accustomed us to think of the best human potential as being a superior level of intelligence. As Stefano Micelli explains, it is "an abstract intelligence, that can shift horizontally and swiftly from one problem to another. [...] In the United States in recent years, alongside the renewed interest in manual work, they have had the courage to seriously question the traditional idea of 'talent' and whether a person's success – insofar as the term 'success' can be analytically defined – could be linked to something more concrete than their IQ".[169]

Ingenuity, listed above as one of the components of talent, includes people's faculty to "sense, learn, realize and devise, by making the most of their intelligence".[170] In a master artisan's training and in the pursuit of excellence in the productive industries in general, intelligence is therefore perceived as a tool that one must learn how to use and to direct. The capacity to read situations, find solutions, learn new methods and open new pathways is the discernible attribute of a well-formed, mature, developed intelligence that has been encouraged to engage in healthy and stimulating pursuits.

> In music, business and sport, talent can take on the form of excellence only after enduring a long period of refinement of the practices that govern a specific field of activity. In-depth studies undertaken in a variety of sectors estimate that it takes about ten thousand hours to master the gestures and the competences required to become fully expert in a particular field. [...] Another crucial aspect highlighted in the literature [i.e. the latest and amended literature emanating from the United States] is the need for society to support and cultivate people's inclinations. [...] We all need a guide, a mentor, someone to steer our efforts in the right direction and to help us find a path. [...] Extensive practice and reliable role models are the key ingredients of an effective artisanal training.[171]

[168] *Ibid.*
[169] Micelli, *Futuro artigiano*, p. 163.
[170] See Zingarelli, *Vocabolario della lingua italiana*, s.v. "ingegno".
[171] Micelli, *Futuro artigiano*, pp. 165ff.

This inevitably leads us back to the central theme of Richard Sennett's *The Craftsman*, which sees the culture of craftsmanship and its training and production methods as a model for contemporary economic and productive growth. Sennett recognizes what could be defined as crafts' "democratic" nature, by virtue of the opportunity craftsmanship offers anyone willing to learn a method and develop those qualities that Sennett believes every human being possesses. To prove his point, and referring to studies on the prehensile capabilities inherent to the hand's bone structure, Sennett explains:

> [T]hough some hands are larger, some endowed at birth with wide lateral stretch, the real difference between able and clumsy hands lies in how each hand is stimulated and trained. Even biologists who contest most strongly the image of human nature as a "blank slate" take this view. [...] [The brain's] resources are apportioned or applied unequally in different individuals; dwelling on that fact, society can poison itself. Make no judgments of fate; stimulate the human organism as much as possible. The narrower realm of craftwork addresses the issue of unequal talents in a perhaps more focused way. The innate abilities on which craftsmanship is based are not exceptional; they are shared in common by the large majority of human beings and in roughly equal measure.[172]

Sennett therefore makes a very clear distinction between exceptional innate qualities – which we can identify as "talent" – and those skills we all share: what makes it hard for us to tell them apart, what they have in common, is the fact that they both need to be cultivated in a stimulating and competent environment. Aside from any intrinsic skills, the artisan's motivation in striving for excellence is the factor that can make a real difference.

These views are shared by John Gardner, an American politician and essayist particularly sensitive to the theme of training and welfare:

> Everyone agrees that motivation is a powerful ingredient in performance. Talent without motivation is inert and of little use to the world. Lewis Terman and Catherine Cox found that historical geniuses were characterized not only by very high intelligence but by the desire to excel, by perseverance in the face of obstacles, by zeal in the exercise of their gifts. Some people may have greatness thrust upon them. Very few have excellence thrust upon them. They achieve it. They do not achieve it unwittingly, by "doin' what comes naturally"; and they don't stumble into it in the course of amusing themselves. All excellence involves discipline and tenacity of purpose.[173]

[172] Sennett, *The Craftsman*, pp. 276–277.

[173] John W. Gardner, *Excellence: Can We Be Equal and Excellent Too?* (New York: Harper & Row, 1961), p. 92.

Master artisans support these theses and prove they are well acquainted with the attributes that lead to expertise and in turn to excellence, recognizing talent in their apprentices or subordinates. According to Mazzucotelli and Medicina, "in contrast to the notion of art as inspiration, the master artisans we interviewed describe art as a trade, a skill, more a question of practical application than of creativity; to them art is, as Aristotle posited, a 'reasoned state of capacity to make'",[174] a linear production process through which the creator imposes a predetermined intention on a particular material.

As Alessandro Grassi puts it, "[t]he manual factor is crucial to this craft: creativity, but also manual skills are its essence [...]. The work is creative and non-repetitive; it is about transforming materials. We work the materials and we create something special, something everyone can admire, something beautiful and enduring."[175] Immersion in the life of a Renaissance workshop, observing, assimilating, developing a style and a way of thinking that relate both to production *per se* and to one's interaction with fellow workers and designers, all the way to an understanding of the customer's needs, of a brand's distinguishing features and of the distinctive philosophy of an artisanal enterprise: these are the qualities that make a good artisan, and are even more decisive when it comes to a master artisan's rise to excellence.

Talent is therefore a gift but also a responsibility and a measure. As De Michelis points out:

> [Craftsmanship] begins with the hands and spurns the mould, inserting, whenever possible and justified, a personal detail that conveys the pleasure of surprise and the joy of wonder. Crafts put the focus back on skill, on expertise, on the power of experience. Emphasis is placed on the primacy of the individual, the wonder of the aura, the mystery of beauty, the delight of competition, and the fervour of battle. In short, crafts are a farewell to modernity and to its scarce human values, and the commencement of a new, extraordinary adventure towards an unknown – and therefore somewhat unsettling – destination.[176]

It is no coincidence that when ethical, professional and, consequently, economic values are in serious crisis, as is currently the case, a pressing need arises to reassess the quality of human capital and talent as a driving force for social and economic change – a need of which the world of the artistic crafts is already acutely and maturely aware.

[174] Mazzucotelli Salice and Medicina, *Maestri del fare*, p. 75.
[175] *Ibid.*
[176] De Michelis, "Dopo la modernità".

This is why it is crucial to fully grasp what talent means for a master artisan and what it entails when it comes to the artistic crafts. As we have already said, talent consists of a particular sensibility, an instinctive feeling for aesthetics and creativity, and ingenuity and perseverance in solving problems and in finding new pathways and opportunities. Talent is not intelligence in the commonly understood sense of the word, but has its own specificity that is born and takes shape through direct experience of the problems and needs within its remit.

Micelli describes talent as a form of "horizontal" intelligence, "that is nourished by the world around it and that refers continuously to a deep-seated knowledge of the working environment. The artisans' skills, their mastery, depend on their ability to establish an intimacy with their tools and to grasp the tiniest differences in the materials they are working with. This talent is a form of intelligence on which relationships are forged within and outside the workplace".[177] Talent is also able to transpose itself and the world around it into the artisans' actions and into the artistic product that is the outcome of their vision, design and manual skill.

In the context of the artistic crafts, it can be said, therefore, that "talent" is and includes:

– *inspiration and an inclination for quality*: a talented person is able to do things well and with ease. In the artistic crafts, this is manifested in manual skill and an affinity with the materials, in the ability to envision beauty in the raw material, and in the creative perseverance to find that beauty where it is not immediately visible;

– *awareness and responsibility*: a talented craftsperson has learnt and fully comprehends that the cornerstones of craftsmanship, namely practice, research and teamwork, can never be disregarded, nor the essential features and production objectives of artisanal work, such as authenticity, tradition and innovation, shunned;

– *intuition combined with learning*: the presentiment that a particular piece of wood is capable of producing the magnificent sound of a cello is of no use without the knowledge of how to fashion it as such. True talent lies in observing, grasping, assimilating, and putting one's creativity to the test, while remaining patient, exercising one's motivation by solving problems, growing and developing despite the frustrations of early failures, in order to reach full maturity and success through a complete mastery of technique and freedom of expression.

[177] Micelli, *Futuro artigiano*, p. 164.

3.3.9. Territory

The International Charter of Artistic Craftsmanship, referred to earlier, opens with an important definition:

> Creative craftsmanship was the first phenomenon to mark man's existence. The crafted object – long before any other evolutionary, organisational or productive form – was the first identifying sign of the presence of human life. In these terms, the artistic handicraft objects contribute to create the identity of a people, intended as [a] collection [of] traditions, knowledge and distinctive marks that make them recognisable and unique.
>
> The artistic handicraft creations are therefore to be considered as an expression of the material culture, linked to the environment where the artistic phenomena and the art objects are manifested or produced.
>
> So objects of artistic and traditional craftsmanship must be considered as a people's artworks, bearing a spiritual and cultural message, as well as being witness to traditions and creativity to be passed on to future generations.[178]

When defining the artistic crafts, the link with territory should not be an *a posteriori* qualification or seen as a purely economic necessity. It is an issue of the utmost relevance. Territory is first an environmental factor and second a social one. The delimitations of and humans' attachment to an area have profoundly influenced the way everyday objects have been created, their shapes, their distinctive decoration, the materials they are composed of, and their production methods.

In her 1991 study on the importance of place in artisanal production, Angela Roncaccioli, lecturer in cultural heritage management at Ca' Foscari University in Venice, discussed how in Italy, for example, the morphology of an environment has given rise to particular craft activities in certain places rather than others. The geological nature of the soil will certainly have favoured the excavation and use of granite and marble. Woodland yielding quality timber in mountain areas – the Aosta Valley, Trentino, Lombardy, Friuli – has fuelled the growth of woodworking and wood-related industries, such as furniture production, inlay and the manufacture of tools for agriculture, carving and sculpture; top European violin-makers, meanwhile, use wood from the so-called "Bosco dei violini" (Forest of Violins) in Val di Fiemme. Metalworking has generally developed in places near iron mines and rivers or streams, while in Sicily, Calabria, Umbria and Puglia the plentiful supply of clay and the hot climate to dry it out has sustained a flourishing ceramics tradition. Sociopolitical conditions have also

[178] International Charter of Artistic Craftsmanship, Definitions, para. 1.

played their part: "The spread of artisanal glassmaking, epitomized by Murano, the art of goldsmithery, which made of Vicenza and Valenza two of the most important centres in the world for this craft, and the entire culture associated with the building of villas and *palazzi* are all closely associated with the Venetian Republic, its trade with the East, and the flourishing aristocracy and bourgeoisie of the time."[179]

And there are numerous other examples of this symbiotic relationship between a more or less "enlightened" patronage and the area's resources, which include both material resources and the working culture they spawned.

The environmental and social situation, the geophysical properties that are conducive to the development of certain activities, and an abundance of raw materials are the principal elements that not only favour certain forms of production and services, but also stimulate artisanal creativity. This brings us to the second fundamental meaning of "territory" in relation to the artistic crafts: the territorial context, or rather the relational networks that give rise to a community.

> The word community evokes goodwill and group solidarity, with its promise to accompany both entrepreneur and worker from the cradle to the grave, as social democracy claimed it would do in its heyday. In this sense, then, the community could project its territory into a wider commercial and reputational space. To cite just two examples from the ceramics and food sectors, Sassuolo and San Daniele are both place names and brand names, and this automatically boosted the image of small businesses in Emilia-Romagna and Friuli regardless of their sphere of activity or level of competence.[180]

Master artisans' community plays a vital role in their training in terms of both the reservoir of knowledge and know-how that they can draw upon and the tastes and demands of local patrons, which in different ways encourage creative experimentation, steering it in a unique direction exclusive to that territory. Paolo Colombo, director of the "Arti e Mestieri" (Arts and Crafts) Research Centre at the Università Cattolica in Milan, points out:

> The "artistic crafts" can be viewed and described as the fruit of a collective effort, whose agents are not simply the individual artisans, but also the "patrons", the professional figures, the public and the critics. The crucial point here is that each one of these contextual elements "revolves", so to speak, around a specific

[179] Angela Roncaccioli, *Aspetti caratteristici e lineamenti evolutivi dell'artigianato urbano: Il caso di Verona* (Padua: CEDAM, 1991), p. 41.

[180] Dario Di Vico, *Piccoli: La pancia del Paese* (Venice: Marsilio, 2010), p. 26.

concept of "art" and of the "artistic crafts", and acts, therefore, within a more or less consolidated framework of aesthetic and productive conventions.[181]

In collating various positions on the relationship between personal identity and a sense of belonging to place, sociologist Gabriele Pollini has outlined the four principal ways in which this relationship comes about. The presence of several individuals in the same place determines the existence of a community and an attachment to it, accompanied by an interdependence between the members of that community (ecological interdependence) created when communal needs are met and problems connected to the territory are resolved.

Lending support to this idea is the strength of *social belonging*, which depends on "the *solidarity* of the social collective, the loyalty of members towards it and their '*sense of affinity*'", and the number of *common cultural interests*, that is to say, "shared value systems (=evaluative symbolism) and institutionalized constitutive symbols on differing levels of generality", while the possibility of dissent and opposition ensures that internal differentiation is preserved.[182]

Personal identity is formed – though not exclusively – by socio-territorial belonging and derives from the territory of reference. This is what is known as "place identity", a spatial/territorial factor that can determine components of personal identity. According to Pollini, this occurs under certain conditions: when there is a supportive community with well-defined roles of its members and when there is a symbolic-cultural system that can be internalized.

It is belonging or having belonged to a socio-territorial collective, therefore, that fosters that aspect of personal identity that relates to a particular area. This sense of belonging enables the assimilation of those shared symbols or values that express and represent the territory (and the relationship with it), where both the individual and the collective are settled and located.[183]

It is not our intention here to enter into a major sociological debate. However, what is crucial to our discussion on the artistic crafts is the master artisans' provenance from (or at least familiarity with) a

[181] Paolo Colombo, "Stabili confini e mutevoli frontiere", in *A regola d'arte: Attualità e prospettive dei mestieri d'arte in Lombardia e Canton Ticino* (Milan: Vita e Pensiero, 2005), pp. 7–9, especially 18.

[182] See Gabriele Pollini, "Appartenenza socio-territoriale e identità personale tra localismo, nazionalismo e cosmopolitismo", in Ilaria Riccioni (ed.), *Comunicazione, cultura, territorio: Contributi della sociologia contemporanea, Atti del convegno 30–31 maggio 2008, Libera Università di Bolzano* (Milan-Udine: Mimesis, 2008), pp. 82ff.

[183] *Ibid.*, p. 86.

particular place and a particular community, from which they assimilate and reinterpret a taste for its objects and a specific way of making them. The materials typical of a certain region, the taste and style that have evolved to become tradition, and the know-how accumulated by a community within its specific limits and potential are part of the shared heritage built up over decades, an ever-expanding store of knowledge and expertise that the new generations can tap into, grafting onto it their own ideas, inventions and innovations. Thus, for the precious cultural morsels of a territory to be reflected in its finest artistic crafts presupposes that the essence of that place will have been fully absorbed. This is no easy task, if we consider that the training methods are not those typically found in schools.

A sense of tradition, familiarity with a know-how, knowledge that has been tested, renewed and passed on as part of a sort of local anthropology and that is distinctive in that it cannot be "standardized", all constitute a system that is geared towards immediate application rather than long-term reach. According to American economist Kenneth J. Arrow, this type of learning can only occur by finding solutions to specific problems, and therefore only when productive activity is actually taking place. Arrow goes so far as to consider learning levels as a cumulative function of investments within the business system.[184] And this is what Franco Lai, researcher in cultural anthropology, and following the school of thought of French ethnologist André Leroi-Gourhan, defines as the "technical environment", or rather, "the sum of a society's technical knowledge". The defining characteristic is the creation of a "pool of tradition" that represents "continuity, providing each generation with all the experience gained by those preceding them". This allows "the capital of accumulated knowledge" of previous generations to settle. The technical environment is neither static nor self-contained, but is rather "in constant flux influenced as much by [...] its contact with neighbouring groups as by its own internal dynamism".[185]

Therefore, the artistic crafts cannot be considered as divorced from a given local context. That context has and continues to put in place a specific method of responding to problems that translates into typical production and decorating techniques and methods, particular tastes and production styles, whose distinguishing features have been shaped

[184] For more on this issue, see Kenneth J. Arrow, "The Economic Implications of Learning by Doing", in *Collected Papers of Kenneth J. Arrow, Volume 5: Production and Capital* (Cambridge: Harvard University Press, 1985), pp. 157ff; Piergiuseppe Morone, *Conoscenza, nuove disuguaglianze e tecnologia dell'informazione* (Soveria Mannelli: Rubbettino, 2004), pp. 77ff.

[185] Franco Lai (ed.), *Fare e saper fare: I saperi locali in una prospettiva antropologica* (Cagliari: Cuec, 2004).

by the territory and its people.[186] "Our own identity is characterized as a whole by the network of relationships that we inevitably build with *others* and the external environment. This is what constitutes *culture*: a fruitful and *dynamic* exchange with the outside world that is constantly adapting and renewing both us and those around us."[187]

This is another reason why Italy is becoming the go-to place for a new generation of creatives with a passion for making, mainly because learning by doing is still emerging as a powerful phenomenon in the country today. Technological developments are "transmitted to the workforce through on-the-job training, giving rise to processes of specialization and division of labour that were practically unheard of in other districts only a few miles away".[188]

If a master artisan's identity has as much to do with the territory of origin as with the profession itself, then we can speak of a collective identity that is transferred into the art object by way of the capable hands of the artist-artisan. This is what is meant by the "typicality" and "recognizability" of a product, a style or a taste. As ethnologist Valeria Siniscalchi writes, "a 'typical' product is both a commodity and an aspect of identity: it becomes 'typical' through at times extremely complex processes that enhance the value of a place or a region, and in this way it can play a key role in defining the identity of that geographical space".[189] It follows that an object will be typical if it conveys a collective identity, carrying with it the traces of a place in the broadest sense, as we have hitherto discussed: it will bear the signs of those geophysical constraints and opportunities, of the historical culture, of taste developed over years, of techniques perfected by the hands of generations of artisans, and of a people's character.

If, as Hegel writes, "the universal need for art [...] is man's rational need to lift the inner and outer world into his spiritual consciousness as an object in which he recognizes again his own self",[190] then master artisans use the artefact to express, through their own ability and ingenuity, a vision of themselves immersed in a given environment, that is both a territory and a community. This "living" geographical identity

[186] See Zingarelli, *Vocabolario della lingua italiana*, s.v. "tipico".

[187] Giuseppe Vitiello, "Oggetto, percezione e astrazione in fisica", in Fabrizio Desideri and Giovanni Matteucci (eds), *Dall'oggetto estetico all'oggetto artistico* (Florence: Firenze University Press, 2006), p. 14.

[188] Emanuele Salsano, *Lineamenti di sviluppo locale: I distretti industriali* (Naples: Liguori, 2002), p. 8.

[189] Valeria Siniscalchi, "Saperi, economia e territorio nella costruzione di un prodotto tipico: i 'tourtons' delle Hautes-Alpes (Francia)", in Lai (ed.), *Fare e saper fare*, p. 141.

[190] Georg Wilhelm Friedrich Hegel, *Aesthetics: Lectures on Fine Art*, translated by T.M. Knox (Oxford: Oxford University Press, 1975), p. 31.

consists of people and institutions that are constantly absorbing and reshaping the same history, the same customs and the same way of thinking. Antonio Sassu, senior professor of political economy at the Faculty of Political Sciences of Cagliari University, explains it this way:

> The territory, especially, is in constant flux, creating and providing those who live there with a continuous flow of knowledge, which generates those processes that affect individual know-how and behaviour. Therefore, the territory is not indifferent to economic factors; it counts because its history counts, because its resources are so diverse and because its processes vary over time and in space.[191]

One consequence of territorial and productive diversification has been the growth across Italy of the "industrial districts" (see Chapter 1), a term first coined by British economist Alfred Marshall. As Clara Bassano writes:

> The main aspect of the district is the interrelationship between the social, economic and political spheres of the local system, whose distinctive elements are: *the community of persons*, who share values, expectations and common languages; and *the business population*, which constitutes a concentration of industries in a geographically defined area. From a historical perspective, and although not exclusively an Italian phenomenon, the industrial district model has found in Italy a fertile ground to assert itself since the 1970s.[192]

This is no surprise, given that Italy's productive system is noted for its territory-based set-up. Furthermore, in its third report, the Osservatorio Nazionale Distretti Italiani (National Observatory of Italian Districts) details how Italy's geophysical make-up and business structure (which includes a remarkable number of small and medium-sized enterprises or SMEs) has ensured that the country is competitive in Europe and globally. It further states that this is the fulcrum on which political and financial leverage needs to be applied in order to boost economic performance.

In recent years, the need to reappraise and enhance knowledge, technologies and local production in Europe has become increasingly urgent, in both academic and political circles. As Lai says:

[191] Antonio Sassu (ed.), *Saperi locali in Sardegna: Tradizione e innovazione nell'attività economica* (Cagliari: Cuec, 2004), pp. 18ff.

[192] Clara Bassano, *I distretti orafi italiani: Tipicità degli assetti territoriali e ruolo della comunicazione* (Naples: Edizioni Scientifiche Italiane, 2008), pp. 45ff.

> Across the Mediterranean world and Europe, artisanal products and foods are being rediscovered and revitalized, and this can be explained partly by the general tendency to reassert local identity in response to globalization and partly by the tourist industry's demand for traditional, locally produced goods. This trend falls within a wider process of "capitalization" that lies at the centre of today's cultural policy in European states (and the EU), and can be described as "national-capitalization". [...] The issues concerning local know-how could be interpreted as a new form of "emergency anthropology". This implies recovering the know-how and techniques that are in danger of extinction, as rural areas are abandoned owing to industrialization and emigration, and with them all those activities connected with farming, forestry and artisanal work.[193]

This is a crucial point when endeavouring to place the value of territory within the framework of a thorough assessment of those artistic crafts that symbolize it: the capitalization of the territory itself.

The Rome-based Symbola Foundation is working along these lines. Since 2005 it has been promoting a development model focused on the quality of tradition and on territory, as well as on technological innovation, research and design. This is what is known as the soft economy, which Symbola describes on its website as "an economy based on knowledge and innovation, as well as on identity, history, creativity and quality; it is an economy that can combine social cohesion and competitiveness, and that draws strength from its community and territory". Symbola conducts research, publishes reports, holds seminars and organizes information and public awareness campaigns. In one of its publications, *Quaderni di Symbola,* Ferruccio Dardanello, president of Unioncamere (Association of Chambers of Commerce), underlines the importance of focusing attention on territory in order to make the most of Italian excellence, stating:

> Our culture is rooted in the territory, and it is only by working at the territorial level that we can nurture the lifeblood of innovation. In this respect the Chambers of Commerce have a role to play, and Unioncamere has been working recently to bring the spotlight back on the best of our traditions, to highlight their merits and showcase what they have achieved and continue to achieve. It is these abilities that help us maintain the competitive edge that makes us stand out from our competitors on the global stage. [...] The originality and success of the "Made in Italy" label lies in this unique ability to imbue an artefact with a sense of the territory, the history and the culture that generated it and to endow a product with meanings that go far beyond its intrinsic value.[194]

[193] Lai (ed.), *Fare e saper fare*, pp. 7–8.

[194] Ferruccio Dardanello, "Premessa", *L'Italia che verrà. Industria culturale, made in Italy e territori*, pp. 9 and 11, www.symbola.net/assets/files/Ricerca%20Industrie%20culturali_1326723510.pdf.

This link with territory, in all the forms we have examined here, is the preserve of master artisans; it lies at the heart of their training, and is inevitably reflected in all their creations, through their choice of materials, the methods they use to transform and manipulate them, and the taste and style of the form and content. The recognizability of provenance is central to a definition of the artistic crafts, as it derives from the prolonged assimilation of the cultural extensions of a community, and since it is embedded in the master artisans' very being, it is immediately visible in their creations and in the way they conduct their overall business. As Lai reminds us: "In artisanal technologies, technical innovation is the result of a combination of 'new' and pre-existing elements. It is the fruit of borrowings and adaptations, and ultimately of 'creative nativization'. People's technical know-how is anything but static: like scientific know-how, it is permeable to external influences and demonstrates 'a perpetual tendency towards syncretism'."[195]

To sum up, the concept of "territory" in relation to the artistic crafts comprises the following elements:

– the territory must be seen as the entirety of geophysical and social features pertaining to a clearly defined and recognized space, and including within it a *knowledge set consisting of the materials, artisanal production techniques, taste and style* particular to the place, problem-solving methods and progressive development and renewal of traditional know-how;

– master artisans absorb the essence of a territory to which they belong and/or refer through a direct, concrete and working knowledge of that essence (learning by doing), developing an acute *awareness of the origins and evolution of the know-how* so that they can internalize them and re-express them in an entirely personal form;

– a master artisan's *creations reflect a status of belonging* through extensive familiarity with the techniques that are traditional to the territory and through a style that offers an original and distinctive representation of the territory's colours and features, expressed in an authentic and recognizable way;

– an artistic craft, in its interpretation of the know-how of a given territory, devotes itself to the continual updating of knowledge and to technological research in an effort to bring a *new vital layer to the entire knowledge set* from which it originated and developed.

To ascertain how and to what extent the value of a territory permeates the work of a master artisan, it is necessary to test the strength and validity of that relationship along three main lines:

[195] Lai (ed.), *Fare e saper fare*, pp. 8ff.

– *territory as a source* of original and authentic raw materials, as a district that has successively developed and assimilated a recognized technique and an artistic-cultural tradition;

– *territory as a network* of human and professional relationships in which master artisans do not play merely a supporting role but rather a leading one in the economic, social and artistic life of the territory itself, capable as they are to provide suitable training of a kind that is not easily standardized;

– territory as heritage, in other words as an asset that is environmental (to be respected, preserved and understood) as well as cultural, logistical and qualitative.

3.3.10. Tradition

> Tradition is the unbroken chain of all innovations and, by that token, the surest witness of the projection towards the future.
>
> LE CORBUSIER, *Athens Charter*[196]

The aforementioned Presidential Decree No. 288 of 25 May 2001 provides a description of traditional and artistic crafts and made-to-measure garments. As we have seen, the definitions distinguish between three kinds of crafts: artistic crafts, traditional crafts and made-to-measure garments. With respect to the traditional crafts sector, the Decree states:

> 1. Traditional crafts refer to those production processes and services carried out using techniques and methods that have been developed over time and handed down via local customs and practices in response to the needs and demands of the resident and floating populations within the territory, taking into account those innovative techniques that are part of its natural development and modernization.
> 2. Such work is carried out using predominantly manual techniques and with the aid of tools and equipment, but excludes mass production and automated manufacturing processes.
> 3. Traditional crafts include the restoration and repair of everyday objects.
> 4. Traditional foodstuffs are produced using techniques that are typical of a local or regional culture, and are largely manually processed and preserved, cured and aged using natural methods.[197]

[196] Our translation.

[197] Decreto del Presidente della Repubblica n. 288 del 25 maggio 2001, Regolamento concernente l'individuazione dei settori delle lavorazioni artistiche e tradizionali, nonché dell'abbigliamento su misura, Article 1(b).

Under national legislation, in short, traditional crafts, including certain agri-food production processes, involve techniques and methods handed down within a particular locality and the predominance of manual work in the construction, restoration and repair of everyday objects. However, this definition renders the scope of the legislation too vague and broad, allowing for even the most modest manual work to be considered as a traditional craft.

The International Charter of Artistic Craftsmanship provides a more focused definition of the requisite characteristics of traditional craftsmanship, clearly highlighting the unique features inherent to craftsmanship. For example, it states, as said earlier, that: "Works of artistic craftsmanship include: [...] creations, production and works of high aesthetic value, whether inspired by forms, models, decoration, styles and techniques that are traditional or historical, or the result of individual creative development and of personal and artistic forms of expression."[198]

Here, the defining feature of artistic craftsmanship is its inspiration from "traditional" forms and techniques. However, this reference to tradition requires greater clarification. It is crucial to understand what the term "tradition" truly encompasses when applied to artistic craftsmanship, and to clearly define the kind of production that can be termed as such.

The Devoto-Oli Italian dictionary defines "tradition" as "a complex of memories, information and testimonies passed on from one generation to another" and, more specifically, as "a set of practices and customs that are handed down from generation to generation and form rules".[199] It can therefore be considered as a process that matures over time, evolving and enduring as the essential vestiges of a community, and is clearly identified by its connection to a territory. Tradition, therefore, has a "residual status", to use Max Weber's term, but it is also a collective memory of customs and procedures that take on a normative value or become an essential aesthetic benchmark. Consequently, there are three areas that need to be explored for the purposes of this study: the formation of the memories, techniques and customs of a community in relation to the artistic crafts; their transmission over time and down the generations; and their constitution as rules that, as such, govern an activity.

If tradition involves the formation, consolidation and transmission of memories, its constitution must be seen as the cumulation and progressive renewal of a knowledge whose roots can be found in an era of productive splendour – for many Italian artistic crafts this corresponds to the Middle Ages, and later to the Renaissance period – leaving traces that

[198] International Charter of Artistic Craftsmanship, Definitions, para. 2(a).

[199] See Devoto and Oli, *Vocabolario della lingua italiana*, s.v. "tradizione".

are still visible in modernity. Throughout this process, the uninterrupted chain of traditional values has been guarded (often jealously and always effectively) by those "ephors" or custodians so typical of Italian culture: the church, naturally, but also the family. The latter would include, more broadly, small communities based on family ties, such as craft workshops, specialized industrial districts, creative teams and family-run companies, where the relationship between team members is characterized by the preservation and, often informal, transmission of know-how. This is very much the Italian way, as Sydney Toledano, chief executive of Christian Dior Couture, points out: "Only in Italy – notably in Veneto and Tuscany – can you find artisans who make shoes and bags in this way. As for suits, no one can cut cloth quite like the Neapolitan tailors. All of this has survived because each one, in their own way, has defended 'the workshop'. It is the great strength of Made in Italy: we thought about centralizing, but the Italians wanted to keep everything in the family, holding on to that sense, that love of their product."[200]

In a territorial community, the terms "typicality" and "distinctiveness" come to life. Production techniques, knowledge of materials and an aesthetic sense develop within it. The sense of community keeps tradition alive, and it is handed down and used as a benchmark, thus ensuring that product specialization – typical of each territory – remains simultaneously credible, authentic and original.[201]

Tradition is not simply a collection of ancient knowledge or skills that can be turned into written instructions, and consequently transmitted indirectly beyond territorial boundaries. In the world of the artistic crafts, tradition thrives on the constant stimulus of the masters themselves, who are engaged in the daily challenge of reinterpreting their tradition and carrying it forward, without succumbing to the temptation to turn out derivative imitations of the past.

Tradition, then, is a form of cultural baggage containing "contextual" knowledge that is not merely a set of techniques that have been handed down, but a *know-how* that also means *knowing how* to choose materials in a specific way, *knowing how* to look at forms based on a typical aesthetic principle and proportions, *knowing how* to endow an object with the aesthetic features of a territory, and *knowing how* to capture and build on the stimuli that a territory, a community or a given challenge can transmit. What results is typical in its content, and typical in the way it is taught, learnt and expressed in the artistic work.

[200] See Paola Pollo, "I numeri? Molto chic", *Corriere Magazine* (12 June 2008), pp. 116–117, especially 117.

[201] Sassu (ed.), *Saperi locali in Sardegna*, p. 21.

In seeking to encapsulate the precise nature of the artistic craft tradition, we need to determine a craft's "level of artistry", to avoid altering the very concept of art as society and its conventions shift. This is because artistic craft technique is based "on a series of theoretical notions and practical skills that can be taught and transmitted".[202] The creation of an artistic craft and the tradition that embodies its values and content is fundamentally dependent on being able to pass on knowledge. Any art that develops into a craft starts out with the apprenticeship, the transfer and continuity from master to student, and this is also true of any communicable knowledge that concerns the craft tradition. Therefore, an object must show traces of a history relating to the birth of an art and its complex development over time. It is a matter of "showing tradition" in its strictest sense: from the Latin *tradere*, meaning "to hand over", which is the root of *traditio*, meaning "the transfer of something you possess".[203]

While the aspect of place and territory may seem more immediately evident as regards the concept of tradition, time is also an important component. Tradition should not be viewed as set in stone or sacrosanct, but rather as a solid basis on which to create our own personal reading of the past and affix to it research, innovation, a personal perspective and artistic flair. Although it may seem contradictory, it is progress that keeps traditions alive: the connection between tradition and innovation is being revived and re-emphasized in many quarters, echoing the words of Le Corbusier cited above.

Stradivari's earliest violins, for example, are known to posterity as "amatizzati", as they were clearly influenced by his master Nicola Amati. Had Stradivari's genius stopped there, we would not have had the extraordinary masterpieces that characterized his school and his style. Nor would we have had the innovations to the cello that transformed it into a solo instrument or those perfect forms that are still used today to create highly contemporary period instruments. Tradition is not only the base on which master craftspeople graft their own activity, but also a guarantee in terms of experimentation and specialization, and may even inspire insights that can bring about a major sea change.

How much importance, therefore, should we give to the link with artisanal tradition? To what extent should artistic objects acknowledge their debt to history, to territory or to proven technical experience, taste and experimentation? Sennett reminds us that, in archaic Greece,

[202] Paolo Colombo (ed.), *Genio e materia: Contributi per una definizione del mestiere d'arte* (Milan: Vita e Pensiero, 2000), pp. 167ff.

[203] See Battisti and Alessio, *Dizionario etimologico italiano,* s.v. "tradizione" and "tradire".

"[s]ocial norms counted for more than individual endowments in the traditional 'skills society'. Developing one's own talents depended on following the rules established by earlier generations; that most modern of words – personal 'genius' – had little meaning in this context. To become skilled required, personally, that one be obedient."[204]

More specifically in terms of economics and the market, this factor should be compared with that of "quality". If we consider the change in consumption patterns in Western society over the last decades, due to increased income, we can see that quality has a decisive impact on the unit price of a product and should be assessed as an economic issue in production terms. When assessing quality, territory and environment, which essentially mean specialization and characterization of the production process, are key considerations that benefit the overall cost structure: "To have safeguarded local production techniques, even though they may have been adapted to new needs, is a distinction as regards modern production methods, and sometimes this is what makes the difference."[205] In fact, territories compete with each other as to which kind of knowledge should be exploited, with the common purpose of defining the most effective global marketing strategy. Competition can take place in terms of standardization, based on low-cost, high-tech production, or in terms of differentiation and typicality, capitalizing on the uniqueness of their history and the weight of past tradition.

The Business Innovation Centre of the Lazio region also highlights the importance of these elements for the quality of the artistic crafts in a report on artistic craftsmanship in the area. It stresses the need to invest in craft professions that are able to maintain links with the past and project into the future. The report mentions those "typical crafts that are firmly rooted in the territory in which they express themselves and that help to forge and change its customs. In a nutshell, it is a question of preserving that ancient knowledge of a constructive art, maintaining both functionality and aesthetics, without resorting to unnecessary self-celebrations".[206]

Indeed, in recent years some of the world's best-known Made in Italy brands have been focusing on the artisanal origins of their products, as they have understood that the Italian artisanal tradition is a hallmark of excellence. As Micelli points out: "This is not a 'nostalgic' cult of all things artisanal, but an awareness that the value of a quality product needs to be grounded in unique skills."[207]

[204] Sennett, *The Craftsman*, p. 22.

[205] Sassu (ed.), *Saperi locali in Sardegna*, p. 25.

[206] Business Innovation Centre Lazio, "Artigianato artistico: arte con qualcosa in più", in *Notes, Quaderno trimestrale su creazione di impresa e sviluppo locale*, No. 2 (2011), p. 134.

[207] Micelli, *Futuro artigiano*, p. 67.

Besides those companies that see the artisanal aspect of their production as a strength and point of pride, there is a long list of businesses specializing in artistic crafts that export widely and whose products bear a "seal of artistic approval" that is proof of even greater excellence. These success stories encapsulate "the three typical characteristics of artisanal work: an independence that converts into entrepreneurship; an ability to communicate and identify with others that converts into a custom-made product; and an ability to reinvent tradition that converts into cultural creativity. [...] As regards the ability to reinvent tradition, it goes without saying that to transform a hand-blown glass vase into a work of art is no easy feat".[208]

The elements that enable us to link the concept of "tradition" more directly to the world of the artistic crafts can therefore be summed up as:

– *knowledge that is accumulated and gradually renewed,* that has its roots in an era of productive excellence and that leaves traces that are still visible in modernity;

– *typical and distinctive production features* achieved via techniques, knowledge and an aesthetic sense that develop, spread and take root in a territorial community;

– *research, experimentation and innovation* as essential values along the path furrowed by tradition, linking with the past and projecting into the future, and reinventing tradition to convert it into "cultural creativity";

– *working processes involving techniques that can be transferred but not standardized*, a blend of know-how, knowing how to look (aesthetics), knowing how to choose (materials), knowing how to endow (aesthetic features) and knowing how to capture (external stimuli);

– *continuity of a professional legacy* that is direct (family) or indirect (school, artisanal and/or artistic community).

3.3.11. Training

> Those who fall in love with practice without science are like a sailor who enters a ship without a helm or a compass, and who never can be certain whither he is going.
>
> LEONARDO DA VINCI, "Of the mistakes made by those who practise without knowledge", *The Book of Painting*

[208] *Ibid.*, p. 98.

The primary definition of the Italian word for training (*formazione*, literally "formation") is "giving shape or form" (from *forma*, shape), and would appear to belong intrinsically to a field such as artistic craftsmanship, where shape is not only the outward element of an object but also the very essence of an idea, that comes to life through the material's innate properties.

The Latin word *educere* – in the sense of "to bring out" the good inclinations and potential of the mind (and the hands) – is the objective of any didactic or social discipline, whereby young people can be led to show, that is, make apparent on the surface, the essence of who they are and have the potential to be, which produces substance in the moment it takes visible form. It is interesting to note that Carlo Nanni, one of the authors of the *Dizionario di scienze dell'educazione*, draws analogies with *artifex* to convey the original meaning of the word "formazione": "An early meaning, that can still be found in everyday language, comes from the concept of 'formare' in the sense of 'to give shape', that is, to configure, fashion or forge, just as a sculptor does with marble, a potter with clay, or a musician or painter with their respective artistic creations. This meaning has also remained in relation to education, which is understood as moulding the human mind."[209]

For the present study, however, the most interesting element of Nanni's definition of "formazione" (training) is the way it is perceived in modern philosophy and pedagogy as associated with the vision of individuals as "constructors of themselves" and with the idea of progress marked by man's technical, practical and manual skills and intellectual capacities. In this context, "training" is considered as the process (and the result of the process) by which individuals

> develop their own potential, master new skills and consolidate existing ones, and learn how to manage their personal lives and relationships with others. This comes about through interaction with the environment and with the tangible historical, cultural, material, as well as human relational possibilities it offers; through the mediation and support of various figures (e.g. parents, educators, masters, teachers, tutors, youth leaders, assistants), institutions (e.g. family, school, church, social groups, associations, mass media), and through individual and social activities that are more or less deliberately undertaken for this purpose.[210]

[209] See José Manuel Prellezo, Carlo Nanni and Guglielmo Malizia (eds), *Dizionario di scienze dell'educazione* (Rome: Libreria Ateneo Salesiano, 2008), s.v. "formazione".

[210] *Ibid.*

At this point in the discussion, we thus need to consider three fundamental points:

– *the specific traits* characterizing training in the field of the artistic crafts;

– *the devices* that best bring out the potential of a person wishing to specialize in an artistic craft;

– *the authors and advocates* of training courses in the field of the artistic crafts.

To understand what training is required to become a master craftsperson, we need to look back at a relatively recent period in the history of artistic craftsmanship: the late 17th and early 18th century, when French luxury production was propelled to unprecedented heights, placing the Royal Manufactures on a par with Italian craftsmanship, which had hitherto set the standards for the aesthetics and quality of artefacts. French historians Pierre Goubert and Daniel Roche refer to this period in their 1987 work *L'Ancien Régime*, in which they examine the relationship that existed between school education and workshop experience and the causes of constructive tension that fuelled the extraordinary French productive machine during those years.

It is well known that artists and artisans worked side by side in the palaces of the nobility, making it difficult to distinguish clearly between art on the one hand and craft on the other. "But it is also important to understand what blurs these boundaries and where pinnacle and base sometimes coincide", explain the authors. "The first thing to keep in mind is that practising any art involves acquiring manual skills and techniques. This is the outcome of an apprenticeship, which always takes place in a workshop, under the guidance of a master who passes a personal experience and methods on to the aspiring artisans and artists, instilling in them an identical passion for his or her own work."[211] This is the first, fundamental point: art and craftsmanship are a combination of manual skills and techniques, which are passed on by a master to the artist or the craftsperson through the master's own experience.

The authors continue, however:

> Between the Royal Academy [of Painting and Sculpture] and the Academy of Saint-Luc [the painters' guild], which groups artisans and artists, there are certain procedures for passing on skills that are not one-way, even if Saint-Luc is destined – like all the other provincial academies – to provide the Royal Academy with a constant flow of new, innovatory talent [...]. For their part,

[211] Pierre Goubert and Daniel Roche, *L'Ancien Régime, Volume secondo: Cultura e Società* (Milan: Jaca Book, 1987), pp. 321–322. First published in French as *Les Français et l'Ancien Régime, Tome 2: Culture et société* (Paris: A. Colin, 1984).

the artisans emulate the academics in order to obtain the same recognition; from 1706, they have benefited from preferential statutes that allow them to impart knowledge in a very similar way – with a few differences – to that of the academics; after 1751 they also have their exhibitions. Both reap the benefits of an increased enthusiasm for the crafts; the Royal Academy has used this as an opportunity for new reflections and new ideas, while Saint-Luc encourages a new school to be set up for artisans, who now appear to have reached the peak of their creativity, and the salons encourage this emulation.[212]

The main point we wish to underline here regards the distinction – not only between artists and artisans, but also between knowledge and practice, science and manual skill – that is found only in the modern age, and the consequent separation in education of these two (in fact inseparable) dimensions of artistic workmanship. Even if, only a few decades ago, historians

realized that crafts and trades were very much present in the classical world, the importance of training and the study of the processes used to teach the skills and the attitudes of future master artisans have been ignored for even longer. […] There is no doubt, however, that even those so-called mechanical arts that correspond to what we usually identify as *artisanship, have always provided, in all Western civilizations, an important educational model, well before and better than schooling as we understand it today.* […] It is not our intention to look back nostalgically at the artisanal training practice of "learning by doing" (as Dewey called it), as opposed to the formal education typically provided by schools throughout the ages, but rather to discuss *the dichotomy, of at least three thousand years' standing, between the hand and the mind, in other words the distinction between the two respective training models, at times despised or regretted, under- or overestimated.* Of the two, however, formal scholastic education has always widely prevailed over on-the-job training in the eyes of officialdom and cultural tradition.[213]

This dichotomy has had a negative impact on the training of young people who want to combine creative and artisanal work in their careers. The aforementioned research and interviews conducted by Medicina and Mazzucotelli Salice with master craftspeople from different sectors led to an in-depth reflection on the many aspects of craftwork and workshop dynamics:

[212] *Ibid.*

[213] Antonio Santoni Rugiu, *Il braccio e la mente: Un millennio di educazione divaricata* (Scandicci: La Nuova Italia, 1995), p. 6.

> The workshop is firstly a factory, in other words a place where, with tools from the past, the mastery handed down through the centuries, and day-to-day experience, materials are transformed into original and unique finished products. [...] This does not mean that artisanal work is simply a question of performing a task. On the contrary, it puts "doing" on a par with "thinking". In the field of crafts, and particularly the artistic crafts, production not only involves making an item, but is a synthesis of intuition, conception, design, prototyping, creation and assembly.[214]

As in any profession, culture is the precious commodity that makes the difference. This is even more so in a creative context such as artistic craftsmanship, where dexterity is essential and gained through practice, but the hand is directed by the mind. In this case, technological innovation, design software, experimentation with materials, familiarity with traditional working techniques, rules of perspective, and drawing skills go hand in hand with such notions as marketing, communication, art history, painting and sculpture, architecture, and foreign languages and cultures. The work is carried out in a factory (a "laboratory" in the true sense of the word) that is also a shop (a commercial undertaking, involving purchasing, sales, marketing and communication), and a school, because this is where new generations of masters are taught the trade, but also where masters and pupils exchange expertise and knowledge in a sort of "continuous training".

This is why the workshop is the most suitable place for training, so much so, in fact, that the teaching structure deployed within the workshop remained fundamentally unchanged from the Middle Ages until the early 20th century. In past centuries, the title of "Master" was awarded only after a lengthy period of learning, naturally on the basis of both the intentions and the talent of the aspiring candidate.

Many went or got no further than the level of simple worker: only the best, in fact, eventually became Masters, and were moreover awarded the title by a committee appointed by key figures in the craft or trade in question or by members of the guild to which they belonged. This always followed a training period of around seven years and the presentation before the committee of a so-called *chef-d'oeuvre*, thereby obtaining the right to receive a salary and to continue the apprenticeship. Only after the completion of the final stages of the apprenticeship (which could last from four to ten years) were artisans allowed to open their own workshops.[215]

[214] Mazzucotelli Salice and Medicina, *Maestri del fare*, p. 64.

[215] See Santoni Rugiu, *Il braccio e la mente*, pp. 63ff, and Mazzucotelli Salice and Medicina, *Maestri del fare*, p. 68.

Throughout this time, the focus was on the trainees' growth within the workshop, through their contact with the materials and tools of the trade, working alongside the master, observing and absorbing the methods used. This direct and unique relationship between master and apprentice is a channel for formal and structured learning but also for equally effective informal and indirect learning.

As Franco Cologni puts it:

> A master is not merely a person who knows how to perform their trade but also how to teach it: and masters and pupils are what we need, not doers and charlatans. We need masters who still know how to convey, through competence and example, the greatest lesson that Greek culture bestowed on us: the "know thyself and thou shalt know the universe and the gods" inscription that greeted visitors to the Oracle of Delphi, and that has lost none of its relevance today. There is nowhere better than a school to reiterate this exhortation: know yourself, discover your potential, and make the most of it![216]

According to Santoni Rugiu, craftsmanship in the late Middle Ages

> was a cultural and pedagogic revolution as important as it was considered unimportant by historians in general and by historians of education in particular. When underlining the contribution made by Locke, Rousseau, Pestalozzi, Froebel, Dewey and all the other more recent pedagogists – who reaffirmed the value of hands-on experience without detracting from the sacred principles of contemporary education – it should not be forgotten that the primacy of those training models, that were the opposite of the aristocratic and intellectualistic models of the theory of formal discipline, is historically and undeniably the merit of the medieval arts.[217]

The great value of this approach is that it is completely suited to the modern day. This is not only because the length of training needed to become an excellent craftsperson has in no way been reduced, but also because this model is perfectly reflected in the most tangible consequence of the training environment: the selection made by master artisans and artistic craft firms from among aspiring apprentices and pupils from the various high schools, if not, as is very often the case, from members of the family who have grown up in that very workshop. When hiring young people as apprentices, masters take a number of factors into consideration, many of which relate to predisposition rather than innate

[216] Franco Cologni, "La regola e la passione del sapere", pp. 12–13.
[217] Santoni Rugiu, *Il braccio e la mente*, pp. 63ff.

talent. This is because masters are well aware that a propensity – for work, dedication, collaboration with colleagues, learning, mental and manual flexibility, and discovery – is one of the key ingredients for a workshop to flourish and the trade to be properly learnt. This potential can only be realized by following a path that teaches gifted young men and women how to channel their creative flair, which tools they need to cultivate it, and how to broaden their culture and increase their skills in order to structure it, giving them what it really takes to turn ideas into reality. Succinctly put, it is a path that allows them to bring out (*e-ducere*) their creative genius.

The high value of training lies not only in keeping the artistic crafts alive and giving direction to young people with creative abilities, but also in boosting the capacities of a workshop or artisanal business for innovation. Richard Sennett makes this point in very concrete terms, seeing training as crucial for the life and economy of a business:

> The well-crafted institution wants to respond to this desire [of most people to believe that their lives add up to more than a random series of disconnected events], once it decides that loyalty matters. Workers who have been retrained by an institution are much more bonded to it than are in-and-out workers. Loyalty especially matters to a business when the business cycle turns down; workers will stay the course, work longer hours, even take pay cuts rather than desert. […] But figuring out how to build on existing skills – to expand them or use them as a base for acquiring new skills – is a strategy that helps orient individuals in time.[218]

In today's globalized marketplace, the competitiveness of any productive sector is played out in the spheres of creative originality, territorial exclusivity and top quality. Training should thus respond to the need for continuous, cutting-edge technical, as well as entrepreneurial, managerial and professional skills, to ensure that a business is able to stay in the market, introduce technological and aesthetic innovations that are in line with productive and territorial specificities, and maintain a lively and stable relationship with customers and consumers. In the great uncertainty that pervades today's economically advanced societies, human resources must be seen as a necessary investment to increase economic competitiveness, provide qualified job opportunities, maintain high standards of social protection and safeguard social cohesion.

Having considered thus far the extent of training required of master artisans, we now need to think of this path specifically in relation to the

[218] Sennett, *The Craftsman*, p. 266.

complex and interconnected world for which young people must be prepared by giving them a formal, distinguishing qualification. As Ugo La Pietra neatly sums up:

> Artisanal culture is similar to musical culture: if I don't practise the piano or violin for at least three hours a day, I won't be able to master the instrument. In the same way, learning how to create a mosaic or a metal object requires dedication. This is why in the past you had to go to school, then become an apprentice, followed by years as a workshop assistant if you wanted to learn a skill that was not that easily transferable.[219]

The *savoir-faire* of craftsmanship – which led to the creation of the Made in Italy mark, which is still a sign of excellence, a benchmark and a source of international economic success – is not only multifaceted but represents entire sectors of typical products. Together, these dimensions must be perfectly synchronized for the overall machine to work. Neither the function and functionality of individual levels, nor the way in which they complement each other can be formally codified. Consequently, they are part of that unspoken knowledge that has nothing to do with the secrets of production or the treatment of materials, but with an interplay of different types of expertise and, therefore, of people, ideas, skills and "thinking hands", all of which are unique both on their own and when combined.

Just as the term "professional training" acquires a dense and specific meaning when it comes to the artistic crafts, "refresher training" (or "ongoing training" as it is more commonly called by experts and legislators) is enriched by a value that can be applied to all areas of work. In a workshop, in close contact with a master craftsperson and in a complex and organic interplay of skills that gives rise to teams in which different areas of knowledge are intertwined, there is a great awareness (yet again) of "how" expertise can be brought up to date. As to the "what", it is clear for all to see.

The problem-solving abilities that are developed in a workshop – and that a school education does not always adequately convey – are acquired and consolidated along a certain trajectory that cannot easily be circumscribed. In a work team based on artistic craftsmanship, where a company's core values and goals are reasserted every day, only a shared awareness of the meaning of (even radical) changes in the mental approach to the production processes allows all those involved to push themselves beyond their existing know-how and to try out new

[219] See Mazzucotelli Salice and Medicina, *Maestri del fare*, pp. 75–76.

ways of doing things. This happens thanks to the tacit transmission of expertise and multiple skills, in the combination of daily gestures and in the search for solutions to new problems.

Returning to the concept of primary training, these observations clearly show the need to reinterpret the word "training" in "artisanal" terms and to place greater emphasis on the

process of socialization in the workplace, by developing training courses aimed at excellence. During such processes, in fact, young people do not learn merely how to carry out the procedures they are told to perform, but they learn the trade: pupils acquire the core values of the workshop or company in which they are placed – such as the meaning of work and the concepts of organization, collaboration, team spirit and quality – and develop a considerable level of personal motivation.[220]

In conclusion, the training of a master artisan has multiple dimensions and different levels of knowledge, skill, expertise, dedication and collaboration. Training courses should thus focus on the following:

– *knowledge of the artistic craft* regarding its history and its different uses and sectors, guiding new pupils towards a specific field of study and learning;

– *familiarity with and primary use of the tools of the trade*, be they traditional, recently invented or highly technological, in the knowledge that these represent opportunities for and not limits on the artistic craft itself;

– the development of an aptitude for collaboration and the *capacity to work in a team*, to help aspiring master artisans to realize that the *accruing of expertise* is essential for resolving problems, fostering innovation (in terms of creativity, technology and communication), and the solid structuring of a craft firm or enterprise;

– making it possible to *come into contact with the workshop as early as possible*, so that pupils waste no time in developing their vocational motivation and learn from the master craftsperson the best ways of nurturing their own creative aspirations and of positioning and channelling their passions, inspirations, intuitions, determination, skills and talent most effectively;

– *the continuous updating and refreshing* of workshop know-how, to enhance internal expertise and, moreover, provide the chance to redirect existing skills to new areas of application, or to reuse them innovatively and nimbly by interpreting traditional production methods in a contemporary and original way.

[220] Mazzucotelli Salice and Medicina, *Maestri del fare*, p. 77.

ALBERTO CAVALLI

4.

PERCEPTIONS OF THE ARTISTIC CRAFTS IN ITALY: A QUANTITATIVE SURVEY

4.1. SAMPLE AND QUESTIONNAIRE DESIGN

As outlined in the previous chapter, we began our project by identifying the concept-terms that are used most frequently in legislation to determine craft excellence, and subsequently by consulting a number of experts on how they deemed this "excellence" should be assessed. We felt it was then important to also gauge the extent to which the connection between the best procedures and products encompassed in the definition of "Made in Italy" and the artistic crafts is a conscious, or at least evident, part of the collective Italian perception.

Our motivation was that a quantitative survey on this topic – which could include a more general assessment of the role of the artistic crafts in the future of the Italian economy – had never been carried out before, or at least not with this end in mind. We also believed it necessary to compare awareness of craft excellence across a variety of productive sectors and geographical areas in order to create a more accurate assessment matrix, and to establish whether Italians still considered it important to safeguard and promote Italy's finest artisanal output.

It came as no great surprise, therefore, to learn that the artistic crafts not only constitute an important part of our tradition, stretching back thousands of years, but that they also have a key role to play in our country's future, in its economy, in its employment opportunities (especially for younger people) and in the general quality of life.

Such was the opinion of the insiders, but also of the broader Italian public, as revealed in the findings of the wide-ranging survey conducted by AstraRicerche in mid-2012 on behalf of the Cologni Foundation for the Métiers d'Art. The study was based on 1,042 interviews with a representative sample of resident citizens aged 18 to 58, corresponding to an adult population of 33.5 million.

The sample was designed to provide as realistic and accurate a "snapshot" as possible, focusing on a section of the population that was still working and distributed across the five macro-areas into which the national territory had been divided: the Neo-Northwest (Piedmont, Aosta Valley, Lombardy), the Triveneto (Trentino-South Tyrol, Veneto, Friuli-Venezia Giulia), Centre-North (Liguria, Tuscany, Emilia-Romagna, Marche, Umbria), Centre-South (Lazio, Abruzzo, Molise, Sardinia) and Neo-South (Campania, Apulia, Basilicata, Calabria, Sicily).

The questionnaire was designed under the direct supervision of Enrico Finzi, sociologist and president of AstraRicerche.[1]

The sample group was initially asked to freely express their own understanding of the terms "crafts" and "artistic crafts". It was then steered towards more precise and detailed definitions and given a list of selected professions as reference.

In our context, "crafts" can be described as a set of productive activities that require a substantial proportion of manual work, knowledge of the materials, skilled use of tools and expert workmanship. These activities may lead to the creation of a finished article or may involve producing components which will form part of a more structurally complex product. Even when the work is mainly carried out by mechanical or electronic tools, human supervision and intervention is always required. The craft may be typical of a specific locality, encompassing traditional techniques and traits and local cultural values, or it may bear no reference to a particular place. In general, the manual work employed by the craftsperson is of a higher absolute value than the capital invested.

The precise definition provided in the questionnaire therefore went as follows:

> Crafts are a set of productive activities that require a substantial proportion of manual work, under full human supervision and with knowledge of the materials, skilled use of tools and expert workmanship. Artisanal businesses generally consist of a few people or even just one person.

The sample group was asked whether they were aware of this meaning of the term "crafts".

The same process was adopted for the term "artistic crafts". Once the open-ended definitions had been collected, the interviewees were told that the artistic crafts form a bridge between past and future, between creation and execution, constituting a legacy of diverse "know-how" perfected over time and combining the aesthetic trends of different

[1] www.astraricerche.it.

historical periods. They are a fusion of tradition and innovation and preserve manual skills – even when new technologies are also employed – where aesthetics and functionality meet to transform an everyday object into a work of applied art. Straddling art and craft, the artistic crafts combine manual skill and design in a creative synthesis which constantly strives for excellence. Master artisans generally produce small series of high-quality, valuable, unique articles, placing them on an altogether different footing from crafts, and even from works of art, which are one-off pieces, devoid of any practical function. The artistic crafts are an expression of the territories, the culture and the identity of Italy. They are continuously evolving and adapting in order to survive and preserve the significance of their cultural and historical roots. Many artistic crafts have been "rediscovered" because of their excellent quality, many have become part of larger and higher-profile production chains, and many have transformed themselves, adopting new and unexpected guises compared with how they are commonly perceived.

The question was formulated as follows:

> "Artistic crafts" are those where – thanks to the artisan's manual dexterity – everyday objects are transformed into works of applied art, combining design and manual skill in a creative synthesis of excellence that is expressed in the production of one-off pieces or small series (using traditional and/or new technologies). Can you honestly say that you knew what "artistic crafts" are?

At this point, the interviewees were given a list of 25 artisanal professions deemed representative of the artistic crafts. The list was based on a series of studies that had identified certain categories of Italian artistic crafts as being particularly noteworthy.[2] Using the recognizability and relevance of the main sectors of so-called Italian "excellence" as the starting point, the professions presented to the sample group were:

– artisan furniture makers;
– cabinetmakers;
– ceramic artists;
– chefs, cooks, food designers, pastry chefs;
– clockmakers/watchmakers;
– costume designers;
– designers, web designers;
– embroiderers;

[2] See, in particular, Paolo Colombo, Alberto Cavalli and Giaochino Lanotte (eds), *Mestieri d'arte e Made in Italy: Giacimenti culturali da riscoprire* (Venice: Marsilio, 2009).

– glassmakers;
– goldsmiths, silversmiths;
– jewellers;
– landscape architects, gardeners, garden designers;
– leatherworkers;
– metalworkers (for artworks, jewellery, etc.);
– mosaicists;
– photographers;
– picture framers;
– printers, paper-makers, paper artists;
– restorers;
– makers, or self-producers (architects, designers, etc. who create and produce their own products);
– set designers;
– shoemakers;
– tailors, pattern-makers, cutters;
– violin and other musical instrument makers;
– weavers, knitters, textile designers.

To make it clear which activity was covered by which artistic craft, each item on the list was accompanied by pictures illustrating the making of the products concerned.

The sample group was then asked a series of questions, including what they knew about these activities on the list, whether they owned any objects made by the artisans, whether they intended to buy such products, and how they viewed the future of the artistic crafts in Italy.

Once their knowledge of these artistic crafts had been established and their awareness raised, the respondents were asked what characteristics they thought an "excellent" master artisan should possess. They were shown a series of characteristics and asked to what extent they believed each one played a role in determining excellence. They graded their responses on a scale of 1 to 10, with 1 being "not very important" and 10 being "vitally important". The suggested characteristics were those that had emerged from the comparative study of Italian laws, directives and regulations (as discussed in chapter 2), with the addition of those proposed by the experts we interviewed, and whose opinions were summarized at the beginning of chapter 3.

The characteristics were:

– authenticity, non-manipulation, respect for the materials;
– creativity, ingenuity, imagination, vision;
– dedication, responsibility, hard work and effort over many years;
– competence, expertise, consummate knowledge of the materials and working processes;
– expression of the culture of a place, of a particular territory;

– family tradition, professional legacy passed on from parents or other relatives;
– innovation, taste and ability to find new and effective solutions;
– interpretive (non-mechanical) execution of the design;
– mastery, innate talent developed through experience;
– follower of a school or membership of an artistic and/or artisanal community;
– originality, distinctiveness, uniqueness;
– title of Master, conferred at the conclusion of specific training, experience and study;
– tradition, continuity over time, age-old experience;
– training, long apprenticeship;
– vocation, strong motivation from an early age.

The final part of the survey concerned the future of the artistic crafts in Italy. As well as seeking to highlight the characteristics that an "excellent" master artisan should possess to be successful and, consequently, to contribute to the development of the country, the sample group was invited to consider a series of detailed points concerning the survival and the relevance of those professions today.

The proposed characteristics of the master artisans of the future were:
– ability to communicate, market oneself;
– ability to communicate with the designer;
– ability to run/manage their own small business;
– ability to use new technologies;
– behaving in an ethically responsible manner;
– capability of training young people, passing on expertise and experience;
– cultured, well informed;
– experimentation with new materials and production solutions;
– informed about the products of other "master artisans";
– knowledgeable of the history and traditions of one's craft;
– knowledge of one or more foreign languages;
– passion, pride in one's work;
– possessing a marketing culture;
– studied for a long period;
– taking care of the distribution of their own products throughout the world;
– trained by expert "master artisans".

Once again, the list was based on information obtained from the interviews with experts in the applied arts and with leading figures from the world of the artistic crafts, and following a careful examination of international, national and regional legislation pertaining to this field. It was felt that the sample's responses might provide valuable information and some useful pointers when reflecting on the kinds of attributes that would be required of master artisans who might wish to project their talent and professionalism more effectively on the global stage.

The final question in our study concerned the longer-term survival of the artistic crafts, with the aim of exploring the sample group's perceptions of their relevance today, their vitality, competitive strength, and economic and cultural importance in an increasingly globalized marketplace. Respondents were asked whether they strongly agreed, somewhat agreed, somewhat disagreed or strongly disagreed with the following statements regarding the artistic crafts:

– they will recover their value because they are one of the most powerful expressions of "Made in Italy";

– they will decline and partly disappear because Italy does not know how to appreciate and make best use of its rich heritage and excellence;

– they will recover their value because in many countries there will be greater demand for high-quality, hand-made, original and unique products;

– they will decline and partly disappear because many "master artisans" will retire or die without having trained young people to follow in their footsteps;

– they will recover their value because they will create employment and offer opportunities for professional development;

– they will decline and partly disappear because technology and globalization tend to standardize tastes and products;

– they will recover their value because enthusiastic, new customers will appear in both traditional and emerging markets;

– they will decline and partly disappear because the ruling class in Italy is increasingly uninformed about and shows little interest in culture;

– they will recover their value because greater numbers of young people will feel attracted by traditional and respected crafts;

– they will decline and partly disappear because there will be increased competition from other excellent artisans in other countries, who to some extent will take the lead on the world stage;

– they will recover their value because certain forms of Italian excellence cannot be exported or relocated to other countries;

– they will decline and partly disappear because many families' incomes and living standards will be lower, even those families who, until recently, have been affluent.

The questionnaire was compiled in April and May 2012 under the direct supervision of Enrico Finzi and based on the knowledge gained over the years by the Cologni Foundation for the Métiers d'Art. It was administered to the sample group in June 2012.

4.2. SURVEY FINDINGS

The survey initially focused on the sample group's knowledge of the artistic crafts (as defined above), those which, thanks to the artisan's manual skill, transform everyday objects into works of applied art, combining design ability and manual skill in a creative synthesis and producing excellence that is expressed in the one-off or limited-series production of objects using traditional or new technologies. The findings show that 20% of Italians are completely unaware of the existence of the artistic crafts, 50% know something about them, and 30% are broadly well informed. One immediate problem that emerged from the survey is that unawareness is at its greatest among young people and at its lowest in late adulthood, decreasing steadily as age increases, suggesting a risk of a progressive "divorce" between the "Bel Paese" and one of its main sources of beauty and success.

More specifically, almost 40% of the sample gave their own definition of crafts as "it's a profession, a manual activity", linking them with manual skill, well ahead of the second definition, "it's a form of production that is non-industrial, not on a mass scale" (26.1%), and the third, "it's a traditional activity, carrying on traditions" (22.5%).

Manual proficiency and precision were spontaneously cited by 9.7% respondents, while only 7.4% of the sample mentioned art or artistically inspired creativity. It was reassuring to see that only 0.4% associated crafts with a type of work "that is outdated, in decline" and a modest 0.6% highlighted the work as "badly paid, insecure, menial".

When presented with the set definition of "crafts", 58.3% of interviewees responded that they were fully aware of the meaning of the term, 39.8% answered "yes, in part", while only 1.9% responded with a definite "no".

When it came to the set definition of the "artistic crafts", 59.2% of the sample responded that they were fully aware of the meaning of the term. However, the complementary data are cause for concern, namely that 40.8% had no idea what it meant. Of those who did know something about the artistic crafts, 25% mentioned "an artistic or cultural connotation", 15.9% stressed that they require "great manual skill", 14.1% associated them with both manual skill and intellectual ability, whilst only 12% highlighted the "traditional" aspect of these crafts.

The sample were then given the list of 25 of Italy's leading and most representative artistic crafts.

Data concerning the reputation of many of the artistic crafts listed were reassuring. A massive 80% were aware of those connected with *culinary arts, food design and pastry-making*. This is interesting and likely due to the recent renewed prominence (including in the media) of chefs in Italy. The response is even more significant if we consider that in France, for example, where the artistic crafts are listed and regulated at the national level, and its culinary culture is certainly well acknowledged and respected, all those professions dealing in ephemeral practice are not considered *métiers d'art.* Therefore, chefs do not appear on the official list of the Institut National des Métiers d'Art, nor among the trades listed in Decree No. 98–247 of 2 April 1988.

Shoemakers also obtained 80% recognition, owing perhaps to the many luxury designer brands in Italy producing internationally renowned footwear.

In third place came *photographers*, recognized by around 70% of the sample. This reflects an Italian trend as seen in the work of leading exponents and self-declared "image artisans" such as Mimmo Jodice, Fulvio Roiter and Maurizio Galimberti.

Similar results were obtained for *ceramic artists* (70%) and *jewellers* (67%). Although their contribution to Italy's GDP is very different, these two professional clusters are strongly rooted in their respective geographical areas; for ceramics, there are centres of productive excellence, or that have long-standing traditions, in all regions of the country, and the jewellery-making centres of Vicenza, Padua, Arezzo, Marcianise and Valenza still have international standing.

It is surprising that the artistic crafts associated with *fashion* and *textiles* were only placed sixth (66%), while *woodworkers* (many linked to the design world) followed with a recognition rating of 64%. These two sectors are highly strategic for the "Made in Italy" label, but it is usually only the designer who has the high profile, while the artisan who translates the designer's idea into a fine product is often relegated to the background.

Gold- and silversmiths and *restorers* obtained 63% and 61% respectively of the sample's recognition rating. *Glassmakers* received 55%, as did *clockmakers/watchmakers*, while those professions connected with *cinema and theatre costumes*, *gardens*, *leatherworking*, *web design*, *printing and paper* and *picture framing* all received 53%. Just behind, at 50%, came *metalworkers*, *mosaicists*, *embroiderers* and *cabinetmakers*. The lowest ratings – around 40% – were assigned to *weavers*, *knitters*, *violin and other musical instrument makers* and *set designers*.

In some respects, these data are unexpected. Violin-making in Cremona was inscribed in the UNESCO List of Intangible Cultural Heritage in 2012, yet it was recognized as an artistic craft by only 42% of those interviewed. At the same time, the list reflects the extraordinary variety to be found in this field. It should be added that it is a world that is much loved by many Italians, although ratings are not uniform, with appreciation generally greater among women and older cohorts and in the regions of Lazio and Abruzzo and further south.

As regards ownership of an artistic craft product, 48% of interviewees stated that they possessed an article created by an artisan jeweller and 46% that they availed themselves of the services of culinary and pastry-making "artisans", while the creations of ceramic artists rated 45%. The lowest ratings were for mosaicists (10%) and, unsurprisingly, set designers (9%). The average number of owned products was equal to 7 out of the 25 listed. This figure was slightly lower when it came to the purchasing intentions for artistic craft products, with a result of 5.9 out of the possible 25. The indication of purchasing intentions therefore tends to be low. This is a clear sign that the downturn is forcing Italians to curb spending, but also suggests that the artistic crafts need to communicate and promote themselves more effectively and in a more targeted manner.

In terms of the importance of the artistic crafts for Italy's future, the sample group's responses produced results that were partially in line with the previous ones. Professions related to fine cuisine, which were the most cited and well known, also obtained the highest average score as regards their fundamental importance for the economy, culture and identity of Italy, with a score of 7.7 on the scale of 10. Professions associated with fashion and design, restoration, jewellery and goldwork, as well as those relating to certain traditional crafts (glassmaking, weaving, clockmaking/watchmaking) scored around 7, although they were unevenly weighted. At the bottom of the ranking, and just making the grade, came picture framers, mosaicists and embroiderers. These crafts are perhaps less well known, less high-profile, less well promoted or seen more as niche professions.

The survey then posed a fundamental question relating to craft excellence: what characteristics did the respondents consider to be essential in determining excellence in the above-listed artistic crafts?

The responses reveal that there is a reassuring collective culture in this regard. Leading the ranking, with 76%, were creativity, ingenuity and imagination. Originality, distinctiveness and uniqueness scored similarly highly, as did tradition and experience.

For the respondents, therefore, excellence in the artistic crafts can be found in a dynamic balance between creativity and tradition, with a strong emphasis on the uniqueness of the object. Interestingly, these findings complement the results that emerged from the experts' responses, and underline the extent to which creativity, considered to be deeply rooted in Italy's cultural DNA, is an integral part of both purely artistic creations and the finest artisanal products.

Competence, expertise and consummate knowledge of the materials and working processes were also found to be very important (75%): a craft object must be "well made", or to put it better, perfectly executed. This kind of perfection can only be achieved with "dedication, responsibility, effort, lifelong learning and hard work over many years" (72%), and must include a high degree of "innovation" (71%), which is developed on a solid grounding of "mastery, innate talent" (71%).

The master artisan is not, therefore, a mere executor, but a careful and capable interpreter. In all, 70% of the sample group underlined the importance of an "interpretive (non-mechanical) execution of the design". However, the link between the master and territory was given equal importance, with craft as "an expression of the culture of a place or a territory" rated by 70%.

Training was recognized as a core value of excellence by 69% of the sample group, immediately followed, at 68%, by "authenticity, non-manipulation, respect for the materials". Some 57% of those interviewed underlined the importance of the vocational factor, as well as that of coming from a family that has carried forward the profession over a long period. The "official" title of Master was considered less relevant (53%): although the qualification is objective, as it was conferred (until the most recent educational reform) by an art institute, the sample group believed it was less important than "workshop" training, as indicated above.

Many Italians were surprisingly well acquainted with the nature of the artistic crafts, and there was a noticeable mix of esteem, affection and pride surrounding them. The fine crafts (both traditional and newer forms) aroused a genuine sense of "Italian pride" (although this was usually stronger among women and older cohorts). This was confirmed by the response to a specific question requiring an overall assessment – on a scale of 1 (minimum) to 10 (maximum) – of Italian master artisans, their products and their expertise: the average score was a very high 8.7 (64% gave a score of either 9 or 10). Emilia-Romagna, Liguria and the entire Centre-South gave a score of almost 8.8, while Piedmont-Aosta Valley-Lombardy rated them 8.6 and the Triveneto 8.5.

Enrico Finzi, who led the research, describes the findings as both surprising and reassuring:

> It was surprising in that our initial hypothesis stated that our fellow citizens were "divorced" from most of the artistic crafts. This divide was due to the ascendancy of large-scale industrialization and mass-produced articles, resulting in a fall in sales of high-quality artisanal products, along with a decline in the sector's employment and image. This hypothesis proved to be mistaken and overly pessimistic. Italians' relationship with the artistic crafts turned out to be strong as regards their widespread awareness of them, their feeling of ownership and, most especially, their attachment to them. Indeed, we should rather be speaking of a genuine intimacy, a close (and loving) bond, that runs counter to the stereotype of a nation that has become coarse and deprived of its roots and collective memory.

Ranking of criteria by perceived importance

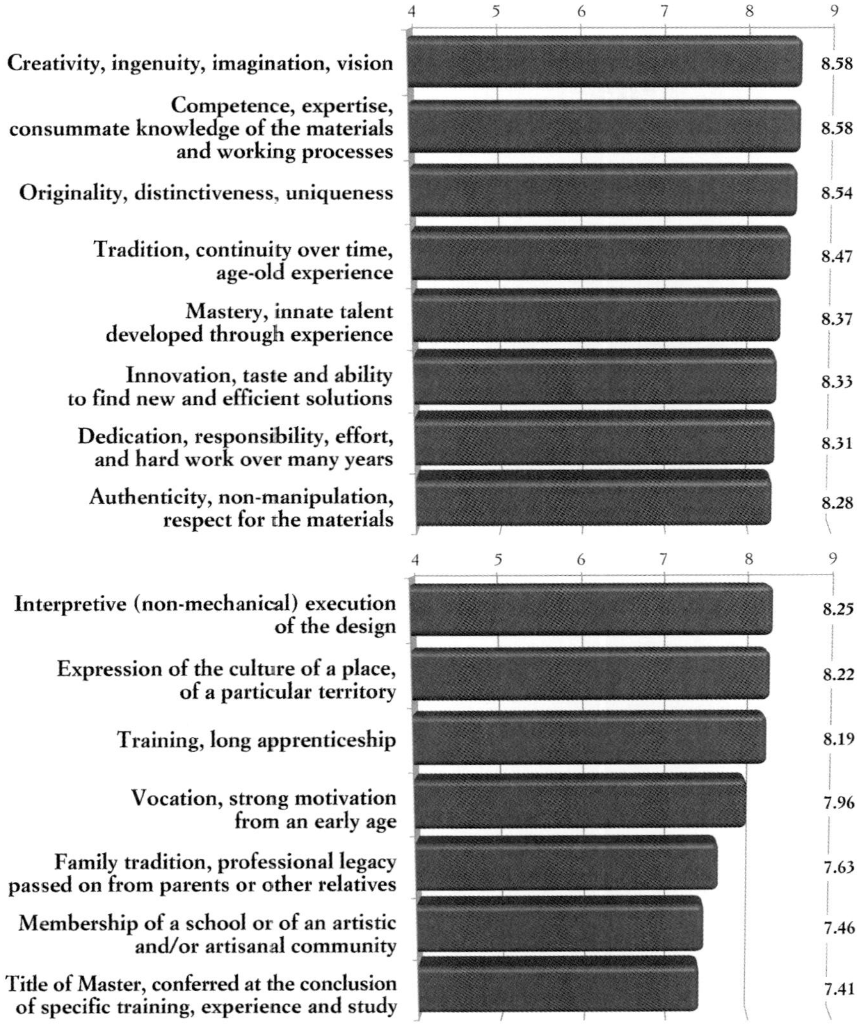

Finzi goes on to say that the data collected from the survey provide nothing but reassurances for the present and future, if it is true that "Made in Italy" – as perceived by society – is also (and at times especially) based on high-quality crafts, and not only in the "fashion" sectors, which receive greater media exposure. So our country can go on calling itself the "Bel Paese", proving that the picture of gloom and doom painted in the wake of the economic and social crisis is unfounded.

4.3. FUTURE SCENARIOS

And what of the future? Opinions varied somewhat but were largely positive.

The first question was: "According to many Italians and foreigners, Italy boasts extraordinary excellence in many 'artistic crafts'. In your opinion, what are the main reasons for this excellence? In your own words indicate the characteristics of Italian 'artistic crafts' that you think have made our country a world leader."

According to 25.6% of the sample group, the characteristics that determine "excellence" in the Italian artistic crafts can be attributed to tradition, history, artistic legacy and long-established practices. A further 19.2% cited originality, creativity, ingenuity and imagination as typically Italian attributes, whilst passion was afforded less importance, scoring 11.2% and ranking only marginally higher than recognition of the quality of products, materials and working processes (11.1%).

Significantly, therefore, the respondents recognized that if the Italian artistic crafts are to continue to uphold that excellence in the future, they must be grounded in a profound understanding of, respect for and promotion of tradition, albeit accompanied and given a contemporary edge by that creativity and that originality (in the sense of both innovation and authenticity) that are the hallmark of Italian products.

The sample group was then invited to give an *overall judgement* on the Italian artistic crafts, on their products and competence, on a scale of 1 (minimum) to 10 (maximum). The average score was very high, at around 8.71. Of those interviewed, 35.9% gave a score of 10, while 28% gave 9, 20.1% gave 8, and 8.1% gave 7. The percentages of those who gave a score of 6 or below, or who replied "I don't know" were insignificant. Once again, women turned out to be more appreciative of the artistic crafts than men, and the older cohort gave a higher score than the younger. In terms of geographical distribution, the responses were similar across the country, although scores in central and southern Italy were generally higher.

In the next phase, the group was invited to reflect on the *characteristics of the master artisans of the future*. When asked whether these should be assessed according to a fixed set of criteria, the sample group's responses seriously call into question any attempt to adopt a radically "objective" approach to such an undertaking. Some 71% of those interviewed said, in fact, that an essential characteristic of an excellent craftsperson is "passion, pride in one's work", echoing the views of the experts and master artisans interviewed.

The sample group also stated that the master artisans of the future should be capable of training young people (58%), know the history and traditions of their craft (55%) and be able to run their small businesses competently (51%).

Lastly, the survey focused on the future of the artistic crafts in Italy. Respondents were asked whether they "strongly agree, somewhat agree, somewhat disagree, or strongly disagree" to a series of statements in this regard. The statements were formulated in such a way as to convey both hope for the future and possible negative scenarios, ensuring that the collected data gave comprehensive information and controlled responses.

Of the sample group, 30% said that they were pessimistic. Reasons cited included: lower incomes of potential buyers; the standardization of tastes and products due to high-tech globalization; the disappearance of many master artisans in Italy who had retired or died without being able to pass on their know-how to younger generations; growing competition from quality artisans in other countries (including emerging economies); Italy's inability to appreciate and make best use of its own rich heritage and excellence; and, above all, the severe shortcomings of Italy's ruling classes (not only political), perceived as being increasingly uninformed and uninterested in culture.

However, some 70%, while sharing these concerns at times, declared they were optimistic that the artistic crafts will recover their value (22% unreservedly and 30% moderately so). Reasons cited were: the artistic crafts are one of the most powerful expressions of "Made in Italy"; local traditions of excellence cannot be relocated to other countries; and there will be greater demand in many countries for high-quality, hand-made, non-standardized, original products (also prompted by new, enthusiastic customers in both traditional and emerging markets). Once again, the most enthusiastic or positive assessments came from women and from the older cohorts.

For 70% of Italians, therefore, a great future awaits the artistic crafts in their country, as they will offer employment and professional growth opportunities in a time of high unemployment. So much so that (according to 64% of interviewees) more and more young people will feel drawn to traditional and respected professions, and no less than 87% believe that these professions can be integrated with new technologies, in a kind of "craft excellence 2.0", bringing together time-honoured experience and the digital society.

These figures confirm just how important the artistic crafts are in the collective culture and reveal that within the future there beats an ancient heart. The pace of development has been speeding up over the last 250 years, even more so in the last 60, and this is bound to produce new experiences and massive innovation. Yet, at the same time it drives us to reclaim the past, especially that timeless expertise which is then used for both traditional and contemporary applications (in printing, for example, with the Gutenberg screw press and web design). It is as though the flood of technology-driven transformations compels us to retrieve those "prerevolutionary" values and experience, almost as if to assimilate and offset this forward thrust. The same is true of global standardization processes that have been aided by type-approved, standardized mass production. While few would deny the benefits these processes have brought, there are many who like (or would like) to see something other than the mostly characterless products that are the same for everyone, everywhere. They prefer items that are original, distinctive, one-off or produced in small series, the fruit of manual skill and individual creativity, expressing local traditions and in some sense going against the flow.

This all points to a revival of one of the great Italian skills, namely the ability to offer the world something beautiful that is also well made, blending functionality and aesthetics, comfort and beauty, practicality and art. This is a key factor of success, provided that the excellence of the product is accompanied by competent global communication and marketing practices.

Interviewees' perceptions of the future

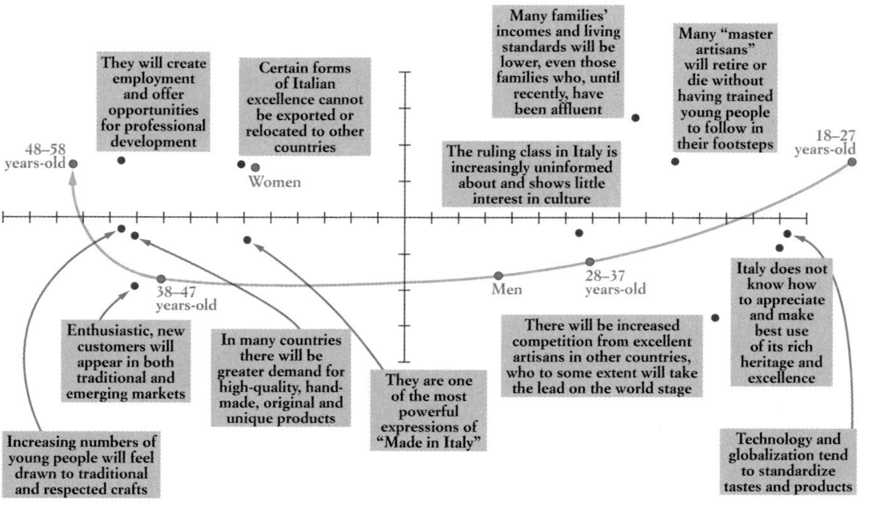

ALBERTO CAVALLI - GIOVANNA MARCHELLO

5.

MASTER ARTISANS IN MILAN AND LOMBARDY[1]

5.1 THE NOTABLE FEATURES OF THE ARTISTIC CRAFTS OF MILAN AND LOMBARDY: AUTHENTICITY AND BEAUTY

The inexorable march of change that has characterized Milan's economic and cultural life is closely tied to the city's identity. Emblematic of this identity is Milan's cathedral, a towering symbol of an art and a technique that has raised our sights to ever greater heights.

Charting the excellence in authentic Milanese goods makes for a fascinating journey through workshops and factories where the creative muses of art and craft have never failed to inspire. However, as often happens with keywords and as we have already said, even the term "excellence" risks losing some of its meaning. That is why we need to establish specific assessment criteria to define it properly in the field of fine craftsmanship.

In the search for a uniquely Milanese authenticity that is both contemporary and impeccable, we cannot overlook that artisanal contribution which gives a product its very soul. The time has come to think differently about the new "culture of making well", because what we need are true masters – people who are also able to teach and pass on a know-how that is constantly evolving and that lies behind the real, visible, tangible "difference" that is so highly prized.

We chose to interview artist-artisans who, drawing on their considerable first-hand experience, could share their views on what constitutes excellence. They are professionals who have placed their

[1] Sections 5.1, 5.2, 5.4 and 5.5 were written by Alberto Cavalli. The interviews with Lombard master artisans in section 5.3 were conducted and written by Giovanna Marchello.

"manual intelligence" at the service of an ideal beauty that naturally translates into an objective concept of excellence. In a world of cultural tautology, where everything looks the same and identical products can be found everywhere, with no soul or history of their own, the key to Italian excellence lies in the expertise of small workshops that provide the intellectual fuel for those sectors where Italy leads the way. The Lombard masters who participated in this study have played their part in this narrative, which tells of a land that gives rise to unique objects replete with cultural meaning.

As all good master craftspeople know, excess can be detrimental. Anything that is not essential to the product's beauty, to its design functionality and to its ease of use is pointless and redundant. It is the master's role, therefore, to seek out what is essential, no more and no less. By the same token, to establish what constitutes true Italian excellence, we need to acknowledge that fine artisanship is a vital part of it, contributing invaluably to the culture, know-how, research, intelligence and creativity of this country.

Contemporary crafts are steeped in tradition, reinterpreting and shaping it to suit the demands and expectations of a world in constant flux. As we have said before, today's artist-artisans are the indispensable professional partners of designers and creative talents.

Master craftspeople are an increasingly rare and treasured breed. To be considered as such, they must have a solid technical background combined with creativity, passion, talent and precision. They must know how to tap into their local artistic heritage and resources, drawing inspiration from them and adapting them to modern needs. They must also be able to evolve into a new kind of artisan, embracing the challenges of the contemporary world, while making best use of their own tried and tested methods, vision and identity.

Handcrafted, creative Italian products are much sought-after and highly regarded across the globe, an extraordinary cultural and economic resource. There is a legacy of tradition, research and creativity running through all the strategic sectors of high-end Lombard production, from Como silk and Cantù lace and furniture to fashion, from the ceramics of Lodi and Laveno to the quality firearms of Val Trompia, from violin-making in Brescia and Cremona to wrought iron and stonemasonry, from gold- and silverwork to jewellery and restoration. Nor must we forget fine food and wine. It all adds up to a globally recognized excellence that thrives on quality and efficiency, but also on passion and a willingness to embrace new technology, contemporary tastes and research. For this reason, we need to ensure that our "Living Treasures" can hand down artistic crafts to a new generation of masters who will continue to unite tradition and innovation and steer the sector towards the future. We must also reflect once more on the criteria underpinning the excellence of these masters, to better understand its origins and ensure it is passed on.

There are few areas in Europe with such a wide and thriving array of businesses, professions and traditions as Italy, and Milan is its beating heart. The city is a vital crucible of art, craft, vision and openness, and any study of the "authenticity" of a Milanese or Lombard artefact requires a perspective that crosses local boundaries, through the broader prisms of taste, luxury and research – in a word, excellence. There is, however, a need to rediscover and revitalize this excellence, both in terms of production and distribution and in terms of communication and training.

While there is an ongoing debate over the merits of craftsmanship versus technology, there is no question that "the great skill of the workforce enhances the quality of Italian products, making them major players in international markets and confirming the intellectual vitality of their creators. In short, late 19th-century Milanese and Lombard culture has come of age".[2]

5.2. BETWEEN CULTURAL INDUSTRIES AND DESIGN: A QUINTESSENTIALLY LOMBARD VOCATION

The pursuit of the delicate balance between fine craftsmanship and technological innovation, between interpretative ability and the preservation of a strong cultural identity, seems to have found renewed vigour in today's productive sector in Lombardy. While this sector is no stranger to large-scale industry, it is also engaged in rediscovering its deeply authentic roots, a heritage that, in some cases, is in danger of being lost altogether.[3]

There has been considerable technological innovation and cross-pollination thanks to thriving, dynamic production chains, notably in fashion and design. In Lombardy, this frequently intersects with the consummate craftsmanship of a district that is historically linked to the production of very high-quality and luxury goods. This union clearly demonstrates Lombardy's historical role as a cradle of the long-standing and time-honoured tradition of artistic crafts, several of

[2] Marina Messina, "Questi sono capi d'opera", *Mestieri d'Arte & Design*, No. 5 (April 2012), p. 42.

[3] See Alberto Cavalli, "Tradizione e innovazione", in Paolo Colombo (ed.), *A regola d'arte: Attualità e prospettive dei mestieri d'arte in Lombardia e Canton Ticino* (Milan: Vita e Pensiero, 2005), pp. 199–224, especially 199.

which continue to this day in the area. One perfect example, as already mentioned, is violin-making in Cremona, which UNESCO inscribed on its Representative List of the Intangible Cultural Heritage of Humanity in December 2012.[4]

However, if we look at the present (with an eye to the future), it is clear there are some occupations, representing a large part of the sector's domestic production, that have a certain vocational appeal. These professions, and the production chains they are integrated into, can ideally be incorporated into macro-sectors, such as the fashion and design industries. These sectors are considered as one of the pillars of Lombard identity of the last 50 years, and rightly fall within the above-mentioned definition of cultural and creative industries.

A recent European-wide analysis of the main cultural and creative clusters, conducted by the European Cluster Observatory in 2010, shows that:

> The Lombardy region plays a leading role within the entire European Union. By number of employees, the Lombardy region ranks third in Europe, after the regions of Paris and London, while Lazio occupies the eighth position, and Veneto the twenty-third. If you take into account the population-employment ratio in the analysed sectors, the Lombardy region rises to second place, overtaking London, which slips down to thirty-second. For all the other Italian regions, population figures are significantly higher than employment in the sectors analysed. The same result is reached when analysing orientation towards the cultural and creative industries at European level, with the Lombardy region emerging as one of the most exciting areas.[5]

Lombardy's success in this respect can be attributed to several factors: the region's environmental and strategic resources; a long-standing heritage of artisanal know-how dating back to the medieval and Renaissance periods; and the exponential growth of the city of Milan, which brought together and cleverly exploited local resources. As a result, Milan has grown into an international communications hub and a centre for economic and cultural relations. Overseas, it is seen as a benchmark for Italian taste and style, hosting trade fairs and events of global importance. Yet, behind each successful fashion or design company (including their respective supply and production

[4] See www.unesco.org/culture/ich/en/RL/traditional-violin-craftsmanship-in-cremona-00719.

[5] Pier Luigi Sacco (ed.), *Il sistema delle Industrie Culturali e Creative in Lombardia: Elementi per un nuovo modello di competitività territoriale* (Milan: Fondazione Università IULM, 2011), p. 42.

chains), and behind the accolades, lies the individual toil of hundreds of thousands of people. This work is not always given the recognition it deserves, even though Lombardy's master craftsmanship undoubtedly gives the region its competitive edge and determines the excellence of its output.

In Lombardy alone, despite the downturn that has hit this sector since the financial crisis of 2008, there are a host of small businesses still in operation,[6] employing well over half a million people.[7] Obviously, not all of those are artist-artisans or master craftspeople. But if you take just the examples of Como silk production, Cantù lace and furniture, the textiles of the Val Seriana, Vigevano footwear, the boatyards on the shores of Lake Iseo, fashion, design and wrought ironwork, it is easy to see why this region, with its range of industrial districts, is fertile ground for the two worlds of fashion and design. These worlds are multilayered and catalyze desires, investments and ideas. It is in their nature to be ground-breaking and forward-looking, built as they are on the solid foundations of tradition and legitimacy.

If by design we mean a culturally conscious creative process[8] that can be applied as much to the wood and furniture industries as to fashion, boatbuilding, textiles and other areas of Lombard excellence that are particularly susceptible to innovations in style and taste, then it is precisely these sectors that provide the "ideal development area for Lombardy in the cultural and creative industries, thanks to its historical primacy in this domain. Even within today's European context, where the geography of the cultural and creative industries is undergoing rapid change, these sectors still possess the productive force, the know-how and the skills to drive growth".[9]

In this respect, the master artisans and their work are not merely an outcome of age-old practices but an expression of the entrepreneurial and interpretive capacities running through the entire system. Design-oriented craft "does not refer simply to the rediscovery of traditional crafts, but rather to the encounter with new technologies, new materials and a product culture imbued with a strong sense of history".[10]

Therefore, what lies behind the "Made in Italy" label is an entire reserve of players who make up the various communities, be they

[6] See Unioncamere Lombardia, www.unioncamerelombardia.it. Figures for the first quarter of 2013.

[7] Unioncamere Lombardia, Ufficio studi e informazione economica per lo sviluppo locale (Office of Economic Statistics for Local Enterprise), *Dossier Artigianato*, April 2010, p. 11.

[8] See the website of the Associazione per il Disegno Industriale (Industrial Design Association), www.adi-design.org.

[9] See Sacco (ed.), *Il sistema delle Industrie Culturali e Creative in Lombardia*, p. 44.

[10] *Ibid.*, p. 46.

business, cultural, scientific, technological or artisan. This is what fundamentally binds ideas to a territory and cannot be exported.

From the 1950s onwards, Italy developed its own practical model of modernity, "based on the ability to experiment in small series production, to connect with creative cultures outside the factory and, above all, to establish an integrated working system drawing on the productive (and cultural) energies of the whole territory".[11] Consequently, it is the contribution of creativity and culture, both closely associated with excellence in the artistic crafts, that makes the difference, and constitutes the competitive edge of a number of genuinely "excellent" businesses. Italian economist Giacomo Becattini's school of economic thought

> has, since the 1970s, developed a model describing industrial districts as systems based on the positive presence of small and medium-sized enterprises that compete within a limited geographical area. This model developed out of a new understanding of industrial development processes [...] that could create highly complex relational systems beginning with the districts. These districts may appear weak and diffuse, but they can actually produce synergies and adapt to new circumstances, bringing fresh, vibrant strategies to expand into more mature markets.[12]

A design culture, a deep-seated passion for one's "profession", the ability to communicate with both designer and client, a sensitivity to tradition and an openness to innovation form both the operating and the methodological paradigms of Lombardy's master artisans:

> These [attributes] lie at the heart of the Lombard system of creative industries and are its connective fabric. There is a long-standing and time-honoured design tradition in Milan and Lombardy that, in light of the current scenario, has undergone reconfiguration over the last few years. This could provide the basic structure around which all the specificities and sectors can be organized. Of course, design will increasingly come to mean not merely the conception and production of an industrial object, but the entire set of stages involved in devising and realizing any product [...]; this is design as a cultural aptitude.[13]

The artistic crafts are the fruit of those "knowledge and skills sets, based on concept, design and execution. In other words, they have been

[11] Andrea Branzi, "Milano distretto per l'innovazione", *Impresa & Stato*, No. 62 (2003), www.mi.camcom.it/milano-distretto-per-l-innovazione.

[12] *Ibid.*

[13] See Sacco (ed.), *Il sistema delle Industrie Culturali e Creative in Lombardia*, p. 51.

formed through the intelligent use of both intuitive skills and practical experience".[14]

This "Lombard vocation" is crucial, not only when producing goods of high cultural and creative value but also when passing on the UNESCO-protected "intangible heritage", which has also recently caught the eye of the regional legislator.[15] It was necessary, therefore, to ascertain the extent to which this "vocation" is linked to a form of excellence that thrives on artisanal know-how of the highest standard.

With this end in mind, we felt it appropriate to interview a cross-section of Lombard masters, entrepreneurs and key figures closely associated with the sector, such as Pino Grasso and Renata Casartelli, using as a starting point the assessment matrix discussed earlier. This matrix uses concept-terms that define the parameters of excellence as laid down by legislators. However, it is impossible to assess the specific importance of each category without direct feedback from the artisans themselves, and a significant sample at that. The sample was spread across different generations, and the selected participants had already been recognized for their "excellence", having either been awarded prizes, medals or special commendations, taken part in a significant number of exhibitions, or received recognition from peers or from older experts and historians of the applied arts.

These masters gave us an invaluable insight into a working life dedicated to a single quest: the expression of beauty through formal perfection. Through their words we have gained a more pragmatic understanding of the term "creative industries" when used in connection with the world of fine crafts. And we can see more clearly how certain requisites can be important indicators (including in future, more nebulous scenarios) of a truly exceptional level of ability.

5.3. CRAFTS AND CREATORS: INTERVIEWS WITH LOMBARD MASTERS

Having identified the characteristics of craft excellence outlined in the previous chapters, we then tested them on 12 great master artisans in Lombardy. These were chosen from a variety of production sectors of economic and cultural importance for the region, or because they represent virtuous examples of collaboration between the artistic crafts and design.

[14] Silvia Mazzucotelli Salice and Isabella Medicina, *Maestri del fare. Indagine socio-economica sulla domanda di mestieri d'arte a Milano* (Venice: Marsilio, 2012), p. 26.

[15] See www.aess.regione.lombardia.it.

As touched on earlier, the selection was based on the following: recognition by their peers; the collection of objects conserved in the Archive of Ethnography and Social History of the Lombardy Region;[16] meticulous research into examples of excellence recognized in workshops and ateliers, taking care to include young, upcoming artisans who have already shown great promise (for example by winning major competitions or gaining international renown); awards received, participation in key exhibitions, level of customer base, and recognizability in their contexts; and the opinions of experts and scholars.

The transmission of know-how was also taken into consideration in identifying the masters: talent, in fact, has to be not only acknowledged but also cultivated and fostered. It is interesting to note that in the interviews the artisans substantiate the view that

only through commitment, learning, diligence and hours and hours of practice can young people really get to know themselves and give a true name to their dreams and skills. The world of the métiers d'art once again helps us to understand the right framework in which education should be set, if we want it to be effective.

Transmitting know-how is now of vital importance to artisans, if the new generations are to tackle the challenges of the contemporary world. Yet one does not become a master in the space of a few months: it takes years, it takes dedication, and it takes determination.

Talent is, of course, essential, but so is the humility to listen and learn, through observation, the master's secrets, and making them evolve through one's own personality. In *The Voice of the Master*, Gibran also wrote: "Learning is the only wealth tyrants cannot despoil. Only death can dim the lamp of knowledge that is within you. The true wealth of a nation lies not in its gold or silver but in its learning, wisdom and in the uprightness of its sons."

Today it is vital to ensure that this knowledge is transmitted, that it grows strong roots and that it is not wasted. Because it is in this "rectitude" that we need to seek the competitive advantage that will help us live a happier, more fulfilling life, in which we will be more aware of our value as men and artisans of the future.[17]

Another factor that was taken into consideration (maybe less objective, but nevertheless central) is the passion and dedication that characterizes the 12 master artisans selected for the interviews. Their

[16] See the website of the Archivio di Etnografia e Storia Sociale, www.aess.regione.lombardia.it.

[17] Franco Cologni, "Know-how fosters integrity", *Arts & Crafts & Design*, No. 4 (April 2014), p. 114.

words manifest an unconditional love for their trade, the spirit of that "new Renaissance" often evoked by Franco Cologni:

> The world of design is rediscovering its points of contact with the "makers", fashion designers reinvent themselves as dressmakers, and even politicians employ screwdrivers and other tools in their metaphors, to make us believe that they are fixing things. In short: there is a lot of talk about the crafts and the intelligence of the hand. And if all these words were to lead to a tangible, lasting effect, I would be truly happy to acknowledge that we really are facing a revolution.
>
> But is it really happening? Or is it just (as Dame Shirley Bassey sings) a case of "history repeating"? It would be naive to think that all that glitters is gold. And perhaps it would be unfair to the world of the crafts and to all the commitment, work and excellence they represent, if we merely identified these activities as a quick and easy way to get out of this crisis: the *métiers d'art* – as we have said more than once – are a cultural asset and a competitive advantage, but if we want to promote, protect and diffuse them, we cannot just talk about them.
>
> We need to appreciate and love them: we need to understand that artisans are not divinities, but that they provide outstanding interpretations of designs. That designers (or stylists or creative artists) are not gods, but professionals who are bringing a new vision into the world. We need to reconnect the ends of the broken dialogue between competences, not with ineffective billows of enthusiasm, but by recognising and restoring roles and the knowledge involved. We need, plainly speaking, to implement policies that will allow everybody to give their very best: to grow, to change and to improve.[18]

The interviews involved a series of open questions based on the matrix. Care was taken to draw out, either explicitly or more subtly, which criteria the masters themselves deemed essential for reaching and remaining at the pinnacle of their craft. Below are summaries of their articulate responses: they are presented in such a way as to allow them to give their visions full flight, while respecting the matrix's structure.

Each interview is preceded by a short biography and, in the words of the artisans, how they found themselves starting or perpetuating their craft.

[18] Franco Cologni, "Knowing and loving authenticity", *Arts & Crafts & Design*, No. 3, (December 2013), p. 106.

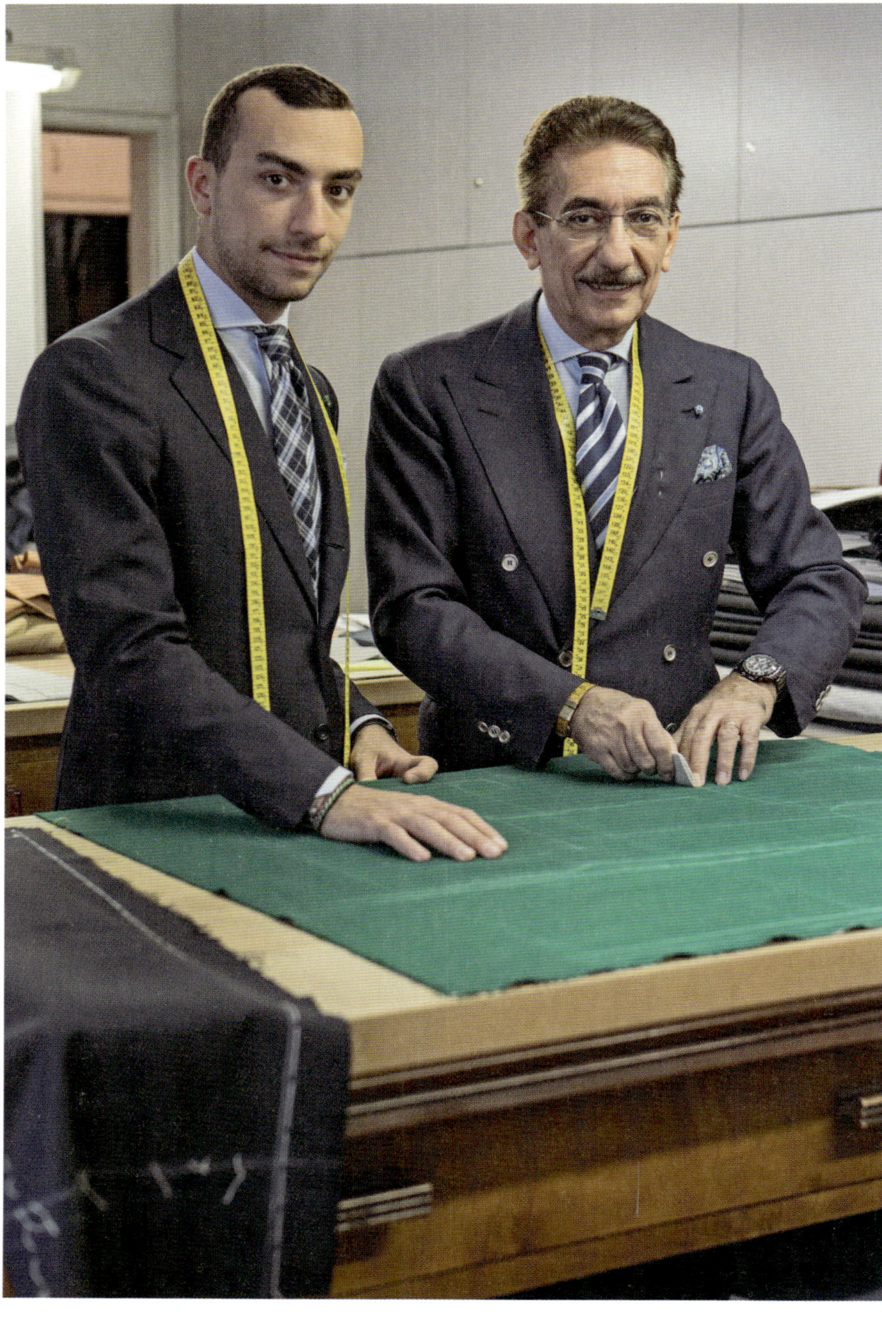

5.3.1. Carlo Andreacchio, master tailor

Carlo Andreacchio, with his wife Rita Maria, runs the "A. Caraceni" bespoke tailors. The celebrated Milan establishment was founded by Rita Maria's father, Mario Caraceni, who named it after his own father, Augusto.

Augusto Caraceni was born in Ortona, Chieti, in 1893 and, as a young boy, he and his brothers learnt the art of tailoring from their father Tommaso, who had a tailor's shop in the town and was known throughout the region. When the eldest brother, Domenico, opened a tailor's shop in Rome, he invited two of his brothers, Galliano and Augusto, to work with him. In the 1930s, Augusto moved to Paris, where he launched a highly successful tailoring business, whose clients included some of the most famous names of the time. Augusto returned to Italy in 1939, having in the meantime gotten married and fathered four children. In 1946 he opened a tailor's shop with a partner at 16 Via Fatebenefratelli in Milan. Augusto's son, Mario, joined the business, and when his father died in 1972, the shop was renamed in Augusto's memory: A. Caraceni bespoke tailor was born. Over the next two and half decades the business prospered, acquiring an international clientele thanks to the determination and commitment of Mario, who stayed faithful to the traditions. He won various awards, including the Sant'Omobono and Milan Tailors' Union prizes. He retired in 1998, leaving the company in the hands of his daughter and her husband, both of whom had worked with him for the preceding 20 years, Rita Maria as administrator and Carlo as a cutter.

Carlo Andreacchio has been a member of the Academy of Tailors since 1997 and was awarded the gold medal by the Milan Tailors' Union in 2002. Since 2004, their children Massimiliano and Valentina have also been working in the business, which had fascinated them since childhood. They continue the family tradition and are ready to take over when the time comes.

You come into this craft either because it is a family affair or because you are born with this instinct, as is my case. I don't come from a family of craftspeople, but I have continued the business started by my father-in-law's father, Augusto Caraceni, a business that my wife and I took over almost 20 years ago. My son has learnt this craft from me. After leaving school, he told me that he wanted to become a tailor. I was pleased with his decision, but I had to see if he was capable and so I entrusted him to one of my master tailors, telling him: "This is Massimiliano, but from this moment on he is no longer my son, he is just a lad who has come here to learn. You must treat him as you would anyone." My son is left-handed, and this tailor told him that if he sewed with his left hand he wouldn't be able to teach him. So my son learnt to sew and cut with his right hand. It was in his blood. In six years he learnt to make a jacket, and three years ago he joined me in the cutting room. I have taught him the secret of the Caraceni cut.

In this job, you are constantly put to the test. Besides technique, your relationship with the client is also important. Our shop is welcoming and private, but I do everything to maintain a formal, discreet relationship, which I believe is crucial in this profession. Some ten years ago I set up an in-house school, taking on five young people. It worked well because three of them have stayed on. But it was a big investment in terms of both time and money, one you can't always afford.

Authenticity

When a client steps through the door of this tailor's shop, he must know that here he will find everything, that he will be made welcome and that his every desire will be fulfilled. This is part of the concept of authenticity. I also think that it is very useful to be able to trace all the steps in the production chain, which in my case is totally possible. We know where all our (exclusively natural) materials come from and often we even find ourselves giving advice to our suppliers of linings and fabrics. Every phase of the work, carried out using traditional techniques, takes place in our workshop, an essential factor in qualifying a suit as a Caraceni. Our signature is the label – sewn into the breast pocket because it must never be visible – bearing the name of the client and the year of production.

Competence

I believe that competence develops also from the interaction with the client. For tailors are also a product of their clients, who have travelled the world, bringing back with them all these ideas for innovations in style or techniques or materials. It also happens to me.

But the bases of a craft can only be acquired in a workshop. It took me a few decades before I felt ready to manage a client directly myself, even though I was probably quite capable well before that. I am always self-critical, while being totally aware of my skills. The bottom line is that we are constantly facing new challenges and must never become complacent. The wonderful thing about our work is that you can never feel that you have arrived, that you have nothing left to learn. If a client tells me he has had a suit made, let's say, in Japan, where there are no great masters in this field, and he shows me a special detail that I feel is valid, I will always take it into consideration.

Craftsmanship

Our work is 100% craftsmanship. I select the materials myself, together with my son. We all try out the new fabrics, because our clients are not guinea pigs and deserve the very best. To make the perfect suit, you need precise measurements. We take 26, all based on the client's physique. If you calculate measurements simply on proportions – waist, chest, hips – you don't achieve the same result, because we are all made differently. I can create the perfect suit for each of my clients, one that fits all his measurements and flatters as well. A well-made suit lends personality and confidence; you will never get the same effect with a ready-made suit. Shakespeare had the right idea when he wrote that "apparel oft proclaims the man". Our delivery times are rather slow as a consequence, with a single suit taking an average of three months to complete.

An article is masterly made when the whole is pleasant and gratifies the eye. A job well done doesn't lie in individual details but in the overall result, in the harmony it creates. Perfect execution is obviously also important, but what counts is the resulting equilibrium.

Creativity

Creativity is fuelled by the craft itself, your experience, and years on the job. If you lose your creativity, it's all over. Creativity exists even in artisanal work, precisely because you are creating a work of art!

Interpretation

The craftsperson is definitely an "interpreter", but precisely because we are talking about an artisanal product, there is never total perfection. If I make ten suits for the same client, each one will be different because they are made entirely by hand. In my case, while not dealing with "fashion" in the strict sense, I need to be aware of changes in taste and incorporate them in my suits, updating them.

I think that Italian artisans have qualities that others don't possess. Unlike their English counterparts, for example, Italian tailors would never send out agents, preferring to deal with their clients personally and directly, inside their ateliers. I think that this can also be attributed to cultural factors, a form of respect for the client, which for me is fundamental.

Originality

I would use the word "originality" to describe everything I do. Tastes change in our field and so do volumes, silhouettes and fabrics. I adapt to the times without compromising either on my techniques or on my signature trademark. In our craft, we always have to take risks and bend the rules, but it's a delicate balancing act. Our client is looking for a very specific kind of product and silhouette. We must be able to satisfy his taste, his desire, without betraying either our line or our style.

Each garment we make is unique and original as it is fitted around the specific measurements of that client. Given that each of us is made differently, none of our suits will ever fit two people in the same way, even if they share the same body shape.

Talent

Talent is fundamental and it applies, in varying degrees, to both the creative and the practical side of tailoring. Talent can also be acquired by practice, but creativity is innate.

I think that a talented youngster responds with appropriate questions to what they are taught, while a master cannot be said to be truly "complete". What really distinguishes a master is their capacity to ask the right questions and find the right answers.

Territory

The tailoring craft has a long tradition in Italy. It has a regional dimension, too, in the sense that the great majority of tailors come from the south of the country, which used to be much poorer, and this was one way people had of ensuring their children had a career. For me, Milan is the capital of tailoring. Milanese style reflects my vision of male suits, which must never be showy, never overstep a certain limit. In this sense, the suits we make cannot be called either Italian or Milanese. I would describe them as international.

Italian tailors used to be second only to the English. Today I would say that we Italians have stolen the top spot. A lot has changed even in terms of the origins of the fabric. In the past, 90 per cent of the cloth we used came from England and only 10 per cent from Italy; today, the proportion is 60/40. We tailors keep Italy's name at the forefront internationally because many of our clients are from abroad.

My ties with my homeland were stronger in the past. I am still very fond of it, but there are many problems on an institutional and bureaucratic level, as well as laws that in some way limit or even hinder our business.

Tradition and innovation

Ours is a craft with ancient traditions. Volumes change, details are added, and proportions altered as clothing fashions evolve. But here we work in the same way as we have always done. We have never used computers. We have a website, of course, because as my son quite rightly tells me, this is important in today's world. But we still do all our

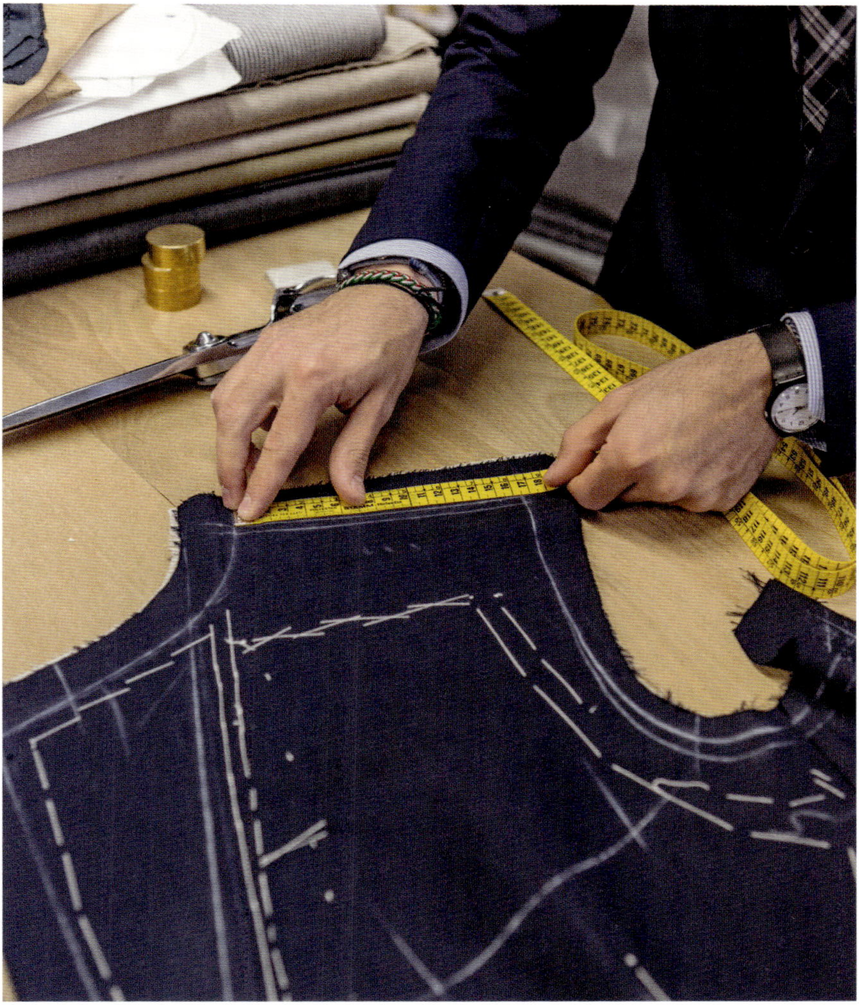

bookkeeping by hand, and the same goes for our archives, complete with all the details of the fabrics and suits we have made for every single client. The greatest innovation we have seen has unquestionably been in materials, because they are of a superior quality and much lighter than in the past, before the days of central heating. It is also true, however, that modern fabrics do not last as long. My son altered a suit of mine from the 1960s and it is still perfect.

The secret of Caraceni tailoring lies totally in the cut. This is our tradition and our innovation. It is a real secret, one we hand down from father to son. Grandfather Augusto, who devised this particular technique, instinctively created a system based on sophisticated rules of engineering. My suits have been unpicked in attempts to find out this secret, but nobody has ever discovered it. The most significant changes in this trade have ensued from labour protection legislation: while irons used to weigh between seven and nine kilos, they now weigh no more than three. Ironing used to be much more tiring, but the results were much better.

Dialogue is not the norm in our craft as there is a lot of jealousy and envy. Each of us does their own thing and keeps their own secrets. "It all dies with me", they say, but I think they're wrong. We Caraceni (and I consider myself a Caraceni to all intents and purposes) have always had a different attitude. Grandfather Augusto used to come in early and get the pattern ready so that he could explain it to the other tailors.

Training

I have always had a passion for clothes. Even as a small boy I would look at what people wore and imagine how I would have dressed them. But my parents didn't want me to be a tailor and so I tried to please them by studying accountancy. I learnt the initial rudiments from the workers in the clothing company where I was in charge of admin and sales. I would spend my breaks in the workshop with them, where they taught me all they knew.

At the age of about 25, I started to take private lessons: every evening from 7pm to midnight I would go to a tailor in Piazzetta Giordano here in Milan. It takes ages before you can use the chalk, scissors, needle and thimble. Meanwhile, I started working in the tailor's shop belonging to my father-in-law, Mario Caraceni.

In our job, the pattern is not drawn, it is created. It's hard work. The work of the cutter is very stressful as it entails great responsibility. If a tailor makes a mistake while sewing, it can be rectified. But if you make a mistake when cutting the fabric, the whole thing has to be thrown out. To this day, I am still learning from my job, from interaction with the clients, and from exchanges with peers. I don't really believe in pattern-making schools, mainly because I think they give students false hopes. They purport to teach them cutting, sewing, English, mathematics, history, etc., and prepare them with three or four hours of practice a week. At the end of the course they hold a fashion show and everyone's happy. But, in fact, they know practically nothing – I see that when they come here as interns. Here, instead, in this tailor's shop, they truly learn the craft. Above all, they learn that it is hard work and they find out straight away if they can put up with the suffering: your back hurts from the long hours spent bending over, your eyes get sore from sewing…

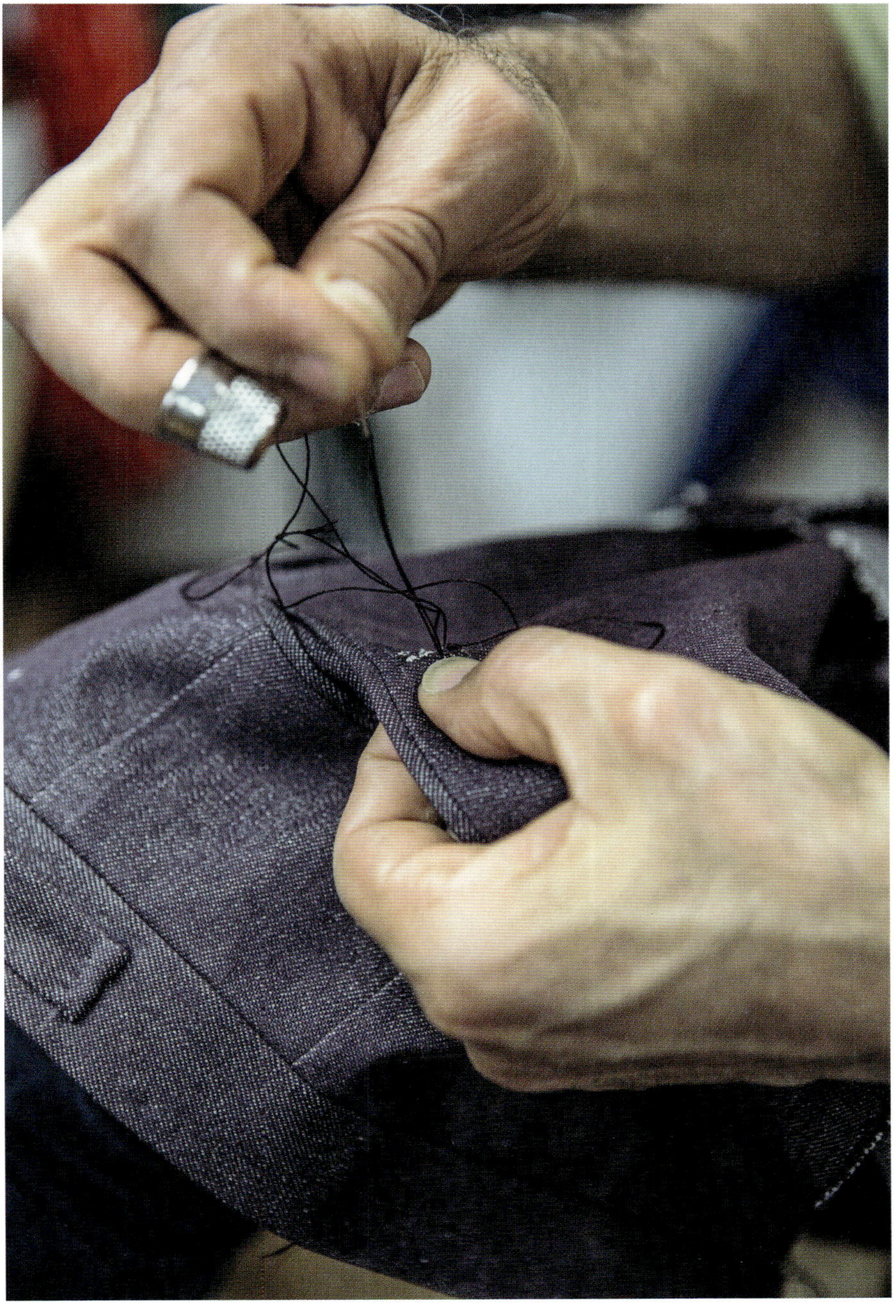

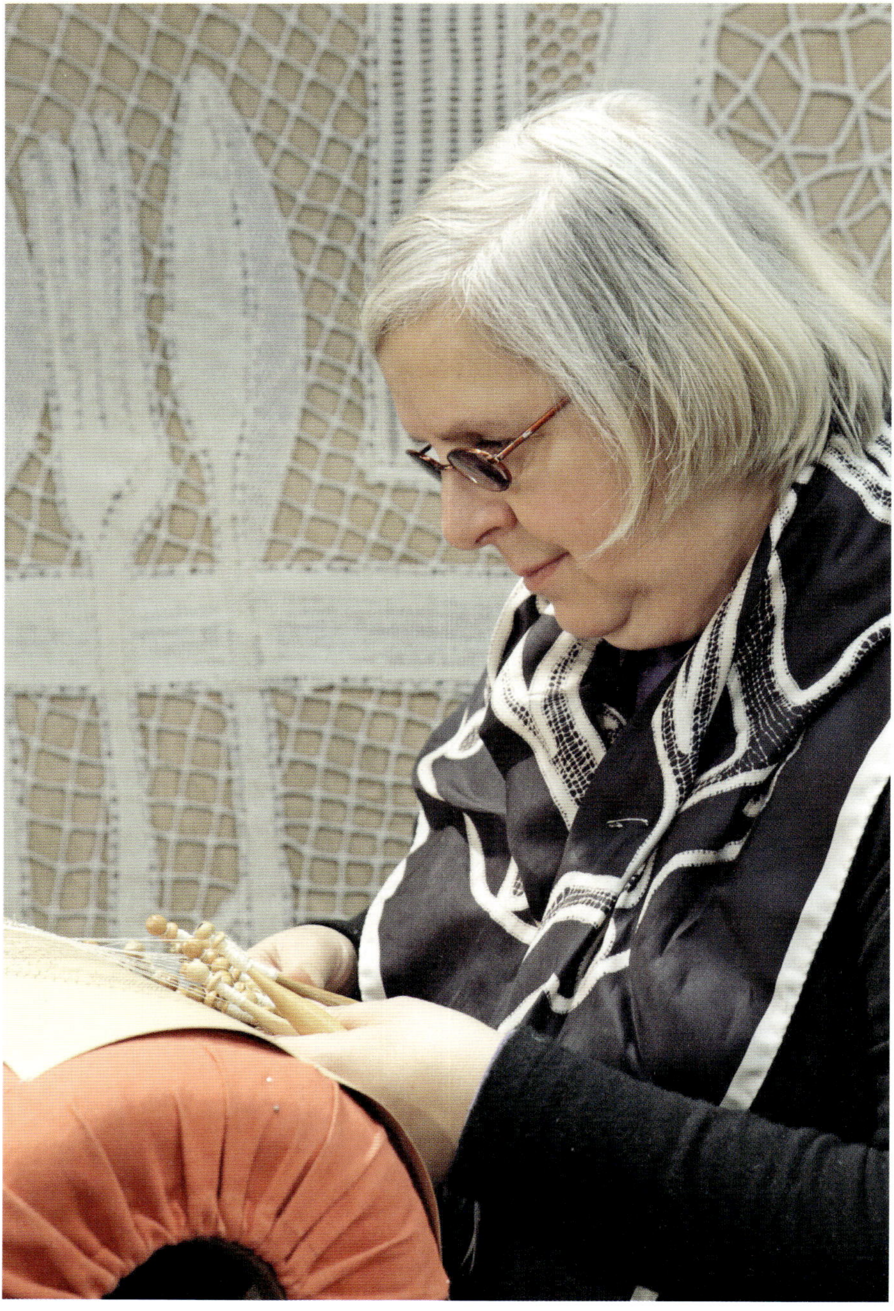

5.3.2. Renata Casartelli, lacemaker and promoter of Cantù lacemaking

Renata Casartelli attended the textile division of the State Art Institute in Cantù because the lacemaking section had closed in 1972. Her story is one of a dogged pursuit of a particular type of lacemaking known as Cantù or bobbin lace. Owing to her poor eyesight, as a little girl she was not allowed to learn this technique, which she was taught by an aunt only at the age of 19. But the fact that she had had to wait so long to get her hands on the bobbins only served to fuel her strong passion for the craft for which her city was historically renowned. That excellence was in danger of extinction, so much so that she decided to do something to ensure that the craft of lacemaker, along with centuries of know-how, would not be lost forever. The Cantù Lace Promotion Committee, which she heads today, was set up in 1993, the year the city decided to dedicate a biennial to this glorious art. Today, the Committee "proposes itself, where possible, as a mediator between the spirit of initiative, production capacity, and creativity in the area of lace and the potential of a sector which has acquired completely new characteristics with respect to the past. A sector which is being globalized, in mass-produced markets, but which still manages to place these quality products, which are destined by their own nature to be excluded from the mechanisms of throwaway consumerism, at various levels in an increasingly well-defined and recognizable manner". Her experience in advertising and as a newspaper editor has led Casartelli to devote much of her time to the promotion of bobbin lace. The author of many books, she is also the go-to person for many designers, notably Alessandro Mendini. In addition to being a lacemaker, Casartelli is a skilled framer, but in 2012 she suffered an optic nerve infarction in both eyes, just a few months apart. Her strength in the promotion of bobbin lace and in her love of her frames, however, has never waivered.

Casartelli specifies that she is speaking here on behalf of the Lace Promotion Committee, which is neither a workshop nor a laboratory but an association whose aim is to keep the ancient tradition of lacemaking alive. Thus, her responses do not come from her as an artisan, but as a representative of a world at risk of extinction. The Committee represents some 40 women lacemakers (but there are many others who work in the anonymity of their own homes). Through its organization of the International Lace Biennial, the Committee brings together 28 associations and amateur courses. In her words, "where there is a teacher, there is always a school".

I come from a family of artisans who made floor tiles with marble chip. My grandparents, however, were builders and they built some of the original pavilions of the Milan Trade Fair. In the 1930s, they had more than 200 people working for them, but they were always craftsmen at heart.

My mother was not a lacemaker. My grandfather wanted a son and so she grew up with a more entrepreneurial approach, in charge of contracts for the family business. This is why I had to learn lacemaking from an aunt.

The Lace Promotion Committee is not a workshop; it doesn't tick the right boxes to qualify as such. By holding bobbin lacemaker groups, meetings and courses, the Committee aims to promote this tradition so that the know-how is not lost, so that it doesn't die out.

Authenticity

Any piece made exclusively by one person and that is made in the workshop declared as the manufacturer, is authentic. Some pieces are described as typical of Cantù , but they might have been made in other places in Italy. So, if a piece is certified as "Cantù lace", it must be made in Cantù. And it has to be made by hand. Authenticity also requires the use of traditional techniques and materials. As for coloured lace, if it is made by a bobbin lacemaker from Cantù, it has the same quality of authenticity, even if it is a non-typical variant and therefore less immediately recognizable.

It is difficult to fully appreciate the work done by bobbin lacemakers, because it entails a huge commitment in terms of hours, even for small pieces. I think each piece should be given its own certificate, which would mean the work was properly recognized and authenticated. As it is impossible, when using standard patterns, to attribute a value that is easily acceptable by the market, we have also involved designers. Because if we link the high manufacturing costs to a famous designer, we have a greater chance that its value will be understood and appreciated. When patterns are created by a designer, theirs is usually the only name mentioned, but I think it would be only right to include that of the artisan.

Competence

Competence is the experience you build over the years, doing the same things over and over. There is no improvisation here. At a certain point, after so much practice, competence becomes a part of who you are. This experience allows you to tackle a certain stitch or solve a finishing problem, also through experimentation. This is not always accompanied by good taste, which is why the lacemaker needs to be guided by someone more expert.

Artisans often have gifted hands, but that does not mean they also have creativity or are good self-managers. I think there are fewer and fewer craftspeople who have all these complementary aspects and who manage also to be commercially successful.

Craftsmanship

The bobbin lace we make in this area is exclusively hand-made. The lacemaker must be careful when selecting the thread, because it must not break or fray. Bobbin lace can also be machine made, but it is obviously not the same thing.

With artisanal bobbin lace, each piece is unique and different, depending on whether it was made in summer or winter, if the lacemaker was in good health or ill while she was making it, how tightly she pulled the thread and so on. It consists of braiding and twisting lengths of thread, which are wound on bobbins, according to a specific pattern marked on a stiff card that is attached to a pillow with pins. The lacemaker interprets the pattern, but to do so perfectly, she must follow the method correctly. This is why someone must have originally taught her the correct method for each stitch. She must apply the techniques in the purest and most honest way possible. When well made, bobbin lace stands up on its own: it is almost rigid. If it feels like a flimsy piece of cloth, however beautiful it is to look at, the lacemaker did a poor piece of work.

Creativity

Creativity is, in my opinion, an innate gift and the basis of everything. "Creative" also describes those craftspeople who, if they have that famous talent inside them, once they have gained expertise in their work, reinterpret it, adding something of their own. I think that this is one of the cornerstones of the "Made in Italy" tradition. Ideas can come from anywhere, and creativity is almost always a reworking of something that evolves, the outcome of a journey.

Even bobbin lacemakers can be creative in their work. Two pieces of lace based on the same pattern can turn out quite different because one lacemaker solved the finish in a personal way, modifying it without, however, changing the nature of the design.

Interpretation

It's not a given that an artisan is always able to do a perfect job. But, quite often, an attempt to create one thing leads to something else that's perhaps even better than what was originally intended. That's what craft is. Artisans find a way to use materials that may, for example, have defects. Take a piece of wood: it has to be used anyway, because it is fine wood and has been bought and paid for. Sometimes, a flaw becomes a feature.

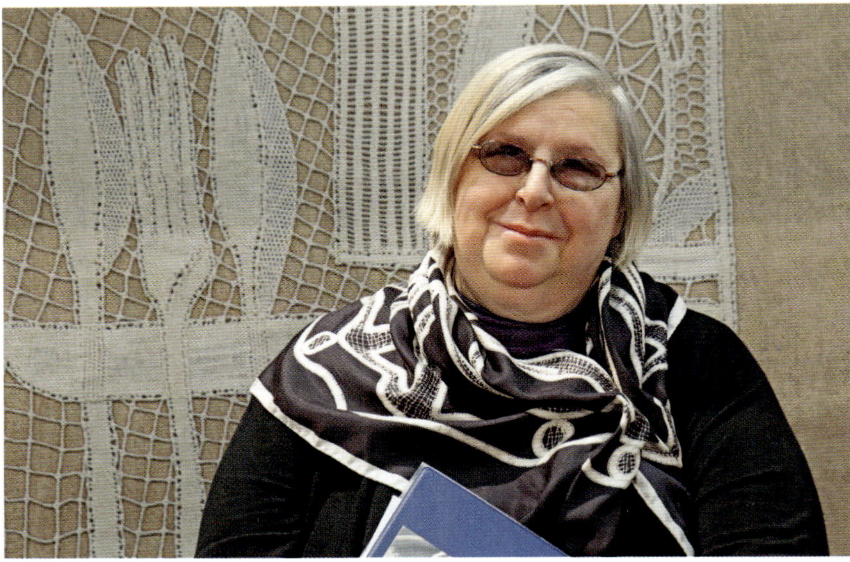

Our workshops here in Brianza have become famous because they manage to interpret the ideas of so many designers who come here for their prototypes. Ours, in fact, is a truly customized production. We know our materials, how they react, what options they offer. There is a foundry here that produces pieces for Ron Arad. They told me that he arrives with an idea, he describes it to them, and their task is to produce the object accurately based entirely on his words alone. That's the skill of our craft companies!

Originality

I think originality is more about the creative aspect than the place of origin. This is also because, with any handicraft, each piece must be finished differently, despite having the same characteristics.

It is normal for someone doing creative work to take risks, to challenge themselves, most of the time without even being aware that they are doing so as it is almost routine. In my opinion, women are less inclined to risk, which is why they may be less successful. The creative woman is capable of making ingenious pieces, but she rarely dominates. Perhaps it's because she always keeps both feet firmly on the ground.

Talent

Talent makes the difference. However, it's difficult to see it in a bobbin lacemaker's work because the talent may lie in the pattern creator, or in her teacher, while her skill is proved by the fact that her lace stands up on its own.

Those who are good at a craft manage to combine all the aspects of execution and interpretation. Talent in young people can generally be seen in the articles they manage to produce. But in the case of the bobbin lacemaker, I think that real talent emerges if, once she is totally familiar with the technique, she starts to create her own patterns. Personally, I see talent more where there is creativity.

Territory

Bobbin lace has developed in every region in Italy. When our Committee published a book entitled *Fili e parole*, literally "threads and words", based on a questionnaire that we sent out to 21 production districts of Italy, we realized that we all make the same things, but call them by different names. Consequently, there isn't even an official national glossary for each different stitch. What makes the lace produced in Cantù unique is the large size. Classic Cantù bobbin lace is also always made in colours that range from optical white to ecru. We have experimented with colour, in an attempt to come closer to design, but we decided that it was perhaps better to stick with the classic white, which makes Cantù bobbin lace more recognizable, because we are more accustomed to seeing it like this.

Brianza women have always been hard workers, toiling in the fields in summer and in the stables in winter, where they made their lace. There were a good number of manufacturers in the district, at least 40 or so, one alone employing more than 1,500 homeworkers. That was a lot of bobbin lacemakers, if you think about it. Today, although we are more expert, we know that a bedcover is an almost impossible endeavour owing to the huge cost of making large pieces; it is also hard to break into the luxury market, the only potential outlet for such pieces.

Our Committee currently represents some 40 bobbin lacemakers and there are 30 or so associations, schools and amateur courses throughout the district. Then there are the women who make lace on their own, at home. We are therefore talking about a few thousand people. Through the organization of the Lace Biennial, the Committee holds exchanges with all the other local bodies. In my opinion, however, there is a more open and social vision in other parts of Italy. Here we tend to dig ourselves in behind the fact that we have reached high levels of perfection in this art, and are therefore superior to others.

As for materials, the linen and cotton used for the lace are still the same, but today they come from other sources. In the past, we used a special Cantù yarn, which was produced with a high amount of twist. It no longer exists and so we prefer to use a Spanish thread, reckoned to be the best among those currently available.

Tradition and innovation

In Italy, lacemaking developed in the 15th and 16th centuries and was mainly carried out for the nobility because it was very expensive. It is an art based on craft practices that have evolved over the centuries. What makes the typical, unique Cantù tradition stand out from other regional variants is the production of large pieces – tablecloths, bedcovers, curtains – worked in small sections on the pillow and then sewn together, with invisible seams, by specialized embroiderers. The Cantù district had very skilled pattern-makers, men included, whose wonderfully inspired designs made these large artefacts possible. Once there were many manufacturers in this area. The craft was learnt at home and in workshops, but now that the latter have disappeared, it is only handed down in families, from mothers, aunts and grandmothers, or through beginners' courses. Groups spring up spontaneously and go on for years, with women taking part every week, some even for 20 years or more. Then there are others who do just a year's training and continue on their own. We even get 30-year-olds who, having started a family, want to learn or perfect their skills. This is how this craft is passed on today.

The Lace Promotion Committee organizes the Lace Biennial. Through our exhibitions, our local know-how can be compared and merged with the skills of other lace-producing areas. More than innovation, I would call it an exchange of knowledge that has brought progress on the technical and design sides. We are the very opposite of science and technology! What we are proposing as a Committee, with our "Lace and Design" project,[19] is based on a concept that developed with the Triennials in the 1930s (here I refer to the dawn of design, Gio Ponti, Buzzi), which led to the creation of innovative pieces that were breaking away from the past.

Training

In Cantù, every woman has always made bobbin lace, since we used to learn this art at home and at school. I wasn't allowed to make lace as a little girl, however, because my eyesight was poor. Perhaps this was why this huge desire grew inside me, together with a stubborn refusal to see this culture lost. So, when I was about 19, I decided to learn from an

[19] A project organized by the Committee on the occasion of the Biennale, where famous designers are invited to develop a design which is then realized by the lacemakers and exhibited.

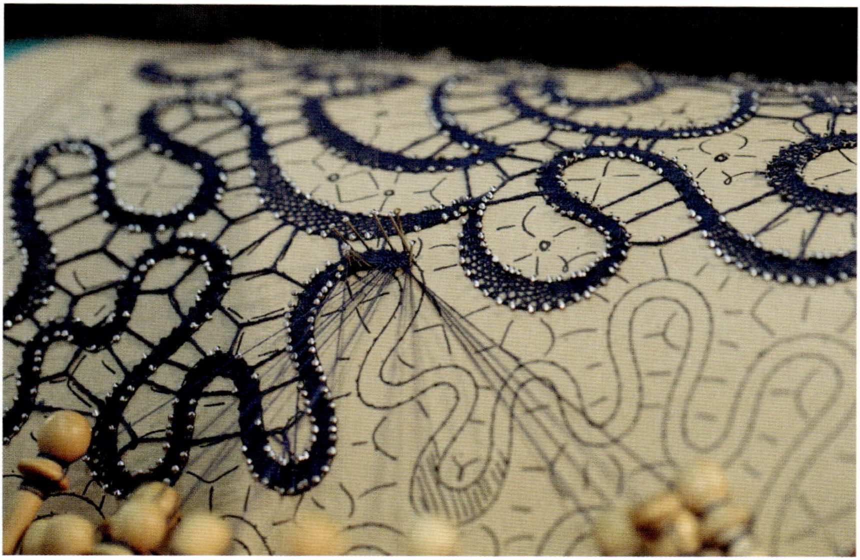

aunt, and then I dedicated my time to the Lace Promotion Committee. In my four years of bobbin lacemaking, I never achieved excellence. But I did come to realize, also thanks to my other professional experiences, that if we didn't want this craft to die, we needed to give real visibility to the know-how in this district. There are still many active bobbin lacemakers in Cantù and the Committee truly believes in the value of design. We have therefore sought to bring designers on board, even at a high level; this is an activity that calls for a huge commitment in terms of hours, even for small pieces, and it is hard otherwise to get its economic value appreciated today.

In this craft, you never finish learning. Suffice to say that on our specialist courses we even have lacemakers in their 70s. But, once you learn, you never forget – it's like riding a bike. Among other activities, our Committee organizes courses for both beginners and experts.

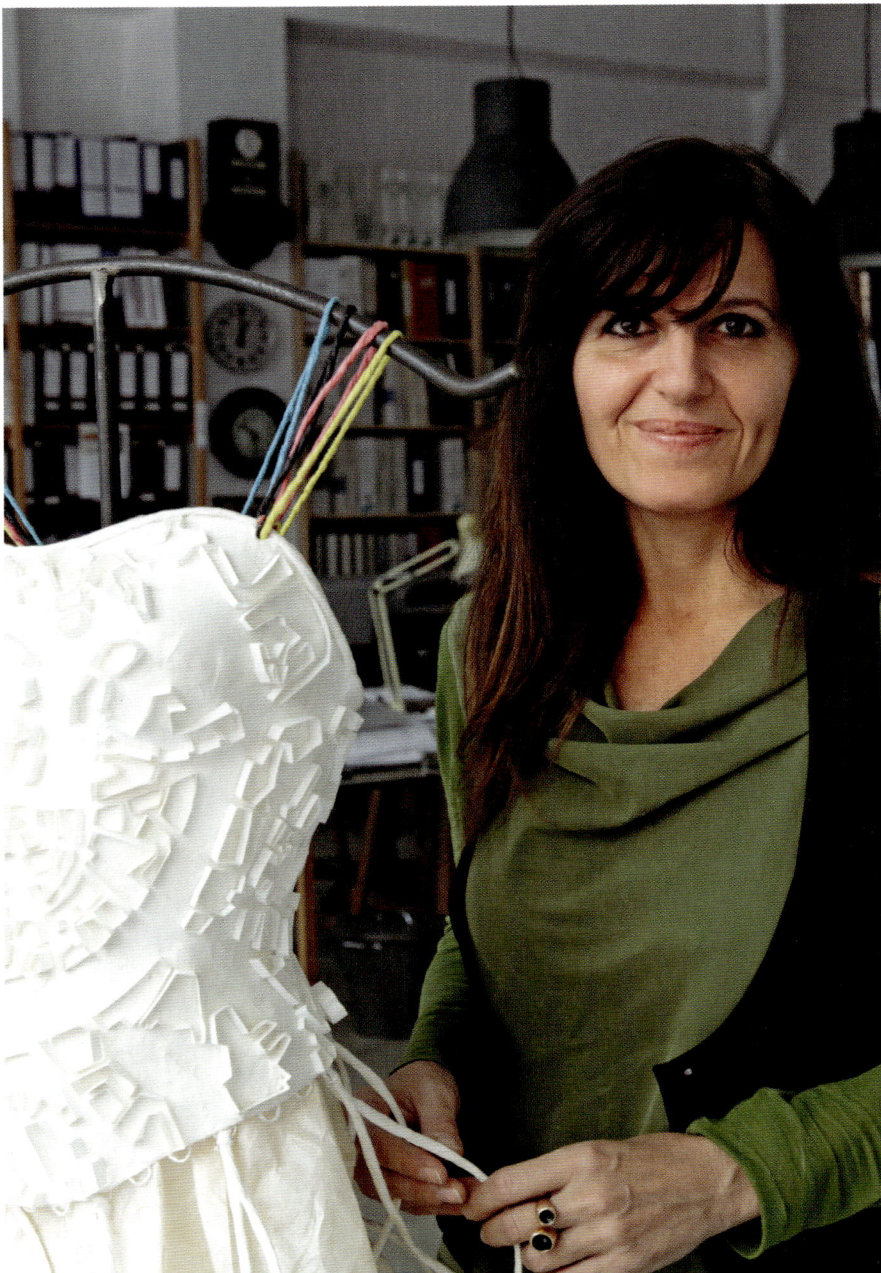

5.3.3. Caterina Crepax, paper artist

Caterina Crepax was born in Milan in 1964. She graduated with a degree in architectural design from Politecnico di Milano and works as an interior architect, as well as being active in the fields of graphic design and the design of exhibition stands and of stage sets in public places. Since childhood she has nurtured another great passion: paper. Daughter of the famous comic book artist Guido Crepax, creator of the legendary comic strip character "Valentina", she has inherited his dexterity and imagination in turning a simple sheet of paper into a fantastic 3D construction. This lifelong relationship with paper has drawn her into the complex, surprising world of contemporary art. She has a particular interest in recycling, reusing commonly used paper materials such as receipts, shredded documents, the perforated edges of computer printouts, and printers' waste. Crepax loves the ironic game of metamorphosis – the transformation of paper into precious "fabrics", into glorious clothes with surprising details, refined objects of desire. Cuts, folds, creases, pleats, puffs, inlays and folds in relief, when repeated ad infinitum, *become rich surfaces, complex structures. She mixes normal, oriental or fine paper with everyday paper to bring to life original creations that are a fusion of art, fashion design and pure fantasy: fragile and aggressive paper armours and sculpted dresses often inspired by the animal or plant worlds or by architectural details, at times illuminated from the inside.*

Although I do not come from a craft background, manual skill runs in the family. My father was a comic book artist with a passion for paper. He had an uncle, an engineer from Venice, whose hobby was making weapons in papier-mâché. So my father was in turn inspired by people who, although not artists, were clever with their hands. Moreover, my grandmother used to make very beautiful, sophisticated pictures using pieces of cloth. In this sense, my family had a big influence on me.

Even if I do all my work myself, I try to pass on my know-how. In addition to technique, I also teach my students a creative approach; I encourage them to try out new things. I currently have two young set-design students working with me. They help me with everything – from the work I do for the Creative Academy (the Richemont Group postgraduate design school) to the production of my paper clothes and the creation of a diorama or a set for one of the exhibitions dedicated to my father. I try to convey my passion for "making" to my son and he, like me, has observed and learnt. This is how transmission comes about.

Authenticity

I would define authenticity as a set of factors that make an article recognizable not only to the eye but also to the touch, and thus includes the material it is made from. I am thinking of a piece of restored old furniture, the authentic character of which is unique and unrepeatable. In fact, I am not a fan of reproductions. I understand that it's more difficult in the craft business, but it is always its character that makes an object authentic.

The authenticity of my pieces is not linked to the use of traditional materials or techniques because this is not a "craft" that already existed. Nor does my work call for modern materials or techniques. Similarly, the place of production or the connection with a territory are not relevant to what I do. However, I do think that the signature of the author is an essential guarantee of authenticity, and I am absolutely in agreement with shared authorship in the case of projects conceived by a designer and realized by a craftsperson. I think it's right that everyone's contribution is recognized.

Competence

Competence is a complex concept. It is not just a case of having "gifted hands", it's also knowing how to pass on a craft, which would otherwise just be an end in itself. I don't see why those who are capable of doing can't also be capable of teaching. Competence lies in knowing how to manage this ability, transmit it, present it and make the most of it. This approach comes perhaps from my architect training, because I never think just about the object itself, but also how it will be displayed: in its space, how it interacts with other things and places. It is a combination of different elements, not necessarily all manageable, but for me this is part of competence.

You definitely gain competence with practice. I felt I was competent when I could say "I can make anything", because I realized that I had mastery over my materials. Sometimes a complex object is made up of simple parts. However, it does take a somewhat artistic eye to envision how it will all work as a whole.

Craftsmanship

I like the old term "artisan-artist" to describe those who set up a small school in their workshop. I don't really see myself as a designer, as I think of a designer as someone who creates an object that can be reproduced, even if some designers have started to make only unique pieces.

I'd say something is masterly made when every aspect has harmony, even in apparent disharmony. In this, we have much to learn from nature. To respect the original design, be it yours or someone else's, is to reproduce the image with attention to detail, which I like to refine even when you can't see it. The result must not be "perfect", but perfectly made. And you can't leave anything to chance: every detail must be carefully thought through.

All my works are made entirely by hand, and no machine could replicate what I do. I have made a few "series" of artisanal products, but each article is inevitably different from the next, and therefore unique. What makes the difference, however, is the idea, the inventiveness. That's why I always say that I straddle the worlds of both art and craft, because there must always be that extra something.

Creativity

For me, the creative approach to artisanal work consists of channelling all your feelings into what you are making, and thinking outside the classic concept of an object. I make clothes, but fashion is of virtually no interest to me, and I don't follow it. I let myself be distracted by what I see and this distraction becomes functional, concentrated into the creation. I don't think inspiration in a historical or modern-day sense is important. What really matters is being a great observer, gathering ideas from what surrounds us – from nature, from architectural details, but also from things that are ugly – and conveying them through self-expression. Even a damp patch on the wall can become a beautiful decoration for a dress. For a while now, I've also been adding the element of light to my paper creations, which allows me to develop new dimensions or highlight certain details and the material. What is really missing today is the "time" for a project, because clients want everything yesterday.

Interpretation

I agree with the definition of an artisan as an interpreter who manages to transform a concept into a perfect product. When I made my paper reproductions of the clothes created by designers for the runway show in Brazil, I felt it was important to restore the garments to the designers, to make them recognizable, therefore, but reworked by me – abstract, stripped of their colour, and back-lit. It was completely anarchic, but also completely perfect; all the details of the clothes were still there, but with the addition of something personal. I have often come up against a reality – in the form of standardized production – that gives me no satisfaction whatsoever. It amazes me how banal the content can be, when you could for example play with the combination of the shape of the garment and the design. There is definitely a kind of carelessness that exists today.

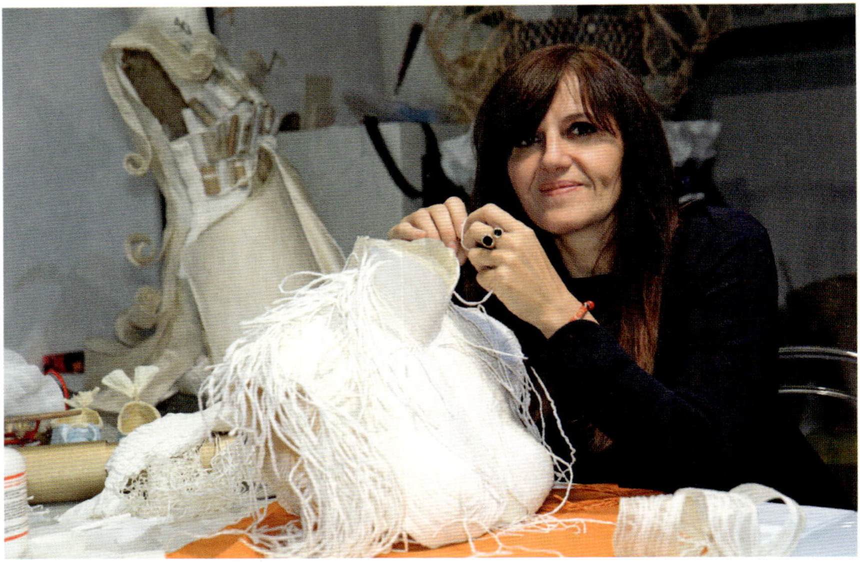

This is why it is important to know how to "interpret" other people's concepts, their inspiration. Perhaps this is where the challenge of craftsmanship lies. Architects and designers today do not know the materials, so they put themselves in the hands of artisans. I think that Italian artisans still have this ability to interpret, although I have found some examples that come close in many places outside Italy. Brazil has great imagination, clever designers, but its workmanship is not always on a par. Indeed, many of its designers come to work in Europe. And then there are countries where there are great manual skills but little interpretive capacity. The all-round ability of Italian artisans is the result of a system that is built on the old concept of the workshop, of learning from grandparents, from parents, as I did. I think there is also an underlying desire for innovation in Italy, which is more cultural; perhaps in this we have been, and still are, bolder. Or reckless even! What we have inherited is unique.

Originality

I think that something that's original is innovative rather than close to the origins. My creations have often been called original because they are different, unexpected – objects that could be almost antique in their manufacture but that are actually modern, made from paper, white, abstract. Perhaps this is why I am sometimes labelled as a designer, because my work is seen as something original.

I think that knowing how to take risks, to push the boundaries is almost instinctive, unconscious. For me, it's not to break away; it's something I do for myself. In this sense, I may be more of an artist, because I have to give external expression to what I have inside. This is how you create originality as perceived by others because what you do is original also for yourself. I once did an origami course, but I don't much like reproducing identical objects. I therefore make every detail by hand, even where those materials can be bought readymade.

Talent

I see talent as also linked to results, to success. An undiscovered talent is a lost talent. Talent that emerges, owing to life's fortunes or an ability to find an outlet, is real talent in this sense.

Working with my hands has helped me enormously to express my talent. It has given me confidence, made me faster and more efficient, able to get straight to the point. There are some very talented artisans, however, who take forever to make things. Whereas I think time management is also important; it's not enough just to be creative. In this sense, the relationship between artisan and artist is interesting.

You can see the talent of successful people, obviously, in what they have done and what they manage to convey to you. But talent is also about managing to capture the potential in young people, in other words being able to see how far they can go. I see young talent in mental alertness, in rapid problem-solving. Other times it takes longer to emerge, and that for me is more of an artistic talent, less artisanal. What for me is fundamental is the passage from an idea to its realization.

Territory

My craft, perhaps owing to its uniqueness, does not have real links with this territory. There are some processes that are typically Italian, like papier-mâché, but that is not my material even if I have fun with it.

In Italy, there are many paper manufacturers that produce very high quality stock, but the ones I use come mainly from the Far East.

Especially through my work with the Creative Academy, I have met other paper artisans specializing in different fields: book-binding, origami, paper jewellery and papier-mâché. At times we meet at paper-dedicated exhibitions, but I have never worked on a joint project. I could do this craft anywhere in the world; I don't think that territory is significant in my case.

Tradition and innovation

I think that certain things are "primordial". It's as if they were embedded in man's DNA and you can therefore also discover them on your own. Paper is one of these. In eastern countries, there is a tradition linked both to its manufacture and to its use. In Europe we also have a long history of exceptional paper production, but I think that the use I make of it is unique. For this reason, there are no set techniques and my entire path has been one of innovation.

There are lots of different kinds of paper and using them in different ways gives results that are always new and original. Working with the paper mills has helped me to learn more about this material, to select the paper best suited to my purposes.

I have also experimented with everyday paper, which I have turned into skirts, fringes and decorations. When the paper doesn't respond as you expected, and you change in mid-creation to adapt the result to your requirements, you build new competences, new ways of working that are therefore "innovative".

I found myself involved in a dissertation on the restoration of contemporary paper art, for which there was no study material. I enjoyed the experiment, but I always think that things don't necessarily have to last forever, that it is a good thing that they come to an end.

I am always very open to collaboration with other artisans. Working with a metal artist, for example, gave me the idea of using metal elements to create a feeling of movement. I also like "interferences", as in the case of a painter who painted my clothes, or the four jewellers who created pieces especially for my busts.

Training

Since I was a little girl, my path has been influenced by my passion for paper. This passion came in part from my father, who not only drew, but also invented and created out of paper, especially for my brothers, elaborate war games with toy soldiers. This is what gave me the idea that a blank sheet of paper can be used to make a three-dimensional object, something luxurious even. When I finished regular high school, my father, who realized that I was an original character and feared that my creativity would be stifled, suggested that I follow in his footsteps and study architecture at university, firm in the conviction that I would then find my own way. My affinity with craftsmanship continued to emerge even during my university years. I liked making 3D models, the miniature versions of the future project. Even afterwards, when working as an architect, I learnt how to make things, to try to understand how they function, to extract their elements, and not just limit myself to designing a project.

I feel lucky to be able to work with paper as an "exception" to the rule, rather than being pigeon-holed as an architect, with all its strict regulations. I started to develop my creative identity in 1995, with a

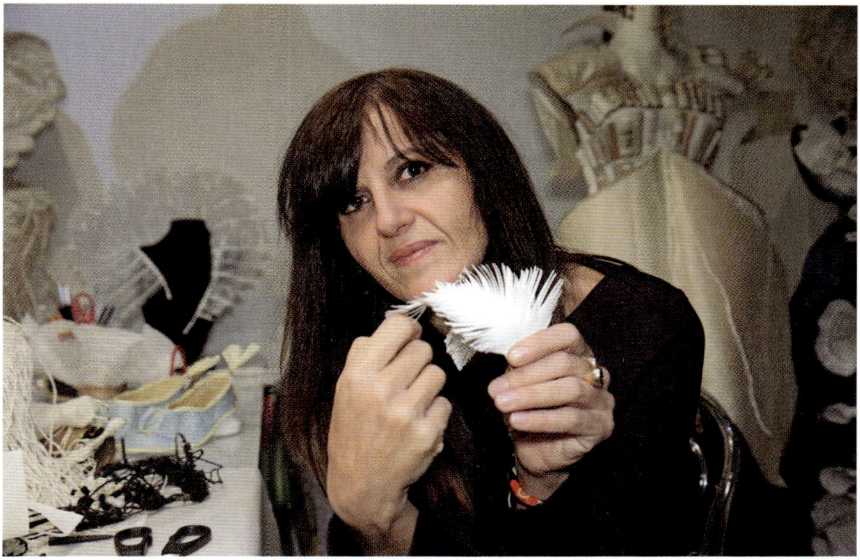

display of paper clothes for the International Furniture Show in Milan. Improvising, experimenting, creating my works from nothing, I realized I had acquired a certain skill when, seven years later, I undertook a major project in Brazil: a paper interpretation of 20 garments, each one by a different designer.

There is no school that teaches these techniques. I have never even done a fashion-related course, because my clothes are not made for wearing. Instead, I often find myself giving classes, and I have seen that it works, because I manage to transmit a desire to try, a desire to make.

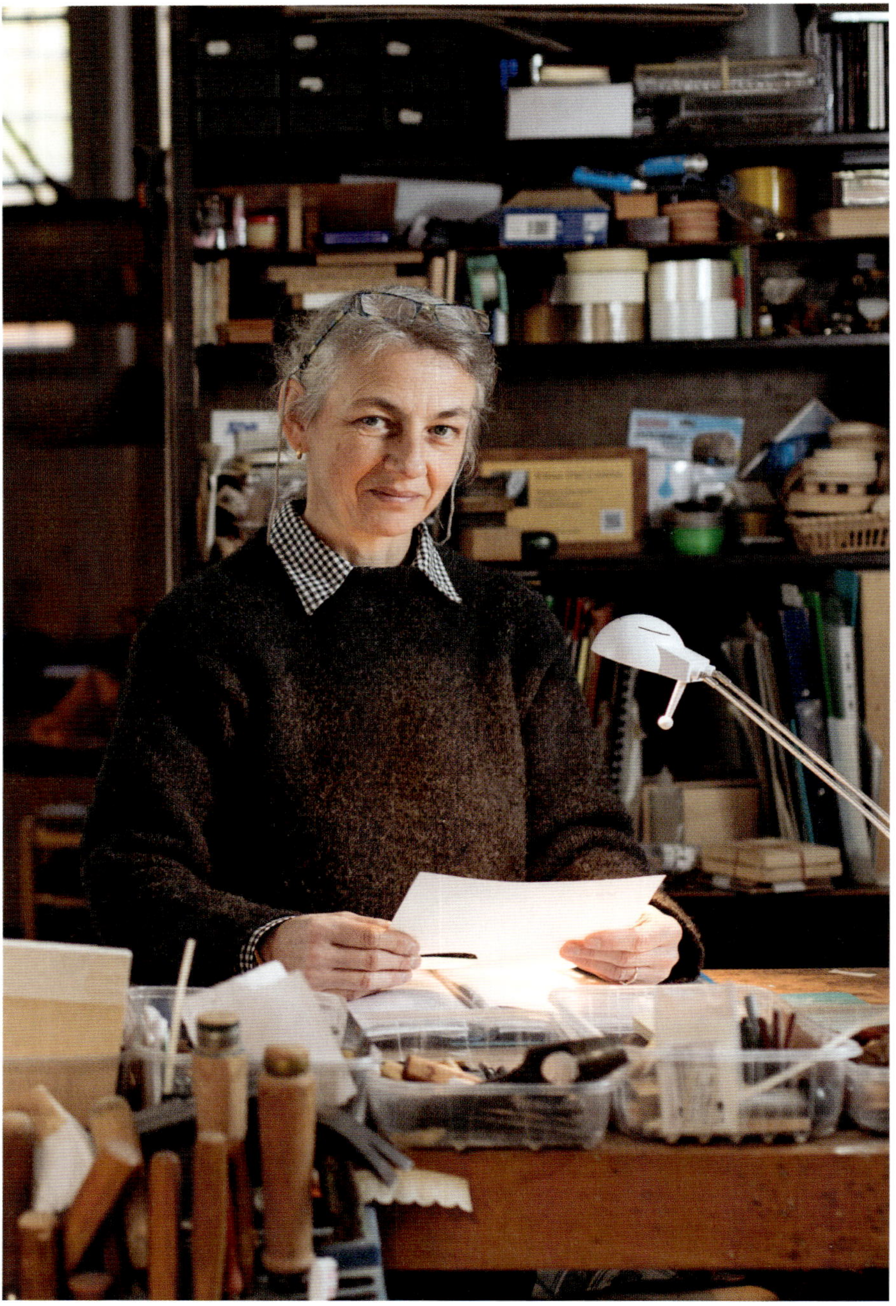

5.3.4. Elena Dal Cortivo, violin-maker specializing in parchment rosettes

After completing high school with a diploma in sciences, Elena Dal Cortivo enrolled at the Civica Scuola di Liuteria (the Municipal Violin-Making School) in Milan. She graduated in 1984 with the qualification of "lutherie heritage operator and conservator", having done her dissertation on the viol in England in the 17th century. In the 1980s, she took part in a series of seminars on early lutherie run by Gerhard Söhne in Pamparato, Cuneo. She subsequently started working as a luthier in Vicenza, making Renaissance lutes, Renaissance and baroque viols, and medieval rebecs and mandolas, occasionally also reproducing parchment rosettes for harpsichords and baroque guitars. During this time, she was a frequent visitor to the workshop of Fabrizio Reginato, maker of viols and other bow instruments in Fonte Alto, Treviso. She also played the recorder and baroque trombone. Dal Cortivo moved to Milan in 1991, where she opened a lutherie workshop at 13 Via Pastrengo and continued to make and restore musical instruments and reproduce parchment rosettes. Thanks to her natural gift for attention to detail, her reproduction of rosettes gradually took over from her violin-making activity and became her main business in 1999. Today, Elena Dal Cortivo is one of the most highly regarded practitioners of this rarest of crafts.

My mother was a teacher, my father a lawyer and jack-of-all-trades – electrician, plumber, tailor. I got my manual skills from him, whereas I have inherited nothing of the spoken word, an art essential to both teachers and lawyers!

When I started to make rosettes for my own instruments, various luthiers saw them and asked me to make them for them, too. Meanwhile, I took part in several exhibitions and my name became known around the world. There aren't many of us specialized in this particular craft.

I work on my own and I don't need an apprentice. People sometimes write to me or come to visit to see how I work. Obviously, if someone really wanted to learn, I'd most likely welcome them.

Authenticity

The issue of authenticity is a very complex one. Materials and workmanship are obviously determining factors and they must be of high quality. In the case of objects with a tradition, respect for this tradition is part of their authenticity. Even when there is innovation, it does not necessarily make an object less authentic, because it can be authentically innovative. My creations are all either copied from ancient patterns or inspired by them.

In my case, the place of production has no impact on authenticity.

But my signature is a must. In the case of a one-off special design, I would also agree to putting the designer's name on my rosettes. I like to think that one day, in the future, restorers will come across rosettes that I made and signed.

Competence

Competence means knowing how to do your job well. An expert artisan knows everything about the history of their craft. It's a quality you acquire in the workshop, from books, from experimenting, and from observing what already exists in order to understand how certain things are made, and why. To my mind, competence in your craft and competence in managing the relationship with staff and apprentices, for those who have them, are two very different skills. One requires practical skill, the other an ability to work with others. Teamwork is probably more relevant in certain branches, and in those cases competence of this kind may well be important.

Craftsmanship

Every bit of my work is manual. Even the small amount I do on the lathe is still done with my hands, and obviously I choose all the materials I use myself.

I suppose that doing something in a masterly fashion implies respect for tradition, the materials and the processes. However, it is hard for me to describe my craft in terms of tradition as there is nothing to compare it with. I think perfection in what I do is closely linked to precision. You need a certain natural manual skill, then the work follows.

Like all hand-made products, each of my rosettes is different. If they were made with a laser, in series, they would be too perfect, too cold. As a whole, my artisanal rosettes look perfect, but if you look closer, you can tell they are hand-made. What counts is the overall impression, the first glance, which gives an artisanal product its special, unique character.

Creativity

I don't know if the word creativity applies to my work, because I always use historical models as a basis. Creativity in my craft is perhaps more a matter of experimentation.

Interpretation

While I agree that the artisan is an interpreter, I am puzzled by the definition of a "perfect product". My work neither entails nor requires modernization of a concept, because the aim is precisely to reproduce or recreate classic patterns, even if, because they are made today, there are clearly differences. I don't think that the ability to interpret a

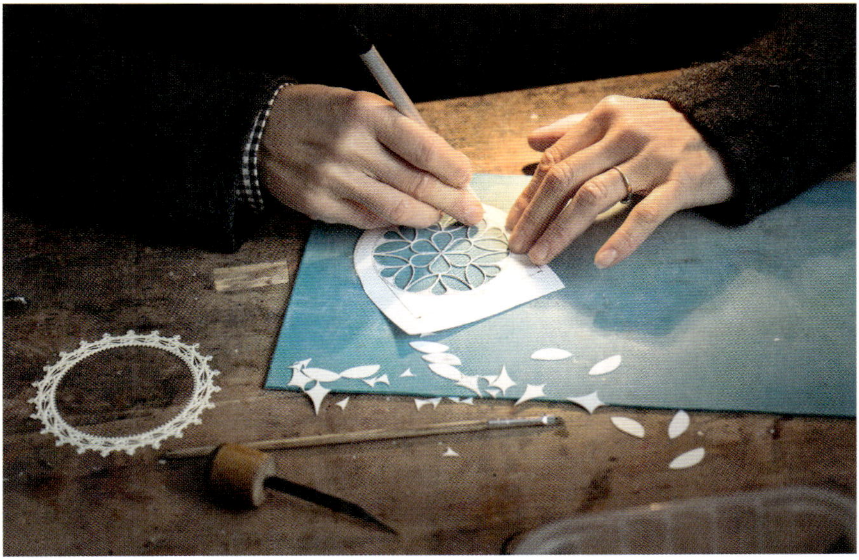

concept is necessarily an Italian prerogative. I do think, however, that it comes from a combination of culture and work approach. For my part, I'm very happy to have developed this very special craft, because it is something I can really relate to. I think that there are only a few people as lucky as me.

Originality

Even something innovative is original. The rosettes I make are "original" in the strictest sense, because they are reproductions of antique ones; innovation lies perhaps in the fact that I have invented the entire creative and production process.

My originality consists in having created a niche for myself that previously didn't exist. From what I've seen, my rosettes stand out from others, maybe because of their refined workmanship, but I've also seen some very beautiful ones made by other artisans.

I can't say if I have stretched the rules in my craft, but I have definitely taken a risk in throwing myself into this enterprise. After my first exhibition, I sent out my catalogue to various luthiers and took part in lots of fairs. That's how I started. In this domain, I don't think it is possible to talk theoretically about the importance of pushing the boundaries versus sticking to tradition, it is something that must be weighed up every time. But I do think that it is important in my job to stay within the boundaries of tradition, even if it is not codified.

Talent

It is my talent that enables me to perform this craft and in this I am fortunate. I can therefore say that talent is fundamental. In my case, talent in terms of execution, more than creativity, is crucial, even if taste plays an important role. Talent is something you are born with, but you have to hone it with practice. When I cut out the third layer of the rosette, for example, the outline is not traced on the parchment and I have to do it all by eye. I find this easy, so for me that's also a talent.

Talent in young people is immediately obvious from the precision of their cutting. With experience, it gets easier. A consummate craftsperson has practised a lot and is therefore faster at achieving the desired result.

Territory

Rosettes are generally made by the people who make the instruments, so I think that territory is primarily linked to lutherie itself. The origin of the material – the parchment – is not really a determining factor. What is important is quality, together with thickness and colour.

As the rosettes are accessories for the instruments, I mainly interact with luthiers, both in Italy and abroad. In this respect, the internet gives me access to the whole world. I also work with antique instrument restorers, mainly from France. Lastly, owing to the nature of this craft, I think I could do it anywhere, even if my ties are with Milan.

Tradition and innovation

The origins of this craft are as old as lutherie itself. Instruments have always had rosettes, and I realized that in the past they were made by people who specialized in this craft. In fact, I found practically identical rosettes on instruments made by different people, an indication that these were made by the same hand. Because it is not a codified craft, everyone creates their own technique, tools and personal style.

The rosettes are made from several layers of cut-out parchment, and the relief is achieved by layering them one on top of the other. The parchment is made from goatskin. The only technology I use is AutoCAD to plan the patterns, which are nearly always copies of or inspired by antique designs. I use hot animal glue, as they did in the past, because modern glues don't work as well.

I generally deal with luthiers, and it can happen – although not very often – that they ask me for special shapes or modifications to the original pattern, or personalized rosettes with their initials.

Training

I graduated from the Violin-Making School of Milan, which, until the mid-1980s, was in Via Pastrengo. I soon realized that I had a natural

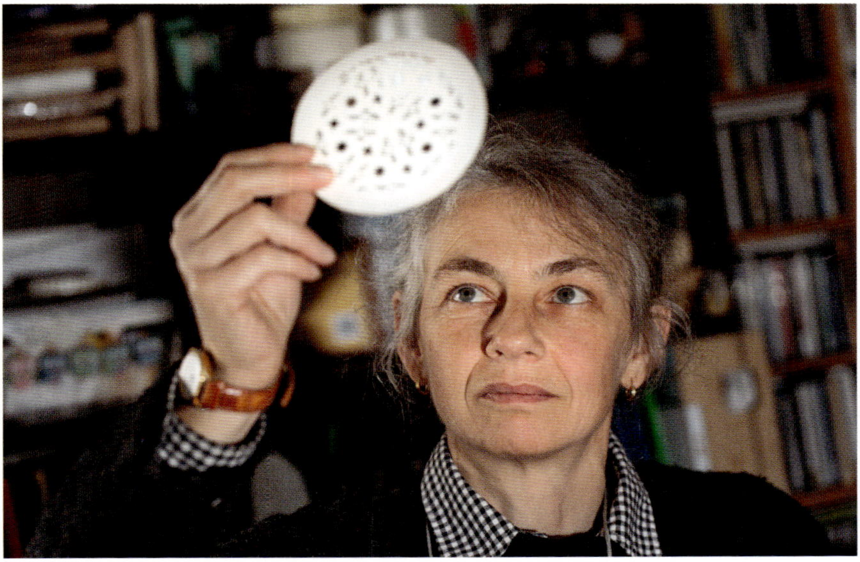

gift for making things by hand and for music. After school I worked in a workshop in the province of Treviso and for a while I made instruments in both Vicenza and Milan. Making parchment rosettes developed from there. These decorations are used on the sound boards of baroque stringed and keyboard instruments and as fronts for the keys on harpsichords. Luthiers normally make their own rosettes, but often they don't have the time or aren't good at making such minute pieces. My curiosity and my fascination with the task led me to experiment, slowly collecting the most suitable tools until I found a system that worked. It was a very gradual process, lasting some 15 years, until I decided to devote my time exclusively to making parchment rosettes. There being neither schools nor courses for this specialization, I would really like to teach the technique to anyone wanting to learn, because I think it would be a shame if my knowledge and skills were lost.

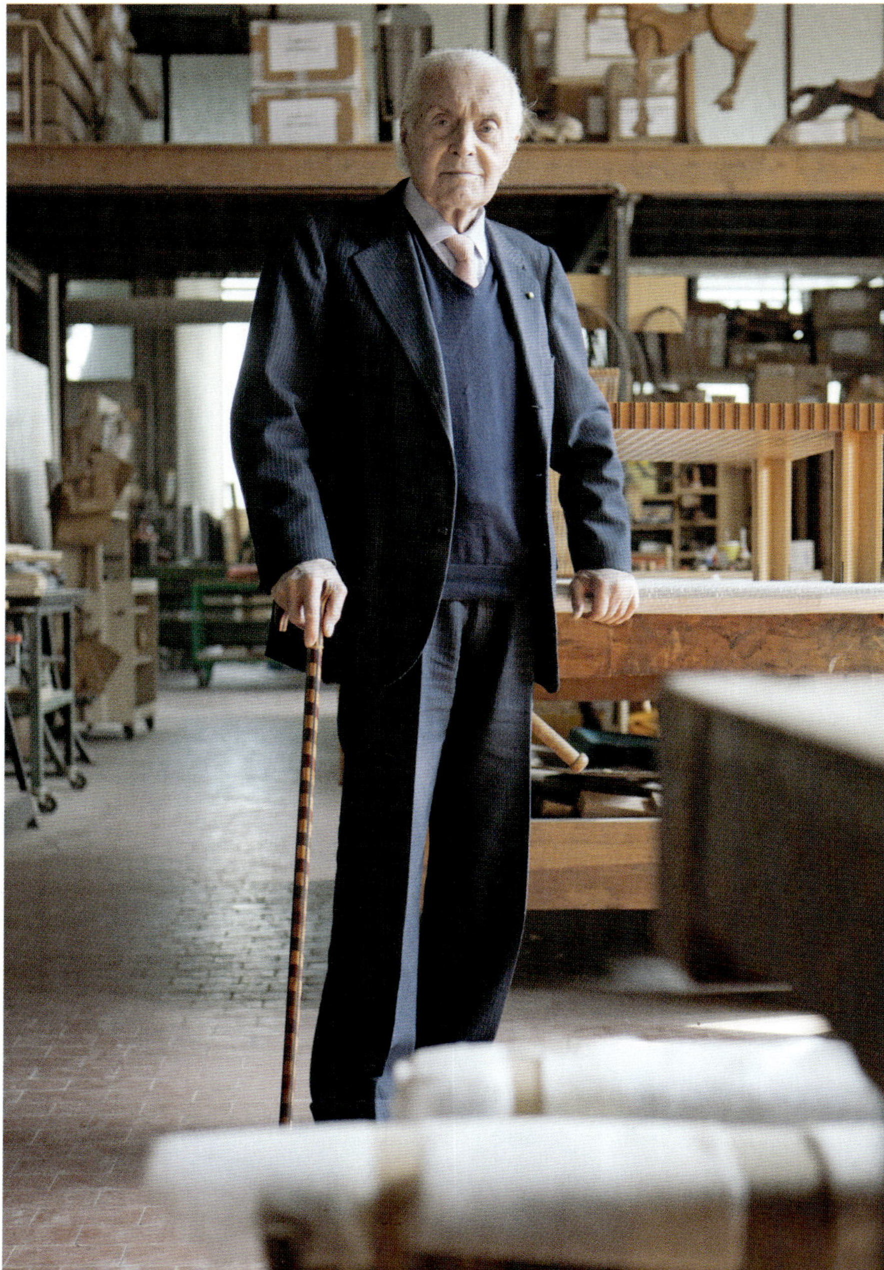

5.3.5. Pierluigi Ghianda, cabinetmaker

Pierluigi Ghianda (1926–2015) was known as "the poet of wood", for the love with which he worked this material and for his expert knowledge and deep respect for a living matter that never dies, not even after hundreds of years. In his workshop, he assembled all the elements of a piece of furniture without nails – as this could "wound the wood" – using only joints, from the simplest to the most complex. The crowning example of this technique was his Kyoto (Frattini) table: 1,764 dovetail joints forming a chiaroscuro pattern of more than 1,600 square holes.

Ghianda's products, made from fine wood such as rosewood, ebony or the more common pear wood, were executed with rare perfection, honed and polished with an expert and patient hand. His work was sought after by the most prestigious companies, including Hermès, Rolex, Knoll, Rosenthal, ClassiCon, Dior, Memphis, Rochas, Pomellato, De Padova, Loro Piana and Thomas, and he collaborated with celebrated designers, such as Aulenti, Bellini, Frattini, Max Bill, Boeri, the Castiglioni, Sottsass, the Vignelli, Monzini, Raggi e Puppa, Sapper, Eileen Gray, the Noorda, Barokas, Cibic, Slegten & Toegemann and many others. For more than 70 years he demonstrated an enthusiasm and love for his craft that set him apart as an old-fashioned artisan, comparable only to the great masters of the past.

Ghianda travelled extensively and not just because he received requests from all over the world. He furnished two floors of Trump Tower in New York, a renovated house by Frank Lloyd Wright in Rye (New York) in collaboration with Emanuela Frattini Magnusson, as well as private residences in Paris and Saint Petersburg. He was fond of Japan and its extraordinary woodworking tradition. Other than that, he travelled mainly in search of fine, rare woods. On one occasion, he went to England specifically to purchase the trunk of a centuries-old elm that was due to be cut down at Buckingham Palace. He also toured Switzerland, buying up the wood from wild pear trees when the Swiss Government liberalized their felling.

This business has existed since the 19th century; the Ghianda brothers were all carpenters, but unfortunately they did not live very long, so turnover on the job was high. My great-grandfather, however, was a blacksmith: they called him "Ghianda del farè", Ghianda the smithy. Brianza developed around the family workshops, where everyone worked, even the women. So much so that they used to call it "a woman's job", which wasn't true, because it was hard work. They said it to make it sound less important, because women's work has always been underrated. Although, in fact, women are way out in front. Without a man, a house continues, but if the woman is missing… This is a natural state of affairs.

When D'Annunzio made his famous flight over Vienna, back when aircraft were made of wood and cloth, my father and my grandfather were making the wooden propellers. My father could tell if they worked and were balanced simply by spinning the propellers and see where they stopped. I learnt to keep things simple from my father, to "work 25 hours a day" as we say in Brianza. My daughter Beatrice works in the company. She is responsible for the details, which are in fact the most important things.

Authenticity

Authenticity is a rather otherworldly concept. It is closely linked to an object's maker, to their knowledge of the wood. Because for them the material has no secrets; they know how to work it skilfully. This is what makes them unique.

We create all our articles in-house, none of the production stages are contracted out. This makes our brand a guarantee of quality and authenticity. We have collaborated with great architects and designers (Gio Ponti, Gianfranco Frattini, Gae Aulenti, Mario Bellini and many others), but our products bear only my signature. The design is obviously not mine, but all you need to do is look at its shape to know that it was designed by Gio Ponti.

Competence

First, you need to know which quality of wood is best for any given job. Pine is ideal for frames, for example, and the variety from Val di Fiemme, with all its veins, is fantastic. Once seasoned, it never changes, because when all the humidity has been removed, its compactness means it doesn't absorb any more from the atmosphere. And then, of course, there must be the ability to create all those details that aren't necessarily functional, but that add that extra touch. I believe there is only one way to do something well, and this goes for everyone, from those with the simplest tasks up.

Craftsmanship

When you make something, manual skills are important. You need to be able to perform certain procedures, like joints, that call for considerable precision. Today, we have machines that make incredible products, but the human hand is always superior, and it is needed to give that touch that no machine can. The term "cabinetmaker" defines the most skilled carpenters, the ones most familiar with wood and whose hands are trained to work perfectly.

The key to everything lies in the choice of material. For every job there exists the perfect wood, which I have always selected personally. The craftspeople who are not interested in doing special pieces need only two or three kinds of wood. But for me, even a thousand wouldn't be enough; someone would always come up with a request for another kind, because when they come to me it's always for special articles.

Woodworking is an art that has to be understood. Using just the sense of touch, you can understand if a job is done well: you feel it in the shape, the joints. My workers would ask me: "*Luisin*, is this good?" And I would touch it and say: "It's good!" Industrial production lacks the hand that can tell you: "No, it's not ready yet."

In my opinion, a masterly execution is expressed through touch. The Neapolitans described this in the simplest and most sensual of ways: smooth and polished as a "nun's bosom". The old folks in Brianza were more explicit and used terms that my mother disapproved of…

Creativity

Creativity comes from our heads. There are those who invent the impossible. Danilo, who used to work for me, was fantastic. He was a simple man. This architect used to call and say: "I'm coming at five, will Danilo be there?" He only came if Danilo was there. They would greet each other and, as soon as they started working, argue over how to do it. "Let him do it himself, then", Danilo would grumble. It was always the same story. But in the workshop there were no hard feelings, nobody was ever offended. Work is work. If what you are doing with your hands is special, then you can say what you like. When Frattini came to visit, we would go out for a drink together, but at work it was a constant battle. And yet…

Interpretation

We have always known how to invent in Brianza, through interpretation. This ability of ours comes from afar. Until the 19th century we were governed by the French, the Spanish and the Austrians, who each added something new to what was already there. While the workshops always stayed the same, the customers would change. First came the French, who had their own ideas and we worked to satisfy their desires. Once one lot went, another lot arrived, and they all wanted different things. This meant that whatever they asked for, you could make it, because you already had. And there was always a lot of competition among the workshops, everyone was always trying to "steal" your craft. This is how Brianza's fame was born.

Originality

I think that originality and innovation are one and the same. Mine lies in the finish, in that touch I talked about earlier. Of course you have to take risks. You must always try things out. I have always done so. I would have been crazy not to, I wouldn't have achieved anything.

Talent

Talent is everything. If you don't have a flexible mind, for understanding, for knowing, for finding an improvement, you'd be better off looking for a different job.

One example of this is my former employee, Danilo, whom I mentioned earlier. I think that the good Lord gives these gifts only to a few. He could do anything, repair watches, this and that, and always to the limits of perfection. When architects came – and they all did – if they wanted something particular, Danilo always came up with an ingenious solution.

In young people you can see talent in how they hold things, how they look at them. Because if you're clumsy, if you drop things, that's no good, it means you weren't born to do certain jobs.

Masters manage to make the joints for a drawer without even thinking. They've seen it once and they do it. It's as simple as that.

Territory

Brianza was a land of country folk: in the summer they worked in the fields, in the winter in their workshops. This is our history. When the summer came, they would put their wood away under the porch and take it out the following winter. This is why Brianza furniture is epoch-making. The carpenters worked up to a certain point and then started again the year after. This meant that the wood dried out and became stable. We used to say that the seasoning process required one year for every centimetre. In other words, a piece that was three centimetres thick took three years to season, if it was five centimetres thick, five years. It was the year that marked time. From one year to the next, some of the wood would bend, so that each piece would be cut and used to make something in that particular shape. We followed nature. This knowledge has been lost, and nowadays people buy timber that has already been dried.

Wood comes from all over the world. The further north you go, the paler it becomes. For example, Scottish maple is the best, but you won't find ebony in Scotland. It is nature that makes the difference. I travelled all around the world at the beginning: if wood arrived from Ecuador, I felt the urge to go there myself, and find out what was there, to have that sense of knowledge that you need in order to work the material.

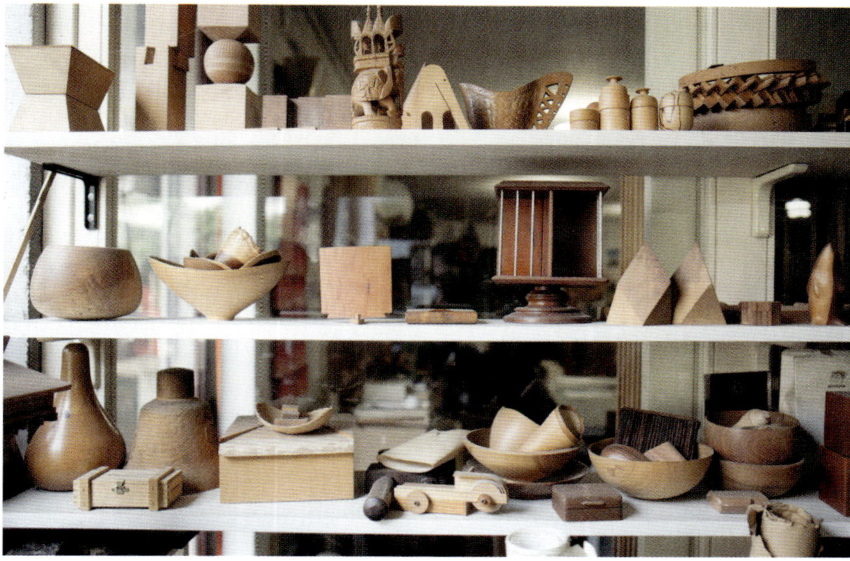

Nothing is possible without passion. Being born in Brianza was definitely an advantage from all these points of view.

Tradition and innovation

We used to make a distinction between carpenter and cabinetmaker, because the latter could work ebony, which in my view is more beautiful than any other natural product. The Italian word for cabinetmaker, *ebanista*, comes from *ebano* or ebony. Today, a cabinetmaker is someone who works wood well, who can create sophisticated details. One can be a carpenter without ever feeling the need to define oneself as a cabinetmaker. It doesn't usually matter what name we give to someone who has the know-how. By the same token, some give themselves this title without deserving it.

Every great craftsperson has made something that has never been made before, as is the case in all things, even music. Human individuality leads to the realization of ever different things, which then naturally become a heritage of humanity. In cabinetmaking we can only invent a solution that is a little out of the ordinary, a tiny joint that might only be visible under a magnifying glass. Perhaps we don't even feel the need to innovate any longer, whereas in the past things were different. We used to watch what others were doing a lot. In those workshops with a certain history or special manual skills, secrets were jealously guarded. When rumours circulated that someone had made something new or special, or had invented a little machine for a special process, the others immediately tried to do the same or more.

At school they teach you to speak, write and sing, but to write a poem or become a musician you need to practice. So the workshop is really important. Today it is much less important to know about the wood, because everyone uses semi-finished products and it's all greatly simplified. But cabinetmakers are always asked to make special things, so we have to have every possible kind of wood to hand and know how to work it.

In the past, anything that was difficult was made only by hand, but now a modern workshop will have at least 30 to 40 highly sophisticated machines for every imaginable process, and it's a pleasure to work these machines.

In my life I have developed many projects with architects and designers, and through this exchange we have always found solutions to everything. I have watched cabinetmakers working in Japan and in other parts of the world and I have always learnt something, even if, generally, the path we have followed has many elements in common.

Training

I started out as a carpenter, like just about everybody in Brianza. We would come home from school and had to walk through the workshop to get into the house. We started early, at the age of six or seven. Until then we were free to do as we liked, but even kids of primary school age had to work. It was mainly a case of being in the workshop, sweeping up, holding a piece of wood for one of the craftsmen, helping move things about. It was normal for the whole family to work, even a dozen or so people. These were artisanal workshops because there was just a man and his four tools, no machines. When I started, we used a band-mill, a band-saw, a jointer planer and planer thicknesser (which was one tool) and a circular saw. And that was it! Everything else was done by hand. Manual skills were what counted in those days. Now the manual part is limited to retouching, because we have machines that make articles that there's no sense in making by hand. But in the old days, drawer joints were only made by hand and they were works of art.

I have learnt from my craft, from what I have seen on my travels, from my relationships with architects and designers, and from my workers, real master artisans.

I have held courses in the past, but I soon realized that they were a waste of time. There is no point talking, you need to be hands-on. So I started to take my work with me: I didn't say a word, I just demonstrated how to make a joint.

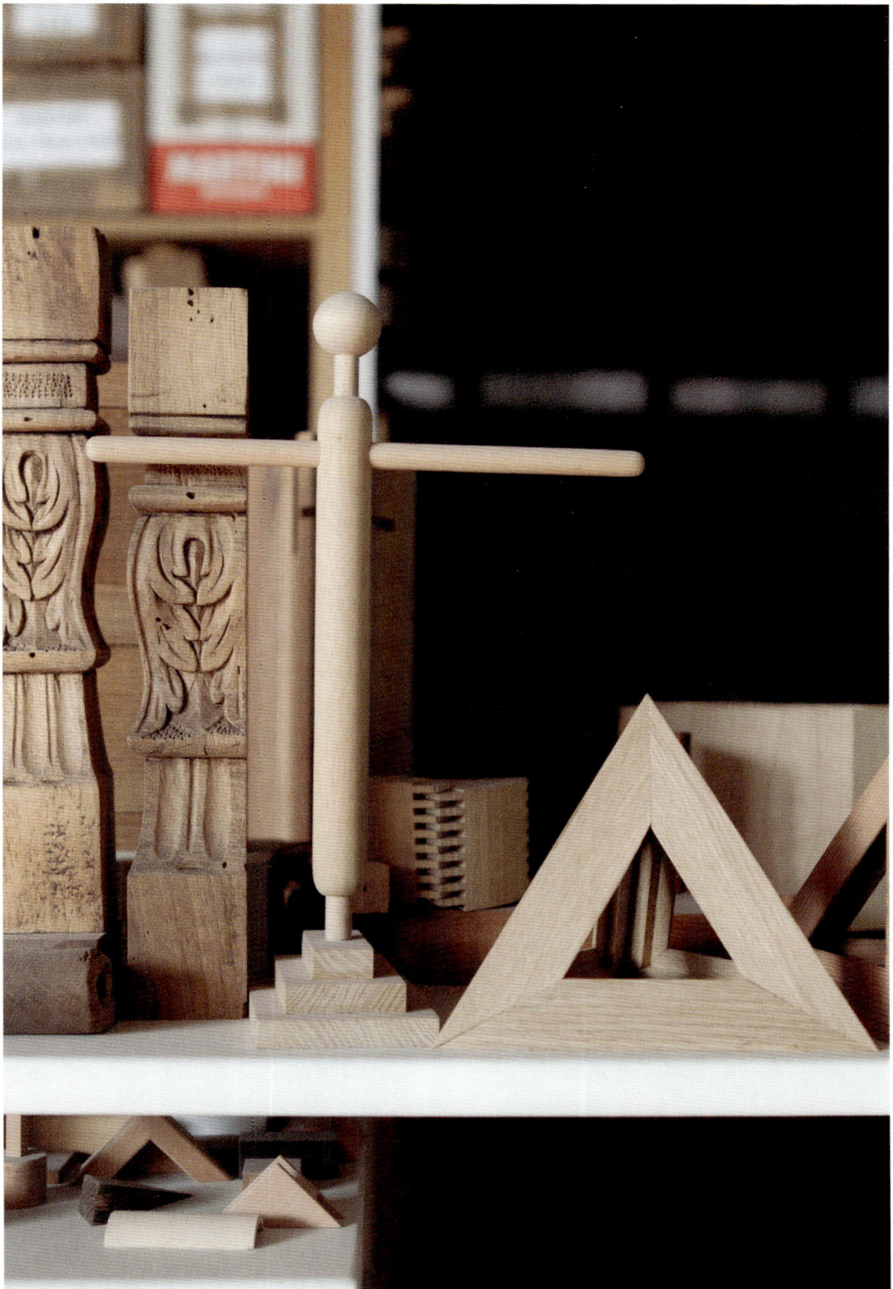

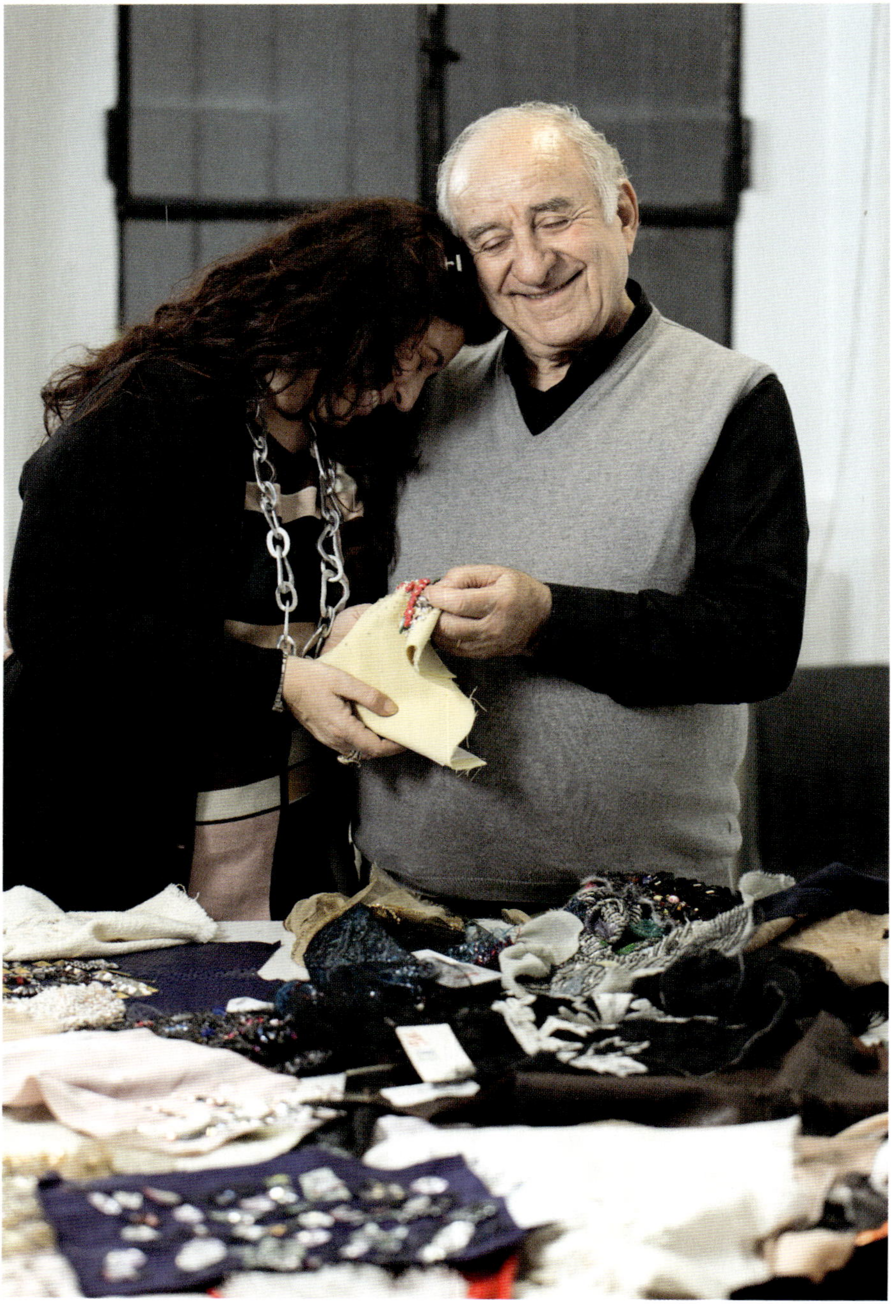

5.3.6. Pino Grasso, embroidery

Pino Grasso entered the world of embroidery in the 1950s, abandoning his medical studies and taking a job with an artisanal company that made couture embroidery. In the early years, he spent time in various workshops specializing in embroidery, trimming, small businesses producing embroidery material in both Italy and Paris, learning about the various manufacturing techniques. It was in Paris, on the French haute couture scene, that he made important, useful contacts and friendships with some of the biggest names in the field of fine craftsmanship, such as Alfred Gaydan and Alexandre for passementerie (a world that has now almost completely disappeared), from whom he learnt different techniques. At the embroidery factory in Mesrine, which he frequented regularly, Grasso deepened his knowledge of design, the sourcing and selection of embroidery materials, and key production techniques. Soon after, he met and became friends with François Lesage, owner of one of the oldest and largest embroidery establishments.

On 28 October1958, Pino Grasso took over an embroidery workshop in Milan, personally supervising all the stages of preparation and production. He dealt with the customers himself, developed the designs, sourced the materials and oversaw each stage of production. Over time, he came to work with the best designers in Italy, including Schuberth, Fabiani, Ognibene Zendman, Sorelle Botti, Senes, Mosè, Rosandrè, Rina, Galitzine, Veneziani, Marucelli, Mila Schön, Valentino, Lancetti, Raffaella Curiel, Gianfranco Ferré, Gianni Versace, Giorgio Armani, Dolce&Gabbana, Gai Mattiolo, Bottega Veneta, Emilio Pucci, Genny, Roberto Cavalli, Etro, Prada, Graeme Black, Albino, Francesco Scognamiglio, Angelo Katsapis and Alessandro de Benedetti. He currently has a team of embroiderers working for him, but he still follows each stage closely and approves every article before it is delivered to the client. In 2010 the Centre du Luxe et de la Création in Paris awarded him the prize Les Talents du Luxe et de la Création in the Invention category.

In 2011 the Cologni Foundation for the Métiers d'Art dedicated a solo exhibition to Pino Grasso, which was held during Milan fashion week in the prestigious hall designed by Galeazzo Alessi at Palazzo Marino in Piazza della Scala.

Today, his business continues thanks also to his daughter, Raffaella.

The family of one of my classmates at school worked in embroidery. He didn't like it, however, and he asked me if I wanted to take his place. At the time, I was a second-year medical student. I thought about it throughout my 18-month military service and when I came home I made the decision. Today I am handing the workshop over to my daughter, who has worked with me for many years and by now knows all there is to know. My grandchildren are too young for the moment, but who knows? Maybe in the future.

Authenticity

To recognize work done by the Pino Grasso atelier, you need to go back to its origins: the idea, the design that shapes the idea, the mind that chooses the materials, the colours and the combinations, the hands that do the work. Just as you can recognize a designer's style, in our work we are sought out and recognized for the way in which we realize the designer's ideas. Authenticity is therefore essential.

In my case, what counts is knowledge of the materials' potential and the desired objective. It goes without saying that, as it is all made in my workshop, the production chain is totally traceable. A determining factor is then your proximity to the designers; this is what distinguishes a product made here from one made in China or in India.

It would be useful to be able somehow, through a signature or a label, to identify the work as having been carried out in our workshop. In my opinion, it would be useful for designers, too – a guarantee of "Made in Italy" and authenticity.

Competence

As I see it, competence is when, before I even realize an idea, I already have in mind how to go about it: the material, the fabric, the technique and the style. It is an expertise that comes with experience, and above all, from the passion of working. My job is a chain that starts with the designers and ends, through me, in the hands of the embroiderers. Managing the relationship between both ends is crucial.

Craftsmanship

Our work starts in our brain and manifests through our hands. To achieve excellence, a craftsperson must have sentiment, soul, taste. The difference between a skilled craftsperson and a master artisan is that the former does a good job and the latter produces an excellent piece of work.

A masterly execution must firstly reflect the designer's original idea. Secondly, it must satisfy your creativity and your soul, but always leave you questioning if you could have done it better. No less important is that the reverse of an embroidery should be as beautiful as the right side. And lastly, an indication of a job well done is when the customer tells you so themselves. I think it's wonderful when you look at one of your pieces and feel that you could still improve it, or when you see pieces done by others and think that they have surpassed you.

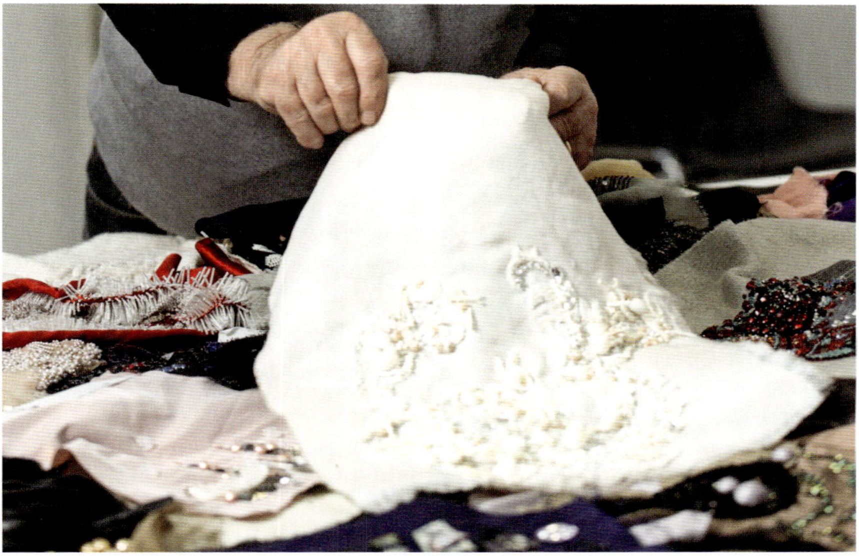

Dissatisfaction and incompleteness spur you on to always do more and better.

I select all the materials personally, but I also get ideas and suggestions from my embroiderers. With time, I have learnt to delegate more; I have understood that when you centralize, you become fixated on a single issue, whereas you need to be able to see the value in the ideas of others. Young designers also communicate better with their peers, while my 80 years of age make it more difficult for them to do the same with me. The exchange between young minds generates new ideas, and it is more spontaneous.

No piece of our embroidery is alike; each one bears that imprint that is the imperfection of manual work. This is what makes each piece unique. Nothing of what we do can be reproduced on a machine. And even when we make several copies of the same embroidery (since we work for fashion houses, many of the garments are made in more than one piece and size), the hand is always different, and two pieces with the same pattern are never identical, like handwriting. Our embroidery expresses the soul that comes from the hands that made it, which is actually the ability to add that extra special something to a product.

Creativity

Italy is full of creative minds, generating thousands of new ideas. There is nothing left to discover: the skill all lies in elaboration. Ability, talent, creativity are necessary to transform those ideas into what you want to make. You might even think up something new, which is what I do when I manage to cut myself off from everything around me. In my opinion, creativity consists in enhancing what already exists. Ideas grow out of a stimulus, they never just happen on their own.

Interpretation

I think that artisans are "interpreters" that can transform a concept into a perfect product. But they mustn't do so mechanically, they must always add something of their own.

The basis of our work lies in the ability to read the designers' minds, to feel their sensibilities, to transform their ideas into a creation, an expression of their spirit. In other words, it is the ability to interpret their style.

To do this, it is vital to give a project a contemporary feel. If you don't do that, it's not complete. But you must always bear in mind who it is being made for. In this respect, Italian artisans have the right kind of edge. We talked about this in relation to the artisans in India, whose embroidery style is very much tied to their culture and their traditions. Italian artisans, meanwhile, can develop a customized interpretation for each designer. We put our talent, our soul and our virtuosity at the service of the project, adapting our expressive skills to the mentality and style of the creator. This is our talent. When I see a Mackintosh armchair, I see the design, but also the skill of the craftsperson in interpreting it. It's a kind of mental elasticity whereby Italian artisans create a symbiosis with the designer's soul. It stems from the fact that Italy has been pervaded by a thousand currents, fashions, invaders, rulers and styles, which have turned it into fertile terrain for artisans able to create and to interpret. It's an innate gift, a multifaceted feature of this country's culture, which is developed and forged through work, by which you learn to interpret but also to pre-empt.

Originality

When you succeed in transforming an object, adapting it to the needs, tastes and times of the designer, while preserving its integrity, you combine originality and innovation. You capture the essence, reworking it and adapting it to the here and now.

As for me, my ability to stand out, and therefore to be original, lies in the fact that people can say "Pino Grasso made this"!

It is extremely important to take risks and to stretch the rules, to know how to capture that aspect of a personality and accentuate its originality. But it should never be overdone, or it can border on caricature. In my case, I know the designers I work with so well that I can give their embroidery a distinguishing feature. So much so that when this feature is too strong, the designers themselves ask me to moderate it because it is too real, too overpowering.

In our work, no reproduction of the same design is an exact copy, because each piece is made by a different hand and a different mind.

Talent

Each of us has a talent. What counts is the ability to discover this talent, through ourselves and others. Skill lies in perfecting the talent through passion, analysis and instruction.

With my embroiderers and designers there is a sort of reciprocal inspiration, it is a two-way street. Therefore, I would say that talent applies to both creativity and implementation.

Experience and an enthusiastic approach to work make talent tangible. You realize you have it when you make something exceptional.

The potential in young talents can be seen in a look or in the questions they ask. Even when the manual skills are there, everything always starts in the head. Everyone can excel in something, be it precision, ability, creativity or speed.

After 50 years of my work being barely recognized, I find it strange to be suddenly put on a pedestal. Therefore, it is difficult for me to give a profound definition of talent because I don't see myself as a master or as someone talented. This is why I would say that it is something that some have, a bud that shows itself when it is allowed to grow and blossom so that others realize it is a beautiful flower.

Territory

For fashion, the capital of decoration has always been Milan because this is where the pattern-makers were. Haute couture existed in Italy, but it was very disorganized and had no international standing. The French, on the other hand, immediately gave themselves rules, and Paris has always been the capital of haute couture. Therefore, these associations of pattern-makers from Milan would go to Paris (and we with them) to buy, at great expense, the models created by the French designers. Meanwhile, we would visit the embroiderers, who would sell us the model and the embroidery sample for the garment. The pattern-makers, with the approval of the various fashion houses, then came back to Italy and presented their garments. Their shows were attended by hundreds of tailor's shops, who, in turn, would buy the models and present them to their clients. This set-up disappeared in the 1960s following the arrival of prêt-à-porter, which sounded the death knell of the dressmakers' shops and with them the embroiderers.

I have Sicilian origins, but Milan is the territory I feel closest to,

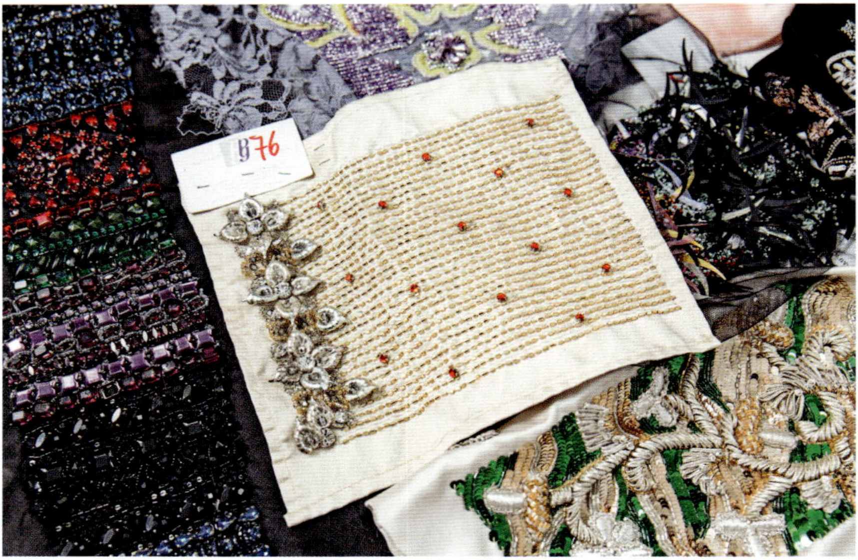

for the culture, the drive, the research, the ideas and the style. Not by chance is it the centre of Italian fashion. While the techniques and creativity are linked to our local traditions, the raw materials may come from any part of the world, even if the basic ones always come from the same suppliers.

There are very few remaining embroidery workshops, and we tend to be protective of our patch. But I have worked with other embroiderers on special projects or even just to lend a hand, as happened with the Atelier Lesage in Paris.

Tradition and innovation

You could say that the practice of decoration is an art that has always existed. It became what it is now in the mid-19th century, when Charles Frederick Worth created haute couture in Paris. When I started, there were still many expert embroiderers working on the outskirts of Milan, while the six or seven embroiderers who worked for the fashion industry were in the city itself. At that time mothers used to send their adolescent daughters to these workshops, where the girls' ability, capacity, predisposition, willingness and sacrifice were put to the test, because eight hours at a loom is hard going. Those who showed most promise were kept on, the rest sent home. The families paid a fee for the training, just as they would in a school.

The techniques and tools have never changed. Some of my looms are more than 150 years old, salvaged from old workshops and flea markets, because they haven't built new ones for decades now. Innovation, meanwhile, lies totally in elaboration, in the use of new materials, even invented ones. Thus, the work keeps pace with the times, which in our case are dictated by fashion, by the designers who encourage us always to be innovative, to stay one step ahead. For my projects I use both traditional and new materials, from Plexiglas to the copper wire from electric cabling, from the fibres of coffee sacks to plastic bottles, plus materials that I have made to order.

A design comes from an idea in my head, but it also emerges from cooperation with designers, embroiderers and pattern-makers. We all work towards the desired result and the process is in continual evolution. For us, a novelty is something that already existed, but which we have changed and developed – because decoration is a combination of taste, colours and execution.

The only impact of technology has been on the organization of our work: the computer plays an important role as a means of communication and for exchanging inputs and patterns.

Training

The embroidery we do involves the application of sequins, trimmings, jet and any other decoration that can be sewn onto fabric. It is a job that cannot be taught, it can only be learnt by working eight to ten hours a day at the loom, in the workshop.

I started on 28 October 1958. I already had a smattering of this craft, but I wanted to be competent in my work, even if I wasn't doing the embroidery personally. I spent several years in Milan and Paris, visiting workshops and manufacturers. I sat down at looms with embroiderers and learnt how to use a needle and a crochet hook. I visited various manufacturers of materials, because if you don't know what exists on the market, how can you imagine a decoration on a garment? And if you know how they are made, you can even ask the manufacturers to do something special for you. You need complete, in-depth knowledge. I even met all the fabric suppliers, because you also need to know what to use for an embroidery, whether it's chiffon or a stiff cloth. Over five or six years I doggedly self-educated, gradually familiarizing myself with this craft.

There are no schools or professional courses in our sector. Consequently, it is impossible to stay up to date unless you do it directly, through research into materials and techniques, working closely with customers and suppliers.

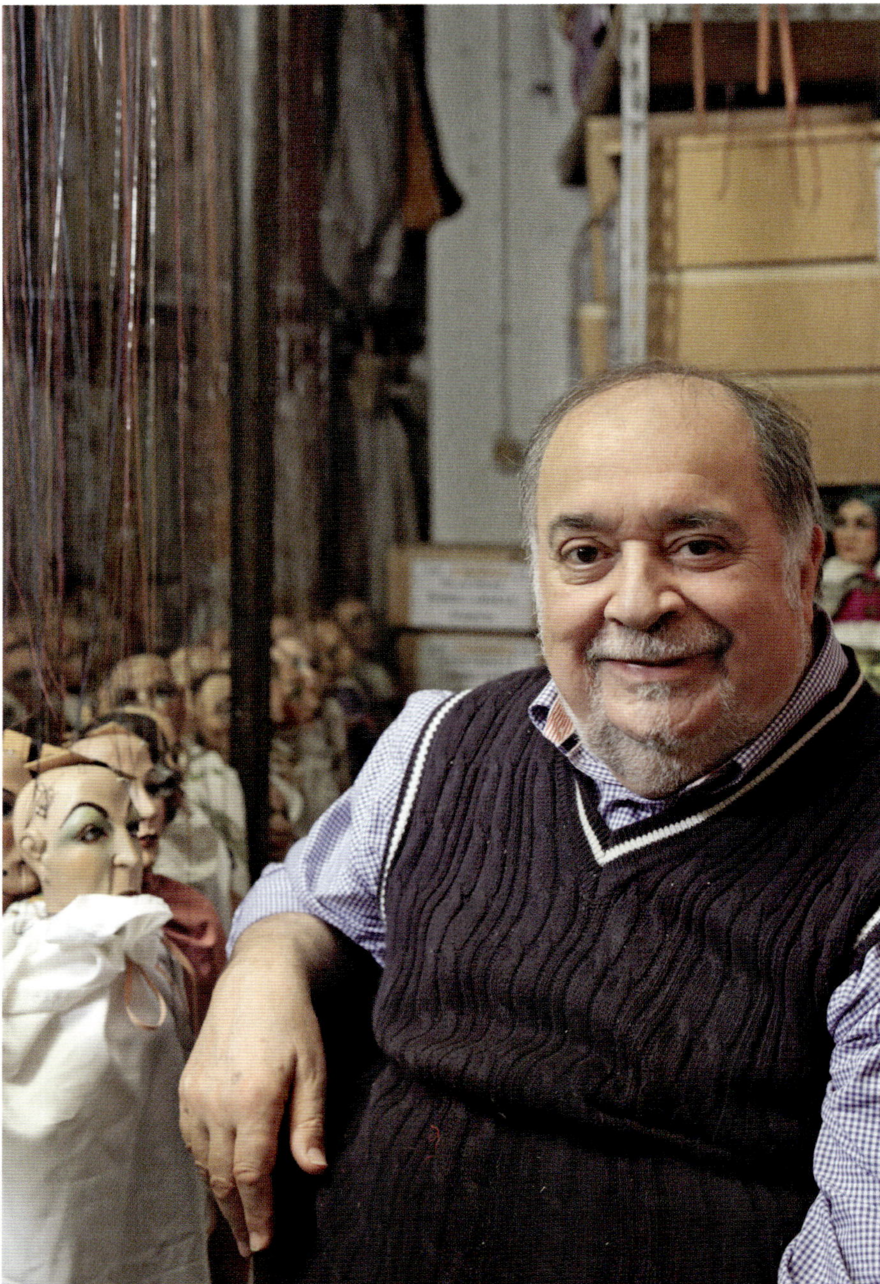

5.3.7. Eugenio Monti Colla, marionette theatre director

Eugenio Monti Colla, was born in Milan on 5 September 1939. His mother, Carla Colla, was a descendant of the famous family of puppeteers, and his father was the painter Cesarino Monti. As a very young boy, he started his apprenticeship on the stage of the Gerolamo Theatre, where Carlo Colla e Figli, one of Italy's oldest marionette companies, had had a permanent base since the beginning of the 20th century. After studying classics at high school, he attended the Faculty of Humanities at the Cattolica University in Milan, combining his studies with amateur theatricals in the role of director. Monti Colla graduated with a degree in theatre history, a course for which he then acted as assistant to Professors Mario Apollonio and Sisto Dalla Palma on the specific subject of theatrical puppetry. After university, while teaching literature at middle school, which he did for some 20 years, he re-formed the family company, which had disbanded some eight years earlier, to continue his artistic activity, performing the traditional repertoire of Carlo Colla e Figli in the role of director, developing and staging new marionette productions.

Over the years, Monti Colla has given lectures and seminars at the Civica Scuola di Teatro Paolo Grassi in Milan on the relationship between official theatre and puppetry, organized cycles of conferences for Cultura a Milano, held in the Grechetto room in Palazzo Sormani, and run seminars and refresher courses for teachers and pupils at all stages of their schooling in Milan and its province. From September 1994 to 2008, he headed the Fiando Theatre School of Animation and from 2002 to 2004 he ran a course on the history and practice of figure theatre at the Brera Academy of Fine Arts.

The marionette company of Carlo Colla (the "& Sons" was added later) was founded in 1861, after the break-up of the original nucleus. The Colla were a family of Milanese tradesmen who supplied the Austrian armies with wood and fodder, and their home was where the Galleria del Corso stands today. They had their own private marionette theatre at home, which was quite common in those days. After the Congress of Vienna, the Austrians exiled them and confiscated their *palazzo* because they had traded with the French, and so they became puppeteers out of necessity. The Gerolamo Theatre had existed since 1868 and it was entrusted to my family in 1906, when they came back to Milan after spending almost 70 years as a travelling company performing all over northern Italy and as far down as Emilia-Romagna.

I am the last puppeteer of the company that performed during the heyday of the Gerolamo Theatre, a legendary space in Milan dedicated to marionettes where my family staged some of the most unforgettable shows in our history. But it takes strength and courage to dedicate your life to this profession. I still feel the presence of all the old Collas I have worked with, and this is a huge joy, because I don't sense "shadows" but people who are still there, and who are hopefully pleased with what I am doing. At the same time, I also feel the weight of 200 years of history. I will leave this activity in the hands of the people who, over the last 30 years, have worked with me to take the company forward. Some of them have been my students while I was a school teacher, and they have followed me in this extraordinary adventure.

Authenticity

Authenticity exists *a priori* in a skilful artisan's work. Because obviously we try to be ourselves in that moment, without faking intention or creativity.

We represent centuries of tradition of a theatre style that in Milan has shaped a certain kind of society. Not living up to that tradition would be a contradiction of the centuries that came before. Piazza Beccaria and the Gerolamo Theatre were a benchmark, a regular fixture for many Milanese. Other habitués included Luchino Visconti, Igor Stravinsky, Gordon Craig, Simone Weil, Paolo Poli, Franca Valeri, Macario, Gian Carlo Menotti and Lila de Nobili. I've heard that Visconti obliged his assistants to come and see the performances at the Gerolamo, saying: "That's where you learn what theatre is." Menotti said to me: "Woe betide you if you use a constructed stage set! They have all to be painted." I think that through us these personalities discovered how much knowledge of baroque, romantic and epic theatre puppets could provide.

If I were to say that none of this ever existed, because we have to put on a different kind of theatre now, that wouldn't be true. I feel the show still needs to have the same kind of impact on the audience as it had back then. I know that audiences have changed; in some respects they are much more superficial and distracted by all this technology. When I put on a chivalric romance, *Il Guerrin Meschino* (Wretched Guerrin), I was chastised for telling the tale of an adopted son going in search of his parents. They didn't understand that it was a journey of initiation, that it had nothing to do with adoption.

Competence

Serious artisans never feel complete, because their work is continually evolving. They can, however, be satisfied with what they have done, thinking ahead to what might come next. Our kind of artisanal work is different from that of someone who creates a Stradivarius. The latter is an artisan with very few liberties, in the sense that the result is preordained, even if perfect.

Competence is a dimension that has to do with awareness. I have to know what my hands can do before I make something. It has happened on occasion that I have said "I can't do this, I'll give it to someone else". I would never want to do an inferior job.

This is a craft that could be taught in a school that doesn't separate the hand from the head. In fact, some members of the company laid the foundations for this craft at school, by doing other stuff. You need to put the person at the centre of the process and always make sure you know what you want to get from that exploration.

Staging a show calls for different competencies. Puppeteers see the marionettes from above, so it's like moving the pieces on a chessboard, without seeing the audience. I teach the puppeteers that it is the reaction of the characters who are not acting that allows you to gauge the impact of what is being performed by the others. You need to understand the importance of those marionettes that are not, at a given moment, at the centre of the action. The position that each character assumes is a direct message to the spectator.

I think that when you are competent in this craft, you immediately acquire a synergy with your team. If you stage trivialities, the others will find it hard to follow you. If my competencies, expertise and knowledge were incomplete or weak, I couldn't expect to have a good team. Although I like to chatter and joke about anything and everything, when it comes to work I have to be the high priest (a definition that may sound pretentious, but it takes us back to the past!) of the temple where Isis was made to move, becoming the first puppet in history.

Craftsmanship

While the place of origin of the raw materials is of no import, it is essential that the work takes place here, in this workshop. I get cross when those who are in charge of a specific division just take care of the initial phase and then don't follow through. I want to see how much responsibility a person takes on, turning a job into a personal experience. As for the choice of materials, since the marionettes are made from a living material, for consistency I try not to use anything synthetic. I hardly ever allow the use of foam rubber, for example, and for a very good reason: Maria Perego, the creator of the Topo Gigio character, told me one day that I was lucky because when I am no longer around, my puppets will still be here to tell my tale, while those in foam rubber are doomed to self-destruction, leaving nothing at all. Synthetic hair is used only for fantasy characters because it has to shine in a certain way, to give them a non-human appearance. It's a choice that becomes a requirement, not just a whim, and is driven by dramaturgical, theatrical and artistic factors.

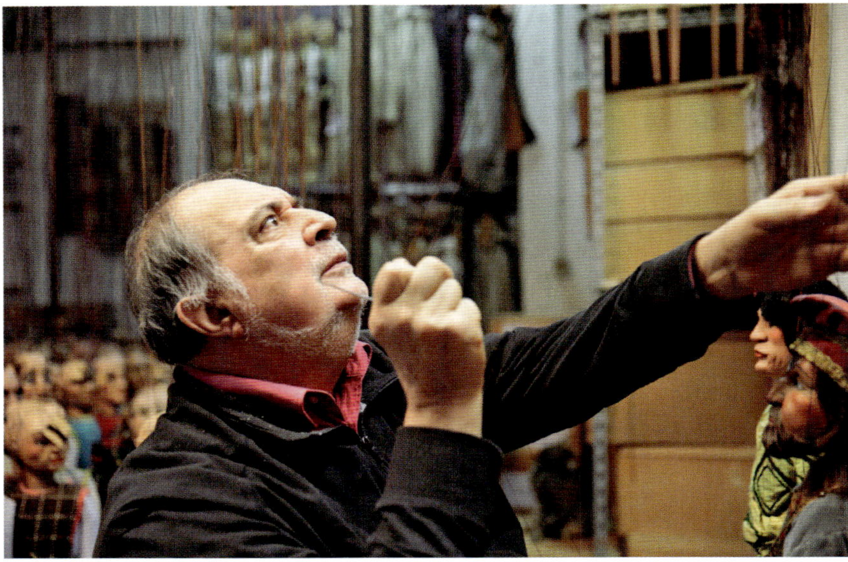

In show business, a masterly executed performance is one that wins over the public, making them come back time and again. It is one that arouses curiosity and has people waiting before the curtain goes up, hoping to catch a glimpse of the stage's secrets. Audiences are surprised when they see that the marionettes, which seemed so tall during the show, are in fact much smaller, and we humans look like giants next to them.

A truly excellent performance is one in which you give your all, you are completely immersed and you realize you are a means and not an end.

Creativity

Where do I get my creativity from? Half of it is madness, without a doubt. The other half is a desire to do something that throws the human soul up in the air, allowing it to find the roots of something simpler, more naïve, more down-to-earth. I am also inspired by the people I am closest to, by what they give me, even unconsciously. I am generally delighted when I am asked to put on a show, because it means that the person has got right to the heart of what needs to be done, or rather, of what I know how to do.

It is also important to know, however, that if a job has been commissioned, your creativity must be confined within certain boundaries. I can't produce a zebra when they ask me for a dog.

Interpretation

We need to establish whether interpretation means liberty or libertarianism. I think we are permitted a certain degree of freedom in what we do. However, when it becomes a form of anarchy, and I try to squeeze everything that comes into my head into a performance, it's harder to judge. Liberty is, in my opinion, to dramatize a text without any prejudice towards that text. Anarchy, on the other hand, is using that text to narrate things that have nothing to do with it. Liberty is a two-way street, and this applies to any work, be it art or a performance: the liberty of execution must respect the liberty of both the spectator and the author.

Originality

There must be originality in the work we do, because we are not making copies. Therefore there must be a purpose that takes it one step further than what we've already done.

I think that originality lies in combining all those functions the theatre has always had – the functions of magic, of illusion – and amplifying them a hundredfold. I don't completely believe in Artaud's style of theatre, but if I did have my marionettes make polenta on stage, I would do all I could to make sure you could also smell the polenta. Because the audience has to be amazed that mere pieces of wood can do these things. During the performance nobody is aware of what is going on behind stage, because they enjoy the illusion, the colours. The spectators let themselves be taken in. I think that, thanks to the huge, infinite potential of marionettes, a show must be a combination of religious rite, town festival, dance and fun.

When you prepare a show or create the puppets and the scenery, pushing the rules is all important. When I found out that the Teatro Regio in Parma wanted our *Attila* to inaugurate their Verdi celebrations, I was terrified, because it was, after all, a puppet show. But I also thought that no other opera theatre could put on a performance like ours: we can have horses on stage with no problem, or tigers, lions, elephants – it's no big deal. These are the great risks we take. I bewildered a lot of people, I think, by staging *L'Après-midi d'un faune* by Debussy with marionettes. But they had to admit that it was good, that it could be performed in this way.

Talent

To begin with, talent forces you to discover if you have it, which seems a pretty fundamental point to me. Second, you mustn't think that just because you discovered that you have a talent, you can stop there, because it might just be a skill. If you presume yourself to be a great artist, you are destined to disappear. And then, if this talent doesn't attract others to you, it isn't talent at all!

Talent can't be acquired, but it can empower what you have. A glimmer may become a bright light, but if the glimmer isn't there, all that is asked of you is not to dampen the flames of others. Standing in a circle, holding hands if possible, is in itself a way of experiencing one's talent. It entails humility, simplicity, understanding what it means to follow others, which is already learning and can develop into a talent, even when there is none evident.

I think that my primary task is to turn everything that I feel into a possibility for the persons who work with me. Because this is how you come closer to the others. I see what steps we can take together. A person might simply choose to fill a niche. I like lots of niches, architecturally speaking, because together they make a wall.

Territory

Milan has a long marionette tradition. It saddens me that people today don't understand the potential of the marionette theatre, which in the 19th century was a purveyor of information. It told of the war of independence, Garibaldi, the wars in the colonies, World War I, fascism – all in an ironic way. The puppeteers did it all: epic, opera, operetta, from Manzoni's *The Betrothed* to *Wretched Guerrin* and Goethe. And the people learnt. The great puppetry traditions have all died out.

Nobody else does puppet theatre like us, and I don't mean in terms of quality. I believe this is because it is extremely costly to do things the way we do. It takes more than a thread that moves a pair of glasses, because that would only be trickery, not research.

I feel my ties are to Milan – the Gerolamo Theatre, the Piccolo, the Scala – because of its history, tightly interwoven with that of the Colla family.

Tradition and innovation

At the start of the 19th century, Milan had 40 puppet theatres that put on performances all year round. Some of them featured many different companies, including foreign ones. The puppets were originally moved using a central wire, then a revolutionary control system with strings, invented by Thomas Holden, arrived from England and was immediately adopted by several companies.

In our family company, we created the costumes, the stage materials and the electrical devices, while the marionettes and the scenery were contracted out to great artisans, artists of sculpture and stage sets. The eldest of the four Colla siblings, who died aged 89 (she was already in her seventies when I was small) was my favourite aunt because she had

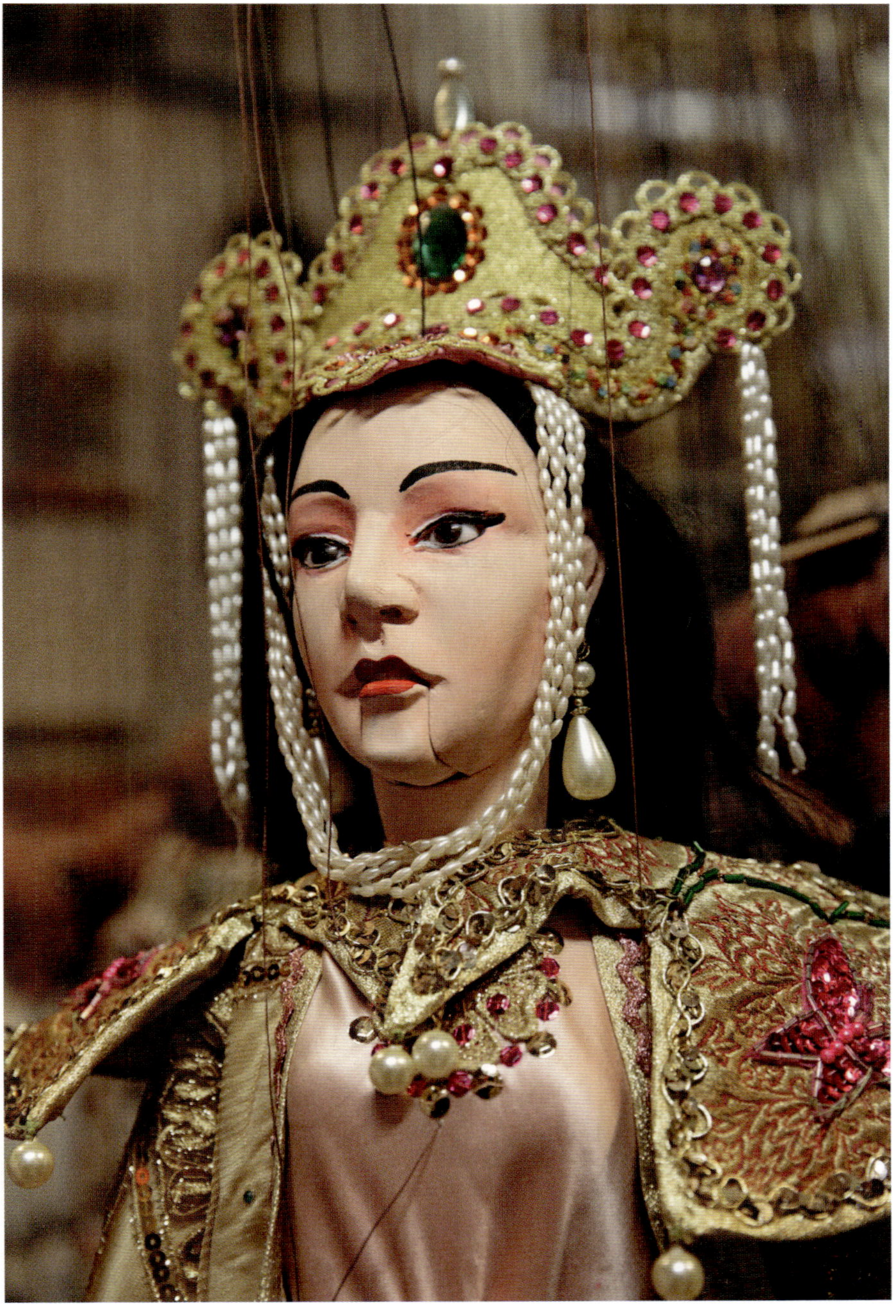

realized that the sacred fire burned inside me. She told me all about the past, all the shows I had never seen. So I knew where to get the materials from, when they had been used, how and where. My mother, who was herself a puppeteer, also had a workshop that supplied hair to all the hairdressers in Via Montenapoleone, where we used to live, and to all the opera theatres that needed wigs and hairstyles. The likes of Pierluigi Pizzi, Dante Cavallotti, Beni Montresor, Filippo Crivelli and other big names of show business frequented my mother's workshop. I also met characters such as Walter Chiari, Ugo Tognazzi and Wanda Osiris. It was my mother who taught one of my students how to make the wigs for our marionettes, which she still makes today.

I was born in time to know and live with my wonderful uncles and aunts on the stage and to discover that, while they considered themselves just "artisans", they were in fact exceptional artists. All this inspired me to make sure that craftsmanship became the heart and soul of this job, naturally involving people who came out of the Brera Academy or who had studied artistic design or attended engraving and sculpture schools. In this way, we started to make everything ourselves, not just the costumes, jewellery, armour, wigs and shoes, but even the marionettes and the scenery.

We have introduced lots of innovations, including the lighting and mechanics of some stage tricks. We have worked hard on some of the features involved in expression, such as mouths, hands, wrists, eyes and even ears, because when the puppets sing, they must act with all their bodies. I will never use rear projection: I want my clouds to be made from tulle so that all children will be amazed by them. Even the voices have changed, since they are no longer spoken by the puppeteers, but by recorded actors, who knew how they spoke in the early 20th century, the same ones that we used at home. I like the idea of having our parts read by the great voices of people who are no longer with us, whom we will no longer hear on stage, such as Maria Callas, Giuseppe Di Stefano and Eduardo De Filippo. Being metaphors, metaphysical artifices, puppets can be represented by these famous voices. And lastly, innovation also implies that the director must be at the service of the author.

Training

My training was a miscellany of experiences. First, I was lucky enough to be born into and grow up in a family that had two centuries of theatrical puppetry behind it. Already by the age of three I was spending my time backstage at the Gerolamo Theatre, and this, I believe, was where I got my imagination, my dreams and my illusions from. After studying the classics at high school, I enrolled in the

Faculty of Humanities at the Cattolica University in Milan, graduating in theatre history under Professor Mario Apollonio, to whom I then became assistant.

In the mid-1960s, I put together a retrospective exhibition on the puppetry material of the Carlo Colla e Figli Company, saving the exhibits from destruction. The Milan City Council had wanted to knock down the Gerolamo Theatre to build a new road, prompting the Colla family, finding themselves without a base, to disband the company. The exhibition was the catalyst for the company's recreation, a choice that led us to be invited to perform, first by the Piccola Scala in 1967, and then by the Spoleto Festival.

I learnt everything there is to know about the theatrical business from the Colla family; I especially liked the fact that they were very critical, very severe. When I became the company's director, I still didn't really know what it entailed. The first thing I discovered was my desire to write. Then came the idea of subjecting myself to the demands of the stage and performance, because these needed to be liberated from the stiff 19th-century canons and to evolve both in terms of the marionettes' movements and the scenery. It was a great moment of self-transformation. The other important thing that I learnt is that art is not inherited with the chromosomes. I realized that it was pointless to think of it as a "family company" and that it was necessary to expand it to include people who had both enthusiasm and other key skills, such as sculpting and painting.

I still don't know if I am totally familiar with this craft, and that's what I like about it. Because it means that it is a path, for the moment, without an end, one that forces me to call everything into question and to rethink the theatre's potential in playing an educational role.

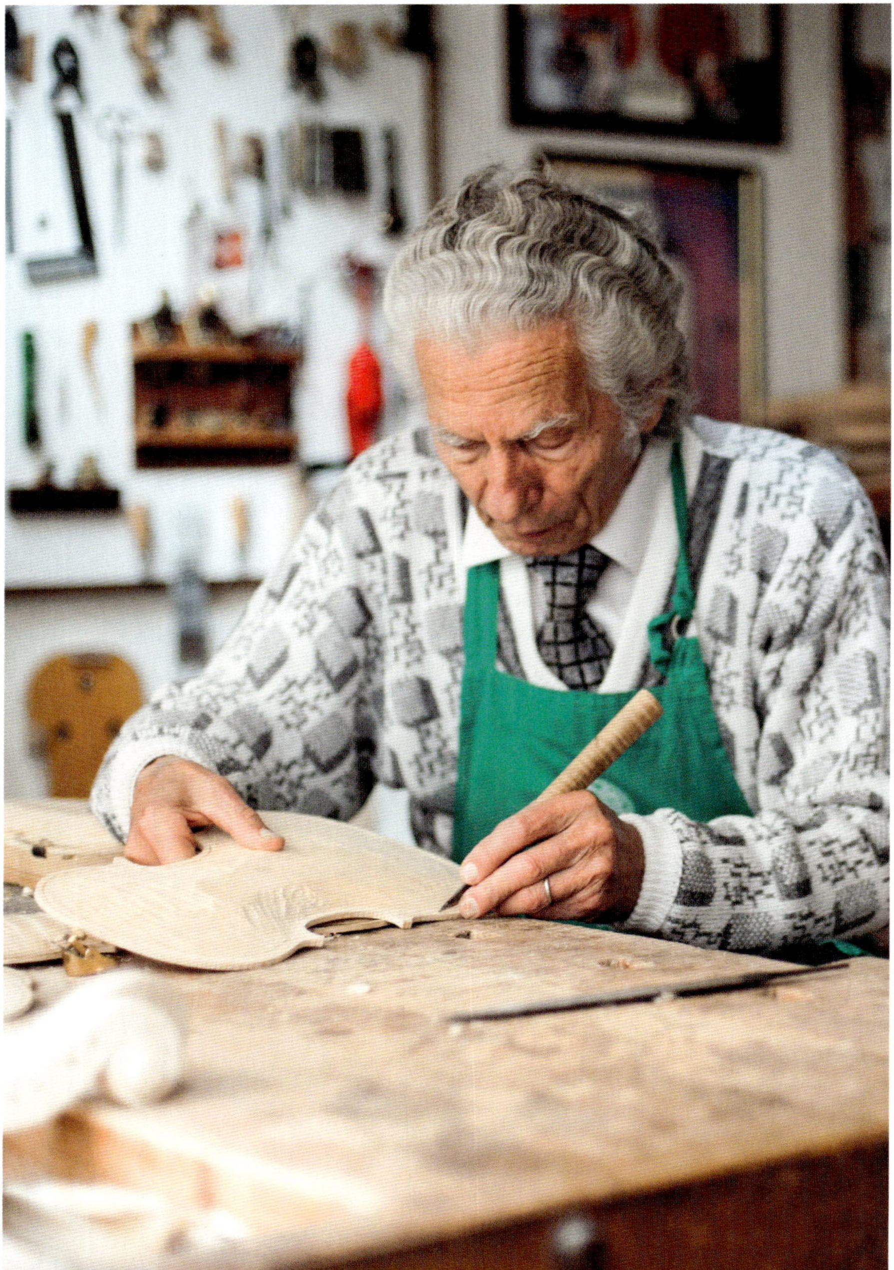

5.3.8. Gio Batta Morassi, violin-maker

Born in Cedarchis di Arta (Udine) in 1934, at the age of eight Gio Batta Morassi and his family moved to Camporosso, where his maternal grandfather managed a sawmill. He went to primary school in Camporosso and professional high school in Tarvisio. It was here, that, on account of his exceptional wood-engraving skills, in 1950 he obtained a four-year scholarship from the Udine Chamber of Commerce to attend the International Violin-Making School in Cremona.

After graduating in 1955, he joined the workshop of the Hungarian maestro, Peter Taràr. A few years later, and following a series of vicissitudes, Morassi took over from his master, who had meanwhile emigrated to the United States.

Famous as a maker and restorer of bow instruments and still active in Cremona, Morassi founded the Associazione Liutaria Italiana and the Cooperativa Editoriale Liutaria publishing cooperative, and organizes courses for young luthiers. He works as a consultant for the Teatro Comunale di Firenze and the Maggio Musicale Fiorentino, both in Florence, and for the Accademia Nazionale Santa Cecilia in Rome.

Morassi is also very well known in Japan, where he is considered one of the foremost exponents of Cremona's illustrious tradition.

Everybody knows that, in matters of wood, I am an expert. My maternal grandfather was a specialist at choosing the trees and felling them, and with parents and grandparents who managed a sawmill, I have been familiar with this subject since I was a young boy. However, I came to violin-making quite by chance. Now both my son and my grandson work in my workshop. We welcome students who come here to hone their skills, but they stay only for short periods. You can't take on a real apprentice like we used to because we no longer have the time to train them properly.

Authenticity

The instrument is authentic if it corresponds to what is described on the label (name, surname, date and place of construction), in other words if the maker is recognizable. We know that when an artisan first starts to work they do it in a certain way, but with the passing of time, depending on the life they live, the contacts they have with other people, changes come about. This usually happens to all violin-makers. Even Stradivari had his "amatizzato" period, when he learnt from Amati; then there was his golden age, from about 1705 to 1720, when he produced his most beautiful instruments; and finally his decline, his old age. Here again the issue is complicated because according to statistics Stradivari made about 1,200 instruments. I have researched lots of violin-makers from history and I am convinced that Stradivari didn't make as many as that. There was no electricity, not even for lighting. You do your best work in natural light. He didn't even have any machines to help him; he had to cut his pieces of wood with a saw. He had eleven children, of whom two became violin-makers – Francesco and Omobono – but we have no idea where their instruments ended up. Therefore they must have been passed off as Antonio's. But this probably happened at a later date, because we know that if Antonio's violins are worth 10, those of his sons are worth 2, 3 or 4 at the most.

All my instruments are certified, but there are lots of forgeries out there, as is also the case with many antique violins. Everything can be forged: stamp, signature, certificate. The only thing you can't copy is the instrument itself. Copying is one thing, imitating is another.

Competence

Competence has to do with sensitivity. An expert can say if an instrument plays well or badly even without playing it. True, you might be wrong, but if a badly made instrument plays well, it is pure chance. Some things can't be taught, they can only be learnt through experience. There was this man in Cremona who had invented a device for measuring if a piece of wood responded well or not, acoustically speaking. We would argue about whether it was better than a person's sensitivity. One day he came to my workshop with three pieces of pine wood, one very good, one normal and one no good. He challenged me to guess which was which. I picked them up and identified them all. He was flabbergasted!

Violin-makers cannot be violinists because their hands and fingers are too stiff from the work they do. While they don't have that musical sensitivity, they must know how to try out an instrument in the various positions. When a violinist says that one of the notes doesn't sound right, I have to fix it. You need a good ear, you need to have listened to many instruments – not just Italian, but from all over the world. Often, especially when musicians are young, while achieving a high level of perfection in sound or in execution, they don't explore the performance potential of the instrument. This, too, takes a certain degree of maturity. The violin-maker judges the work as well as the sound. The violinist judges the voice. I can hear immediately if it is a false voice or a long-lasting one.

In competitions, the winning violin becomes the benchmark for the next competition. But then after a lapse of time this instrument may not play so well any more. That's because when a violin is made of the finest thicknesses of wood, it plays well immediately, but the fullness of its sound is artificial, while it would sound more natural if the violin had been played a lot. On the other hand, if its components are thicker, the violin doesn't play well at first, because it needs to be played, the wood must vibrate continually. That's why violins in thin wood are used in modern competitions, and those who fall for them like amateurs are the violinists themselves. Why do antique violins still play well today? Because they have been played continually for hundreds of years. A violin that has been shut away in a museum display cabinet, even a Stradivari, needs to be played for several days before it regains its sound.

Craftsmanship

Almost all the work on the instrument is done by hand, especially those parts that are crucial for acoustics, such as the fitting of the bridge. Accessories for the instruments (chin rest, tailpiece, fingerboard, end pin, bridges, etc.) are bought ready-made; nobody makes them by hand any more, but they still need to be worked and adapted to the instrument.

We can tell one kind of wood from another, feel the differences between harder and softer veining, when we gouge it, saw it and use a hand plane. We need to be able to tell the difference with the sensitivity of our hand, by touch. If something is made by machine, you feel nothing, you can't sense this difference. This is crucial. Factories exist where they can make the entire instrument on machines, and many luthiers also use special – very small and very sophisticated – machines. Those luthiers usually keep the machines hidden in their cellars, so that nobody finds them out. But you can tell! It takes a well-trained eye, but the machine always leaves a trace. Whereas the imprint of the hand is completely different.

Creativity

Creativity comes above all from nature. From nature or from works of art. It is something that happens in the moment. It is not a system or a rule. It comes about while working, it is part of the process.

Interpretation

Between the design phase, which involves reasoning and planning, and the actual making of an instrument, aesthetic variations may occur. There is no fixed rule. Interpretation is important, as long as it is done by someone competent.

You may be born with a talent, but the context is also important: the place you live, what you have the chance of experiencing and studying. The animal kingdom, for example, provides important inspiration (I'm thinking of certain snails you come across in the sand). In Italy we have a bit of everything, from sea to hills and mountains, and this allows us to observe and absorb many different things.

You could say that each country has skills linked to the local area, to its way of living, to its culture, and even to religion.

Originality

It's a bit like the difference between a copy and an imitation… The violin shape can't be changed. Many violin-makers dream of inventing a new shape. I did, too, when I was young: I developed a Morassi model, but that style, that line already existed. Everybody has copied Stradivari, but they have interpreted him in their own way. Only Stradivari made and can make his violins. Personality is the most important thing; man's mark is unrepeatable. By observing the scroll, you can see if the violin was made by a professional or an amateur.

The scroll is the most significant imprint of a violin-maker, a mark of their personality, of their style: mine was inspired by a spiral designed by the famous architect Giacomo Barozzi da Vignola. Varnish, too, is a distinguishing feature; when some of my pupils used my formula, their varnish actually turned out differently. But that's normal: I got ten different results from ten different pupils.

It is important to take risks, but the outcome depends on the individual, on their courage, and even on whether they can remedy any mistakes arising from the risk they decided to take.

Talent

Talent is fundamental. If you don't have any, you'd be better doing something else. Talent is everywhere, even in your non-professional life: it is the ability to see things, to understand them. It doesn't have an exact origin, it's innate. Through work, you acquire experience and practice, but talent is something that only nature gives.

You can always spot talent immediately in a young person. There is always a sign, even in a child.

The talent of an accomplished craftsperson is indescribable! There are things that can only be understood by living together: you need to share all the good and bad moments that life gives us. You can't describe it in a few words.

Territory

Historically, Italy has always been at the forefront of violin-making. In addition, we know that the Italians have always had genius, flair, that special something. Eighteenth-century Neapolitan violins, all crooked and uneven, were made by Alessandro Gagliano, who studied in Cremona, and his descendants continued the family tradition almost

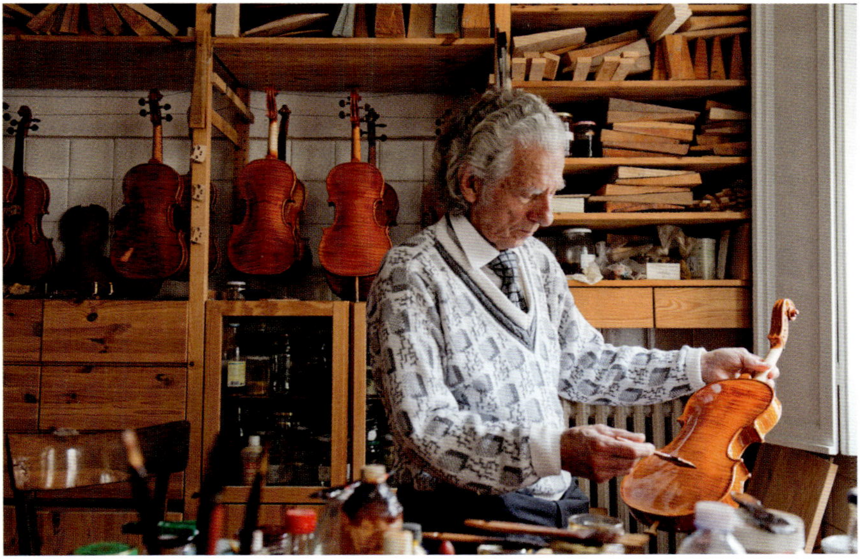

until the end of the 20th century. Their bent violins proved to be very popular and typical of the Neapolitan personality. Nicola Amati was the best of them all, in my opinion, both for his taste and for his design and refinement. Better even than Stradivari.

We are keen promoters of our violin-making in Cremona, but some very beautiful instruments have also been made in other countries. I have had a violin made by Amati and one by Jacob Stainer, who was a wonderful violin-maker. It is difficult to tell them apart, yet Stainer never came to Cremona and Amati never went to Austria. But they met in Venice, which was a musically important city, and had contacts with Innsbruck, Vienna and Budapest. That's how they copied each other.

The sound of the Italian violin stands out from others because of its timbre, the quality of its voice. The violin strings were originally made of catgut, which gave the instrument a much more beautiful, mellow sound. While that sound is extraordinary, most violinists nowadays prefer to use synthetic strings, from which they manage to obtain considerable results, especially in terms of power. Today's violinists want quantity, but this is wrong because what counts is quality.

The best wood for resonance is found in the Italian Alps, in Val di Fiemme, in the Cadore and Tarvisio districts. Up to the border with Austria, the wood has formidable acoustic qualities. The further north-east we go, the worse the wood gets. This is why in past times the violin-making schools in those countries couldn't achieve the same standards of instruments – the quality of the wood didn't give the same results. When I started my workshop years ago, I discovered that this high-quality wood also grows in the Tarvisio forest. Production is limited, but in this way I can provide beautiful wood also to other violin-makers, exporting it all over the world. Suffice to say, there used to be nothing in Cremona, and the same goes for the wood. But, over the decades, we created what Cremona represents today on the violin-making scene.

Tradition and innovation

Lutherie comprises three arts – sculpture, painting and music – and a scientific component that combines the technology of wood, chemistry and acoustic physics. I have always supported the principle that training is fundamental and essential for the continuation of this art. It takes schooling, internship, tradition; there are no short cuts. Without sufficient preparation you also jeopardize the legacy of the ancient instruments we have, because if masterpieces end up in non-expert hands, they will be destroyed instead of being preserved.

The secret of a Stradivarius lies in the varnish. Even Einstein, who was a fairly good musician, wanted to understand how it was that Stradivari's violins played so well, but after six months he gave up and went back to nuclear energy. Of the great French violin-makers, Jean-Baptiste Vuillaume managed to make technically accurate copies because he had the original Stradivarius violins in his hand. He was able to open them up and study them, but even he wasn't capable of recreating the same varnish. Half the world has gone mad trying to find Stradivari's original formula, which doesn't in fact exist. That's because it depends on the type of resin, on the environment. If the varnish is made in Cremona, it has one effect; if it's made in another city, with different climatic conditions, it changes completely. Nature never makes two things alike, not even the wood we use to make violins. Each piece must be treated differently, like people. Even twins have two characters, two mentalities, that make them completely different. We therefore need to approach the wood in the right way. That's the experience you get in the workshop, and it takes years to acquire.

Computer technology has done a lot to enable us to see and study Stradivarius and Amati models. While it is easier today, the mental process is missing, which is important because, when you make everything by hand, you train your eye working on the instrument. We also have modern materials, such as carbon fibre, that allow us to make the end pins of large instruments lighter, or the bows. With certain studies made into historical instruments at our disposal, and by using highly technological means, we can make incredible progress. There are ways to analyse an old violin soundboard, using a simple photo, to establish its origins and the date when the tree was felled. On the other hand, for working the wood itself, machines don't have human sensitivity.

There are certain principles – be they technological or inventive – that come from experience, practice and sensitivity. When you talk to other master craftspeople, you exchange know-how and something interesting and unexpected always comes out of it. These exchanges really contribute to the progress of our craft. In the end, despite advances in information technology and other technological and scientific developments, what counts for an excellent final result is the human touch, an expression of the maker's sensitivity, mastery and talent.

Training

I was pretty gifted in woodwork and artistic drawing, so when I finished middle school in 1950, the Udine Chamber of Commerce awarded me a scholarship to study violin-making in Cremona. At that time not even the inhabitants of Cremona themselves knew where the school was. It consisted of a single classroom inside the Carpentry Institute. The teaching body was unfortunately not up to their task and there was no master violin-maker. As a result, almost everyone opted for a different profession: some chose carpentry, others became office clerks. I, on the other hand, sat the test to become a master luthier and stayed on at the school, where I taught for 23 years. We called on two great masters from Milan, Giuseppe Ornati and Ferdinando Garimberti, considered to be the 20th century's best violin-makers, and the school slowly made a name for itself. Being in contact with these masters meant I really learnt about the craft. In parallel I opened my own workshop. The initial years were very difficult – selling a violin was no easy task – but we were used to fighting and I didn't lose heart.

It was one long learning curve. Like becoming a surgeon, it takes practice and sacrifice, as well as plenty of talent. You dedicate so much time to making an instrument, it's a very long, complicated process. This is why I say that the violin-maker's work must be fun, because when it's a passion it's not hard work. I think it's extremely important to stay up to date and, especially, to keep in contact with the top experts at the international level. You need to look around, be curious, while remaining critical. I have travelled a lot, all around the world, from the United States to Japan. A couple of years ago, I went to China, where I got to see first-hand the gigantic steps they are taking in this sector. I was greatly impressed: their lutherie and violin teaching courses are excellent, and they are starting to win the most prestigious European awards.

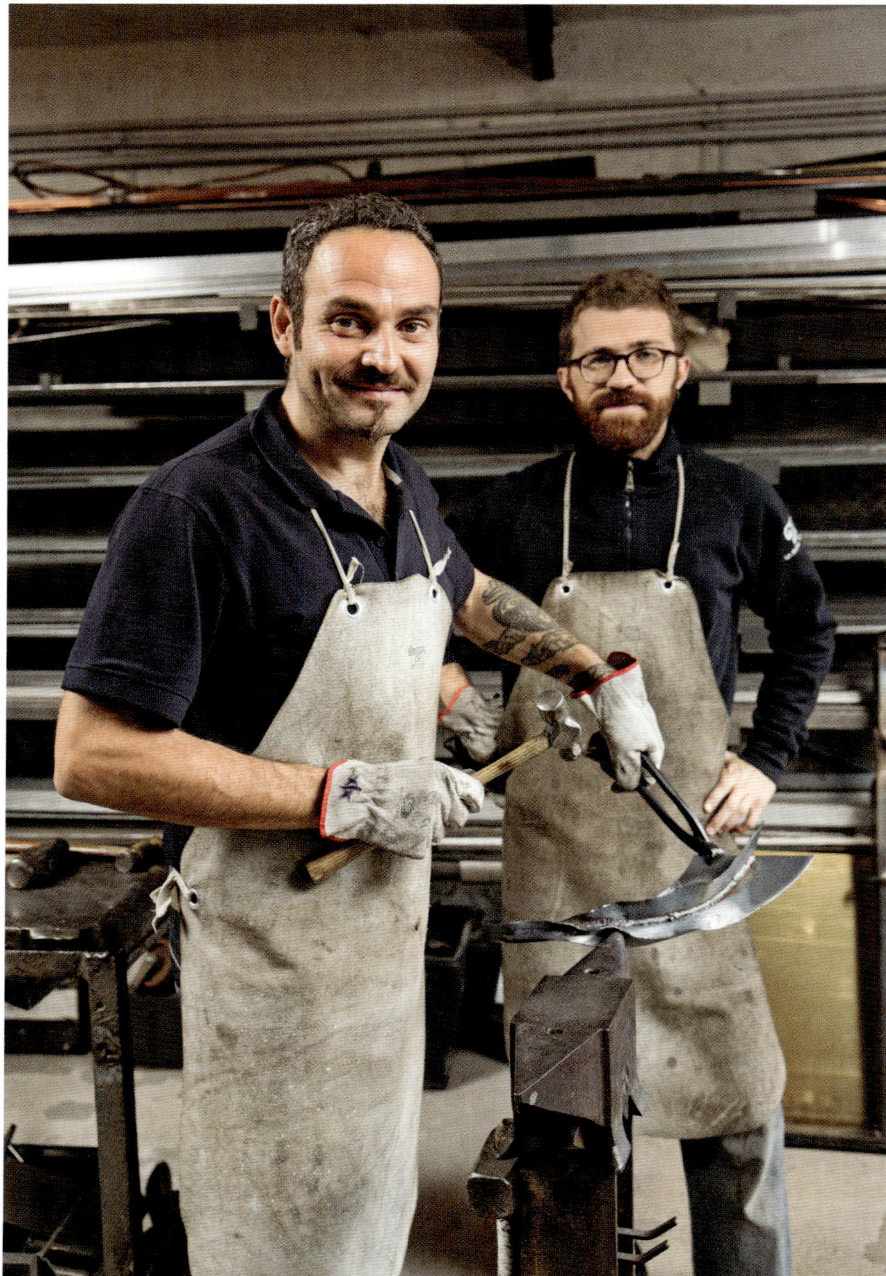

5.3.9. Alessandro Rametta and Andrea Capriotti, metal sculptors

Alessandro Rametta and Andrea Capriotti are the soul of La Fucina di Efesto (The Forge of Hephaestus), a Milanese workshop named after the Greek god of fire and metallurgy that has taken metal sculpting to new and glorious heights. Through their knowledge of the different materials and willingness to push the technical and creative boundaries, they transform metals, in particular iron, into exquisite designs and shapes. The duo, together with sculptor Nicolò Mulazzani, have explored many and varied levels of experimentation with passion and enthusiasm, resulting in the creation of unique collections and a singular manufacturing philosophy.

Rametta is skilled in both traditional techniques and innovative applications that focus on studying and reinterpreting the qualities of iron and other metals. Since the dawn of humanity, these materials, with all their expressive potential, have undergone transformation when they encountered fire. To this day, their alchemic and poetic properties are sources of inspiration for the craft world. Research and experimentation in this field thus aim to enhance the aesthetic impact of metals and their assorted and variegated chromatic contrasts and combinations.

Rametta and Capriotti have conducted extensive research on the different metals (iron, hard and mild steel, copper and brass) and techniques (often using heat) with the aim of enhancing the natural beauty of the raw materials.

[Alessandro Rametta:] My grandmother was a seamstress, and I grew up with her, among tailor's chalk and tape measures. We like to use the expression "metal tailoring", because very often our approach is similar to tailoring. In sculpture, especially, we lay out paper models on skeletons, then we trace them onto the sheet metal, shape it and model it.

Our workshop is a crossroads that has seen many young people pass through. But for the moment there are only two or, sometimes, three of us because we have limited space. Independence and interdependence are important in any training relationship. You need to have a vision of the entire creative process, which goes from imagining the spatial positioning of a work to its realization and installation. On principle, we try not to succumb to that possessiveness towards our craft that is typical of many artisans. Knowledge can only lead to further knowledge, and this means progressing, growing. If you build a wall around yourself, you end up eclipsing yourself.

Authenticity

Authenticity is the fruit of individual genius, achieved through your own sensitivity and experience. In our case, even our tools are emblematic.

Only a few craftspeople nowadays work with a forge, a hammer and an anvil. Even the untrained eye can tell the difference between a product that has been made in a forge and one that has not. The fact that our works are recognized proves that they convey this authenticity.

A joint signature is absolutely necessary if something has been created by two people. It is a combined effort, a synergy between designer and artisan. This does not, however, negate the fact that a badly made good idea is in any case a bad piece of work. And vice versa, any well-made bad idea is still a bad idea. No way around it.

Competence

You have competence when you start to have a vision of the whole, to imagine how a specific piece will look, its spatial impact, every crucial detail. It is the ability to understand the constructive and aesthetic requirements, while knowing what difficulties you will face. We are obliged to go into this detail. We can't say "I will think about it as I go along". The material itself demands it. This approach is essential because iron is not an easily worked, pliable material; even making a simple hole calls for effort. Despite this, you will still come up against problems and the unexpected. Only practice, experience, study and perseverance will teach you how to overcome them.

We believe that you can get great inspiration from books, and even from talking to people, because it opens your horizons. For us, human resources are a value to invest in. It is important to establish a real rapport with your team, and even the relationship with the client requires dialogue and empathy. We are pleased to say that the people we work with are also our friends. Relationships endure because a good job has been done, an experience shared. Otherwise we wouldn't get anywhere.

Craftsmanship

This craft has very long turnaround times, and if you are unable to relate serenely and respectfully to the natural cycles of creation it can be very testing. It's difficult to be an artisan today; it's almost an anachronism, precisely because of this concept of time. Everything moves so quickly, it all has to be done yesterday. Instead, our work teaches patience and constancy.

We have a very empathetic, loving relationship with our material, especially when it is hot. It is also important for us to feel the iron, in a tactile sense.

In our opinion, masterly made expresses two concepts: "knowing what" and "knowing how". On the one hand, it calls for awareness, and on the other for the ability to find solutions. It means completing a task perfectly, by finding the simplest way, while respecting function and the harmonious dialogue between form and space. In this sense we also focus on rhythm. Achieving that aesthetic touch tells us that the job has been well done.

We personally follow each of the production stages, even when they are contracted out: the very idea of abandoning one of our pieces is inconceivable, because they never stop representing us.

Our work is almost the antithesis of series production. Our philosophy is the uniqueness of each piece, the fact that there isn't another one like it. In all these years we have never repeated anything. As we are making bespoke, customized items, we accompany the client through the creative process, and each piece has that touch that makes it unique and completely artisanal.

Creativity

We draw creative inspiration from our practice but also from nature, architecture and art, our relationship with clients, study, research and experimentation. For us, creativity is the ability to listen and to observe. To be there in the present. To create something. We believe in involving our clients in the creative process. The quality of our work is paramount, so we draw on our experience to calculate the exact time we'll need to complete a job without compromising on that quality. This is one of our distinguishing features: we strive to put forward workable proposals while endeavouring to enhance our deep knowledge of iron, a material that will last forever.

Interpretation

We are assuming that perfection is a relative concept. Only nature has a universally recognized aesthetic value. Differences in styles and tastes dictate what is beautiful for one culture or for another. We Italians have a natural inclination for beauty, as evidenced by our cultural, architectural and artistic heritage. We are the heirs of all those who have shaped our history. Our master artists and artisans, from Dante to Da Vinci to Stradivari, are celebrated worldwide. It's in our genes.

The "Made in Italy" label is recognized everywhere as a mark of excellence, and this is reopening opportunities to approach new markets abroad in which to promote our talents, our culture and our tradition. Italy could quite well live off its cultural heritage, in the broadest sense of the word.

Originality

The research, experimentation and manufacturing requirements of every single piece we make are an invitation to reflect on the possibilities the material presents us with. In this way, we combine originality and innovation. It enables us to move forward, seeking originality in everything we create.

Taking risks and pushing the rules is paramount. Our methods border on engineering, arising from a conscious knowledge that derives from our know-how. Iron has a resistance and an elasticity that allow to experiment with dynamics and false equilibrium. We like playing with balance, shifting the barycentre without the structure losing any of its solidity. We have made these discoveries through our research, which centres always on the materials' potential.

We have never reproduced two identical objects. During restoration work we have replicated certain decorations, but always adopting a different approach and techniques.

Talent

Talent is the soul's desire to satisfy and cultivate its own curiosity. We base our relationships on empathy and sympathy, and we try to build an understanding with the people we work with. But it is also important to gauge how willing someone is to step up to the plate, to get their hands dirty. Working with metal is a fairly rare passion.

We hope that over time there will no longer be any distinction between creative and manual talent. Talent works in a cycle, it requires you to imagine, to reflect and then to accomplish your work. It is a passion that must be kept alive. The driver of the soul in both young and old is always the same, although an older person may have the capacity to delve deeper within themselves. We don't think that it's possible to put the question in different terms. We really like those older people who still have that look, that desire to do and discover things.

Territory

Milan has always been a centre of iron and other metals. We are thinking of the Napoleonic foundries, but also of the works of Alessandro Mazzucotelli and the significance of Art Nouveau for Milan, home to the most beautiful and influential schools. Iron is just about everywhere. Even today, Italian foundries are still in operation. Competition from other countries has increased, and this is not a good thing because they dictate the prices. A civilization with steelworks is a rich civilization.

On the former Bovisa industrial estate, there are still many artisanal workshops because there are many suitable locations. There you will still find craftspeople who work iron in the traditional way, to whom we outsource certain large pieces which we can't make ourselves because of our limited space.

Milan is very fertile ground. It has a sizeable support industry, and

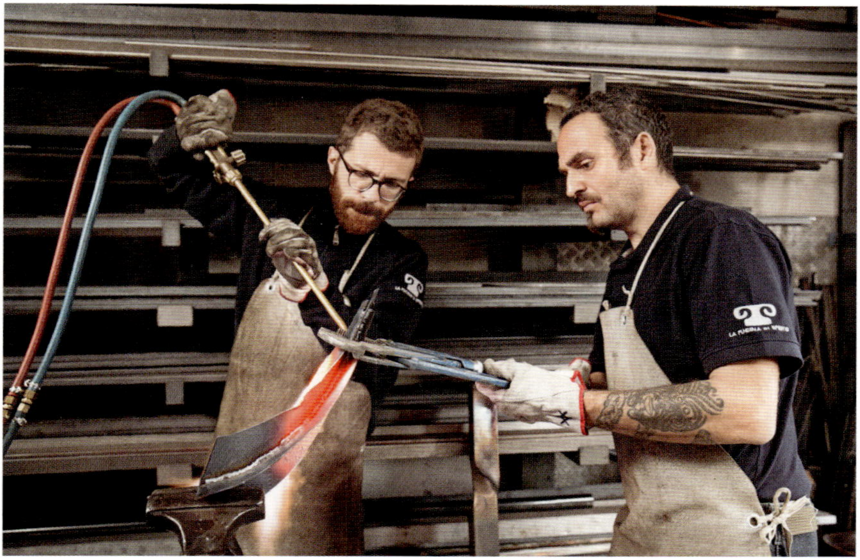

the clients are always very interesting. This enables us to gain inspiration from a variety of angles.

Tradition and innovation

We use traditional techniques such as hammering, forging, twisting and inlay, the latter being a technique only a very few artisans use nowadays. We are tied to certain elements – fire, anvil, hammer – that have always been and always will be the same, but we do try to introduce innovation through design, finishes and a decorative touch that has an artisanal feel. We spend every free moment experimenting, for example to test the response of iron to acids, salt, rust and abrasion. We hope one day to publish the results of our research.

Research and experimentation are vital for us: without them there can be no future. They constitute an investment in our business. Every job is planned consciously, and at the end we go over each phase and analyse the problems that have arisen, because you can't rule out the unexpected. Innovation is inherent in research.

The material has not changed, even if, owing to constant recycling, it is now far less pure. It is more porous, which is obvious from the huge quantity of waste it produces. Besides which, contamination by aluminium or other materials has made it difficult to braze-weld it at melting point, a technique that used to be widespread in the past.

We design with AutoCAD or other similar programs, which enables us to represent three-dimensional objects from every angle. Even so, the finished item is always much more beautiful than anything we could possibly have designed or even imagined.

Technology is the icing on the cake. Today we employ machines for our sculptures that allow us to do plasma cutting, grinding and welding with incredible precision. It has allowed us to evolve. For the more common metal sculptures, however, these applications aren't as useful, because tradition still prefers fusion, such as bronze and lost-wax casting.

We favour an interdisciplinary approach: through contacts with artisans who work with other materials we learn techniques that can be applied to our own materials. It's essential for developing our expertise, for absorbing new methods. And it's reciprocal. We strongly believe in sharing knowledge, and we are convinced of the importance of training young people.

Training

[Alessandro Rametta:] Our experience with metal was a choice dictated by circumstances. I've always liked working with my hands, and after completing technical high school I did an apprenticeship in a workshop that made parts for elevators, where I learnt to weld. I was crazy about metal, enamoured with the possibilities for assembling it, transforming it. Then I studied philosophy at university because I hadn't explored this discipline yet. Meanwhile, my closest friend and I used his grandfather's old forge as a workshop and hangout. That's how I learnt; I was self-taught, driven by my passion for sculpture.

The sculpting process is complex, but when you know the material, it becomes much more accessible, because you don't just assemble it, you mould it. In the end I realized that I wanted to devote my life to this medium. The more time passed, the more I was convinced that this was the right path. Even now, with all the difficulties and the recession, I can't imagine it any other way. A workshop is an exciting place, and working there brings you physical, mental and spiritual peace. It is always very gratifying to see a job finished.

Mastering this craft was a long process. It took me seven years before I could fully take pleasure in the knowledge I had acquired. The beauty of this craft is that it is always different; indeed, experience helps you deal with the difficulties and the obstacles you encounter in every situation. Research, study and experimentation are essential in our job, which we have expanded from sculpture to include design, interior design and restoration.

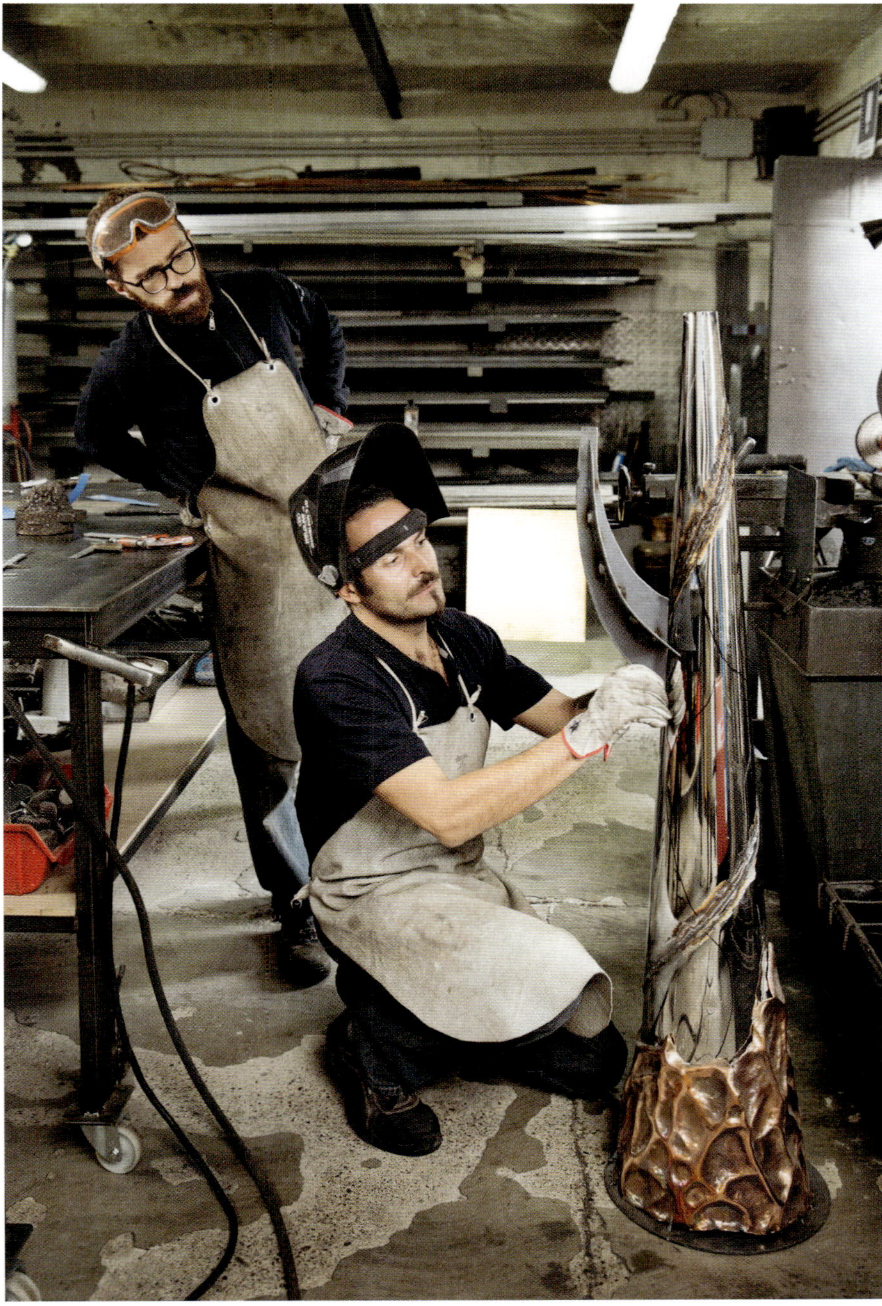

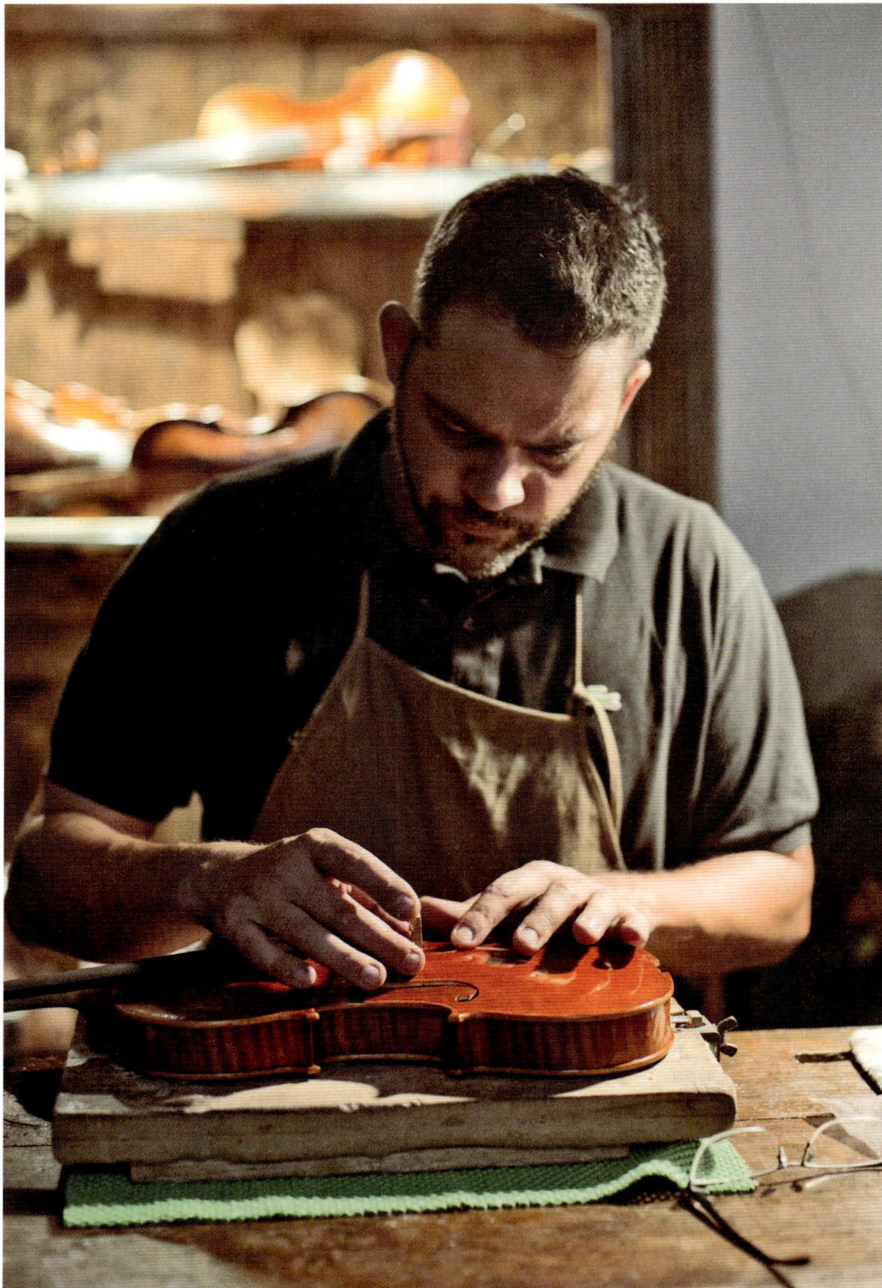

5.3.10. Lorenzo Rossi, violin-maker

A teacher since 2008 at the Civica Scuola di Liuteria *(the Municipal Violin-Making School) in Milan (from which he also graduated with full marks), Lorenzo Rossi started his own business making bowed string instruments in 2003. In 2008 he won two silver medals in the violin and cello categories at the national competition in Pisogne and in 2012 a bronze medal for his cello in the so-called "Lutherie Olympics", the three-yearly international Stradivari competition in Cremona. After obtaining a specialist diploma in the construction of bowed string instruments, he also took up restoration work, attending workshops run by the masters Carlos Arcieri, Guy Rabut and Greg Alf. Participation in these courses of international repute not only ensured he remained constantly in tune with new techniques and materials, but also gave him the opportunity to compare different styles and methods upon which he could develop his own distinctive style. When building modern instruments, Rossi uses models inspired by the Milanese school, while for reproductions he copies traditional antique Italian instruments.*

Rossi chooses the wood himself, and all processes are carried out in controlled environments entirely by hand. He uses animal-based glues and, unless the client explicitly requests otherwise, he prefers amber-based oil varnishes, prepared in his workshop using the ancient recipes he mixes personally. Great care is taken with the base coat, to ensure it seals the wood without clogging the pores and lends depth to the overlying varnish.

For Rossi, fine-tuning a bowed string instrument is the most delicate and interesting aspect of his work. Achieving the right balance is the result of a synergy between musician and maker; together in the workshop the two seek and find the best compromise between the instrument's potential and acoustic requirements, bearing in mind the player's comfort.

My father is a technical drawer, who used to design oil rigs for a US multinational. He is also a great handyman, able to do just about anything in the home, from plumbing to furniture repair. I inherited my passion for craftsmanship from him.

My children are still very small. The eldest has great fun when he comes to the workshop, but I don't know if I would like him to take up this profession. As a dream, from the heart, I would say yes. But it's a complicated life, always under pressure, always on the edge. Beyond the beauty, the appeal of this job, we face the same problems of all craftsmanship.

The issue of apprenticeship is complicated, regulated by laws that often don't meet the needs of an artisanal workshop. Craftspeople always find themselves having to run their own businesses, with little time to spend training an apprentice, which calls for a lot of energy. If you don't have very quick pupils who, by themselves but under your supervision, absorb, build on and develop the lessons you teach, the quality of the work in your workshop will suffer. You need to find the right person with the right attitude. The same goes for recruiting new staff. Hiring somebody right now in Italy is a huge expense, and a big problem that needs resolving for all artisans.

Authenticity

In relation to my craft, authenticity means having personally built all the parts of the instrument and being responsible for all the stages of design, construction and fine-tuning, from beginning to end. This makes it an authentic instrument, made by me. The client demands proof of this, and my certificate of authenticity provides it. In fact, on the international market, certification has become an imperative today for bowed string instruments.

There has always been a lot of confusion in our world. At this moment in the history of contemporary lutherie it would a great thing if there was a documentation protocol for the construction of every single instrument. The certificate is a small step in this direction.

The place of production is absolutely connotative. The name of the author, today as in the past, is strictly linked to the city of origin. Stradivari is Cremona, just as Montagnana is Venice and Gagliano is Naples.

The authenticity of your instrument is provided by your style, by your way of working, together with your signature and certificate.

Competence

A craftsperson is competent when they have been trained – at school and through lots of hands-on experience – in a way that is correct for the product they will create and sell. It is technical competence and more.

Competence must be taught to employees and pupils. Managing relationships is part of the job, there's no getting away from it. I think that in order to have, you must give. If you are the head of a workshop and you have people working for you, your role must be well defined, recognized and recognizable. You have to make sure your team fall in love with their craft. This means explaining it to them, pushing them, giving them the energy and the desire using all means possible, be it laughing, joking, getting cross, reprimanding them. In addition to being in the workshop, you must be able to take your craft to the outside world, show it at its best, manage client relations. That, too, is part of competence.

Craftsmanship

Every bit of this craft is artisanal, nothing is automated. It starts with choosing the wood, which I do in person – Val di Fiemme for spruce or Bosnia for maple – using local sawmills to obtain the sizes I need, respecting the old rules for the correct cutting of the wood to be used for bowed string instruments.

In general, the modern concept of masterly made is achieving symmetrical, almost synthetic, perfection. This is very different from the way perfection was interpreted in the 17th and 18th centuries, and which is my working reference. Nowadays, absolute perfection is mechanical – a depersonalized serial job, with little expressive potential or life. The craftsperson's work, meanwhile, must be fuelled by experience, energy, passion and humanity. Perfection means one thing for a businessperson, quite another for a musician. And something different again for me, an artisan. My task is to achieve the best I can in terms of artistic and aesthetic expression. An imperfection has a very high added value that must be present because it reveals that an instrument is hand-made: it is the mark of the hand that performs the work. Instruments by Stradivari or Guarneri del Gesù are – to some degree or other – distorted and asymmetric. But you look at them and you say: "What a fine job"! Why? Because in the past, to be beautiful and well made, an instrument somehow had to be expressive rather than adhere to geometric and mathematical formulas. It's like the asymmetry of a face. While you work, you do it almost without realizing it, with that information that is yours alone and which gives character to your piece. These are things that you see and realize only when you've finished.

Creativity

Creativity for an artisan may be innate, but you can't define yourself by that creativity. A luthier does a traditional job, governed by many rules. We can perhaps express our creativity in the way we use the tools or in the construction of a customized tool, specially designed to make a given task easier to accomplish. Perhaps creativity can be detected in the overall quality of the work, but it cannot determine the finished instrument.

Interpretation

Interpretation is an attitude you develop as you work. Ours is a very complex craft: every bowed string instrument is the result of a fusion of art, craft and science. Once finished, the instrument is adapted and fine-tuned to the hand and ear of its future player. This means that there is a strongly subjective interpretation on the part of the musician. There is objectivity in beauty, of course, but the finer aspects – which

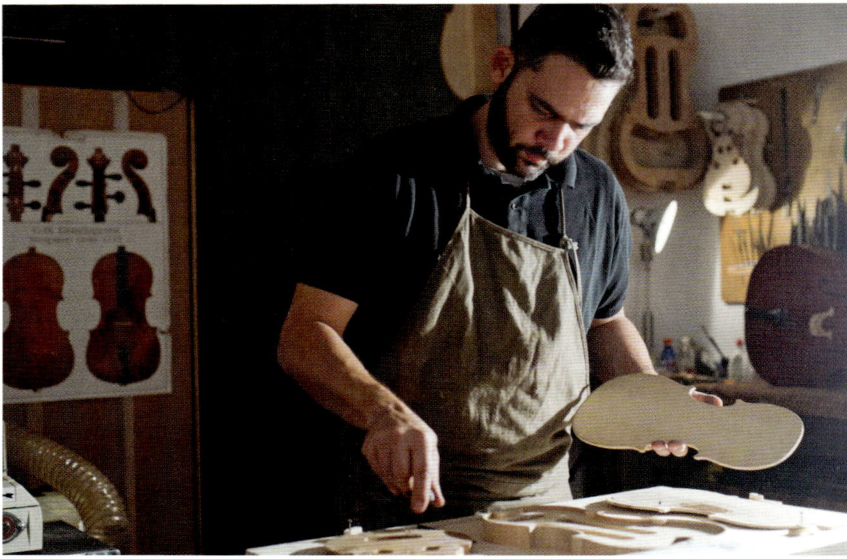

are what give your work that added value – are extremely personal. For this reason, I don't think there is a predetermined point of arrival; it is a continual quest for agreement, a link between musician and luthier.

Perfection is always subjective: both the client and I must like the instrument. Interpretation is vital, because through it you endow your work with your personality. While the client may be more concerned with the acoustics, all the rest is my prerogative. Things are different when you want to reproduce an antique instrument. If a musician requires a copy of the Stradivari 1712, it should be recreated with worn varnish, warts and all. That is a different kind of project.

Italian violins are traditionally considered to be the best, and many people come to us to buy them. Some artisans are better known than others, probably because they have a stronger entrepreneurial spirit.

Originality

Taking risks is essential. People are often gripped by a reverential fear when faced with certain situations, but this must absolutely be overcome. If you don't take risks, you get nowhere. You can't move a millimetre at a time if you have to cover 10 miles. You will never get to the end. Give it a go, start running! The worst that can happen is that you trip and fall. If you hurt yourself, you get up and start again. Absolutely nothing will happen. At the very worst, you make a mistake and do it over. I'm not talking just about the technical skills you use when making an instrument, but also about bumping into the world's greatest musician and plucking up the courage to introduce yourself.

In artisanal production, originality is the personal character that you put into every instrument. We talked earlier about expressing a detail in a certain way, which in the context gives the instrument its aesthetic balance. Getting technical, I have a certain way of making the purfling tips that is my own personal method, both in terms of construction and aesthetics. Originality can also lie in how you make the edge, whether it is thick or thin, or how you work the curve. These are things that happen unconsciously; you look at the instrument and you realize you always do it like that, and hope that it is right and that people will like it.

Talent

Compared with the enthusiasm and eagerness to work, talent counts for about half. If you don't have any talent, you can only get so far, up to the limit that we all have. If you like, talent is a way of measuring a person's objective limits. Those with no limits are probably very talented. When you work, there must be synergy between executive talent and creative talent. Trying to push your own limits ever further is something that must be cultivated a little bit more every day, corresponding to that little extra technique that you then need to "demonstrate" your talent.

In talented young people, you can glimpse skill and, probably, a capacity to reach objectives faster than others. An experienced craftsperson's talent lies in the consolidation of their own craft, their own art.

Territory

The craft of building bowed string instruments is practised throughout the world, although its historical – and consequently its modern-day – importance still resides here in Italy, in Lombardy. There are various longstanding Italian schools based in Naples, Florence, Rome, Venice and Milan. But the most famous is Cremona. Geographical origins are very important in this business, especially for antique instruments, and the antique Italian violin is the best seller of them all.

Training and exchanges with colleagues determine an Italian style that is internationally recognizable. After 10 to 15 years practising this craft, this is something that you will have absorbed, that will always remain with you. The same question of historical ties to territory and tradition goes for the materials. The wood for the back of the instrument, the ribs and the neck comes from the Balkans, whereas the top, called the belly or table, is made from red spruce found in the Alps in north-eastern Italy, the Val di Fiemme in particular. This pine is absolutely the best for resonance. If you make an instrument with a different kind of pine, you won't get the same result.

Tradition and innovation

You need to stay close to the rules in your workmanship, in your search for materials, in your methodology. Now we use band saws rather than handsaws to open the trunks, but the luthier's craft is totally traditional. Since Stradivari, no changes have been made to the violin. There are no other ways. The problem today lies in what is happening on a cultural level. A professional musician, pushed aside owing to cuts in spending on culture or because the orchestra has closed or the theatre has been put under temporary receivership, will think twice before spending 10,000 to 15,000 euro on a violin made by a luthier. They are more likely to buy a factory-made product of average quality at a much lower price. In China, where they churn out 5,000 instruments a day, the factories do everything possible to reduce production times and costs. Mind you, this is nothing new. At the end of the 19th century, artisanal factories in France and Germany produced a huge number of instruments, but those "factories" employed artisans who worked in series production. This was very different from today's mass production.

Innovation in lutherie almost always stops at the experimental stage. In the United States, a lot of effort has been put into scientific research to investigate the construction techniques and wood treatments used by masters from the past. For the construction of new instruments, some people use Computer Numerical Control (CNC) procedures to ensure the outside of the violin always has the same curve. Some are experimenting with all-carbon construction. This concept does not have many supporters in the world of Italian luthiers, and I am not a fan either. Violins are traditionally made from wood. The only "scientific" tool I use is a piece of equipment created by a bow-maker in Cremona who died a couple of years ago. This measures the speed of sound inside a piece of wood. It is an extra source of help, but it is only one of thousands of variables that must be tackled individually every day when making a violin.

This is a very specialist craft, involving a variety of instruments. I make violins, violas and cellos; others make mandolins, guitars and lutes; yet others make viols and double basses. We're all in the same boat, but have very different skills. Exchange of information with the others fosters a collaborative mentality that helps everybody to grow and keeps this craft alive. This dialogue is key, because achieving excellence in our work requires the union of lots of different details. It is more a question of mental than practical innovation.

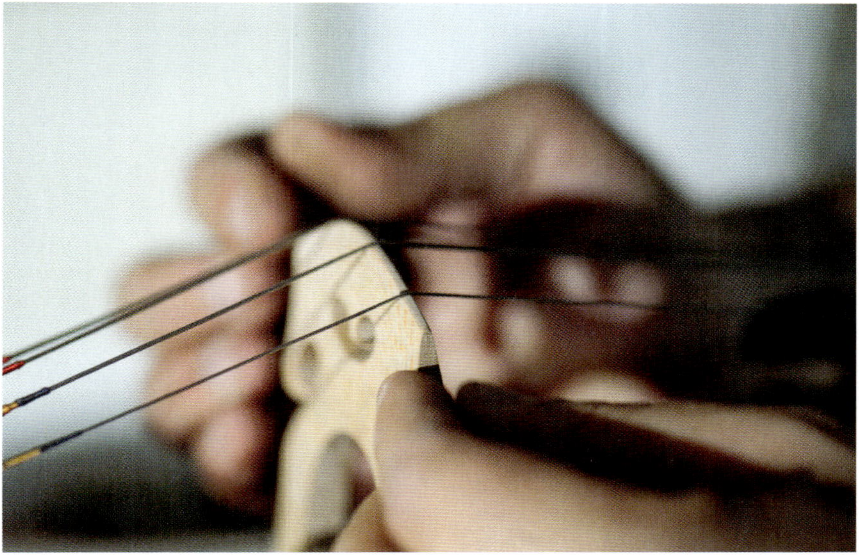

Training

My initial priority was my studies. After obtaining my diploma in mechanics from technical high school, I enrolled at the University of Milan and attended physics classes for the first two years and then switched to materials science. My life changed the day I met a luthier, when I went along with a friend who needed a guitar repaired. I dropped out and enrolled in the *Civica Scuola di Liuteria* in Milan, from which I graduated with full marks four years later. I opened my workshop in 2003, after spending time in the workshops of my former masters to perfect the craft. I've always wanted to understand, to know more. The school offers a very complete and important foundation on which you must then build and develop your own style, strengthening your skills. It is therefore essential to take specialization courses, organized in Italy by professional associations (Associazione Liutai Italiani, Liuteria Parmense and Consorzio Liutai Cremonesi, for example) on specific topics and with contributions from great masters.

Work means responsibility – registering for a VAT number, thinking about setting up a business, meeting deadlines, giving yourself goals. Crucially, if you ever stop, you lose your manual skills, you become unfit like an athlete after stopping training, and then you really have to work hard to recover. Therefore, if you want to move ahead you must be there. Every day.

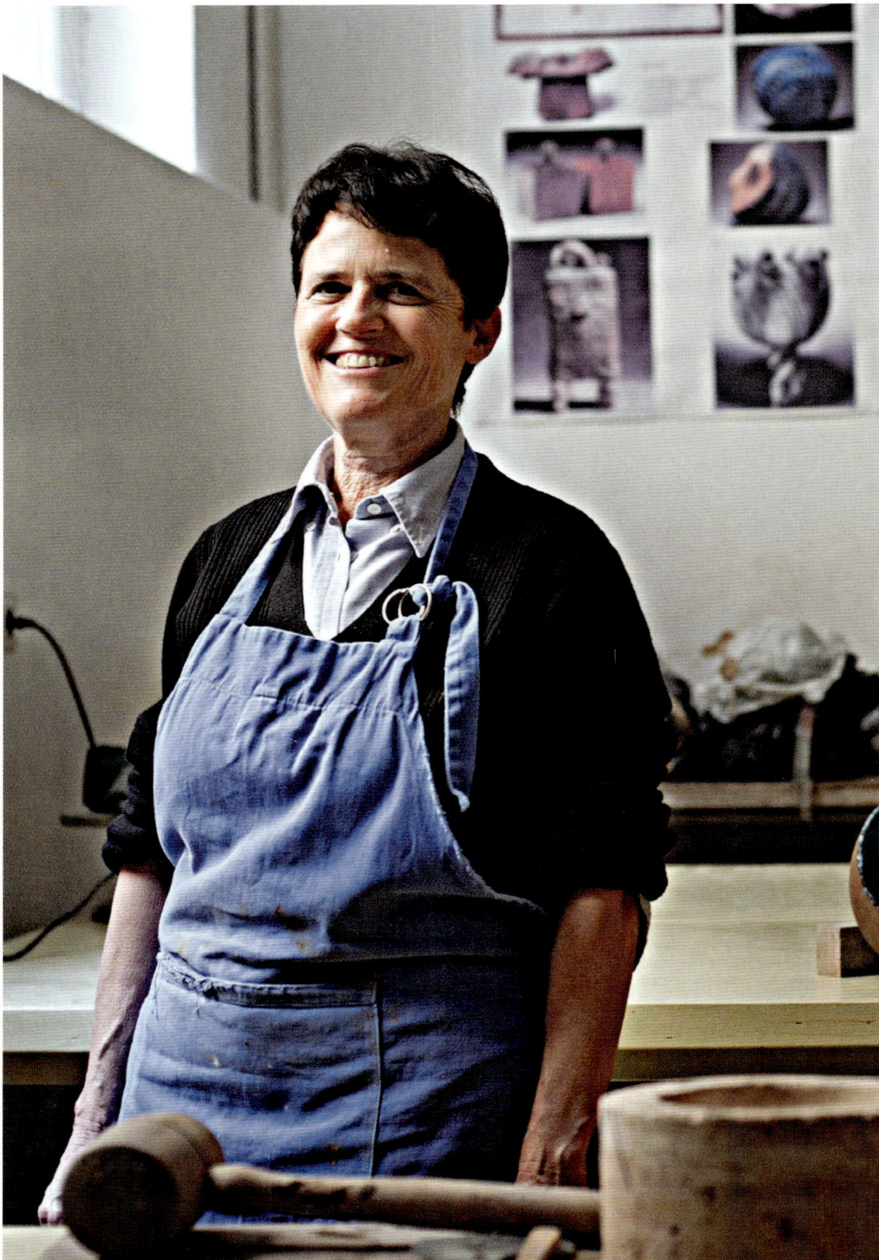

5.3.11. Gabriella Sacchi, ceramicist

Gabriella Sacchi was born in Milan in 1951. After completing artistic high school in Brera, she went on to study architecture at Politecnico di Milano.

In the 1980s and 90s, Sacchi worked as an art teacher and as an editorial consultant. During the same period, she co-wrote a book on art education with the Italian artist and designer Bruno Munari. She founded Laboratorio Nibe in 1981 and Spazio Nibe in 2002, where she devotes her time to creating ceramic sculptures and conducting cultural, research and promotional activities in the field of ceramics. Considered to be one of the foremost contemporary Italian ceramists, Sacchi regularly works with designers and architects, and her pieces have been included in some of the most prestigious exhibitions in Italy and abroad.

In her workshop, Sacchi is in charge of every stage of production, from design to execution, of objects in majolica, stoneware, raku and terra sigillata. Her work covers the themes of travel, memory and the past. In addition, jointly with other professionals, Sacchi organizes and teaches courses on a variety of subjects.

My family has always had very close links with art. My great-grandfather, Gaetano Previati, was a Symbolist painter in the Divisionist style and, consequently, my mother insisted that my education include art. She was the one who suggested that I go to artistic high school. While I have always believed that, if you concentrate and really want to, you can learn techniques, I also think the cultural baggage you receive from your family is very important.

The nature of my work does not allow me to have apprentices, but I do hold courses in my workshop and a few of my former pupils have made a career out of ceramics. As for the transmission of this craft, the workshops of the past – where you had a whole team of people involved in creating an object – no longer exist. Today you work alone in your workshop or with a few, often temporary, helping hands.

Authenticity

The element of authenticity is present when you can attribute a work to a master or to a school with absolute accuracy.

Something can be called "authentic" when its creator is able to assimilate historical and territorial elements and interpret them in a personal style that is also an expression of a personal vision. In this sense, if an object is to have the added value that distinguishes it from a similar object, the materials and techniques used to create it are not enough. At times, even the signature of the workshop of origin might not be enough, because a single workshop may produce works for all manner of tastes.

In the past, I have made pieces for a designer. What I was required to do was mainly the execution of an idea, in the knowledge that what had to emerge was not my personality, but that of the designer. Let me give you an example: when you launch a new clothing collection, it is obvious that it will be the result of the work done by the designer, the tailors and many other people. The tailor obviously has very high technical and interpretive skills, but the fashion show is mainly associated with the designer's name. The relationship between the designer and the tailor is the same as that between the designer and the artisan who makes the object. I think it is right that the different skills be indicated by two signatures, but I also think that the designer will have greater visibility than the artisan. The design skills should take precedence, because the implementation is at the service of the design.

Competence

First and foremost, you need to link the concept of competence to the kind of work you choose to do. The creation of a unique piece calls for all-round expertise. Serial production, by contrast, requires very specific skills. If all you need to do is a certain kind of decoration, competence is simply a case of having "a good hand" and the ability to follow the original. If, on the other hand, the goals are more diffuse and design-oriented, the word "competence" takes on a broader meaning to encompass also design skills and knowledge of the materials and their expressive possibilities. But even that is not enough, because many are the things you should know, and they come from different worlds: culture, art, family, school… And, lastly, there's also the specific expertise relevant to your artistic field, because each material has its own aesthetics.

You also need to be in tune with the contemporary scene, because otherwise you risk making things that have neither value nor meaning. If your goals go beyond producing a very limited output, over time you gain expertise. You become properly competent in your chosen field when you manage to achieve the desired result.

Competence is also essential in managing relationships and in being able to pass on what you know. I have come across some very talented professionals who don't know how to teach, while others refuse to do so because they don't want to transfer their knowledge. I have no problem with sharing my know-how. If someone happens to use my ideas, it irks me a little, but only because I am amazed that they can't be bothered to have their own ideas. It's more a criticism of their mental attitude, because while someone is copying my idea, I am already working on something different. I can't stop at one thing, I have to move on to the next.

What interests me is that people recognize me for the entirety of my work, not just for a single element.

Craftsmanship

I produce very small series or unique pieces, therefore my work is done entirely by hand. Even the relationship I have with the materials is a direct one – for me it is essential to experiment with all of them. Before choosing the six types of clay that I work with now, I tried out at least fifty. At the moment I am using an Italian clay for the few things that I still make in majolica, but I mainly use German or Spanish clays. Almost all my work is in high-temperature clay, a formula which has no tradition in Italy.

In artisanal work, the design stage is very important, as is the idea, the vision, which must be expressed in a way that corresponds to and suits the material.

An object is masterly made when you can recognize the person or the "school" that designed it and realized it.

Because in artisanal production, an object can be made either by the person who designed it, and who is therefore completely familiar with the idea that generated it, or by someone trained to reproduce it, with very good knowledge of the initial idea.

If we look at a fresco in the style of Giotto, only a great expert can, perhaps, tell the difference between Giotto's hand and that of one of his pupils. In industrial production, on the other hand, the many different stages are segmented, and even if the person carrying out a single stage has good practical skills, they will not necessarily be aware of the thought behind the design. In big architectural firms there are people who spend their lives designing door and window frames, without ever knowing in what kind of design context they will be used.

Creativity

When people say to me: "Ideas don't come to me like they do to you", I reply: "It's true, but it's also true that, for about 30 years now, my thoughts have been focused almost exclusively on my work." If I have three hours of free time, I go to an exhibition. When I travel, I visit museums of all kinds. I'm interested in many things that don't necessarily have a link with ceramics. I always carry lots of notepaper in my bag, on which I jot down anything that strikes me in particular. I think this is a feature that distinguishes a creative approach from a repetitive one. A skilled craftsperson might be able to copy things very

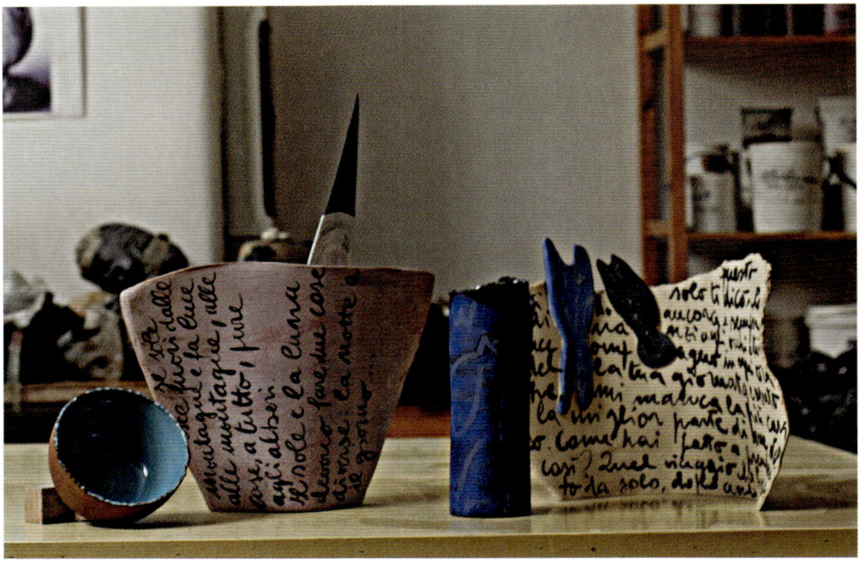

well but their work will have little life, whereas a craftsperson who has "soul" will manage to express this in their work.

Interpretation

According to the dictionary definition, an artisan is a skilled worker who makes things by hand. The artisan turns a design – by a community or an artist – into a product worthy of attention when they achieve the best interpretation of the design itself.

Therefore, it is also important to know how to interpret, because this ability enables you to collaborate with other designers.

Nowadays, there are more designers than artisans. This is having a profound effect on the future of craftsmanship. If you need a decent miniature reproduction of Michelangelo's statue of David to sell in a museum, all you need to do is to find a good, professionally trained craftsperson. But if you want to sell, as part of the museum's merchandising, a product with added value, you'll need to find people who have a more global vision of the artistic object.

Therefore, if we want to talk about the future of craftsmanship, we have first to think about training, which is the essential element. If we truly believe that we still need people who work with their hands, we must look at how schools were organized in the past, the same schools that we are currently shutting down. We need to reconsider the whole concept of training.

Originality

The most interesting artefact is the one that manages to interpret the spirit of the original design. And by "original design" we don't mean just the idea of a single individual, but also the ideas that stem from within a community in any given place. Take, for example, the craftsmanship of non-industrialized countries: it's interesting because it has very close ties to its territory and the needs of the people who live there. A ceramic object created in a remote African country by women who model it by hand and bake it in a wood-fired oven is "original" for several reasons: it is useful, it has been made with the means available, and it expresses local aesthetic taste.

As far as my work is concerned, if an object I've made reveals my personality, irony, calmness, rage or nostalgia, if other people recognize all these traits as being a part of me, then I can say that that object is original. Whereas some very skilled artisans may reach extremely high technical levels but never develop their own identity.

Talent

I think that talent is a combination of natural and acquired qualities. However, I believe that you become talented mainly by accumulating theoretical and practical experiences. If your talent is a natural gift, as was the case with Raphael, you have a head start. But talent must be cultivated, or it will just dry up. There are people who sit down at a piano and play by ear. Others have to study for years before they can play. But in the end there is no guarantee that the one who played by ear is the better of the two, because their talent might not have been nurtured, while the one who worked the hardest during training may well become a concert pianist.

For this reason, I think that talent is an advantage but not the be-all and end-all. The true master manages to mix design skills with the ability to express them in a new way. Unfortunately, schools today focus almost entirely on design skills, leaving no room for practical skills.

Territory

In the past, every region in Italy had its own ceramics production area, for example Lodi in Lombardy. Today, however, there are far fewer workshops specializing in the typical white pottery. In Piedmont there was Castellamonte but, as happened elsewhere, there has been a downturn in the ceramics business, with a sharp drop in the production of ovenware, although they do still make ceramic stoves. Even in Veneto and Emilia many factories have closed down, and other Italian regions have been similarly affected.

We need to rethink the role of Italian ceramics in a world that has changed profoundly, bearing in mind that in Italy qualified craft businesses have never been a close-knit network, unlike in other countries such as England. Moreover, majolica and earthenware, typically traditional Italian ceramics, used raw materials that were abundant in Italy and throughout the Mediterranean basin. Today, the materials you can buy may be local or imported, greatly increasing the available selection, but meaning that ceramic production is not necessarily linked to local materials.

For myself, my work is not bound to a specific territory and I think that, in a certain sense, the world has become our local territory.

Tradition and innovation

Ceramics is an art based on traditional techniques. A great deal of the work is still done by hand, in a series of very simple operations. Even when you use moulds, the pieces must always be finished by hand. In the world of industrial ceramics, technology matters greatly, and enormous changes have taken place. In the tile industry, for example, very little is done by hand. In this field, Italy is at the cutting edge, to the point that people come from China to buy our machinery. Even in the glazed ceramics sector there are many companies constantly developing new products, and their research has an impact on my work. But I am more interested in developing my own style (which does not mean capturing the latest shade of yellow). All I need is an oven with three programmes, even if the market is replete with ever more sophisticated devices offering infinite possibilities.

Mine is a style of work that relies more on personal design than technical means. The internet gives you access to an infinite number of images, which, in some cases, is useful for the design stage. However, I think that, like all technological tools, the computer is a means and not an end.

Training

After specializing in art at high school, I took a degree in architecture, writing my thesis on the rather more sociological subject of land-rent. But I have never worked as an architect. I started teaching art and, in parallel, opened a workshop for the development of creative expression in children. During this period I began working with ceramics in a very spontaneous way. After a few years it became a life choice, and since 1990 I have dedicated myself full-time to ceramics. I immediately became interested in both the design and the production sides, an approach that called for a rather long learning curve.

You need specific technical skills to get to know the materials, and

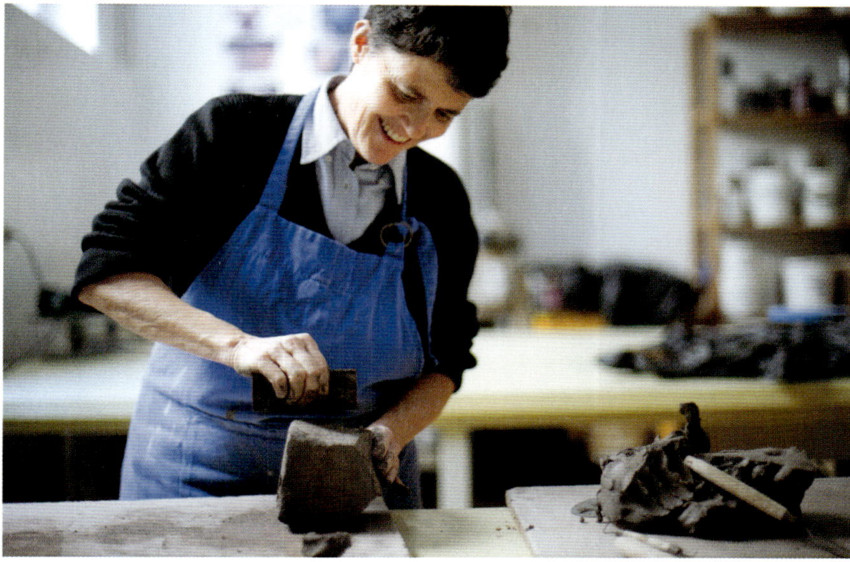

these I gained by attending many training courses in Italy and abroad and through hands-on practice. The general term "ceramics" covers a wide range of artefacts, although the word itself refers simply to objects made with clay and fired.

Given that life is, unfortunately, short, if you do decide to go deeper into every possible technical aspect, I think it is almost impossible for you to ever find your own expression, a style, that will make your work recognizable.

I did my architectural studies during the years of student protest, when everything revolved around the notion of research, and this greatly influenced my training. This is the approach that continues to inspire me.

Work must not be seen just as a daily routine; you must be constantly exploring new possibilities, because this is the only way to stay connected with modern life.

I believe that the quality of my work took a big leap when I decided to explore certain techniques that allowed me to express my vision and my aesthetics, which gave my pieces an identity and recognizability. Even now, if I can, I attend refresher courses in Italy or abroad. There's always something new to learn.

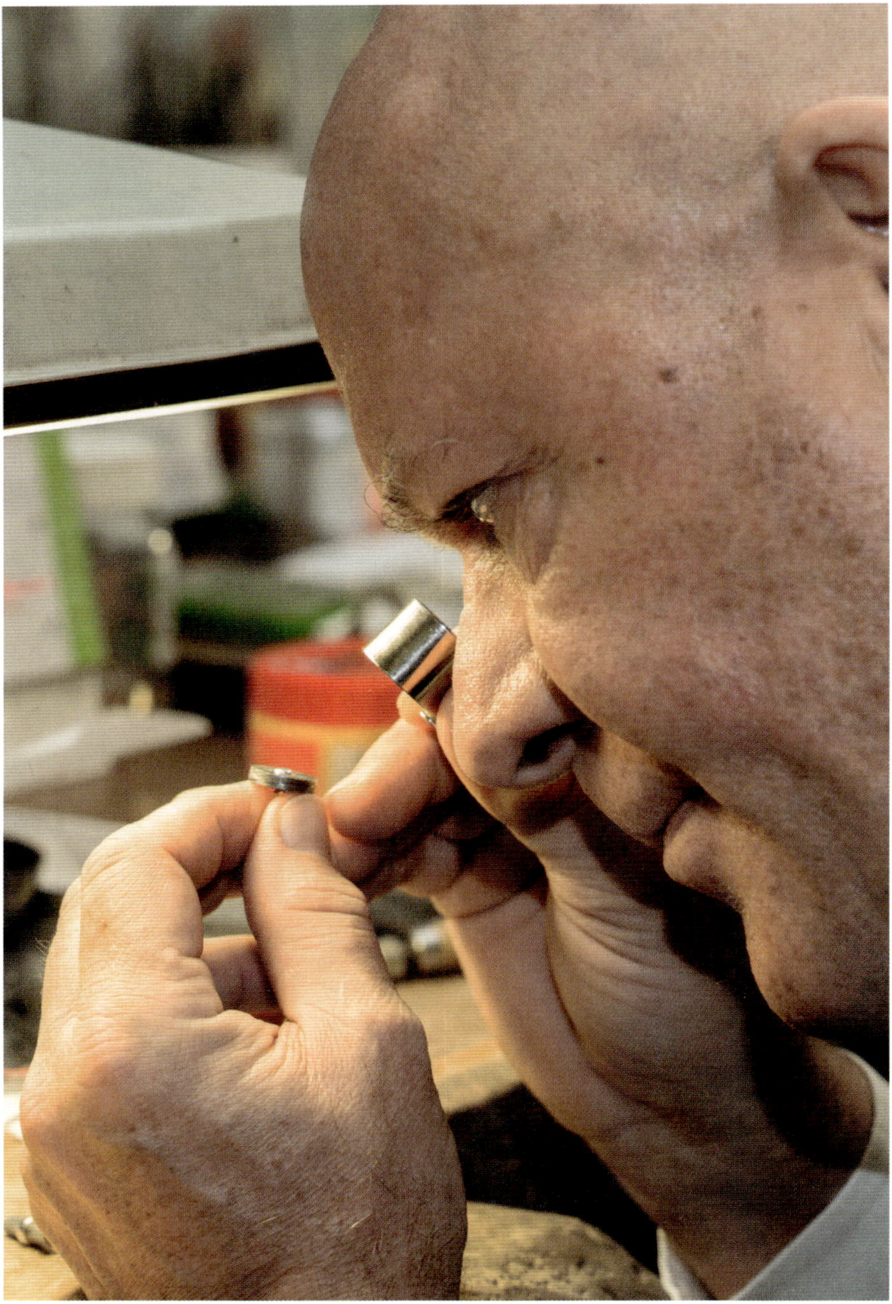

5.3.12. Filippo Villa, jeweller

The Villa family business was founded in 1876 by Benvenuto Villa (1846–1914). A goldsmith, sculptor and alchemist, Benvenuto strove unsuccessfully to find a formula for a black gold alloy. He funded his experiments by making and selling jewellery and sculptures in gold and silver, exhibiting them at the great world's fairs of the era. One example of his fervent creativity was Cubo, *a very modern silver sculpture that can be broken down into separate parts, which won him the gold medal at the famous Universal Exposition in Paris in 1889.*

Benvenuto's son Giuseppe (1890–1961) took over from him as head of the company, developing the production of articles in gold, initially in the workshop in Via San Maurilio and then in Via Manzoni. He perfected the ancient technique of woven gold, eventually patenting the "tessuto Villa", a still unequalled versatile weave of gold threads that fits the body like soft velvet and was bought by all the biggest jewellers of the time. In 1930, his wife Isotta (1891–1957) opened the store at 9 Via Manzoni, in what was formerly the Hotel Continental, involving in the venture her young son Adelio (1922–1954) who had graduated from the Brera Academy of Fine Arts and already showed strong artistic inclinations.

After the Second World War, thanks to the strong personalities of Adelio and his brother Alessandro (1927), Villa established itself definitively as the place to go for quality gems and original models, particularly popular with Milanese high society. This tradition has continued since 1980, when the fourth generation, represented by Filippo (1957) and Marco (1961) joined the company. They sell exclusive pieces skilfully produced by Milan's best team of artisans for a sophisticated clientele of connoisseurs.

Our company has the mark 49 MI, which means that we are the 49th jewellery company founded in Milan. Besides us, only Buccellati, a company just a few years older, is still in business today.

Benvenuto Villa, my great-grandfather, was a sculptor and an inventor – a volcano of ideas. In 1889, he won a gold medal at the Universal Exposition in Paris. His son, my grandfather, was a goldsmith and served some 200 jewellers around the world. It has been estimated that, in northern Italy, one out of two gold workers learnt from someone who in turn learnt from someone who came from my grandfather's workshop. My father, with my grandmother, produced fine jewellery. Now my brother and I manage the company, and my son, who represents the fifth generation, is joining us. He has inherited my ability to make clients happy, the important gift of empathy.

This business takes a lot of commitment, dedication and humility. Statistically, it is practically impossible for the son of a talented goldsmith to also be smart in this field. It's like saying that the son of a footballer is automatically a good footballer. Besides which, being a good artist or craftsperson is one thing, and being business-minded is quite another. So many great artisans of the past were well known and admired, but they weren't successful. On the other hand, a business might be inherited by a son or daughter who does not have the same creative or manual skills but who manages to turn it into a successful commercial venture.

About 15 years ago, the great master Ferruccio Motta agreed to graft all his know-how onto young branches. In the space of five years he taught my team of craftspeople what usually takes 30 years of practice to learn. I make them mix techniques a lot, conceiving and designing pieces of jewellery consistent with their training trajectory. Because if the cleverest cooks in the world make the same dish every day, they will never become great chefs. In this very virtuous situation, we have written the last 25 years of our company history.

Authenticity

I think that an artisan may be more authentic than an artist. Imperfect perhaps, but authentic. Many craftspeople produce everything from A to Z: they represent the entire supply chain. This in itself is a guarantee of authenticity.

Authentic is something made according to certain canons, which in our case are artisanal. Even if the object is a copy of the original model created by a neighbouring workshop, for me they are both authentic. Because craftspeople, in 99.9 per cent of cases, are not designers, they make something thought up by someone else. But if they make it using the right materials, appropriate tools and the correct technique, and by doing so achieve a perfect object, according to the rules emanating from the years and years of experience of the artisans who came before them, then it is an authentically artisanal object. If a craftsperson improves on the technique, so much the better, because from that moment on, what is authentically artisanal will be represented by that increment. If, for example, a chair looks artisanal, but is made in China, and the legs are stuck on with glue, albeit the most high-tech glue in the world, that product is not authentically artisanal.

In my great-grandfather's time all models were patented because there was a law that managed to protect them efficiently. We don't do this any longer, because exercising your rights has become increasingly difficult today.

Competence

You acquire competence in the workshop and you express it when you show in practical terms that you know how to reproduce what you have learnt. I think that, in the craft sector, the human aspect is just as important, and that competence is therefore mainly expressed in relationships.

I am the creative, the person who conceives and designs the jewels, but I also have to be the person who buys the stones, which is a completely different role. If I already know what I'm going to do with a stone when I buy it, it's a big advantage. It's more difficult when the buyer and the designer are two different people. With my clients, I also need to be a psychologist, understanding their tastes and their wishes. Competence is based on these values, which you learn on the job.

Craftsmanship

Ninety per cent of our work is done by hand. A piece of jewellery that is masterly made implies technical perfection, in other words the absence of defects. But, and this is something that very few understand, it is above all a question of balance. If we vary by the tiniest degree the curve on a perfect ring, it is no longer perfect. The most difficult thing to achieve is the harmony of the proportions between colour and volume. It is the same difference you have between a pair of beautiful legs and a pair of normal legs, and just as difficult to define.

Each artisanal product is unique. If a craftsperson makes the same ring ten times, each one will be different. Firstly, this is because I will never find ten identical stones. Series production can also be perfect: nylon stockings come to mind, which are impossible to make by hand. But the beauty of craft production also lies in its imperfections, however small. Uniqueness is what makes the difference, and this difference appeals to the taste of one client rather than another. For this reason, industrial production has to be bland, because it must appeal to the largest possible number of people.

Creativity

From my point of view, mine is more an ability to create arrangements than creativity *per se*. It's like in music: someone composes the tune, someone writes the words, and then someone else arranges them. This is a key figure, capable of turning a song from the fifties into a great modern success. Last but not least, you need to be creative in developing a team of craftspeople who can realize your ideas, translating them into the most beautiful objects. You need to be able to motivate your workers, inspire them. You may have to rein in your own creativity, confine it within certain parameters, if you want an idea to be not only technically and commercially feasible, but also in line with the public's tastes. Going back to the music metaphor, there is no point in writing a song today that will be popular in 20 years' time. Creativity is the sum of many parts: you need to become a doctor for yourself and for your patients – find the right formula, inspire esteem, gain credibility. But you have to keep in mind that in the end you need to pay wages. And also find the time to do other things.

Interpretation

In the old days there were big clients, patrons, the Pope; now our clients are designers. Every artisan dreams that a designer will ask them to turn a concept into a reality. If the project turns out well, it is usually thanks to the artisan, because they are the ones with the technical skills.

I start with the stone: I imagine how I could set it, and this may, for example, lead to a ring. If the piece has been commissioned by a client, it gets more complicated, because you have to find a stone that is proportionate to the size of the person's finger. To get the best results you always need to use stratagems that you have gained from experience.

In Italy we are great artisans. This is directly linked to the fact that our country has always been a collection of small states. Each city had its furniture-maker, cabinetmaker, goldsmith, glassworker. Towns were situated very close to each other, which resulted in healthy competition and a good dose of mutual scorn. The jeweller in Pisa would thus try to outdo the one in Lucca. Each king, each duke, each nobleman cultivated his own artisans, so that his house would be more beautiful than the one next door. And once the work was finished, he would invite his neighbour to come and see the skill of his artisans. Thanks to the creative rivalry and the differences between the various cities, the Italians developed their great workmanship, imagination, versatility and flexibility. In this respect we have surpassed everyone else, even the incredibly brilliant French and English craftspeople. If we had had a single king, a single capital, like Paris, we would have had the same concentration of talent as they had in France. Because they all worked for Paris, French jewellers have reached dizzying heights, but the variety we have in Italy is unmatched.

Originality

I always do the exact opposite of what everyone else does, and nine times out of ten I get it right. You need to have a mindset which is constantly pushing you to pursue new and different ways of doing things, spurning the obvious, taking risks all the time.

Each of our pieces of jewellery is unique, because they are all made by hand. Even when we use the same model there are variations and adaptations in the cut and design of the stones, depending on their size. Even in the case of black burnishing, which is one of our specialities, the result is never the same.

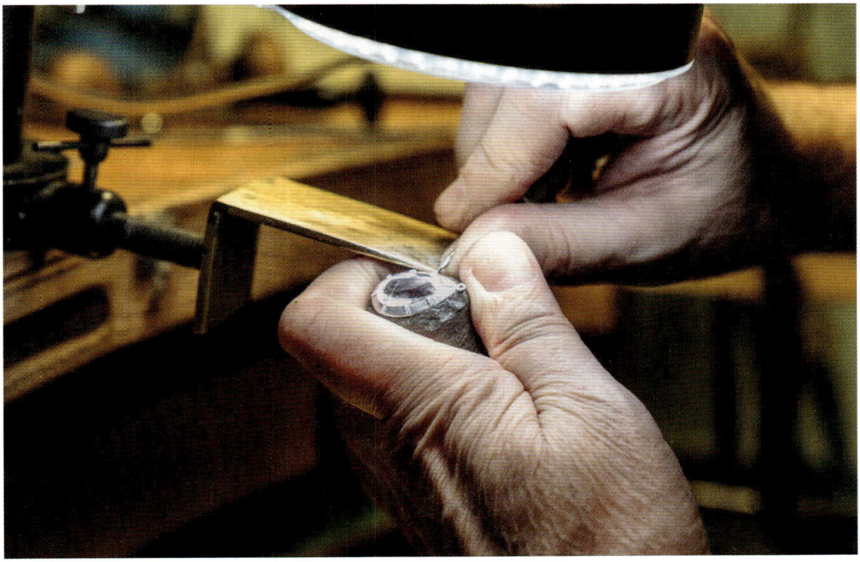

Talent

Those fortunate to have a talent have a huge advantage, but it is not enough on its own. Talent is something you have from childhood, but if you don't discover it and foster it, it's of no use. When you work with your hands, you allow talent to grow and blossom. Some people are even born with the "talent" of developing skills in a variety of contexts.

Talent in a master craftsperson can be seen when, having come to the end of their career, instead of putting their feet up they continue to go forward, repaying the gift they've received. What I mean is that talent can bring great joy, and when you have fully exploited and enjoyed it, it would be a shame as well as unfair should you decide to end it there.

You can see talent immediately in a young person. It might get lost along the way, if it is not nurtured, but the spark is evident from the start.

Territory

Jewellery as we intend it today was created by the French. In Italy, where we have sculptors of the calibre of Benvenuto Cellini, it developed later and, as with other specialities, we have proved to be outstanding in this field. There are excellent jewellers in Milan and in Rome, Florence, Naples, Genoa and Turin. Each one has their own style. But I think it is safe to say that for the last century it has been the Italian style in general that has achieved global renown and popularity. Some of the extraordinary stones still in circulation today date back to the economic boom, when we had some prolific buyers. As well as the stones, we had the jewellers who knew how to set them divinely. The industrial districts like Valenza and Arezzo, meanwhile, had concentrations of great contract manufacturers.

Most of the coloured stones come from Indochina, Africa and South America. Diamonds, on the other hand, which do not exist in either the Far East or Europe, come from a variety of sources, mainly Russia, India, Australia, Africa and North America.

I could do this craft anywhere in the world, but I adore Milan and perhaps would not like to imagine being anywhere else.

Tradition and innovation

There are no short cuts in fine craftsmanship. You start out as a boy in the workshop and you gradually grow. Nobody is really interested in sharing their know-how, and this is true for all the great masters. A master does teach their best pupil better and faster, but this is a privilege you have to be worthy of. A lot you learn on your own, by being there every day and by your initiative and responsiveness. It has to do with the human side of things, courses and schools are always somewhat cold and removed from this dimension.

In our field, the greatest evolution has been in the machinery, which allows you to do things that used to be unthinkable. My great-grandfather, who was also an alchemist, had this dream of creating black gold. Now, like then, it is impossible to do, but I can produce a ring in black gold because companies that have nothing to do with jewellery have invented a system of black rhodium plating. I was the first to use this technique in jewellery, because I have always been curious. But we are more likely to use techniques from the past or from other cultures, a bit like fusion cooking. We seek cross-pollination because it is necessary if we are to move forward and evolve.

Computer technology has enabled design innovation. I don't use it much, because I have an artisan in our workshop who is a "human computer": I speak, he translates. But in the world of jewellery, the introduction of machines for creating prototypes is crucial, even if, in my opinion, it is a rather cold method that lacks the soul of the human hand.

There are countless new materials and new stones being discovered every day. This, too, is having an enormous impact in terms of innovation.

Training

I started very young, at the age of 17. I was a pretty rebellious student and my father, hoping to frighten me, sent me to work in our jewellery workshop. It was one of the happiest years of my life because I started to get a close-up look at my father's work, which I had always greatly admired. But it was from my uncle in the goldsmith factory, where I was taught to be a polisher, that I really learnt to work. That experience nurtured my creative mind and I absorbed so much from working alongside the others.

After completing my military service, I was the first Italian to study at the Gemological Institute of America in New York. My father entrusted me to a very famous diamond merchant, with whom I spent every spare minute of the day, when I was not attending classes, gaining hands-on experience and getting a feel for the job. Two years later I came back to Italy and joined my father in the shop in Via Manzoni. He was at the end of his career and already had his eye on other pastures, whereas I was champing at the bit, full of enthusiasm and ideas. Above all, I had got to know a whole new world that I wanted to bring into ours.

My father unfortunately died too soon, and at the age of 24 I found myself at the head of the company. But I knew I had enough experience to cope on my own. I had made my way in the world of gem merchants and I began to think that it might be fun to also create jewellery. Browsing through thousands of jewellery catalogues, I absorbed and stored up ideas, styles and techniques. My preferred sources were auction catalogues, of which I have a huge collection. In there you find a miscellany of objects, beautiful and ugly, curious and embarrassing, but real, from which I gleaned details that I then transformed into beautiful objects. Meanwhile, the jewellery workshop where I had started out had closed on the death of the old master, and I built myself a new team, made up of the best artisans for each stage of production.

Staying up to date is essential, always. Doing so can even come from an unexpected source. If my workers encounter a technical problem, while looking for a solution they may come in contact with specialists in other fields, such as metallurgy, and by asking for information they learn something. There are no refresher courses; thanks to the skills we have acquired, we could hold them ourselves. For equipment, however, there are specialist fairs.

5.4. MASTER MATRIX

Skill does not run in the blood, according to Eugenio Monti Colla. To put it in another way, while talent is innate, skill is something you acquire in the workshop and should not be taken for granted. For Pino Grasso, the same goes for creativity: “Today, designers are returning to Italy because, although people overseas may be good, they lack imagination.” Imagination, creativity, intuition all stem from the cultural bedrock on which you are raised. That bedrock is the workshop, of course, but the kind of workshop where the Renaissance model still very much predominates, a place where you not only learn a trade but also how to live and think. For Filippo Villa, "each artisanal product is unique" because it is the non-mechanized perfection of the hand that produces the most magnificent works, the ones that speak to the heart. These pieces hide their secrets deep within. "The secret of Caraceni tailoring lies totally in the cut. [...] It is a real secret, one we hand down from father to son [...] and nobody has ever discovered it", confides Carlo Andreacchio with a smile.

The Lombard masters have turned their talent into a vocation, and their manual skill affords them a competitive edge that has taken them to the peak of their professions. With understated but passionate testimony, drawing on first-hand experience, they have reaffirmed the criteria gleaned from our analysis of the requirements of legislators, the opinions of experts and the perceptions of the sample group. For those who, in their daily lives, follow the principle of Albertanus of Brescia and the early Franciscans that "doing well" amounts to "feeling well",[20] craftsmanship is the defining factor.

For any artisan striving to be both authentic and contemporary, "craftsmanship" encompasses a range of other criteria, which for reasons of objectivity and clarity have been itemized and analysed above. These include commitment, talent and on-the-job training. When asked how much craftsmanship mattered in their profession, the masters unanimously answered: 100 per cent.

The masters consulted seemed to think that "training", which is clearly an objective criterion, was only of relative importance. The reason for this rather low rating is not the value of training *per se*, but (according to the masters) because the relevant training schools do not exist, or those that do are either inadequate or lack the necessary programmes. This would suggest that master craftspeople believe that the real teaching process takes place in the workshop and that vocational, artistic or technical training schools are poorly equipped to train aspiring artisans properly.

At the same time, there were mixed views on the importance of innate qualities versus acquired skills and abilities and personal versus relational elements. True masters are able to take risks, know how to capture the *zeitgeist* and can teach and share know-how, but they are also sure of their manual skill and their chosen "profession" and are able to reinvigorate tradition by giving it a contemporary slant. But,

[20] See Romano Benini, *Saper fare: Il modello artigiano e le radici dello stile italiano* (Rome: Donzelli, 2010), p. 179.

above all, they have a social role to play and are sensitive to cultural shifts.

The masters frequently cited culture as an important element, a benchmark. They are referring, of course, to the cultural environment in which they work, but also to culture as an educationally advanced reflection on art, society and taste, and on the ability to create beautiful things and to use that beauty as a competitive advantage tied to manual skill.

Owing to the close links between the tangible and the cultural, between the artistic nature of the work and its reliance on a trade, master craftsmanship would appear to fall justifiably within the still amorphous, but increasingly relevant scope of what European legislation describes as the "creative and cultural industries". Those four words sum up well the ethos of the master craftsperson, who is at once entrepreneur, interested observer of (or in many cases leading player in) cultural phenomena, and, of course, maker who eschews mechanization in favour of intuition and creativity.

5.5. INTANGIBLE HERITAGE AND THE ARTISTIC CRAFTS

Be it stringed instrument making, embroidery, tailoring, wrought ironwork, paper craft, cabinetmaking, puppetry, ceramics, jewellery, textiles, boatbuilding or fashion, Lombardy's production identity, in its most original and authentic sense, has for centuries centred on these sectors and the people who drive them. They have engaged constructively with industry, mass production, the challenges of trade fairs and the pressures of ever-changing fashion and design trends.

Our study aims to show that there may well be a rational way of assessing excellence in craftsmanship, and the leading figures who have so generously shared their time and experience to assist us in this quest have given much more telling testimony than mere feedback on the proposed criteria. They are the personification of those criteria in all their aspects, and with that "simple intellectual probity" championed by the German sociologist and philosopher Max Weber, they have provided invaluable insights into the deeper nuances of the concept-terms that should inform any assessment of artisanal excellence. These nuances are confirmation of a fundamental truth: assessing excellence, as we said earlier, should not be seen merely as a rigid checklist of predetermined views, but as a fluid examination of constantly evolving measurements and visions. The criteria are therefore open to improvement even when, in practice, a level of excellence may have already been justifiably attained through fame, talent or widespread recognition. This is an important point that came out strongly in the interviews: learning is a lifelong process, and curiosity and passion are the key ingredients for achieving extraordinary heights.

Ideally, such heights should not be associated only with the production of one-off pieces. The works of master craftspeople are in fact "hybrid in nature, ranging from one-off pieces to small series and large-scale hand-finished products. In other words, artistic craftsmanship is where the cream of Italian artisans, artists and businesspeople can come together to sow and propagate new ideas with the aim of creating objects that are aesthetically pleasing, useful and of high artistic value".[21]

The master craftsperson is therefore essential, not only to perpetuate that "workshop logic" on which the authentic transmission of know-how depends, but also to transfer into the more industrial forms of production those values that are still closely linked to an idea of excellence that only the most expert manual skills are able to convey. In Lombardy, in particular, these skills thrive on very specific characteristics. One of these is authenticity, most notably in the sense of that *veritas* which is "masterly and appropriate execution, integrity of the elements, being true to the design, adherence to the rules of the art, and legitimacy".[22] Another is moderation, or what might also be called understatement, a characteristic that can still be found in design, in architecture and in fashion, where even the most sumptuous and luxurious works tastefully spurn excess. This quest for simplicity never descends into shoddiness, but is a conscious rejection of ostentation. Then there is elegance, as in "a harmonious quest for beauty that is something more than an aesthetic principle, but is also persuasive, able to strike a chord, leaving aside anything that is ugly or ill-made. This is the 'uniquely Milanese quality' that finds expression in the presentation as well as in the substance, in the graphic font, as well as in the written text, in the wrapping paper and ribbon, as well as in the contents of the package. The packaging is not only a design feature in itself, but also the 'icing on the cake', the finishing touch that overlooks no detail of the 'project'".[23]

Lastly, there is research, which is the consummate awareness of materials and techniques and respect for tradition and its inventive fusion with innovation.

In our interviews, the master craftspeople provide a detailed and forthright response to the question of what constitutes the excellence

[21] Mazzucotelli Salice and Medicina, *Maestri del fare*, p. 24.

[22] Franco Cologni, "Prefazione", in Paolo Colombo, Alberto Cavalli and Gioachino Lanotte (eds), *Mestieri d'arte e Made in Italy: Giacimenti culturali da riscoprire* (Venice: Marsilio, 2009), pp. 11–14, especially 13.

[23] *Ibid.*

that the contemporary world is seeking. For them, the acquisition of know-how is a constant endeavour and the road to excellence is long, nurtured by talent, undoubtedly, but also by creativity, beneficial ties to the local territory, interpretive skills, intuition, taste and originality.

Thanks to these elements, craftsmanship has not only survived through the centuries, but also cross-pollinated and adapted, without relinquishing its DNA or its intrinsic characteristics. Although deeply rooted in history, these elements also hold a key place in modern life. As mentioned earlier, some of the masters interviewed are already included in the directory of "intangible heritage" that Lombardy has catalogued and codified in its Register of Intangible Heritage (REIL).[24] In keeping with the debate initiated by the adoption of the UNESCO Convention for the Safeguarding of the Intangible Cultural Heritage, the Regional Department for Culture intends the Archive of Ethnography and Social History of Lombardy to promote, via REIL,

> new cultural policy measures and interventions to activate processes of renewal and dissemination of regional intangible heritage. Intangible goods are a particular form of public goods. According to the UNESCO definition, they are practices, representations, expressions, knowledge, skills [...] that communities, groups and, in some cases, individuals recognize as part of their cultural heritage. This intangible cultural heritage, transmitted from generation to generation, is constantly recreated by communities and groups in response to their environment, their interaction with nature and their history, and provides them with a sense of identity and continuity, thus promoting respect for cultural diversity and human creativity.[25]

Based on the personal accounts of the masters involved in our study, and in light of the outcomes of the recent *Autentico Contemporaneo* (Contemporary Authentic) project run by Politecnico di Milano,[26] the Lombardy Archive might be persuaded to consider broadening the knowledge, practices and skills it has recorded so far. For, if it is true that, as Eugenio Monti Colla maintains, the puppetry activities of this historic family are unrivalled or that the instruments made by Gio Batta Morassi are rightly considered to be the heirs of Stradivari's tradition, then it is equally true that the *savoir-faire* of Pino Grasso's atelier, the mastery of Carlo Andreacchio and the artistic design skills of Gabriella Sacchi, to name but some, are also a precious trove of knowledge to be handed down and preserved.

[24] See www.aess.regione.lombardia.it/reil/.

[25] See www.aess.regione.lombardia.it/reil/?page_id=2 and www.unesco.org/culture/ich/en/convention#art2

[26] See www.contemporaryauthentic.com.

These masters are aware that their identity stems from a glorious past, and they communicate with the contemporary world in an extraordinary way. Tailoring, embroidery, ceramics and wrought ironwork are "public goods" that Lombardy showcases with justified pride. As such, they can rightly be considered a key part of our cultural heritage, and are also emerging as paradigmatic. We hope that this study will enable us to develop a tool that we can be used to assess and identify an excellence that has culturally solid foundations and that will provide our institutional counterparts with a stimulus – or indeed opportunity – to broaden their scope to include the artistic crafts, which constitute a priceless resource and heritage for Lombardy. If we can achieve this, we believe that our efforts to collect and analyse all the data will not have been fruitless.

ALBERTO CAVALLI - GIUDITTA COMERCI - GIOVANNA MARCHELLO

6.

ASSESSING EXCELLENCE: WORKING TOOLS

6.1. ANNOTATED SUMMARY OF THE OVERALL FINDINGS

The criteria for assessing the artistic crafts were initially drawn from (mainly Italian regional) legislation, analysed and then submitted to a panel of experts for comment. They were subsequently tested on a significant sample of the Italian population and further verified by a group of eminent master artisans from Lombardy, selected on reputation, expertise and relevance. From these findings emerged a clear matrix consisting of a number of concept-terms that together encapsulate the meaning of "excellence" within this cultural and productive context.

It therefore makes sense that, when examining whether and to what extent a master artisan may be considered "excellent", a range of factors should come into consideration. There are personal attributes (creativity, competence, training, talent, interpretation), relational and geographical aspects (territory, tradition) and, of course, features related to the object itself (authenticity, originality, craftsmanship, innovation). However, each of these terms carries a different weight, which should be taken into account in the final assessment. While it is true that each criterion is essential in its own right for ascertaining excellence in a manner that is not wholly subjective, it must also be acknowledged that some are more important than others.

There are several difficulties involved in comparing the findings and developing an assessment matrix. Nevertheless, we must, at the very least, aim to "suggest that a broad and comprehensive assessment paradigm be constructed that uses and is defined by a set of assessment tools with common objectives but different characteristics".[1] A paradigm of this

[1] Massimiliano Mazzanti, *Metodi e strumenti di analisi per la valutazione economica del patrimonio culturale* (Milan: Franco Angeli, 2011), p. 112.

kind could be devised along the lines of models elaborated recently to assess cultural property that has non-commercial purposes. The artistic crafts, as we have already seen, are to all intents and purposes part of that intangible cultural heritage for which assessment tools have already been developed, as is also the case for environmental assets.[2] However, the definition of "cultural property" does not adequately cover the artistic crafts, because a master artisan's work is by its nature bound up with commercial considerations. Therefore, we could not simply adapt and apply to the artistic crafts the paradigms that are currently in place.

As regards the person of the master artisan, it is not always possible to come up with unequivocal, clear-cut criteria when assessing excellence based on mostly objective criteria, such as training and education; for, "while research is the overriding factor in defining and assessing excellence, analysis of the definitions collected [...] shows a profusion of conceptions of excellence that may be alternative to, and consequently in competition with, the dominant one".[3] Furthermore, although all fields of the economic and social sciences produce assessment matrices on a daily basis, an examination of the legal instruments that should provide clear regulation of artisanal excellence reveals a decided lack of well-defined, specific criteria. If legislators have been wary of drawing up an overly restrictive set of codes, perhaps we would do well to remember that "perfectionism is the scourge of assessment, and the quest to attain a perfect assessment enables you to keep putting off unwelcome choices".[4] Therefore, if it is true that "all assessments are imperfect and all measurements are imperfect",[5] it is clear that measurement and assessment mechanisms must also be accompanied by corrective tools. The matrix that has taken shape so far is simply a first step towards an increasingly thorough form of investigation.

It should be borne in mind that a measurement can be considered valid "if it provides a realistic picture that corresponds to the object that is being measured. An assessment is good or bad according to whether or not it produces the incentivizing effects it was initially carried out for".[6]

[2] There are numerous examples. For suggestions for assessing cultural property, see *ibid.*; for assessing environmental assets, see Onnu Kuik, Ståle Navrud and David W. Pearce, "Benefit Estimation and Environmental Decision-making", in Ståle Navrud (ed.), *Pricing the European Environment* (Oslo: Scandinavian University Press, 1992), pp. 274–287.

[3] Fiammetta Corradi (ed.), *Alla ricerca dell'eccellenza: Le politiche per l'eccellenza nell'istruzione superiore in quattro Paesi europei* (Milan: Edizioni Universitarie di Lettere Economia Diritto, 2009) p. 193.

[4] See also Andrea Bonaccorsi, "La valutazione di Bertoldo", *Il Mulino*, No. 2 (May 2013), pp. 257–265, especially 265. Andrea Bonaccorsi is a board member of ANVUR, Italy's National Agency for the Evaluation of the University and Research Systems.

[5] *Ibid.*

[6] Daniele Checchi, "Valutazione: c'è un medicinale adatto?", *Il Mulino*, No. 466 (February

This is one of our matrix's objectives: as well as assessing excellence, it may also provide an incentive for those who might be underperforming in one or more areas. Having identified a master artisan's "weak points", it would be possible to provide them with clear directions as to which aspects require improvement. In this way, the matrix could be used for inspirational and not just assessment purposes. It would be a tool that is consonant with the hybrid nature of artistic craftsmanship, simultaneously covering creative works and the intangible cultural heritage, while remaining closely connected to niche markets and industries.

Before summarizing the findings discussed in this work, we would like to at least suggest an ideal assessment tool that could be applied also to cultural property that has a commercial aspect. This tool could provide meaningful insights into formative and performative excellence as well as into a culture and a technique linked to the territory and to the intangible cultural heritage. It would also be sufficiently flexible to cover a range of disciplines that, while different in many respects, share the characteristics of manual skill and the criteria listed below.

The following concept-terms represent the criteria that would be included in the assessment matrix:

– authenticity;
– competence;
– craftsmanship;
– creativity;
– innovation;
– interpretation;
– originality;
– talent;
– territory;
– tradition;
– training.

These criteria need to be harmonized so that they fit into a useful assessment tool. Therefore, we had to carefully consider about how to proceed in order to develop a matrix that does not claim (as we have already pointed out) to be exhaustive. The result must nonetheless be complete, weighted and manageable within an assessment exercise conducted across a range of domains.

The provisions that UNESCO has gradually put into effect for the safeguarding of the intangible cultural heritage are a potentially useful reference in this regard.[7] These recommend, for example, a careful

2013), pp. 266–272, especially 271.

[7] See http://en.unesco.org/themes/protecting-our-heritage-and-fostering-creativity.

weighting of the units of measurement and data reliability, as well as a judicious preliminary survey of the territorial context. The matrix we are aiming to formulate sets these elements out clearly and, as we shall see later, we will attempt to harmonize them for the purposes of calculation, using clear and rational criteria. Furthermore, in accordance with UNESCO recommendations or requirements, we felt it necessary to adopt a collegial rather than individual approach, delegating the assessment to a board made up of experts, peers and institutional representatives.

Therefore, in keeping (*mutatis mutandis*) with the UNESCO provisions, such an assessment board, which should be created and regularly called upon when evaluation processes are under way, might initially comprise the following members:

– an art historian specialized in the applied arts who has a certain number of published works;

– a designer who has won an internationally recognized prize such as the Compasso d'Oro Award, and who is known to have collaborated with quality master artisans;

– the director of a nationally important museum of applied arts;

– the head of a cultural body active in promoting the artistic crafts;

– the president or general secretary of a national association connected with the artisanal world;

– the director of a school, reputed as excellent, tasked with training budding master artisans;

– the editor-in-chief of a publication dedicated to excellence in the applied arts or design;

– two institutional representatives (one each from the Ministry of Economic Development and the Ministry of Cultural Heritage and Activities and Tourism);

– two master artisans, recognized as such by formal peer review.

The board would be asked to judge, on a case-by-case basis, to what extent the criteria are met, by completing the assessment matrix set out below. However, besides the matrix, a rating system is necessary to harmonize the responses from the diverse sample groups involved and to automatically rank the assessed criteria in the right order. In this way, any weaknesses in relation to particular criteria can be identified so that suggestions for improvement or growth can be provided.

The board would also have the role of verifying the required standards, based on the ideals to which it aspires, so as to establish a minimum level for the affirmation of excellence.

6.2. PROPOSAL FOR AN ASSESSMENT MATRIX AND RATING SYSTEM

In light of the above, we thought it essential to rank the concept-terms in order of importance, based on four criteria:

– *frequency of use* of each term by legislators;

– *recognition of the importance* of each term by the experts;

– *recognition of the importance* of each term by the sample group interviewed for the quantitative research;

– *feedback from the master artisans* in Lombardy who were consulted extensively on each term, although this cannot be rendered numerically.

The interviews conducted with the last group were especially significant in that they provided direct, competent and relevant feedback on the qualities that master artisans themselves feel they should possess, and therefore recognize and ascertain in others. This served as a kind of peer review that was vital in helping adjust data from other sources that were either too theoretical or too emotionally charged.

While the legislators and experts focused on tradition and territory, placing these criteria in first place, they differed on other aspects. The experts saw competence, creativity and interpretation also as extremely important, while the legislators referred more frequently to innovation (in its generic sense) and craftsmanship (meaning prevalence of manual work). The master artisans also considered craftsmanship to be crucial, placing it highest, followed by competence and creativity. Responses from the sample group painted a very different picture: creativity ranked highest, followed by originality and competence. The two extremes of the entire system – tradition and innovation – once again aggregate expectations regarding excellence. Territory, in the sense of a source of both raw materials and inspiration, as well as of a key cultural benchmark, was viewed as a factor that cannot be exported and therefore strategic. Talent, understood as an innate interpretive ability that with time becomes expertise, is naturally also seen as a key factor, although dependent on study, practice and commitment.

The results from the four sources were then harmonized.

The further down the rankings you go, the more the interviewees' views coincide, in terms of both the number of times a criterion was cited and its relative importance. This finding clearly demonstrates that a perception of excellence can be determined when there is a well-defined scale within which "deviation" from a fixed core nucleus is only very slight.

Based on the weighting of the four results obtained, an assessment matrix could be formulated as follows, with *the highest category being the most relevant and the lowest, while still important, being the least significant*:

– *tradition*: dynamic, constant renewal of cumulative knowledge rooted in a time of productive excellence; techniques and working processes that can be passed on and communicated but not standardized; perpetuation of a direct or indirect professional legacy;

– *creativity*: manifestation of a master artisan's personal vision that does not lose sight of the requirements of the trade; ability to balance functional and material limitations with inventiveness; vision and talent to take familiar elements and arrange them in a truly creative way, while respecting the "rules of the art", or masterly made;

– *craftsmanship*: prevalence of skilled manual work; set of skills and knowledge that the master artisan draws upon when working with the materials; masterly execution of an object;

– *innovation*: ability to change something pre-existing by adding new elements; investment in research and new technologies; dialogue between technology and artisanal know-how that yields new and original forms, styles, functions and aesthetics;

– *territory*: source of original and authentic raw materials; network of human and professional relationships; heritage, or rather environmental, cultural, logistical, qualitative and historical asset;

– *interpretation*: non-mechanized, personal and original transformation of an idea into an object; ability to adapt tradition to modern requirements; ability to capture and give shape to the sensibilities of contemporary clients;

– *competence*: consummate knowledge of materials and working processes; experience gained in one's own field; superior level of workmanship that implies a deep understanding of the craft and ease when doing it, as well as highly developed personal skills;

– *originality*: delicate balance of old and new, demanding innovative ways of applying centuries-old techniques to create something fresh and unique; curiosity, search for alternative viewpoints outside one's own sphere of expertise; specific provenance of an object, not only in a geographical sense but also in terms of a school or a master;

– *talent*: natural, innate ability and predisposition to do things well that needs to be nurtured; marked sensitivity in relation to the material and its possibilities; insight that is honed through the learning process;

– *authenticity*: inimitable quality of a product that connects it with its maker; creative endeavour that eschews mass production; techniques, working processes, use of materials and aesthetic sensibility that are true, genuine and result in something unique;

– *training*: school education and qualifications; passing on of know-how via workshop training and continuous learning; knowledge of the craft, its history and context, as well as of its practical applications.

How the matrix is to be implemented depends on very simple

instructions, that must take into account, however, the fact that the study should produce numerical values that can be compared and ranked (these may, of course, need to be improved and are subject to variation and further development).

The board should assess each category by awarding a score to each of the three subcategories into which the 11 concept-terms are divided. However, the concept-terms have been weighted slightly differently, to maintain their order of relative importance. The assessments need to be "projected" into the general context of the matrix, to balance the different marks given with the category's importance, derived from the responses collected from the various groups consulted.

To provide a tool that might otherwise be too complex to use (also for the purposes of calculation), the seven most important categories have been assigned an assessment range from 1 (master's role, history or production is totally absent) to 5 (criterion met in full). Thus, the scores for the first seven categories could range from a minimum of 21 (one point for each of the three subcategories of the seven concept–terms) to a maximum of 105 (five points each).

The remaining four criteria, although still prerequisites for "excellence", have a relatively smaller influence on the final outcome. Accordingly, the assessment range for these concept-terms will go from 1 (as above) to 3. The scores for these criteria will range from a minimum of 12 (one point for each of the three subcategories of the four concept-terms) to a maximum of 36 (three points for each).

This method ensures uniform measurement: the criteria are ranked according to the importance that has been established as objectively as possible; the final assessment will represent the different facets of each category, without important aspects of the work being lost in overly broad definitions.

The results obtained in this way easily allow for the creation of three broad levels of attainment, within which the data can be subdivided and organized.

The calculations are very simple. *Given that 141 is the highest score a master can obtain (105 + 36), we can say excellence has been achieved when the final score is slightly above half: a reasonable threshold would be 80 points.*

An additional category could then be introduced to better assess the scores obtained: *an artisan scoring above 120 (between 120 and 141) may be considered a "master" in the traditional, respectful and etymological sense, or as a "Living Treasure"*, whose practices, history and actions have made excellence an evident and recognized feature of their work.

For those scoring between 80 and 120, although undoubtedly excellent, there are certain aspects that need clarifying, or certain skills that need honing if they are to achieve the status of the highest group. To be fair, the higher status is often accorded to someone who has dedicated an entire life's work to their trade, and therefore it more often applies to older masters than those with less experience.

Lastly, where the score falls below 80 points, the matrix clearly shows where the artisan needs to focus their attention in order to improve, or where investment is needed to trigger a gradual process of improvement aimed at achieving a recognized and recognizable level of "excellence". As previously stated, this working tool then becomes a parameter that, while certainly not exhaustive, will (we hope) help potential master artisans to pursue their own interpretation of excellence with confidence.

Below is the proposed assessment table, compiled according to the process described above.

Main criteria:

Criterion	**Sub-definition**	**Rating 1–5**
Tradition	dynamic, constant renewal of cumulative knowledge rooted in a time of productive excellence	
	techniques and working processes that can be passed on and communicated but not standardized	
	perpetuation of a direct or indirect professional legacy	
Total tradition		
Creativity	manifestation of a master artisan's personal vision that does not lose sight of the requirements of the trade	
	ability to balance functional and material limitations with inventiveness	
	vision and talent to take familiar elements and arrange them in a truly creative way, while respecting the "rules of the art", or masterly made	
Total creativity		
Craftsmanship	prevalence of skilled manual work	
	set of skills and knowledge that the master artisan draws upon when working the materials	
	masterly execution of an object	
Total craftsmanship		
Innovation	ability to change something pre-existing by adding new elements	
	investment in research and new technologies	

	dialogue between technology and artisanal know-how that yields new and original forms, styles, functions and aesthetics	
Total innovation		
Territory	source of original and authentic raw materials	
	network of human and professional relationships	
	heritage, or rather environmental, cultural, logistical, qualitative and historical asset	
Total territory		
Interpretation	non-mechanized personal and original transformation of an idea into an object	
	ability to adapt tradition to modern requirements	
	ability to capture and give tangible shape to the sensibilities of contemporary clients	
Total interpretation		
Competence	consummate knowledge of materials and working processes	
	experience gained in one's own field	
	superior level of workmanship that implies a deep understanding of the craft and ease when doing it, as well as highly developed personal skills	
Total competence		
Total first criteria		Score from 21 to 105

Remaining criteria:

Criterion	**Sub-definition**	**Rating 1–3**
Originality	delicate balance of old and new, demanding innovative ways of applying centuries-old techniques to create something fresh and unique	
	curiosity, search for alternative viewpoints outside one's own sphere of expertise	
	specific provenance of an object, not only in a geographical sense, but from a school or a master	
Total originality		
Talent	natural, innate ability and predisposition to do things well that needs to be nurtured	
	marked sensitivity in relation to the material and its possibilities	
	insight that is honed through the learning process	
Total talent		

Authenticity	inimitable quality of a product that connects it with its maker	
	creative endeavour that eschews mass production	
	techniques, working processes, use of materials and aesthetic sensibility that are true, genuine and result in something unique	
Total authenticity		
Training	school education and qualifications	
	transmission of know-how through workshop training and continuous learning	
	knowledge of the craft, its history and context, as well as of its practical application	
Total training		
Total remaining criteria		Score from 12 to 36

Summary table:

Total first criteria	**Total remaining criteria**	**Total masters**	**Overall score**
			Below 80 Between 80 and 120 Between 120 and 141

As already stated, the table allows for an assessment of each criterion, which is divided into further subcategories so that the single elements that make up each criterion can be more easily distinguished; the points awarded for each subcategory go towards the overall score, which constitutes the final assessment for each criterion. And, as already mentioned, some concept-terms are weighted differently within the assessment process, thus reflecting the importance attributed to them by the four different groups consulted.

The result for each category will therefore be the sum of the scores awarded for each subcategory, calculated on the basis of the importance accorded to the criterion itself. The final figure will be the sum of all the other scores and will determine (based on the criteria assessed) whether "excellence" has been achieved, or if there are areas where improvements need to be made.

6.3. APPLICABILITY OF THE MATRIX

Having defined the matrix, based on scrutiny of the criteria laid down in legislation, and then verified and weighted according to the findings of the surveys of the three groups (experts, masters and population sample), its validity can be tested by applying it to the experience of the master artisans. At this stage, it would be essential, as already suggested, to create an assessment board. Backed by a suitable secretariat to process applications presented by the candidates themselves or to submit cases for assessment, the board would be tasked with assessing artisans operating in all sectors covered by Italy's 2001 Presidential Decree, as well as those artisans whose work is not covered by the decree but whom the board is willing to admit for preliminary assessment.

As any consideration of excellence is bound to deal with a person's individual activity, each assessment should be specific and meticulous. Furthermore, recognition of excellence would be subject to regular inspections, and could therefore be suspended or revoked as the board sees fit.

The aim of this study was to create an assessment tool based on verifiable and objective observations, and subsequently tested on a variety of groups. The tool will evidently require further honing, modification and variation, as it is put into practice, because – to reiterate our earlier point – an assessment process "is good or bad according to whether or not it produces the incentivizing effects it was initially carried out for".[8]

It is our hope that a reasoned and objective assessment of excellence will act as an incentive to preserve, improve and rediscover that extraordinary artisanship that underpins the very best of "Made in Italy" production.

[8] Checchi, "Valutazione: c'è un medicinale adatto?".

FRANCO COLOGNI

CONCLUSIONS: PROTECT, PROMOTE, PROGRESS

Any attempt to investigate and establish a criterion by which to judge something is very often a matter of pure chance. But, even then,

> this criterion will have to be rediscovered over and over, reinvented each time from scratch, plucked again from the air. [...] [I]f the criterion is already fixed, an objective, one-size-fits-all measure or paradigm, our work – be it a shoe or a work of art – would, at best, be nothing more than a modest reproduction of an already established model. If, on the other hand, the criterion has to be constantly re-evaluated and reinvented [...] we have reason to believe that our work radiates an exceptional beauty – something *more* than beauty, even, because it is the embodiment of grace, talent, novelty.[1]

Beauty and novelty, grace and talent – these are the qualities that master artisans strive for or possess, and that are eloquently expressed in their work. Although difficult to pinpoint objectively, they *can* be analysed and broken down into their component parts to gauge how much or how little of each is present in a given product. From a communication perspective, such qualities can be effectively harnessed to showcase the uniqueness of Italian artistic crafts and the workshops, ateliers and businesses that produce them, or to highlight the genuinely typical "artisanal" nature of a product or artefact.

Doing so would give greater visibility to and raise the profile of the finest Italian crafts, encouraging institutional stakeholders to consider including many Italian production processes in the "intangible heritage" that constitutes the *genius loci* of a territory.

[1] Sergio Givone, "Socrate e il calzolaio", in Stefania Ricci (ed.), *Il calzolaio prodigioso: Fiabe e leggende di scarpe e calzolai*, exhibition catalogue, Museo Salvatore Ferragamo, Florence, 19 April 2013–31 March 2014 (Milan: Skira, 2013), pp. 65–69, especially 67.

Lastly, the acknowledgement of these qualities is essential in promoting a know-how that is more than the simple repetition of gestures or the safeguarding of traditions: it is rather the constant interpretation of ideas, the search for solutions, an openness to the challenges of modernity which contemporary master artisans have to confront. These include the blurred boundaries of top-end production processes where a master artisan is called upon to take centre stage. Artisanal know-how can be expressed in the form of memory (as in tradition and the acknowledged value of the techniques), space (understood as both the workshop and the local territory) and time (which is necessary for learning and the cultivation of knowledge).[2] This knowledge, however, must always be translated into processes (be they transmissive, productive or communicative) and products (unique, one-off, manufactured, semi-processed, and so on).

Any attempt to define artisanal excellence, as this study has done, necessarily means devising an assessment tool that can be used to promote the merits and skills of master artisans, and to support them in the transmission of their knowledge. Promotion alone, however, is not enough. Today, the very existence of the artistic crafts is under threat, and this requires them to be open to change without relinquishing their core DNA. At the same time, these activities must be protected with a clear view to preserving and incentivizing excellence.

The study has raised a number of issues: the legislative definition of the artistic crafts; the self-confessed lack of awareness of many Italians on the subject; the somewhat inadequate nature of production regulations; the nebulous, relatively unstructured state of training schools; and the younger generation's relative ignorance of the range of opportunities available to them in the artistic craft sector. On the upside, be it in daily life, the business world or the cultural and aesthetic sphere, the Made in Italy legacy has emerged as a vibrant, driving force in the national economy and has proven itself capable of delivering enduring value despite changing tastes and economic downturns.

This study is the brainchild of the Cologni Foundation for the Métiers d'Art and has been undertaken with both Italian and global audiences in mind. It aims to contribute to re-evaluating the master artisan's role in contemporary society, a role that at times also needs to be revamped and rebooted,[3] including through processes such as the dissemination of knowledge based on "human relations, which means facilitating

[2] See Federica Vacca, *Design sul filo della tradizione* (Bologna: Pitagora, 2013), p. 94.

[3] As Politecnico di Milano's *Contemporary Authentic* project also attempted; see www.contemporaryauthentic.com/.

the sharing, transformation, re-production and incorporation of this traditional knowledge in contemporary forms and [cultural processes], essentially by establishing relations between the masters and the local community and the entrepreneurial system".[4]

I set up the Cologni Foundation in Milan in 1995 and have been its president since. The foundation has always pursued an intensive programme of serious academic work, with the aim of formulating definitions and strategies to provide a more comprehensive understanding of the artistic crafts. This work is part of a conceptual and heuristic journey that has involved numerous generic and specific studies, including on: master artisans in the European Union; leading artisans operating in the fashion world; the master artisans of Milan; and the role of the artistic crafts in the Expos, the international exhibitions that since 1851 have been regularly showcasing around the world the best production processes and creative outputs of the different nations. The common thread that runs through all our academic activity is the link between a master's work and the territory. As can be seen from the assessment matrix devised and analysed above, this is a crucial element in defining the concept of the Made in Italy "excellence" that, objectively, gives Italian production its competitive edge. For, not only does that excellence stem from a way of making things that cannot be easily found elsewhere, but it also derives from a specific historical and constantly evolving model firmly grounded in the relationship between the masters and their community, between artisans and their territory, and between what makers aspire to and what customers desire:

> [T]his instinctive pursuit of happiness, which goes beyond mere survival, is linked to the economic and social renaissance that took place in the first centuries of the second millennium, references to which can already be found in Roman thought, from Seneca to Marcus Aurelius. Man, as a social being, is at the centre of this quest. This is what is meant by well-being, or welfare: disciplined and balanced economic and social growth tempered by love for oneself and for others. This concept of development constitutes progress as it is governed by the underlying principle of the common good – and this is a venerable Italian invention.[5]

If this supremely Italian identity is to survive, then we must be able to show that this vibrant universe of artistic endeavour and design

[4] *Ibid.*

[5] Romano Benini, *Saper fare: Il modello artigiano e le radici dello stile italiano* (Rome: Donzelli, 2010), p. 31.

actually exists; it must be brought to the attention of legislators, the media and the public. The know-how that is inseparable from this identity does not refer simply to the expertise of individual artisans but to the very essence of the Italian productive system, to that sensibility and skill – repeatedly demonstrated and proven over time – in finding effective ways to achieve universally recognized standards of beauty and enduring value.

Artistic craftsmanship represents the best of Italy's know-how; it is the mark of a creative, artistic, yet pragmatic people that has served as a beacon of civilization, forging the Made in Italy mark that conjures up at once notions of taste, substance, technical perfection, formal balance, tradition and innovation, originality and authenticity. As workshops vanish and fewer people opt for skilled manual work in favour of the so-called intellectual professions, our idea of the artistic crafts has become incomplete, if not altogether erroneous. This is evident in the findings of Enrico Finzi's public survey (described in chapter 4), and we are genuinely concerned about how best to promote and raise awareness of the value of the artistic crafts.

The aim of this study, therefore, was to suggest ways to assess, promote and support the artistic crafts and the artisanal workshops, ateliers and businesses that are the lifeblood of Italy's economy and culture.

The analysis of legislation contained in chapter 2 enabled us to identify the objective criteria by which both typical features and genuine excellence are determined. As specifications vary from region to region in Italy, it is important to point out that territorial relationships do not preclude the need for a cross-cutting definition of Italian know-how that transcends (or rather incorporates) the respective dictates of regional legislatures. In chapter 3 the proposed definitions aim to contextualize the identified concept-terms in the versatile and multifaceted world of the artistic crafts, helping to deepen and refine the understanding of each term.

The experts that were interviewed are all prominent in their fields and, through their experience and vision, can be seen as emblematic of the artistic crafts both nationally and internationally. Their testimony provided invaluable insights into what constitutes "excellence", a term that goes far beyond the legal requirements and plays an integral role in the economy, which has turned this most desirable of attributes into a competitive advantage.

Nonetheless, several questions remain. For example, is this competitive advantage always sufficiently well understood and exploited? Is excellence seen as a generator of economic growth and a means of emerging from the current recession? The research commissioned by the Cologni Foundation and carried out by Enrico Finzi, whose findings are summarized earlier in these pages, paints a picture that, while in some respects reassuring, certainly provides food for thought. Moreover, the qualities or characteristics that the sample group attributed to the term "excellence" have provided further significant input for more theoretical considerations; they have also introduced more subjective and less easily mapped values, such as creativity and passion, into the assessment process.

These attributes were certainly not lacking in the Lombard masters that were interviewed, and the views they expressed reflect the thinking of people who have learnt, practised and passed on their know-how for a significant portion of their lives. This "peer review", albeit rendered in a narrative rather than schematic form, suggests that the kind of excellence we are talking about must always be accompanied by a substantial period of practical experience, not in the sense of the daily drudgery of the workhorse, but of an unceasing response to the creative challenges set down by the endless possibilities offered by the materials, by new ideas, by unexpected creative visions.

The consultations with these diverse groups have culminated in a table or matrix – an intrinsically objective and detached tool with more than one concealed danger. The researchers themselves have admitted that the matrix presented here does not claim to be exclusive or immutable, but should be seen rather as an aid to assessment. It provides a precise list of characteristics that the real master artisans should possess, and whose greater or lesser presence needs to be ascertained and considered by a board, as has been prudently suggested. It is also an attempt (successful, in our opinion, although it can be further refined) to introduce in Italy a culture of assessing excellence, a culture that aims to protect and promote the country's great intangible cultural heritage. We hope it will help make it easier to identify those "Living Treasures" (as they are so beautifully named in Japan) who can still be found in every corner of Italy, often hidden away in the background.

Application of this assessment tool will reveal the extent to which the expectations of the researchers and consumers have been met. Like all undertakings with trailblazing aspirations, this project will also be subject to verification and variation. It will be tested, and will contribute to the research that the Cologni Foundation is conducting on Italy's foremost artisans. Perhaps it will also help us to better understand what we should have learnt from the ancient Greeks, namely that authentic beauty must be accompanied by genuine "goodness". As we have seen, excellence thrives on passion, but also on authenticity, legitimacy, creativity and all the other features typical of the "artisan" who is, and continues to be, a true maker of beauty.

The assessment matrix shows that beauty, from a production

perspective, is inseparable from the success of the Made in Italy label. It is, therefore, a beauty that is "participatory", since it stems from a team effort, the result of a fusion of many minds and many hands, each expressing their own but complementary visions, dreams and knowledge. As the findings have shown, beauty of this kind relies on tradition, but it also incorporates novel elements which, while introducing fresh perspectives and new standards when they first appear, eventually take root and become part of that timeless tradition. This beauty is ultimately also the fruit of hard work, personal commitment and extensive training in specialized schools and the workshop. And it also belongs to the realm of dreams, transporting us into an unexpected, otherworldly dimension, which is nonetheless profoundly linked to reality and desire.

According to Enrico Finzi's study, the younger generation appears, at times, to be far removed from this world – and yet the younger generation is what incites us to keep in mind that *la grande bellezza, Italy's great and touching beauty,* must pass through their hands. We must carefully nurture this new generation, guiding it towards excellence and the highest standards of workmanship. They are the makers of tomorrow's beauty, the protagonists of the progress mentioned in the title of this concluding chapter.

I would therefore like to end with a commitment to the future.

The Cologni Foundation for the Métiers d'Art, directed by Alberto Cavalli (who oversaw this research), reaffirms its resolve to assess and promote the work of the great master artisans and to nurture the talent of the new generations. It will do so via two specific initiatives, for which the outcomes of this research will certainly prove useful.

The first is to institute an award, "Maestro d'Arte e Mestiere", which takes its lead from UNESCO and whose aim is to recognize and promote the "intangible cultural heritage" that many of our leading artisans so impeccably personify. This initiative has been developed in collaboration with ALMA (La Scuola Internazionale di Cucina Italiana), presided by legendary Italian chef Gualtiero Marchesi, and with leading Italian schools of arts and crafts, which have at their disposal top experts in applied arts, artisanal know-how and creative *savoir-faire*. We believe that establishing concrete and, as far as possible, objective criteria for ascertaining "excellence" is an important starting point in identifying the most significant and emblematic figures who deserve this distinction.[6]

The second initiative is to create a Register of Artistic Craft Excellence. This international register is the natural corollary of the Maestro d'Arte

[6] See www.maestrodartemestiere.it/en.

e Mestiere award and will be structured along the lines of the Japanese Living National Treasures or the French *Maîtres d'art* directories.

We believe that these initiatives will lead to a fruitful and constructive dialogue with the institutions: our common aim should be to set a possible course of concerted and effective actions that can be shared with other countries or territories, where the artistic crafts are not only an expression of creative productivity, but also – and perhaps more importantly – of culture.

EPILOGUE

ALBERTO CAVALLI - GIOVANNA MARCHELLO

EXPANDING THE VISION OF EXCELLENCE

When we set out to explore the universe of Italian artistic crafts – a process that culminated in a matrix to assess artisanal excellence – we had a dual purpose. First, we wanted to shine the spotlight on the great master craftspeople who dedicate their lives and talent to the creation of lasting beauty. Second, we wanted to help young artisans identify the values they should pursue to achieve a level of craftsmanship worthy of a "living treasure".

Our goal was not simply to define an impersonal matrix, the product of abstract calculations, which might be appropriate for the cold realm of finance but not for the passionate universe of crafts. We aimed to be inclusive, directing a loving and admiring gaze on artisanal excellence. In the process, we identified and analysed 11 criteria that we believe come closest to tracing an ideal path that transcends national boundaries – a universal matrix that highlights and celebrates the rich diversity of the artistic crafts in all the countries where, like Italy, workshops, ateliers and small enterprises flourish, and where the "intelligent" hand of the master craftsperson gives substance to the creative vision of the designer. Thanks to the Michelangelo Foundation for Creativity and Craftsmanship – which endorsed, supported and promoted the English translation and publication of this study[1] – we have taken another step towards developing a common vocabulary that will enable us to recognize, understand and protect artisanal excellence.

Words are the building blocks by which we give substance to our thoughts: we felt that it was important to create a language that could be shared with confidence and ease by all those who strive to safeguard

[1] First published in Italian as *Il valore del mestiere: Elementi per una valutazione dell'eccellenza artigiana* (Venice: Marsilio, 2014).

and promote fine craftsmanship. A brave undertaking, no doubt, and not without its pitfalls. It was nonetheless a necessary undertaking if we were to advance the networking activities of the Michelangelo Foundation, which will help develop (as it is already doing) a fruitful and constructive awareness.

The master artisans who were interviewed for the Italian edition represent not only a particular territory, but also an approach. Their point of view, therefore, is in itself paradigmatic of a perspective that is not confined by national boundaries and speaks to all those who appreciate and seek hand-made perfection. To test our matrix also at an international level, we decided to incorporate in this English edition an additional set of interviews with a selected group of European masters. In doing so, we followed the same methodological approach we used in our original research. As with their Italian counterparts, the interviews with the ten European artisans were conducted by Giovanna Marchello.

The choice of interviewees was based on specific considerations: the relevance of their craft in their territory, their reputation and renown, their ability to interact productively with contemporary design, the cultural context and the relative value of their respective production sectors. We picked masters with lifelong experience of their craft, as well as young artisans whose potential and talent have already been formally acknowledged.

The testimony of these artisans, who devote their skill wholeheartedly to the creation of beautiful and well-made objects, has provided us with an invaluable affirmation of the 11 assessment criteria we had identified in our study and which have proven to be applicable even in contexts that are geographically distant but culturally close. Once again, by the union of similarities and differences, we can generate an important vision: a specialized, evocative and authentic common language by which to discover and observe Europe's intangible cultural property, a heritage that gives us a fundamental competitive advantage and nourishes our identity and value every day.

Fully aware of the long path that lies ahead of us, we would like to draw particular attention to these interviews: the intellectual integrity of the artisans, who recognize the beauty, worth and truthfulness of genuine craftsmanship, provides us with an important insight into the future of the artistic crafts, namely that it is beauty itself that feeds the joy of making, of being, of living. In a world pervaded by tautology it is the joy we feel when a simple object speaks directly to our hearts that can make the difference. Today more than ever.

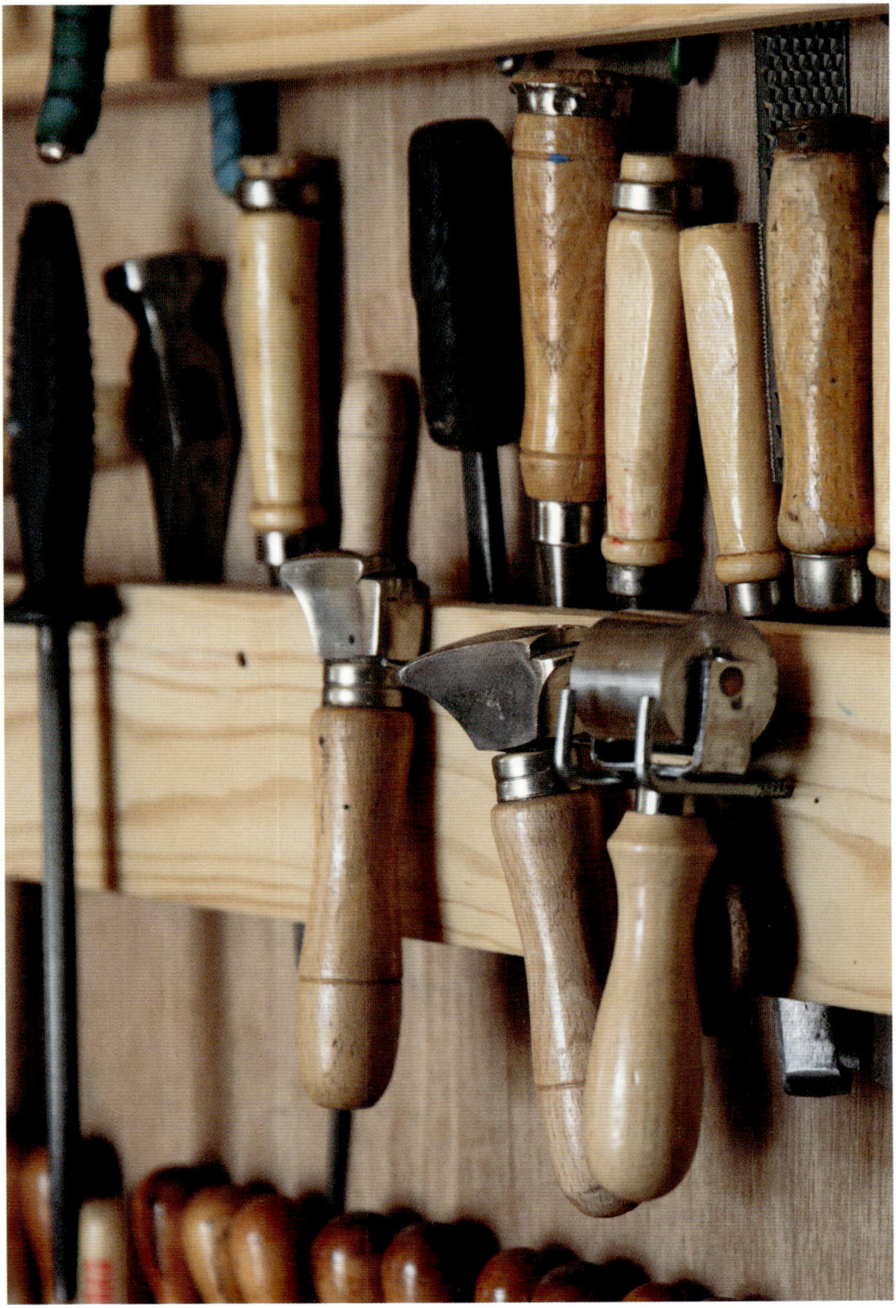

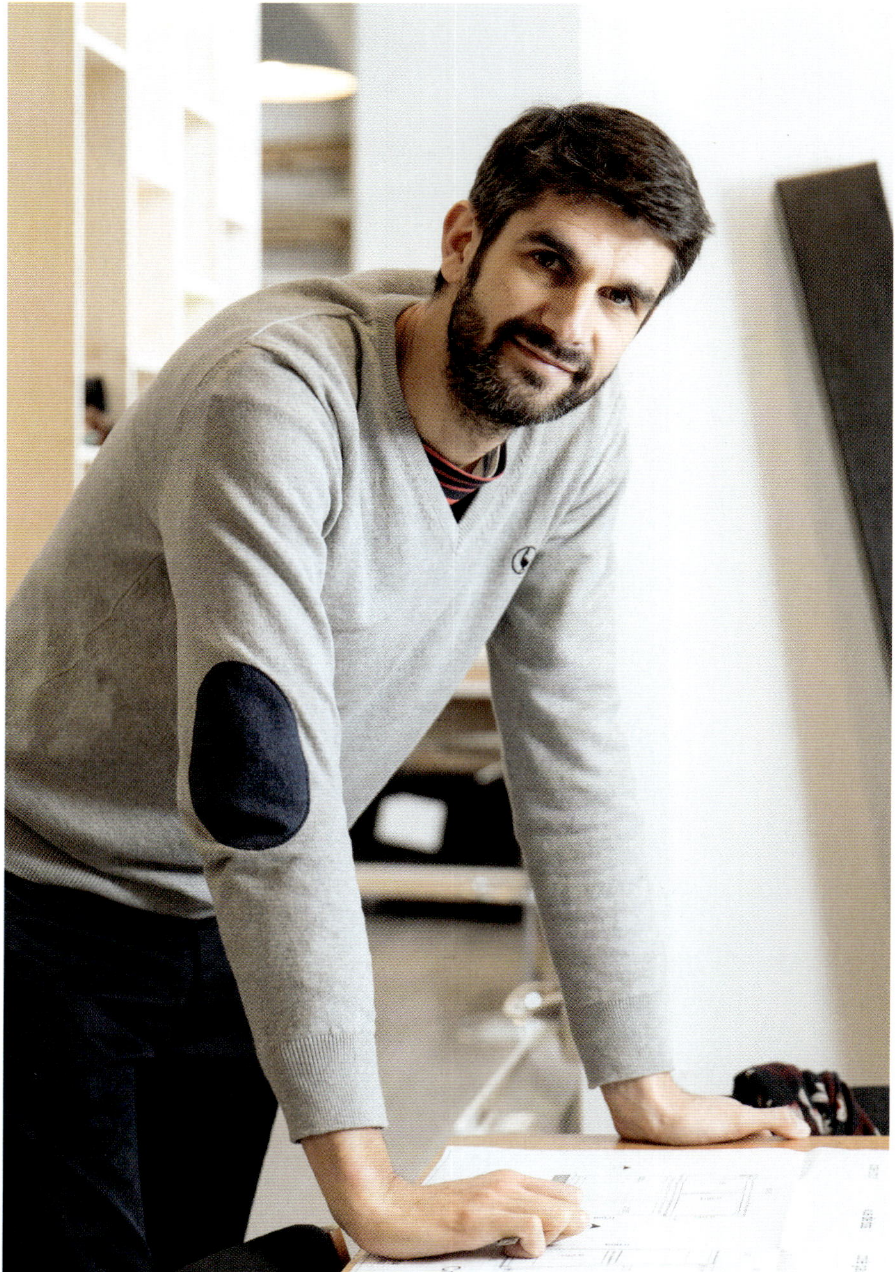

1. LUDOVIC AVENEL, CABINETMAKER

Ludovic Avenel was born in 1984 in Rouen, France. Although none of his family had previously followed an artistic career, he knew from an early age that he wanted to make things with his hands. He started out as an apprentice within a professional school before enrolling at the École Boulle, the college of fine arts and applied arts in Paris. In 2007, aged 23, he was awarded the prestigious Bettencourt Schueller prize for "intelligence of the hand". He opened his own workshop the following year in the Faubourg Saint Antoine, Paris's historic district where skilled woodworkers and furniture-makers have traditionally gathered.

Avenel combines creativity and savoir-faire *to produce exquisite one-off or limited-series pieces in a contemporary style, using traditional materials such as sycamore, wenge and mahogany, alongside more modest or cutting-edge materials such as rubber, cardboard and alucobond (an aluminium composite material). While fully versed in the rules of his art, he firmly believes in pushing the boundaries, borrowing techniques for his furniture from other cultures, such as making a single-piece drawer based on the Japanese art of origami. By playing with the conventions, he seeks to reconcile the two disciplines of design and craftsmanship.*

None of my family has ever been involved in cabinetmaking or design: I'm the first (and only). It's a passion I discovered when I was a child. I always wanted to do things with my hands, and at the same time I enjoyed exploring and understanding the secrets of how things are made.

Today I have a small team: a group in charge of research and the creative side, and three artisans who work with me in the atelier. I pass on my skills, but I learn a lot from them too: each has their own personality and interests, which overlap, and in the end you realize that their individual paths have raised the competence of the whole team. In this way, you can evolve and give to the others.

For me, the transmission process is more about developing curiosity, reflection, understanding. There are many solutions to the same problem, but we tend to choose the one that's based on our personal experience and path. So, if you just teach a technique to someone who hasn't personally experienced other ways of doing it, that person won't know if it is the most appropriate technique to use. The important thing is to find the solution autonomously, taking responsibility. In the end, what matters is the result.

Authenticity

An object is authentic when it has its own personality. To be authentic, it must be consistent, in both its external and internal nature.

It is unique and authentic because it was made by hands that possess competence and expertise. You can be authentic even when you adopt a very contemporary technique, because in your hands it will develop its own language.

The traceability of a hand-made object is crucial. Often my products are supplied with an identity card explaining where the wood comes from, who designed the object, where it was made and by whom. I think it's also educational, because often customers don't know how a piece of furniture is made. The identity card gives them an insight and enables them to have a different approach to the way they buy, because they're more knowledgeable. It's important to create a culture around what we do, otherwise it's difficult to convey it, expressing also the time that has gone into it, even in terms of the biological time that was necessary for a tree to grow and for the wood to dry – on top, of course, of the time the object took to make.

When both a designer and an artisan are involved, I think that it's important to have a double signature, although some egos are probably complicated to handle…

Competence

When you're comfortable and relaxed in what you're doing. When you're not afraid. When the work is not an effort. When it is part of you and your continuation. That's competence. Perhaps competence is also when you realize that you will never finish learning.

There are many fundamental competences that I learnt in school, including discipline, knowledge of the materials, deep respect for the techniques, passion, curiosity… All these go beyond the craft, and concern who you are and your relationship with the material. If you are overconfident, then you could make mistakes. You have to learn the manual skills and how to concentrate on what you're doing. Then, with practice, in the workshop, you improve these skills.

We mustn't forget that we make things for other people, so it's vital to understand the client's needs: you have to listen carefully and be open-minded. The same applies to your team: it's important to understand and accept their needs and interests. We can't be perfectly competent in every aspect of the trade but we can always be constructive. It's an experience that we build on day by day, with suppliers, clients, the team, other craftspeople. For me, this is the culture of truly living the *métiers d'art*.

Craftsmanship

I would say that I do 70 per cent of my work by hand and 30 per cent with a machine. What's sure is that you can't take the individual out of the making, so in that sense everything is 100 per cent hand made.

Cabinetmaking consists of a series of phases: in some, the hand gives added value, while sometimes it isn't important at all, because a machine can do it better. Some objects are more technical and you don't need to see the trace of the hand. But they can only be assembled by hand, and the hand is always necessary to give an object life. A sculpture, for example, would be devoid of life if it were made entirely by machine.

In France, the *règles de l'art* apply to techniques that have been used for a very long time and that we know are better than the others. And since the rules depend on a number of constantly changing factors (materials, techniques, technology, environment), the rules themselves are also constantly changing. I think that the *règles de l'art* define the quality that goes beyond the perceived quality. If we make an object according to the rules that bring about this quality, we respect the ethics of craft. In this sense, "ethics" is synonymous with "transparency".

There are two main differences between an artisanal and a serial production. The first is determined by the simple fact that certain objects or materials can only be worked by hand. The second is that when we make something with our hands, we can tweak it until we achieve the result we are looking for. This is something that can't be done in serial production. And when we do it with passion and pleasure, we transfer a part of ourselves into this object, and we give it its own life. This is a quality that isn't fully defined; it's not mechanical and is subject to the unpredictable.

Creativity

I see creativity as something global: it involves the technique and the execution, the design and the approach. It's about transforming what is part of our daily life into something different. There is creativity in every single phase of the making, from beginning to end, even in the way an object is packaged and delivered.

I am inspired by my daily life, even just talking and working with different people. Some projects come out better when I am pushed for time, when I have a deadline to meet and the urgency spurs me on to get it done. "Creative stress" is exhausting, but effective!

However, as with an athlete, your performance tends to remain stable for a while until you achieve the next level, and then it plateaus again. It takes regular exercise and routine to build up to that peak of creativity that allows you to stray from your familiar path. But it can't happen with every project. The moment comes when you feel ready, and you have the time and the opportunity. What I find interesting in the *métiers d'art* is that there are companies that are always more forward-looking, more conceptual. This happens also in haute couture and in industry, where peaks of research and innovation provide the nourishment to create new paths at all levels. But artisans can't constantly be in the phase of pure research, because they couldn't make a living.

Interpretation

Every project aspires to perfection, but each time, for different reasons, it doesn't come out so "perfect". If I could go back and do it again, I would probably do something in a different way, and the result would change. To interpret is to capture the universe, the environment, the style, the objective of a design. If you are collaborating with a brand, you have to find what that project has to evoke, where it wants to lead you and why. It may happen that the designer or the client isn't clear about the goal, so you have to open a dialogue to define it. If you don't, you can't interpret it, because you would in fact be participating in its conception.

What characterizes many artisans is their ability to connect these different universes and open new horizons: everything is possible as they don't have preconceptions. In this exchange, they make the difference in what we perceive with all our senses, so that every object ends up having a soul.

Originality

I tend to think in terms of stretching the rules, rather than breaking them. If a technique has reached a certain level, it can evolve to the next. But if you don't question yourself, you can't move on. You need to think how you can do things differently, like adding new notes to an existing tune. The techniques belong to everyone, but the path is individual, and what's important is the experience, what we find out in the process, even if it has already been done before.

Originality is tied to the identity, to the style, to the shape. Personally, I enjoy passing from one style to another, without mental barriers. I follow what interests me and amuses me intellectually. Since my work is always very linear, I like to take everyone by surprise by making something completely different. Two objects can be similar in shape, made from the same wood, with the same veins, but look completely different if you approach them in different ways. But even then they retain the qualities of authenticity and originality.

Talent

Talent is extremely important, and it translates into the pleasure of working. You are sometimes faced with unexpected problems and you must find a solution within yourself and move on. The weight of knowledge can be overwhelming, and I think talent is the energy that allows you to be "lighter" and completely open.

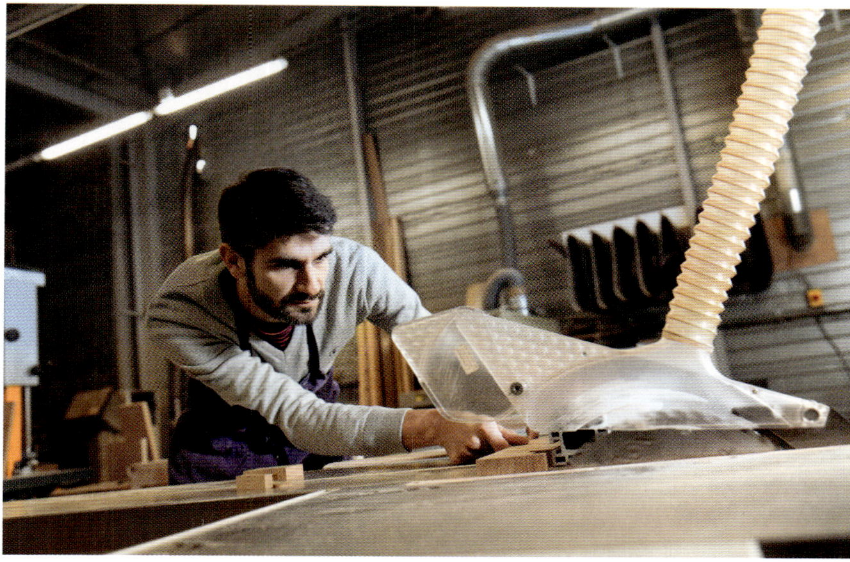

The more you exercise it, the more talent develops and things become easier, more natural. Sometimes you can see this potential in young people, who have a very agile, surprisingly natural approach. I love to meet artisans who have progressed farther than I have, both in their craft and in their research. I find it interesting when the solution comes from someone working in another field, because they have a broad experience but a different point of view. They see things in a fresh and new way, a bit like a child.

Territory

Cabinetmaking has a long tradition in the Faubourg Saint-Antoine. In the days of the guilds, all the craftspeople working here were free artisans, often protected by the nuns of the Abbaye Saint-Antoine-des-Champs. The creativity that flourished here, deriving from the different origins of the craftspeople (Flemish, Italian, German, French…) and their fields of specialization (bronze, marble, wood, lacquering, gilding, varnishing…), was amazing, and was much appreciated by royalty. This enabled the artisans to make some incredible advances in the techniques of veneering and mixing different materials.

When I was a student, I was frustrated because it was impossible to have exchanges with other craftspeople. That's why I settled down in this quarter, where this tradition endures, although much diluted. I often work with leather, marble, glass, bronze, so a project will involve dealing with other artisans. It gives me the chance to share ideas and experiences, and in return to improve my understanding and find new solutions. I believe there is still a lot to be done in this direction, to become closer and more creative. I don't think I could work without this interaction.

For me as a craftsman, the provenance of the wood is very important. I rely on established suppliers with a solid reputation, whose materials can be traced and I can be sure of the quality of the drying process.

Tradition and innovation

The fundamentals of this trade are tied to the raw material we use. Since wood is a living substance, the whole history of cabinetmaking is essentially based on tackling the problem of moisture and hydrometric variations, which are difficult to control. Veneering, which is the core of cabinetmaking, has developed from the challenge of slicing and gluing the wood panels and decorations onto a wooden surface.

Traditionally furniture was designed and made to last, so it was important that it would weather well and continue to be beautiful even with "wrinkles". And if it broke or was damaged, you had to be able to repair it. Today's factories are not concerned with tomorrow. But there isn't a big difference between making something that will last forever and something that won't. If you make something using beautiful materials, it's a shame if it doesn't last, even if it's only from the point of view of sustainability.

The first real innovation in the history of cabinetmaking was the invention of the drawer: every time we find an innovative solution, we create a new vocabulary linked to this technique. Take Thonet, for example, whose bending technique created a new style and a new vocabulary for wood. In this workshop we've developed a novel way of opening a piece of furniture, which I've used in my "bureau à effeuiller" – a desk with a flexible top that can be peeled off: by working the veneer in a supple way, laser-cut and paper-backed, we enable it to bend. We employ traditional techniques but with different procedures.

Cabinetmaking has certainly benefited from many technical and scientific advances. There are new materials and technologies that allow us to improve our handling of the hydrometric variations. The way we design a project has also changed dramatically, and technology, including 3D printing, has greatly facilitated the realization of an object.

The trade is evolving hand in hand with techniques, tastes and lifestyles. The question is: How can I, as an artisan, take all these changes and incorporate them into what I'm doing? Today we have tools that enable us to work on the materials both in a direct way (such as the hammer and saw) and in an indirect way (such as laser and computer-based techniques). It will be interesting to discover what the next level of the artisan's interaction can be. At the same time, it is possible to innovate, or rather to rediscover and reinterpret techniques that have been used before, maybe in the 17th or 18th centuries. In the workshop, things also happen by accident, and the accident can turn into something interesting, as in cooking. It's a big game, where everything is possible.

Training

I realized early in life that I wanted to work with wood. I took the CAP (Vocational Aptitude Certificate, the first level of training in France) and the BAC PRO (Professional Baccalauréat) in woodworking and cabinetmaking, which gave me the foundations of this craft. I went on to the École Boulle in Paris, where I obtained a Diplôme des Métiers d'Art in cabinetmaking and a Diplôme Supérieur des Arts Appliqués in product design and interior architecture. My training was a perfect mixture of practical skills and cultural notions tied to the history of the trade. I believe it took me seven or eight years to feel "comfortable" in my work, to feel that it came easily. But it takes a lifetime really, because you can never perfectly master a trade. What I find interesting is that the more you learn and understand, the more you can "play" with a skill. It's like a musician who, after years of practising scales, can start to change the arrangement of the notes – which are always the same – to create something new. Similarly, in cabinetmaking we can create something new by playing with the culture and techniques. I had exceptional teachers, but when I started working I was alone. Perhaps, if I'd done things differently, I could have progressed faster, but I wasn't looking so much to learn quickly as to live the experience.

Even if you're skilled in a technique, you should always ask yourself, "How could I do this in a different way, and better?" It's more of an introspective path, and this is the progression that interests me, both intellectually and professionally.

For this reason, I always try to keep up to date also with other *savoir-faire*, because the techniques of an upholsterer or a saddler cross over with the techniques of cabinetmaking, and can be integrated into our work.

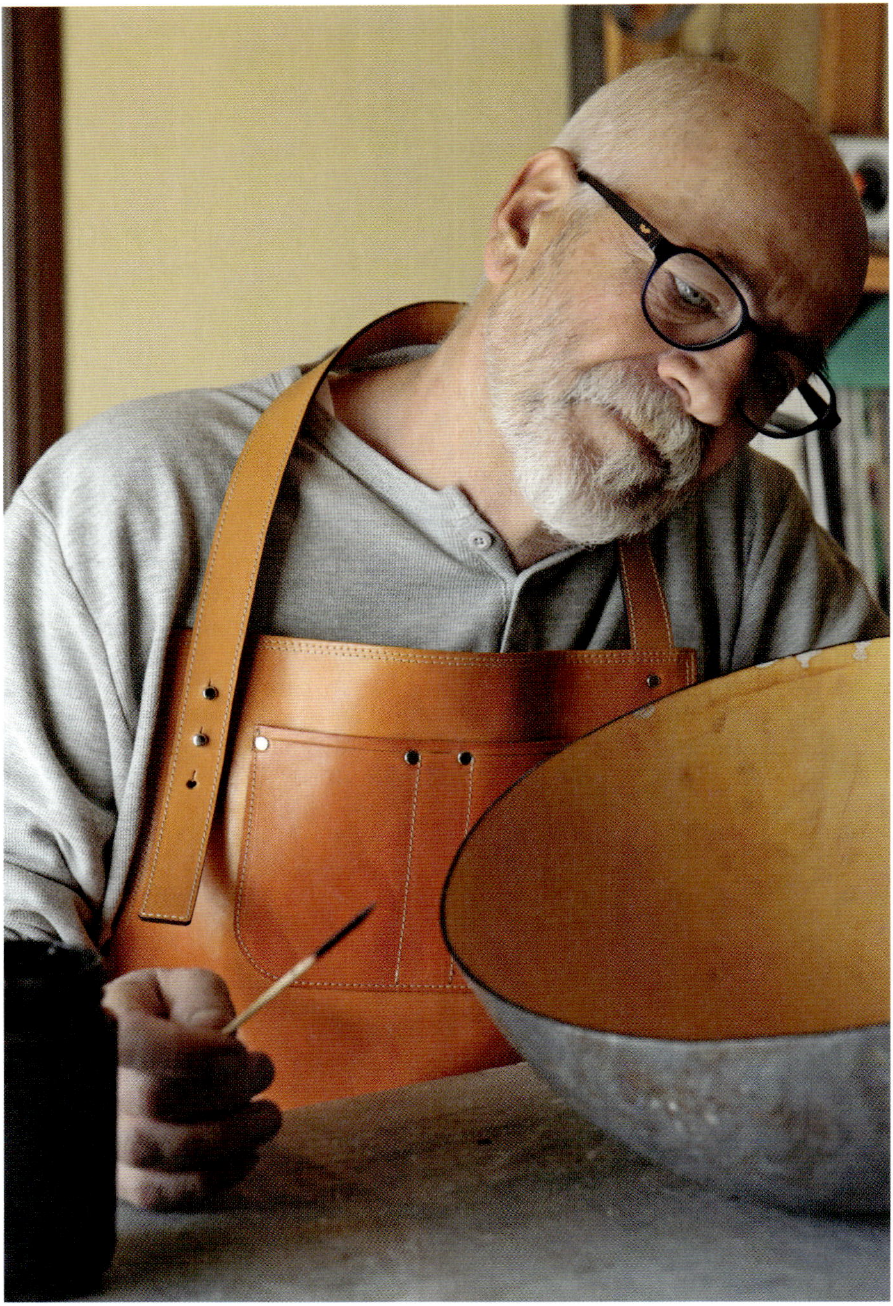

2. JOSÉ LUIS BAZÁN, LEATHER CRAFTSMAN

José Luis Bazán comes from a venerable family of leatherworkers who have practised and handed down their craft for three generations. He was born in 1959 in Ubrique (Spain), a town whose leatherworking tradition dates back to the 18th century, when Italian immigrants arrived bringing the trade with them. He began his training at the tender age of 12 while still at school. He spent his formative years going from one workshop to another, acquiring as much knowledge and experience of the different techniques as possible. Bazán started his formal apprenticeship at 14, qualified at the age of 18 and became a master at 21. He then went on to work for Manolo Ortiz, specializing in bags and suitcases, before opening his own workshop serving some of the major fashion houses such as Luis Vuitton and Chanel. He also spent time in Seville, working in production and design and in public and private training centres.

Bazán has been based in Benaocaz since 2002, where he can give free rein to his creative ability, using leather as a means of expression. He devotes much of his time to research and to developing his own techniques for moulding and engraving, and creating textures and shapes using all kinds of elements and mixing leather with other materials. Adapting age-old techniques to new technologies is his brand signature. Bazán has participated in several exhibitions and has won awards for excellence.

Leatherworking is a family tradition and both my father and grandfather were master craftsmen, so I got acquainted with leather from a very early age.

Having spent 20 years training young people, I now conduct only personalized programmes, one to one, directly on the project that they want to develop. This means that if they want to make a bag, they don't have to start with small leather goods, and in a couple of weeks they can gain the same experience as they would in two or three years working in a workshop with 15 or 20 people. In the past, I have always done it in the classic way, from the beginning to the end. But I no longer believe in this type of training: training is important but it has to be personalized.

My pupils come from all over the world. With me, they also do a "spiritual" training: this is a time of transition and we need a little bit of magic. Some of the young people who come here arrive in very low spirits, disintegrated by what surrounds them. When they leave, they are "healed" by the creative and manual work with the leather.

Authenticity

In the old days of Ubrique, when a master thought that the apprentices were ready to have their own workshops, they presented them to a committee and the apprentices were given a name and a seal with which they would stamp their work. This was their "mark of authenticity".

I think that authenticity today lies also in being faithful to the person you are, whoever you are. It's you in the moment in which you start working, but also in the whole process that precedes the work, because what comes before is days and nights of thinking. I am the sum of all I have done, all the people I have met, all the masters who have taught me, and this is what makes me authentic.

Today, to promote a product of high craftsmanship, we must be able to tell a story. Every piece is highly personal, since it represents the life and the path of the artisan. This is what the market needs and expects: people are tired of buying mass-market products.

In this sense, the signature of the artisan is important. If you buy something that has this degree of personalization, you also want to know the name of the person who made it.

My collaboration with Loewe was the first time the name of the craftsperson was associated with the product of a fashion brand, although not on the actual product, which consisted of 150 numbered pieces, but in the marketing. It was a very important statement, and probably a sign that a new era is beginning for the crafts.

Competence

I think that competence has to do with believing in your ideas. To be competent, artisans must know their craft and understand the materials they use; they must also be capable of creating, designing and researching the project they want to develop. In addition, they must establish a selling price for the product. Then they have to photograph it, market it, promote it and sell it. Their competence must be 360 degrees complete.

As an artisan, what I'm most interested in is creating; the rest is just a problem, especially here in Spain, where the real "craftsmanship of excellence" isn't adequately supported. There is a lot of bureaucracy, the tax system stifles you, and very little energy and investment are dedicated to promoting this culture among the public, which very often isn't even aware if it is buying quality or not.

Craftsmanship

I love new technologies and I'm not bothered if other artisans use them in their work. But I prefer to do everything by hand and by myself. I love travelling and I can go anywhere in the world because all I need is my leather and four tools.

There is no such thing as perfection in an artisan's work, but I consider something to be masterly done when, first of all, the original idea is expressed in the finished work. There are many paths that you can take that will lead you in different directions. For example, leather can have a defect that forces you to do something in a different way. It's a relationship that you are building with what you are creating: at a certain point, it talks to you and it just happens. But when you start to create, you ask more and more of the material, and you have to know when to stop. This is the meaning of "masterly done", and I believe the term "excellence" defines this quality very well. Whether we want to call the outcome an artwork or a craftwork depends on those who look at it.

There is an international movement that supports the spread of artisanal and micro-enterprises (one or two people at most) focused on so-called "creative craftsmanship" and one-off production. I explain to my pupils that if you are making 10 bags, you are simply performing an operation with your head that's multiplied by 10. It's a mechanical process and those pieces don't have a soul. A unique piece, on the other hand, has a soul, because it's your creation, something in which you have been immersed. Unfortunately, artisans are often forced to produce series of products for their own survival. But even if you are making ten bags that are the same, if you do them from start to finish you will have shared a small part of your life with them and each bag will be a unique piece to which you have transmitted your emotions.

Creativity

Picasso used to say that "inspiration exists, but it has to find you working". I always sleep with my notebook near me, so that if I wake up in the middle of the night with an idea, I can jot it down. Sometimes, if I have an idea and also the materials, I might get up and start to work on it at whatever time of night.

My creativity lies in the relationship with the material. There was a time (when I was a teenager, many years ago) when I thought that I could be more creative if I let my subconscious flow by smoking grass. But I realized that it really didn't make any difference, because the creativity is already inside me and I only have to let the material talk to me and guide me. Since I "think in leather" I know what result will come out of a certain process, and that if I do a bit more or a bit less, maybe something completely different will happen.

Interpretation

Some artisans have preconceived ideas and they put boundaries and limits on what they can do. But artisans know their craft and the point to which they can push it, and if you are open, you can do whatever you want. Very often designers design objects that are impossible to make, or totally impractical, because they have no idea of what working with leather is about. However, if a designer has an idea that's beautiful but impossible, my experience enables me to preserve the original idea and to transform it into something feasible. We mustn't forget that we are artisans, and we have to make things that can be used. Otherwise, we are doing something that's closer to art.

The reason the luxury brand Loewe asked me to develop the Bowls Project was that Jonathan Anderson, Loewe's creative director, saw the leather bowls I make and had the idea of reproducing the ceramic bowls originally created by the famous potter Lucie Rie. I spent two months figuring out a way to overcome a critical problem: leather can only be shaped when it's vegetable-tanned, but Loewe wanted to use a very soft, chrome-tanned nappa. I succeeded in finding a solution that works with every kind of leather, even the softest, and so I could start this project with them. But how I did it is my secret!

Originality

I don't know if what I do is original, but I can safely say that I don't see anyone else doing similar things to mine. I believe my originality derives from the way I understand leather, in my relationship with it. There are many techniques that have been developed throughout the ages but I think that only a very small part of the creative potential of leather has been used so far. Moulding with water is one of the techniques that I use most of the time and what I've done is to update it and use it in a contemporary way.

To take risks and break the rules is very important, and I do it all the time. I explore paths that I don't know where they will lead. If I end up burning the leather, for example, I will use it for something else. That's because I really don't like doing things that are always the same and in the same way. If there are 20 objects that look exactly the same and only one has a defect, you can be sure it's mine! That detail, that imperfection, is what gives the object its value.

Talent

Talent is very important in any trade. The talent I'm talking about applies to the "craft" as a whole, the full process, not just a small portion of the job like screwing the bolts, which anyone can learn. In this sense, talent is enlightenment. It's the ability to look for the revelation, to have the patience and determination and the soul to reach the point where the revelation emerges.

With my pupils, I can see if they have talent on the very first day. I give them a piece of leather and I ask them what they can do with it. I never hold back anything that I know, because the other person will only learn what they can learn, nothing more and nothing less. So if I

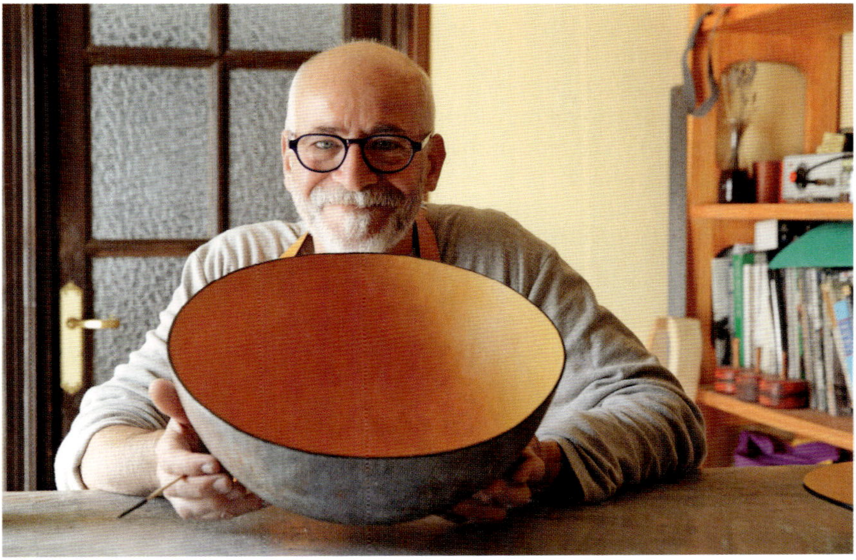

understand that I can fill them up, I continue. I can only show them the path, and they will have to go down that path on their own. Each person is born with a gift, with a purpose in life, and I'm enormously thankful to the universe for the paths it has led me to follow.

Territory

Ubrique's tradition of producing small leather goods, bags and suitcases dates back to the 18th century, and most families who live in the area were involved in leatherworking. Many things have changed in the past 30 to 40 years. First of all, it's very difficult to find artisans who have a full, all-round competence: most are specialized in just one part of the process, such as dyeing, making straps, sewing bags, etc. Nonetheless, all the big brands continue to come to Ubrique to produce their leather goods because of the high concentration of workshops possessing a level of expertise that is, in fact, superior to anywhere else in the world.

For me, the raw material is the most fundamental element. I have a good knowledge of leather and I know what is more suitable for each type of technique. Since my partner and I are very bohemian, we only use vegetable-tanned leather from adult animals. Every time I use a skin, I ask the animal to forgive me, because we must give dignity to what we take. What is left over, I give to my pupils, and I send the smallest pieces to Ubrique where they are recycled. Vegetable tanning was the traditional method in Ubrique until the Spanish Civil War, but then the big industries in Barcelona, Valencia and Alicante started to use chrome tanning, which is very quick and allows you to dye the leather in whatever colour you want, whereas vegetable tanning is possible only with black, brown, red and natural colours. Today the leather comes from Argentina, India, Africa, but it continues to be tanned in Spain.

I've chosen to live in Benaocaz because it's isolated and at the same time close enough to Ubrique, which is useful for many practical and logistical reasons.

Tradition and innovation

The techniques that we use are still very traditional, and some, like the moulding of leather, date back to prehistoric times. There have been many innovations, however, in the materials, in the techniques and in the design.

Most artisans have only a very limited knowledge of leather, so it's difficult for them to stray from the beaten track. What interests me is to see leather from new points of view and to do things with it that are different from what everyone else does. I like to mix leather with wood, ceramic, stainless steel, silver, tin and so on. When I can't do something personally, I ask for the assistance of other artisans, but I like to try to get where I want on my own, to experiment also with materials and techniques that are different from leather.

Over time I've built a network with artisans who have both a good hand and good ideas, but these collaborations are only possible once in a while owing to distance and limited time. There is one group of artisans with whom I am developing a very innovative retail project near Malaga. I am also a member of a small association that meets every two or three years to exchange information, organize training sessions, share updates on techniques, etc. We also keep in touch through Facebook and other social networks.

Training

In the past the training system in Ubrique was very rigorous, and individual progress depended on your personal commitment and determination: you started off as a simple apprentice and only after going through a series of intermediate levels did you become a master.

I began my training at the age of 12, when I was still at school. I wanted to learn from the best masters, and I spent my training years passing from one workshop to the next, taking in everything that I could. First I learnt the *repujado* technique, a typical Andalusian embossed leather, in the workshop of the Urbina brothers. At 14 I started my full-time apprenticeship in a small leather company where I was taught how to

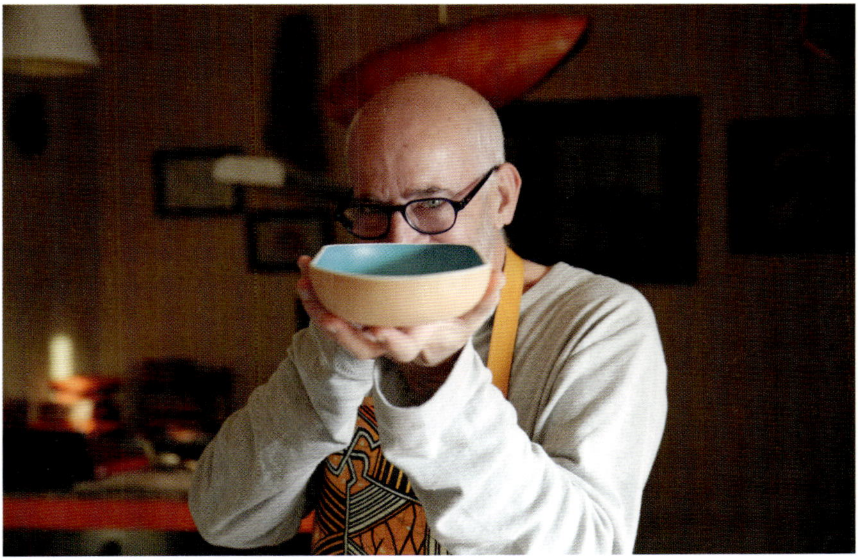

make leather-covered boxes known as *guadamecil*; I literally "stole" the craft by observing Felix Sanchez, who was a real genius but not the master to whom I'd been assigned. Then I moved on to specialize in bags and suitcases with Manolo Ortiz.

My masters taught me not only how to work the leather, but also how to run a business, how to have patience and the values to live by. Above all, I learnt from my father: we had a very close relationship and he always gave me advice. When he knew I was getting bored with what I was doing, he would encourage me by saying, "Don't worry, there are another 400 workshops where you can go!" I opened my own workshop and after a while joined a design group that had just been established by the association of producers in Ubrique: we were specialized leatherworkers at the service of the big designer companies (Louis Vuitton, Chanel, etc.). After a few years I left for Seville, where I worked in production and design and in public and private training centres. Finally I came back and settled down in Benaocaz, where I dedicate my time to training and experimentation.

An artisan never stops learning: you can have a diploma and a seal, but you continue to learn throughout your life. I know I do, every day, even from those who come to learn from me. That's why I consider my work a blessing.

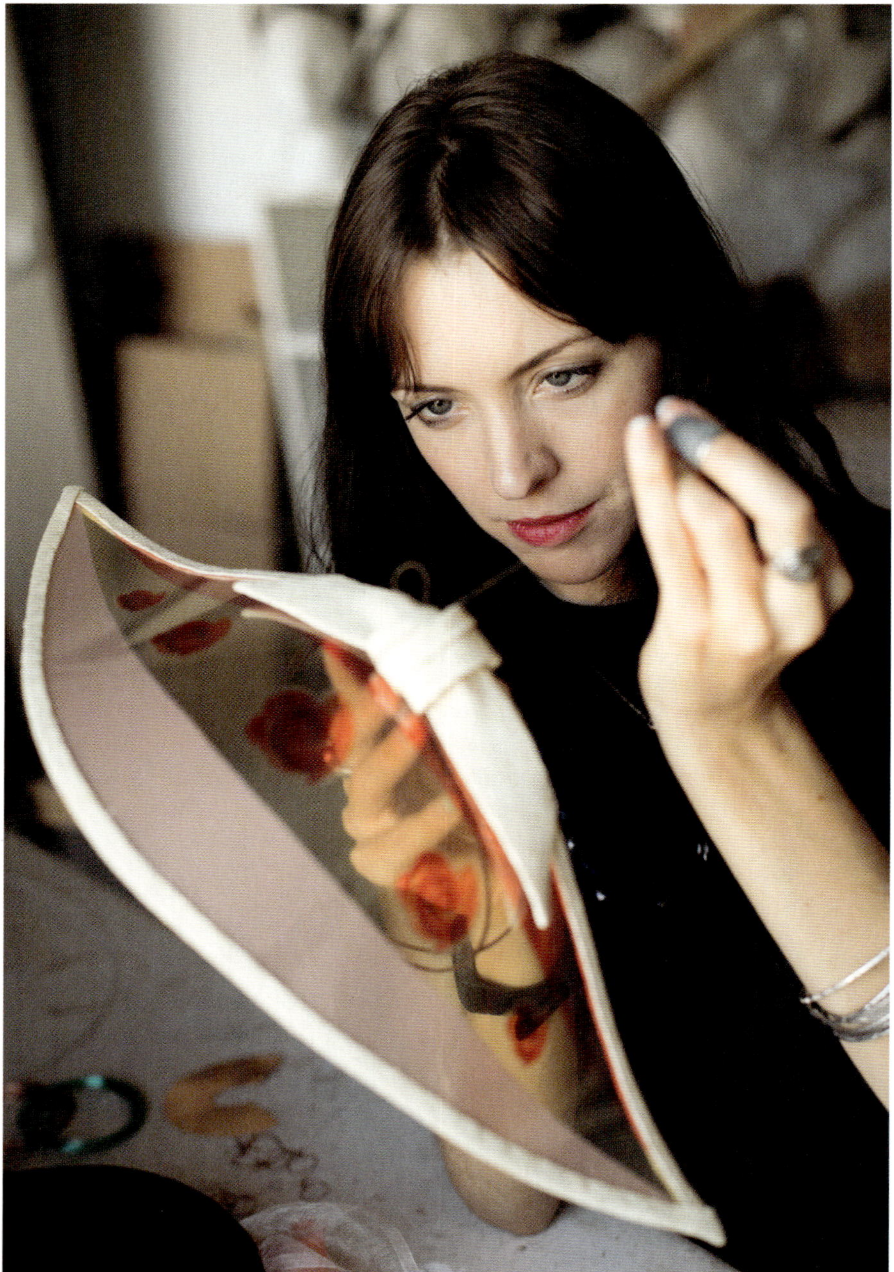

3. SOPHIE BEALE, MILLINER

Sophie Beale grew up on the Isle of Wight (United Kingdom), whose romantic cliffs and blustery sea air continue to inspire her today. She entered millinery

after completing a costume degree, where she discovered a love of making hats. After a course with Rose Cory, former milliner by royal appointment to the late Queen Mother, Beale enrolled on the millinery course at Kensington and Chelsea College, from which she graduated with distinction in 2011 and where she now teaches. After stints with some of the world's most iconic milliners, including Noel Stewart and Philip Treacy, Beale was headhunted for the position of couture milliner at Stephen Jones. She launched her own brand, Sophie Beale Millinery, in 2012, working out of her London studio.

Named Britain's Hottest New Milliner in 2012, Sophie Beale is winner of various awards, including the British Fashion Council and Grazia magazine's national Hat Factor, judged by Philip Treacy and Stephen Jones. Her work was selected from over 100 milliners to join a celebration of Britain's finest millinery in association with the London Olympics. She has also been selected to show at London Fashion Week and is part of the Royal Ascot Millinery Collective 2017. She crafts intricate and sophisticated designs that combine space and lightness, structure and fluidity, texture and depth, innovation and wearability. The brand is sold internationally, with a growing list of high-profile clients.

I am the first in the family to embrace a craft and make it my trade. But I believe it has always been there: both my parents are quite creative, though more on the musical side. My mother is a piano teacher and she has always done a lot of sewing, and my grandmother used to knit. My father plays an instrument too.

My business is still too small to have my own team or apprentices, but at busy times I have someone who comes in and helps with the more basic things. It's the exchange of knowledge for a bit of help! I also teach on the same course that I took at the Kensington and Chelsea College.

Authenticity

Something that's true to its core, to its origins, is authentic. With a hat, I believe that it means it has been made from the start to the finish in a proper way. For this reason, the traceability of the manufacturing process is important if a client wants to buy something that's hand made and completely done by you, or watched over by you if another artisan contributes to its making.

The place where something is manufactured is important for what you are selling it as. For example, the source doesn't matter for many materials, but if you are using a Japanese straw braid, then it must obviously come from Japan. I think the concept of authenticity is also related to the training and to where those skills have been developed: in the case of millinery, we are using very particular methods from this particular place.

Under other aspects, it really has much to do with the romance of it. If you use the same techniques, quality and materials in two different places or countries, it may not affect the final outcome, as such, but it would have more to do with the story of it, the emotions it generates.

Sometimes this aspect is totally detached, and people just buy what you have made, but obviously you need to be linked to customers if you are making something personal. So you need to be there, in that place, with them. It's important that the signature stands out: if the skills are there, then the name relates it to the person who made it.

Competence

I think competence is being able to make fewer mistakes as you go along. It builds up with experience and shows in the final result. And I believe that it's something that you learn in the workshop, while you work, practising and doing things over and over again. Even if you have done a particular thing many times, other things will happen to it when you work in a different temperature or make it into a different shape.

Communication and organizational skills, technological proficiency – these too are elements that need a high level of competence. Being able to control your brand image and developing good communication skills are actually very important today; they are aspects that you have to learn to handle very well.

Craftsmanship

Being so sculptural, most of the work is done by hand. Only occasionally do I make models with elements that can be stitched with a sewing machine, but, even then, they are still hand made. I do everything myself, and I personally follow every step of the process, from buying the materials to constructing the hats.

Being a perfectionist from start to finish, I would say that a hat is masterly made when everything that goes into it, from the skeleton to the trims, is perfect all the way through.

It has to do with the flow, the depth of it, including the design, which must be original and quite intricate, even when simple in appearance. I think that the result must look almost effortless, although a lot of work goes into it. Also, a hat is masterly made when it speaks truly of the original intentions, when the vision that you had in your head has come out in the right way.

Since I create collections that I also sell to shops, I may make more than one piece of the same model, and it will always be as accurate to the original sample as possible. They will all differ, obviously, because each of them is hand made. What makes the difference is always the attention to detail and finish, the quality of materials, and how they have been handled. I think that anyone holding and wearing a hat made like this can always tell.

Creativity

You need to learn how to make quite boring, basic hats before you can take those and push them in another direction.

Being creative means to be quite free with your ideas and allowing yourself to experiment with many different and unusual things, which you must do in a good way but without being held back too much by the techniques. Sometimes headwear creeps into it, but I believe it all depends on finding a new way of making a hat using the traditional techniques and at the same time bringing in your own ideas and modernizing it.

You have to be constantly looking for new inspiration. I look all over the place, but I tend to get drawn to natural elements such as the weather, wind, coastlines, the atmosphere. I am also inspired by period and historical shapes. There are so many adventurous and unusual things throughout history and I am interested in the idea of using them in a really contemporary context, making them look clean and modern.

Another very important and creative part of my work is the presentation, the way in which I convey the mood and look of my collections. In defining the concept of the season's lookbook, for example, I try to portray a woman who looks quite unique but isn't too strong in her looks, not too overpowering.

Interpretation

Since millinery is so deeply fashion-based, it's especially important to keep reinventing and updating designs, even if the craft itself is very traditional.

There are endless ways to interpret something, and although you try to get it as perfect as you can, I don't think anybody is ever purely satisfied with what they do. If you are making a hat for a private client, the interpretation also has to do with understanding what their idea of perfection is, as well as yours. It's bringing the two together, getting as close as possible. You have to look at their personality and the way they hold themselves and their height and face shape and hair colour. People try to set rules for which kind of hat will work with which kind of person, but you really need to have people try them on and see how comfortable they feel. Sometimes what they have seen is exactly what they want, at other times they will want to have changes made. If you interpret it accurately, you bring their personality into the work, rather than yours.

When it's your design, then your personality is already part of it, of course, and therefore part of the natural interpretation. I haven't personally worked with designers yet, but I know that there is a great part of the interpretation that speaks about the artisan as well as the designer. The two elements coming together make the look and feel of the final result.

Originality

In millinery, every hat that you make has to be different, so you need to have a continuous stream of ideas. The balance between tradition and innovation lies in figuring out how far you can push something, and in getting the combination right. A hat can be quite stifling if you stick to the traditions too much, so you must find ways of expanding the tradition, whether in the shapes or in the textures. This works both ways: you could be making something that has an overall traditional shape but is made with metal and plastic. But then again, I think that moves away from millinery, because millinery is defined by traditional techniques, which involve traditional materials. Otherwise, it goes off towards "headwear".

I think that the feature that distinguishes me is the subtle mixture of unusual materials and design. You have to come up with your own signature shapes, more than anything, and I always try to keep to lines that are quite simple and striking. In my hats the ripple shape or a dent in the front come through quite often, together with other details that people wouldn't notice at first sight but that are my signatures. I believe you need to have a thorough understanding of the rules in order to know how to break them in the right way.

Talent

This is very important! To me, talent is a mix between being very dexterous with your hands and knowing how to interpret what you see and getting that to come out in your hands: it's having the ideas and being able to translate them physically.

If you're lucky to have the raw talent, you need to understand how to refine it. At the same time, you can have less of a natural talent but learn your own way of getting your ideas across. I see it as a combination of

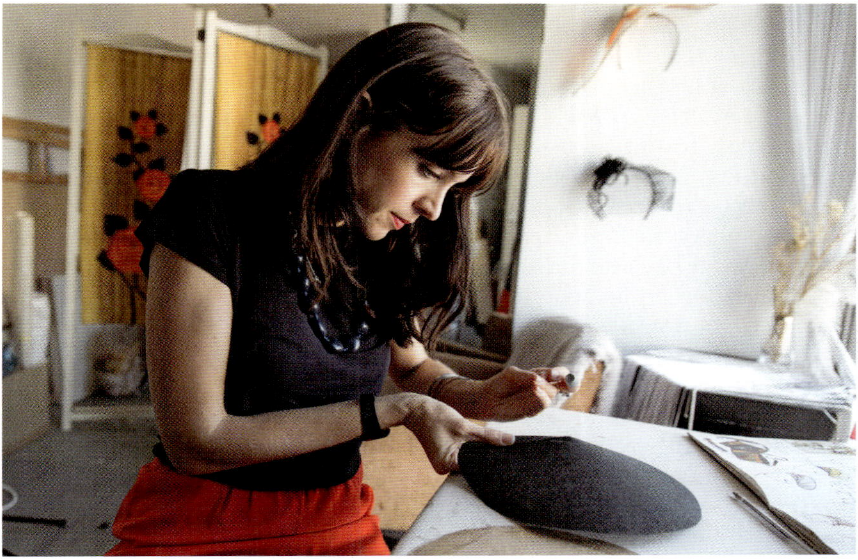

these factors. At the beginning it emerges in learning the technical skills, whereas later on in your career it lies more in being capable of coming up with ideas to express those skills in different ways.

Territory

Millinery is definitely typical of British culture. One thing about millinery in this country is that it's very close-knit and it's easy to get to know the people in the industry. Personally, I find it interesting and inspiring to look at other crafts and trades, such as jewellery, furniture or shoes. But there is no real network with craftspeople outside this community.

Getting the right materials is really important, because they are very specific to this trade. They are selected according to the best places that produce them. Some are made in England, like buckram, which is the core material that we use. Sinamay, meanwhile, comes from the Philippines, while straws come from Italy, and so on. The internet has certainly played an important part in shortening distances, because sometimes the time to get an order is quite unpredictable, and you need to source something else. I think I am located in London more for practical reasons, for the connections to materials, suppliers and press, rather than any other reason. But I would like to get away, for the space and fresh air – perfect for designing and working.

Tradition and innovation

Millinery is a craft, but I suppose it verges on art when the pieces are more like sculptures, less wearable. In terms of "decorative fashion", this craft started in the 15th century. Before that it was either more ornamental, for royal pieces, or created for practical purposes, like the weather. The types of hats we make today, which we would call "occasion wear", developed in the 20th century. Until the 1940s and 50s, everyone was wearing a hat, from the aristocracy to the working class. In the 1960s it became more a case of mass production and people were less concerned about whether the hats were hand made or not. There has been an overall decline of hat wearing among women since the 1970s, but there continues to be a small market for hand-made millinery.

In millinery, the making process is as important as the design. There are many ways to make a hat, even in terms of structure and finish. The use of feathers and silks, the craft of making flowers and hand-stitching the items together are all very traditional and have been done for hundreds of years. Even modelling on the blocks is part of the tradition, and you can find blocks that are centuries old. Although it isn't defined and regulated by a corporation, I would say that there are generally accepted boundaries between millinery and "headwear": the core elements of millinery are the traditional blocking techniques and the use of wires and of the more traditional fabrics like buckram, felt and straw; headwear, conversely, can be anything, and you can completely make it up without any training, as long as you can figure out a way of making it stay on the head. It's very difficult to find milliners who are just designers: milliners always end up making their own hats unless they have a large team.

In millinery, it's the technique that keeps it what it is: the hand-sewing and using your hands to get the finest kind of finish, even when using modern materials. I believe that I have been most innovative in the design and in the use of materials, and that has been mentioned quite a few times about my work.

I tend to look at the modern combinations of fabrics that are used in couture clothing, interpreting them in the way that can be worn in a hat. I also tend to keep things quite simple, letting the materials speak rather than having too much going on in the hat. I try to use different materials myself, like plastics and acrylic, without relying on craftspeople in other trades, and when I use modern materials I always incorporate them along with the traditional ones.

Training

I learnt how to make theatrical headwear studying costume design. After a few years, I realized that what I really wanted to do was simply make hats. I went on to train specifically in millinery, first with private tuition, learning the very traditional skills (one of my tutors was Rose Cory, the Queen Mother's milliner), and then at the Kensington and Chelsea College in London, which has the only Higher National Certificate millinery course in the country. During the year, students develop five or six projects in a variety of styles, from a flat pattern to a theatrical hat, to hats made purely of felt, to pieces that are more in the traditional English style, for a wedding or the races. This allows you to experiment, to look into the materials and open your mind to the different ways of using them.

The final project is designed completely in your own style, using all that you have learnt to make adventurous, fun pieces. It was good to grasp the traditional skills beforehand and understand how to translate them into my own style.

After graduating, I interned first and then started working for other milliners. It's good to learn from the industry, because you have access to a variety of techniques and skills; even though millinery is always very traditional, everybody does things in different ways.

When I started doing my own hats, at first it crossed over with my work at Stephen Jones, where I stayed for three years, and then I threw myself into my own work. It's difficult, of course, especially at the beginning. You have to work and keep trying and balance it until it all comes together. The confidence is built over time and I guess you realize it's happening when you have to ask less questions and instinctively know how to do things.

There are many advanced courses both in the UK and in Australia, where there is a very big millinery industry. Many milliners attend these courses, because even if you are established you can continue to learn new skills. The internet, of course, also has a lot to offer, with websites and blogs that are always posting tips and hints and small courses.

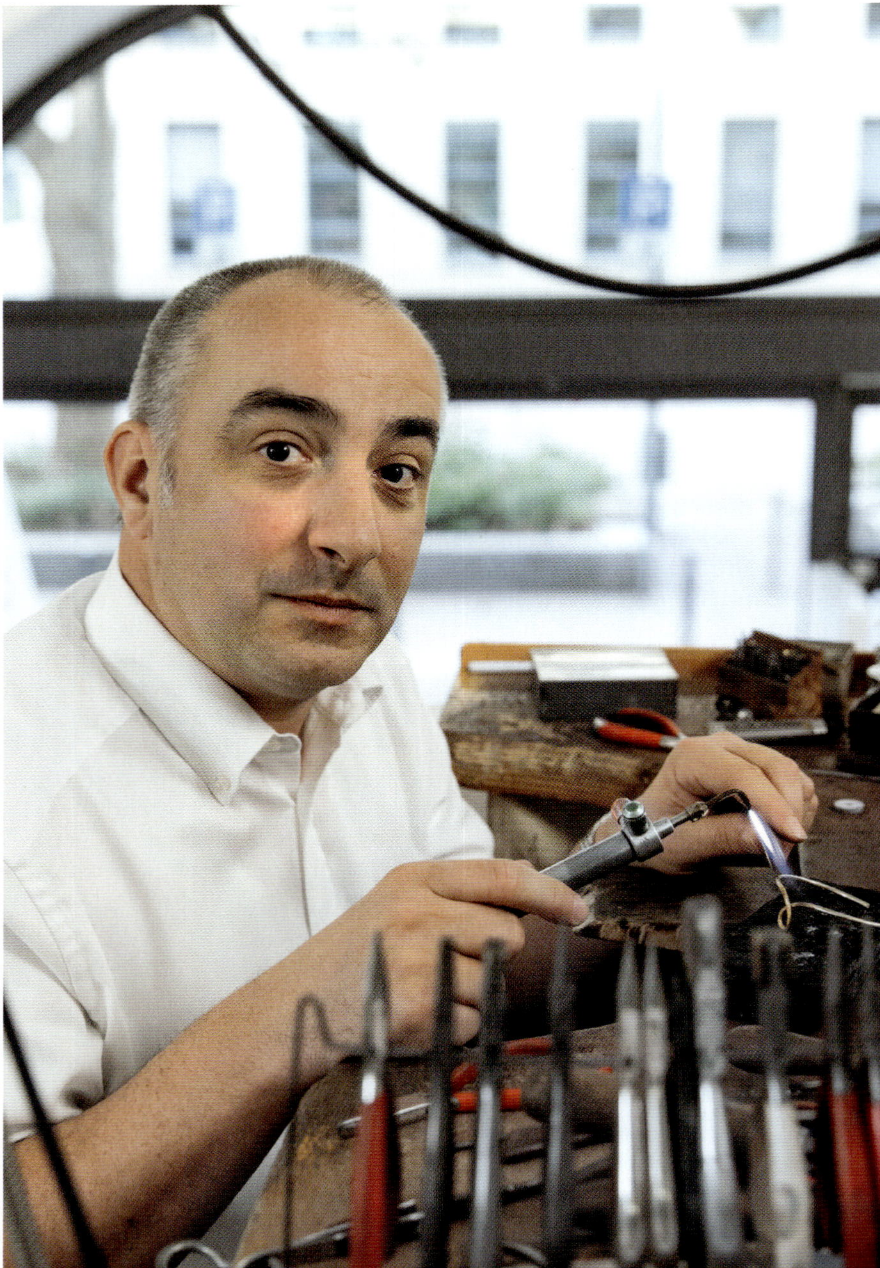

4. MARC-JENS BIEGEL, JEWELLER

Marc-Jens Biegel is the second generation of jewellers and goldsmiths whose prestigious family business in Frankfurt's Börsenplatz has been in operation since 1964. Born in 1967 in Frankfurt-an-Main, he did his apprenticeship under the watchful eye of his father, a master goldsmith. He produced his first ring at the age of 17 for his then girlfriend. Driven by a desire to learn more about the conceptual side of jewellery making, Biegel went on to study product design, first at the Hochschule für Gestaltung in Offenbach and then at Kingston University in London.

On his return to Frankfurt in 1998, Biegel rejoined the family business, keen to apply his newfound knowledge and expertise, which he now runs with his cousin, a master goldsmith. The business combines profound knowledge and experience in the creation of fine jewellery with cutting-edge design and materials of the highest quality. The team uses its expertise both to produce bespoke jewellery for individual clients all over the globe and to develop and produce "ready-to-wear" collections. Owing to its outstanding design, Biegel's jewellery has been exhibited in some of the world's top design museums and photographed for numerous publications.

I work with my cousin, who is the master in our workshop. He was trained by his father, who was also a goldsmith. Our parents were born in Idar-Oberstein, a very important area in Germany for the jewellery-making business, where our grandfather was a diamond-cutter. After the war, when our parents were young, the only options they had were to become cutters, engravers or goldsmiths. My father opened this shop in 1964. He ran the business as a one-man show for almost 20 years, until it gradually became bigger and bigger. Today we are well established in Frankfurt, where we have clients who have been coming to us for more than 40 years. The reason I joined my father's business was that I wanted to be self-employed, I didn't want to have a boss. I still don't regret my choice, but it's getting more difficult for small companies. We might survive the next 20 years, but I don't know if it will be possible to go on in 30 or 40 years' time. In any case, my cousin has no children and mine are still far too young, so it's too early to think about this.

In Germany we have a dual education system that combines apprenticeships in a company and vocational education at school. It's important to acquire a background knowledge which you can develop in the workshop, where you learn faster and, above all, you are closer to what is happening in the real world. But then again, it takes time to do that, which is rarely possible if you are both the master and the owner of the workshop. We value human resources very much and we try to keep people working with us for as long as possible. Two of our former goldsmiths are now teaching at the Staatliche Zeichenakademie in Hanau, and they bring us their more talented students. At the moment we are training two young ladies in their early 20s. Since we are making jewellery for women, we also like to have a female perspective.

Authenticity

The answer is simple: authenticity means credibility. There is always something of me in the pieces I do, and if people can read that, then I am credible and people will give me money for what I'm doing because they feel that I am authentic. Our customers rely on the fact that our products are made here, in this workshop, by us: they come here to buy a Biegel jewel. But they aren't really interested in how they are made, and only rarely do they want to know where the stones come from. To me, too, the process is just the means to get to the product: although I like the process, I'm proud when the product is finished and then I move on to the next one.

I think it's very important to be clear about who does what. We always indicate the name of the person who designed the jewel, whether it's me, my father or an external designer, while the producer is always Biegel. Artisans are artisans because their primary interest is to produce things with their hands, whereas designers design products because they are extremely creative. I believe that the double signature, including the name of the artisan who made the piece, really depends on the complexity of a work. I think that some craftspeople would be proud to have their names mentioned, but then again, others just don't want it, and that's why they do what they do: they want to make things without being under the spotlight.

Competence

In this craft, competence always takes time to build. You have to train for a long period and do the same things over and over again. No one was born a genius from the first day and certainly not everyone succeeds in becoming competent. The process by which we make our jewellery is part of our competence, and if we made it in a different way the end product would certainly be very different.

Competence is also important in many other aspects of the trade. You have to be able to explain what you want to produce to the people working with you, and also tell them how to do it or how to do it better. Also, when you sell your product, if you talk about it and how it was made, your customer will immediately understand if you are a competent person or not. This is very important if you want to communicate about the objects you sell.

Craftsmanship

I made quite a lot of pieces of jewellery myself until I started the Bodysign project, including some of the first prototypes, but after that I simply no longer had the time. I now focus on doing the technical drawings and overseeing the whole production process, as well as the marketing and sales. When you are making an expensive piece of jewellery, you have to concentrate hard and everything that takes your mind away isn't good for the product. That's one reason we have the workshop upstairs, so the people who work there can concentrate. It's a different job profile altogether.

I'd say that for something to be masterly crafted, the idea is the first thing, no matter how it turns out. To get as close as possible to the idea, you must have knowledge and expertise of the processes and materials, which translates into the responsibility to do it as best as you can. This, I believe, is very important: we have to make a product that we can show to people and be proud of. If a product doesn't turn out the way I want it, we just throw it away. This is the responsibility we have towards what we have learnt and what we stand for. If I didn't take this responsibility, all this would never have been possible.

Creativity

Art and design are a great source of inspiration for me. Where the original idea comes from I don't know, often it's simply in my mind. When I see some parts of the jewellery, like the stones, I immediately get an idea of what to make of it and how the story could be told. But this isn't everything, it isn't a recipe. If I go to a furniture fair, like Milan or Cologne, or even a car fair, I see how other designers work with different materials and I try to understand how they might have felt about the product and what they are trying to express with it, and I try to adapt this to jewellery design.

I believe that you can be creative even as an artisan. The material often tells you what to do with it, because working with platinum, for example, is different from working with pure gold. If you want to bend it, it just doesn't work sometimes, and you may have to cut it and work in the way the materials allow you. At other times you may have an idea that you can't complete because the material tells you no, I'm not following you! And you have to rethink it from the beginning.

Interpretation

I would agree with the definition of the artisan as the person who transforms a project into a perfect product. When we are making a ring, we aren't "inventing" something new but we are working on archetypes. Anyone would read this product as a ring, even if that person comes from a totally different culture. Similarly, in many different cultures a ring would look similar: I am interpreting, in my personal visual language, the original idea of a ring.

When I am making a ring designed by someone else, I am interpreting an archetype of jewellery and at the same time giving it a contemporary feel. What is fundamental is that you can recognize it for what it is, or no one would want to have it.

Originality

Having been trained as an industrial designer, I think that the design is the most important thing, no matter how you realize it. Whether you make it with your hands or use tools to help you should always depend on the result you want to obtain. The knowledge and competence that we have in our workshop is what enables us to be original, not the materials, which in the end are always the same.

So, originality in the sense of "coming from the origin" is what we do here in our workshop, something that has been learnt and handed down for hundreds of years. My father learnt it, and I learnt it from him. The other meaning of originality is probably "individuality", which is what distinguishes the artisans but also the customers, who see themselves not as someone in a mass, but as individuals who are looking for a very original product.

To attain this, I need to break the rules, and in fact I keep on doing so over and over again. You have to take risks to achieve other things and continue your trade. I take a risk even in the simple fact of being here every day, because I never know what will happen tomorrow. Being self-employed is always a risk, but you must learn to live with it.

Talent

I would compare it to the importance of talent in sports: it's always good if you have a talent for football or tennis, but it's not enough. When you want to be a professional, you have to have the gift and also the training. Likewise, in this field it's crucial to have a feeling for the material, which I would say is equivalent to having a certain talent. If you don't, you get stuck at a certain level and never go beyond. When I go to my supplier in Idar-Oberstein to buy the stones, I know immediately what I could do with them. This is because I have both a creative talent for designing things and a great knowledge of how to make this product in an efficient way. Anyone can design a ring, but what I try to do is to design a story, of which the product is just the end.

I can honestly tell within two hours if a young person has the talent to become a good artisan. We give them a simple job to do and just watch

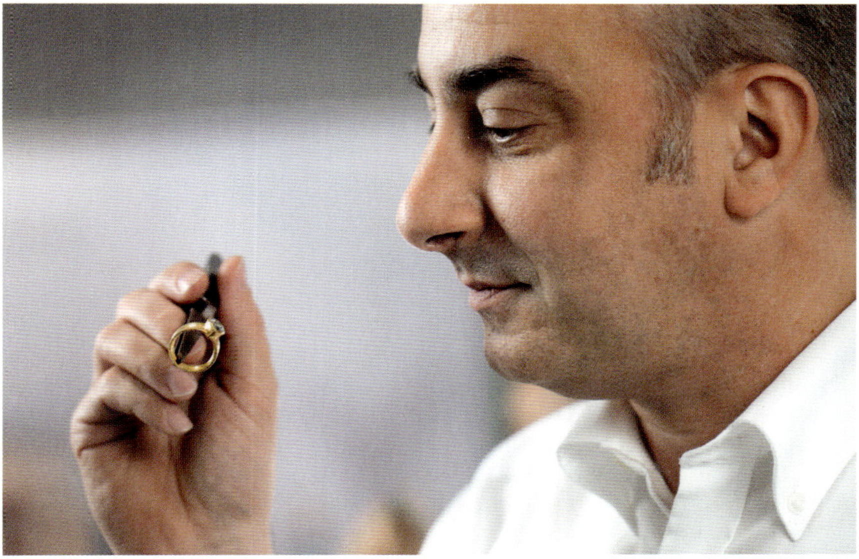

how they work, how they use the tools and how they concentrate on what they are doing.

I suppose that the talent of a master, like my cousin or my father, lies not just in making the jewellery but also in the ability to reflect on what they do and to communicate it and even teach it to others. This is the definition of a *meister* in Germany: when you are a master you are allowed to teach.

Territory

Goldsmithing is a longstanding tradition in Hanau, a town some 30km east of Frankfurt: it became a big capital of the jewellery trade in the 18th century, when the French Huguenots settled there after escaping to Germany during the persecutions. Hanau is the seat of the leading school for jewellery art, established in 1772, and also of a beautiful Goldsmith Museum. Another important centre is in Pforzheim, near Stuttgart, which concentrates more on mass production such as for the chain and gold ring industries. Then, of course, there is Idar-Oberstein, 130km south-west of Frankfurt, with its long tradition of stone-cutting, engraving and setting.

The raw materials we work with are all precious, because this is our speciality and competence and what we like to do, so to me there is no alternative. I really feel safe when I work with these materials, because I know how they react and I can do whatever I want with them. I select the gems with my cousin and I have people I can refer to for advice. But at the end of the day, I'm the one who decides. More than 60 per cent of precious metals, such as gold, silver and platinum, is recycled. The diamonds (which are in high demand at the moment) come from South Africa and Russia, while the other gemstones come from all over the world.

Tradition and innovation

The jewellery business tends to be very traditional and conventional. And since I'm not just a maker but also a designer, in this shop we have pursued a more contemporary approach. The question I asked myself, more than 20 years ago, was what jewellery would look like if it were designed by a contemporary product designer. I realized that the large furniture companies developed incredible projects with designers, and relied on their craftspeople only to make them, not to design them. This wasn't the case with jewellery, which was almost always created by the artisans themselves. At the same time, jewellers weren't catering for the tastes and needs of a more contemporary clientele. That's how, in 2002, I came up with the idea of collaborating with designers from outside this business to create pieces that combined craftsmanship and design. I launched the project (called Bodysign: Body + Design) at the Cologne Furniture Fair in 2003. It totally changed our company, because it opened a new horizon and enabled me to experiment with new and different things.

I believe the biggest modern innovation in this business is marketing, in which all the big companies invest huge sums. You can be the best craftsperson producing excellent products for a very reasonable price. But if no one knows it, no one is ever going to buy them. In this sense, the internet has been one of the most important technological advances of recent decades.

In terms of the making of the products, most of the techniques we use in jewellery haven't changed at all. You will always need an expert craftsperson if you want to obtain a certain result, like setting stones, for example. It has to be hand made, and it would never work in any other way. We use tools that are about the same age as the company and they are still the best. Unfortunately, the quality of some of the new tools is very cheap, you don't even have to be a goldsmith to realize it: if I knew where to find a supplier for the old stuff I would certainly go there. At the same time, we employ modern instruments like cutters and work with suppliers who make elements that would be a waste of time and money to do by hand (like the casts for some simple settings) or for products that are specifically intended to have a clean-cut design.

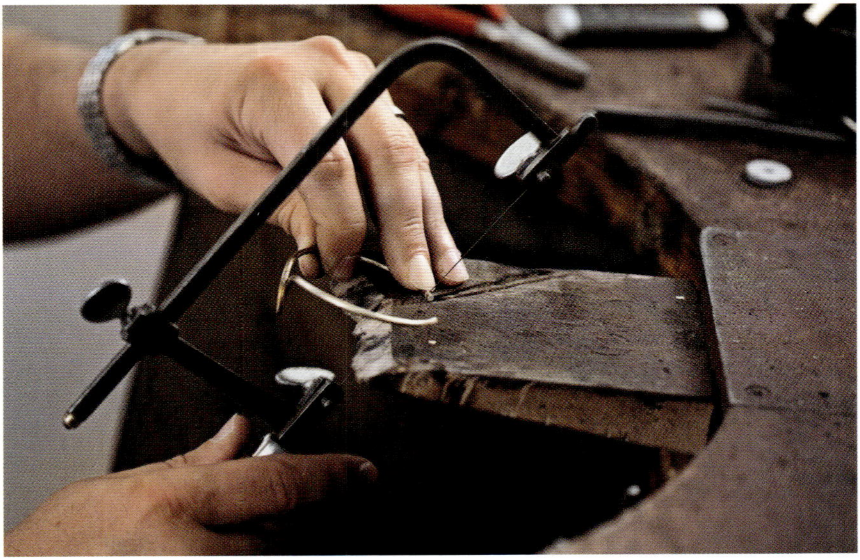

Training

I did my apprenticeship in my father's workshop in Frankfurt. Being a master goldsmith, my father was qualified to teach the trade, and he has, in fact, trained many pupils during his career. We got along well and I'm happy that I could learn from him. My training lasted four years, after which I realized that making jewellery wasn't enough for me: I wanted to go beyond the viewpoint of the craftsperson and explore this wonderful universe also from that of product design. For a jewel is also a product, although this doesn't necessarily imply that it has to be produced industrially. What I was interested in was to approach jewellery-making from a new conceptual perspective. For this reason, I spent another five years studying product design, first at the Hochschule für Gestaltung in Offenbach, near Frankfurt, then at Kingston University (formerly Kingston Polytechnic) in London. When I came back to Frankfurt in 1998, this different outlook allowed me to open new horizons not only for myself but also for the family business.

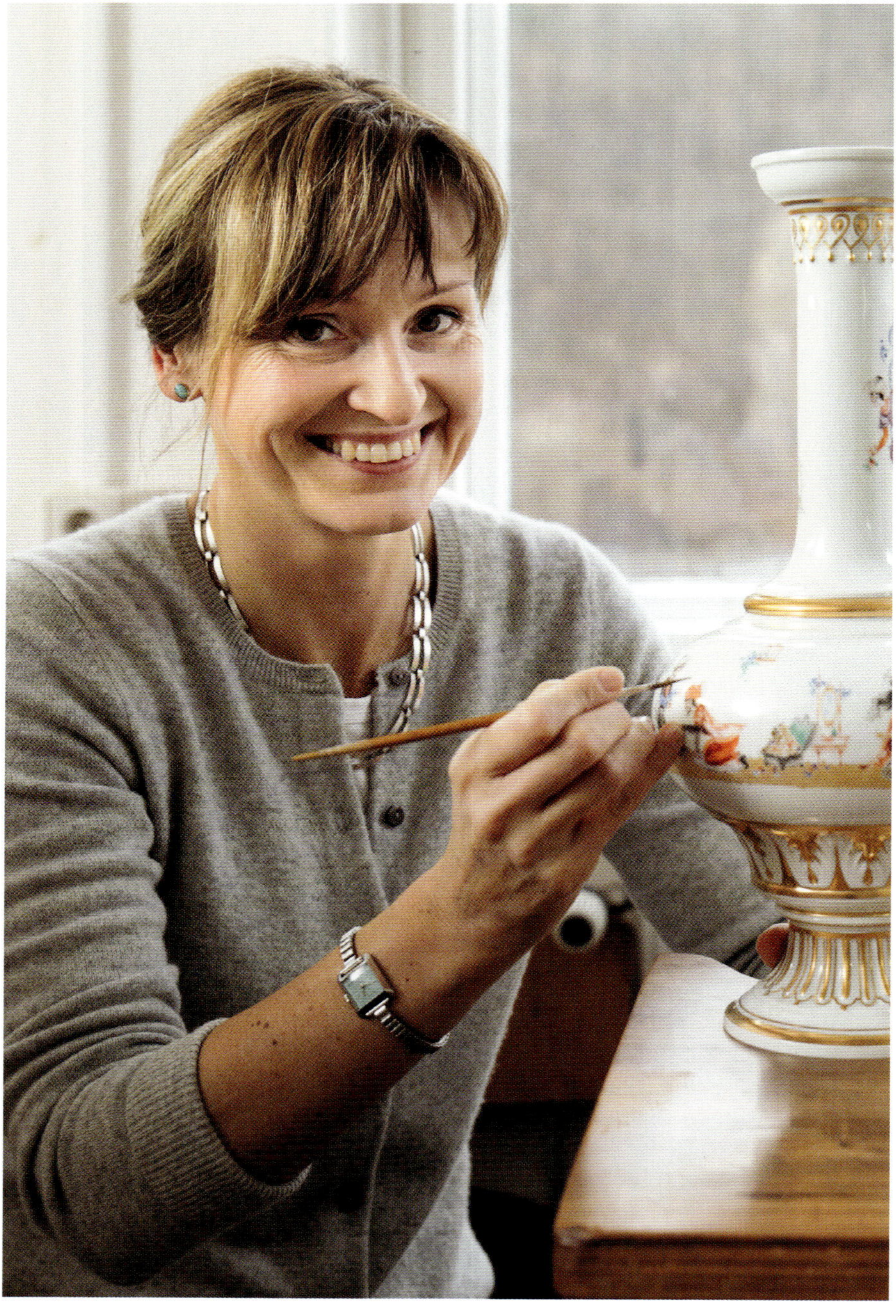

5. ELKE DANNENBERG, PORCELAIN DECORATOR

Elke Dannenberg has followed in the footsteps of her mother and grandmother to become a porcelain decorator at the renowned Meissen Manufactory, near the Saxon city of Dresden. She began her training aged 16 at the factory's drawing school, where she spent the first year learning different techniques using a variety of tools and materials, before moving on to porcelain. Starting with relatively simple designs and figurines, she gradually progressed to more complex and sophisticated shapes.

At the end of four years, Dannenberg passed the examination and began work in the manufactory, where she was fortunate to be chosen to develop the designs of a well-known porcelain decorator of the late 20th century, Professor Heinz Werner. Some 25 years on, Dannenberg continues to reproduce and interpret the Meissen Manufactory's most celebrated designs with the same recipes, tools and techniques that have been in use for more than 300 years.

To work at the Meissen manufactory is an important and long tradition within many families in this region. My mother and grandmother were both painters at Meissen. So when I turned 16 and didn't have a clear idea of what I wanted to do in life, they suggested that I follow in their footsteps. I was fortunate enough to find that it matched my talents and desires. I love my work and it makes me happy to paint day after day.

I am currently training a young colleague who has just finished the Meissen school and is going through all the departments to learn the different techniques. We see each other three times a day: I show her how to paint and she asks me questions. The Meissen school is very selective, and there are only a dozen students admitted every year. This is also because the turnover here is very low, since most of us work in the company our whole lives.

Authenticity

Meissen is absolutely authentic: it has the roots and the final product, and you can follow each step from one end to the other. Nothing comes from outside. So even if some little things have changed in the final product, because new techniques have evolved, the output is always the same, whether it comes from the past or from the present.

Each object produced in the Meissen manufactory bears at least four marks: the Meissen trademark (the crossed swords in underglaze cobalt blue), the year of production, and the numbers denoting the identity of the moulder and of the decorator.

I'd say that it's important that the artisan's signature (or number in our case) is on the piece. It's part of the object's authenticity and adds value to it. It's a guarantee that it's hand made by a person who has all the knowledge that comes from Meissen's history. There are collectors who specifically request pieces by the same decorator, and we all have our own "fans".

Competence

To be competent is to be a master of your craft and to know what you are doing. In the beginning, you have to put many things in your head and in your hands. You have to learn what happens to the material, everything is very tricky and something can always go wrong. An example is the many colours we use, and you have to get familiar with each one of them. Every colour is special; you have to know how to mix the powder with the turpentine oil, how to apply it on the porcelain, always remembering that it will change after the firing and glazing. All this belongs to the knowledge that you develop working here.

Craftsmanship

Everything is hand-painted. Working in a production plant, we obviously have a given amount of time to complete each piece, depending on its complexity and size. But we have enough freedom to alternate between different activities in order to keep our senses sharp and receptive.

I always choose, mix and test the colours myself; I try them on the porcelain, send them to be fired and check the result. Each artisan and artist working at Meissen is integrated into the process. Although we operate within our individual frameworks, we all have our share to do in the process, and it has to be perfect all the way through.

I find it very important to receive feedback from our customers, which happens when we meet them on Meissen open days or on the trips that the company organizes to Japan and the Far East.

Creativity

Normally we have to follow the originals. But when we take an old pattern and put it on a very different shape, we can keep being creative. For example, in the vase with the Arabian Nights pattern, I have to interpret Professor Werner's design on a shape he never used. So, before starting I have to think how to adapt the story and the motifs on it. In this case, I invented a tale called "Palace Stories" in which I created five rooms where different things happen, and in between each room are little details like the animals and the flowers. On the neck of the vase, which has the shape of a tower, is the lover who climbs into the room from the window. All the characters and decorating themes were originally created by Heinz Werner, but the fascinating thing about his Arabian Nights is that you have endless stories to tell, always remaining very faithful to the original.

Interpretation

One very interesting aspect of the Meissen manufactory's heritage is that we have many collectors who are always interested in having new editions of their favourite patterns. The Fine Arts Department is in fact dedicated entirely to these very special products. To give these clients the new products they're looking for, we have to constantly interpret the old patterns to make them interesting and always unique. In fact, we produce these pieces in very limited numbers, usually between 10 and 100 pieces for each new edition.

There are two ways in which we can interpret an original creation: the first is that we reproduce what the artist originally did on a specific shape; the other is that we reproduce it on a new shape. And since we are not machines, we always put our personality into what we are doing. What I believe is truly important for me is to do my work honestly and with full awareness, giving it my undivided attention.

I think that it's important to update a design. In the background you have your tradition, but it has to become contemporary. The way we eat, for example, has changed many times in the last 300 years: today we have dishwashers, we use just one plate, we eat exotic food like sushi… Some very modern shapes we are using today actually come from the 18th century, but they are simple and meet modern tastes. This is an interpretation of history that keeps it fresh and up to date.

Originality

At Meissen we have the unique combination of a very long and unbroken tradition dating back to the 18th century. This means that every piece made at Meissen stems directly from its roots, and in this sense is close to the origins. Then what makes it so special, so different and original compared with other manufactories are the colours, shapes and variety. No other company has as huge a range of moulds and colours.

At Meissen we often combine old shapes and old designs with new shapes and new designs. The shape of the vase I am painting in the theme of the Arabian Nights, for example, was created in 1721, whereas Professor Werner designed the pattern in the 1970s.

I suppose what really makes my work original, compared with other decorators who have painted the same pattern in the past, is similar to handwriting: every painter has an individual style, although

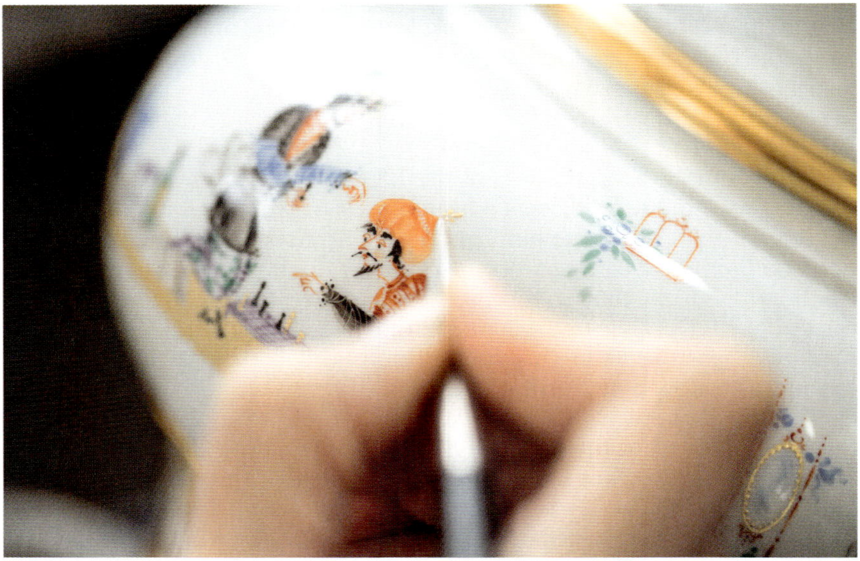

it's imperceptible at first glance. The head of the department will always be able to tell what I've painted, because she will recognize my "handwriting". In the same way, I can always spot my work, whether it's in a museum or in a shop.

In our work, it isn't important to break any rules! On the contrary, it's imperative to paint the pattern and to follow it in a very rigorous way. Then you can do very little things to the design (I try to leave my personal mark in the expression of figures), but I must always follow that pattern, because that's what the customer is looking for. Only when you are developing new designs, or new combinations of patterns, can you put all your thoughts and creativity into the realization.

Talent

I'd say that talent is the basis, together with patience. You have to be patient because it takes a long time to learn, and even after you've learnt you always have to concentrate on what you're doing. You have to leave every other thought to later in the day, when you have finished working.

There can be a time, in the very beginning, when no one knows what's inside you. That's when the teachers you have in the first years are fundamental, because they can discover, encourage and guide your talent.

I believe that when a young person is talented, you can tell by the way they keep to the topic and try to understand and discover it by themselves; they don't wait to copy a sample, but they can visualize an image in their heads and recreate it in painting. To do this, you need to have both your basic knowledge and your own imagination.

Territory

Böttger was able to discover the way to produce porcelain because a deposit of the most important ingredient, kaolin, was found right here in Meissen. Luckily for the king, the kaolin that was extracted from the Meissen quarry was – and still is – of the best possible quality, which made Meissen porcelain the finest in Europe. The factory was originally situated inside the Albrechtsburg Castle and moved to its present premises in the Triebisch Valley only in 1864. The traditional recipe for the porcelain is still a secret, and likewise the recipes for the colours that are used for the paint, which are known to no more than a handful of people working at the manufactory.

In my work, it hardly ever happens that I'm faced with a problem that I can't solve. But if I have a question, I know where and how to ask. In general, the artisans and artists working here don't have any exchanges with other artisans and artists from outside, with the important exception of the projects that are developed at the Meissen Art Campus with emerging and established international artists.

Tradition and innovation

The Meissen manufactory was established in 1710 by Augustus II the Strong, who was a passionate collector, after the secret of making porcelain was discovered by the chemist J. F. Böttger. Meissen porcelain is still produced in the same way as it was 300 years ago. We still use the traditional recipe and the same moulds, the same colours, the same brushes, the same techniques. All of Meissen's skills are passed on only inside the House's workshops. Furthermore, the Meissen manufactory has managed to preserve its vast collection of historical documents and impressive archive of moulds (more than 700,000). For this reason, we can continue to reproduce objects that date as far back as the beginning of the 18th century.

Although everything is still rigorously hand made, new technologies and innovations have made work much safer and more precise, and have also enabled Meissen to increase its quality standards exponentially. In particular, the firing techniques have changed since the days of the 10-metre-high "Round Ovens", fired with coal, which have been replaced by modern gas or electrically heated ovens. Porcelain manufactured today is therefore much smoother and brilliant than in the old days.

Training

More than 25 years ago, I started my training at the Drawing School of the Meissen porcelain manufactory, to which I was admitted after a strict selection process. We spent the initial phase just doing warming-up exercises on paper, in order to become relaxed and familiar with the material and the pencils. Then we started to approach perspective, nature, the human body, etc., which we practised drawing on a wide variety of supports – from drawing paper to packing paper to cardboard and so on – using many different techniques and instruments, including water colours and acrylic paint. At the end of the first year, our individual talent was assessed, and we were assigned to different departments, where we began our training on porcelain. I started by decorating figurines, which, being three-dimensional, is a rather different technique from painting on a flat surface. You begin with little figurines that have a simple decoration and year by year you advance to more elaborate and sophisticated shapes. After four years, you take a final examination, which includes an oral, a written and a practical test. If you are successful, you can start working in the manufactory.

A few years later, the Meissen manufactory was looking for internal painters to develop the designs of Professor Heinz Werner, one of the best-known Meissen porcelain painters in the second half of the 20th century. Professor Werner created more than 100 very famous decorations, including the Arabian Nights, which is probably the best loved. I thought it was a wonderful opportunity, because although I liked painting figurines I was also interested in broadening my knowledge and, on top of this, I could learn from Professor Werner personally, because at the time he was still working in the manufactory. I applied for the position and was chosen. We worked together to readapt and reinterpret his designs on old and new shapes, and I still continue today on my own.

Painting on porcelain is a fluid process. Once you have the basic knowledge, you train yourself every day, while you look for the best way to compose a pattern on porcelain. It's a process that can take many years, but this really is the time necessary to come to such a wonderful product.

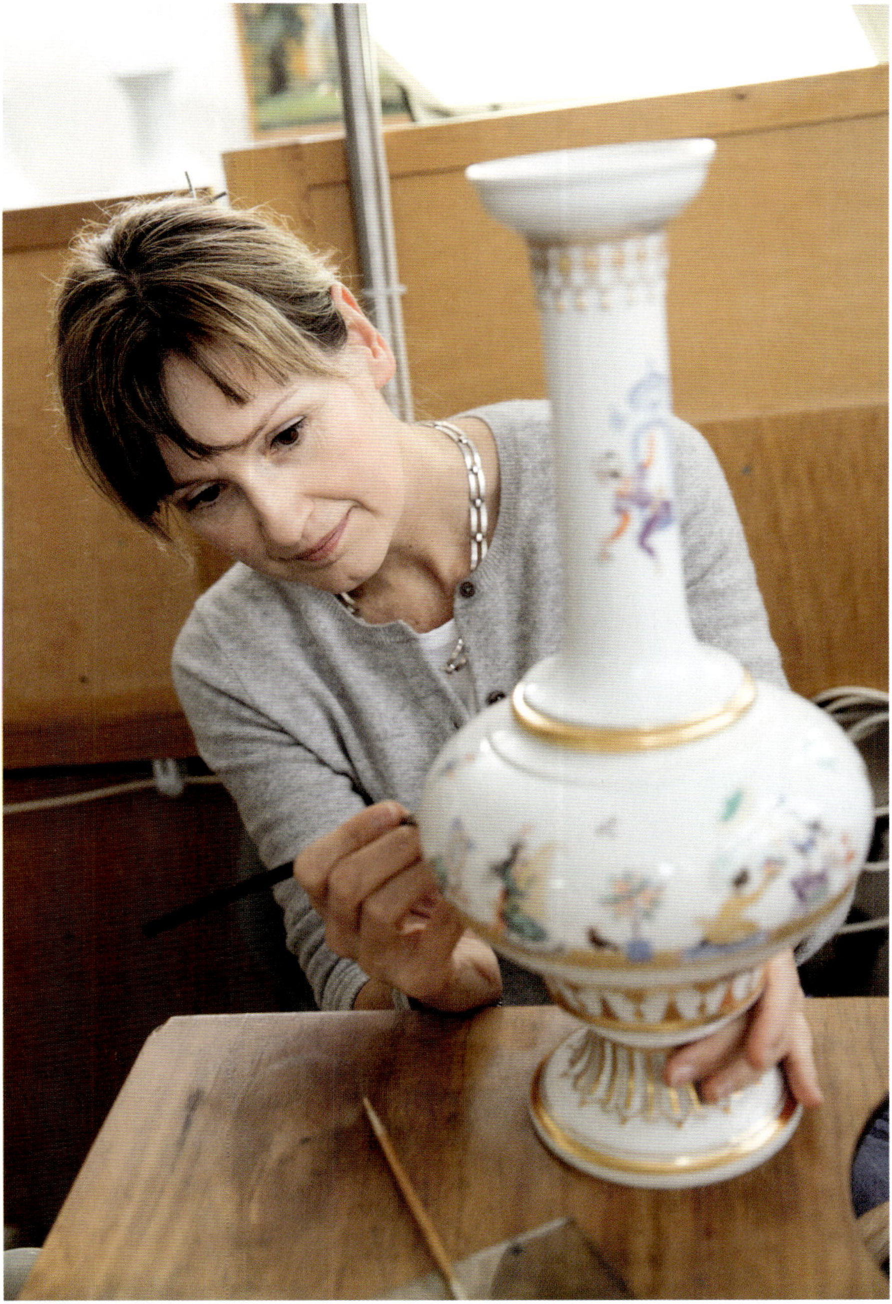

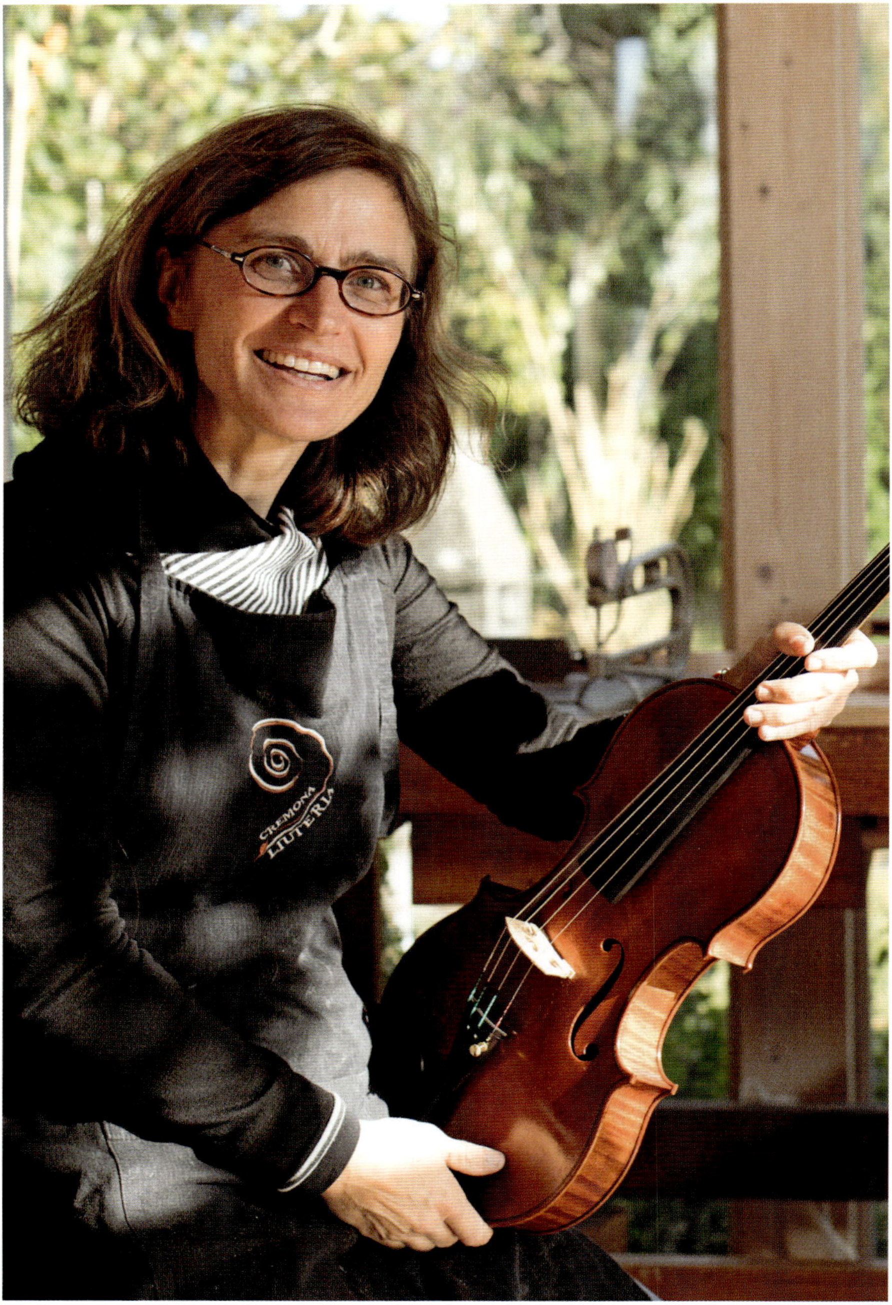
CREMONA
LIUTERIA

6. ULRIKE DEDERER, VIOLIN-MAKER

*Ulrike Dederer was born in Stuttgart in 1969. After finishing secondary school, she was admitted to the International Violin-making School in Cremona, where she studied for four years under Vincenzo Bissolotti, gaining valuable hands-on experience in Francesco Bissolotti's workshop in her final year. She graduated in 1993 and in the same year passed the apprentice examination (*Gesellenprüfung*) in Mittenwald. She spent the next 12 years restoring string instruments at the Atelier Jecklin in Zurich and Machold workshop in Vienna. She worked for numerous musicians from Vienna's famous orchestras and renowned soloists such as Heinrich Schiff, Günter Pichler, Julian Rachlin and Janine Jansen. In 2002 she passed the Master Examination (*Meisterprüfung*) in Innsbruck.*

These years of experience gave her the expertise and inspiration she needed to start making her own instruments: in 2005 Dederer moved with her family to Zurich, where she established her own workshop. Since 2008 she has focused on making new instruments, in modern and baroque style, in the tradition of the old Cremonese violin-makers.

Her instruments have won numerous international awards, including 1st prize and gold medal for viola at the 13th International "Triennale" Violin-making Competition in Cremona in 2012. Her instruments are played by orchestral musicians and soloists such as Patricia Kopatchinskaja and Ursula Sarnthein.

Although I am the first to embrace this profession, my family's role has been crucial, because they gave me their support and encouragement, first of all in playing an instrument.

I think that having someone to work with allows you to progress together and also to pass on your skills, perpetuating the discipline of violin-making. It would be a shame, and also unfair, to keep all this knowledge to myself. Even the greatest luthiers in history have handed down their legacies, and not necessarily through their own families. Antonio Stradivari's trade, for example, wasn't continued by his children but by other people, such as Carlo Bergonzi, and to a very high standard. In any case, it has been observed that after three generations the trade starts to decline, which means that it's vital to keep the transmission line moving.

Authenticity

I think that an authentic instrument reflects the person who made it. I try to combine the choice of the wood with the model, the sound, the varnish, etc. If everything goes well together, the instrument is authentic. If I were just trying to make an instrument in the same way as Stradivari,

I would end up losing my authenticity, because I would go by a path that's too far removed from who I am. Of course, it's always someone else who has to judge.

When you use traditional materials and techniques combined with classical wood and a classical shape, you can be more authentic than if you try to do something very original just to show your personality and character. I believe that authenticity doesn't emerge from strange things. That's why I like restoring antique instruments, because through them you enter someone else's world.

If, like Stradivari, you are such a gifted master that you can instruct, train and guide your pupils to do things in the way you do, and there is a continuity in your work, it can be authentic in the same way as if you made it yourself. But as far as I'm concerned, I wouldn't put my signature on an instrument that was done in my workshop but by someone else.

In any case, I believe that the issue of the signature is relevant only if the instruments are interesting, but we will only know in 50 years' time if an instrument that's made today is interesting or not.

Competence

Apart from the competence to make an instrument, which is obviously fundamental, you have to know how to build a relationship with your client, who buys the instrument not just because it's well made but also for the background of competence and knowledge you have put into it. Competence applies to both sides, in fact. There are people who go to dealers to try a hundred different instruments, thinking that the wider the choice, the better. Other people hear or try your instruments and decide that it's what they are looking for. The making of an instrument is a process that involves both the violin-maker and the client, because the sound is fine-tuned together so that the result is the right one for the musician.

Craftsmanship

If you make violins traditionally, the process is 100 per cent by hand. And you must be dexterous, because if you can't work with your hands, your ideas remain stuck in your head.

I can't say whether violin-making is more of an art or a craft. I think that what really matters is to consider both sides, because if you focus just on one, you lose the other, which is equally important. In fact, when violin-making developed, those making them weren't just craftspeople, they were also mathematicians, engineers, physicists, chemists, theologians and artists, like Leonardo da Vinci.

To me, the combination of all perfect details doesn't make a perfect violin. Guarneri del Gesù was all but perfect, yet his instruments are works of art, not only for the sound, which is incredible, but also for the execution, even if it isn't done "by the book". Stradivari, on the other hand, was a genius who worked in a more meticulous way.

If perfection doesn't define a "masterly execution", perhaps passion does. The instrument you make must contain your knowledge of the history, of the theory, and of the time and place where the instrument was made. Each instrument has an aura that must give you an emotion. Some instruments are well done and beautiful but they don't speak to you. Often, they are made in a factory. This means that they can be of a good technical quality but without a soul, and you can tell how the instrument will play just from the way it looks.

Creativity

Violin-makers are always creative in their work because the material they use is never the same. This means that each time I take a piece of wood in my hands I have to decide how to use it: how thick, how arched, and so on.

Not even Stradivari, who was a genius, "created" anything new, because when he started the violin already existed and was already made to a very high standard.

When I set out to make my own violins, I started from what I'd learnt during the years I'd been working on antique instruments: I created a classical model that reflected my personal characteristics. In the end, the aim of a violin-maker is to make an instrument that the music needs and the musicians want. The reason we use this type of wood is simply because it gives a certain type of sound, and if we play music from the 18th and 19th centuries, we also need the instruments that will give the sound of that period. I believe that the violin-makers are so tied to the musicians and to the musical world that, from this point of view, we can't push our creativity beyond a certain point. If, for example, a composer and a musician were specifically looking for a completely different sound, then they could ask a luthier to make something completely different. But unless that instrument proves hugely successful, it would end up being one single instrument made for one single composition.

Interpretation

Normally, a musician who comes to me has already tried my instruments and is looking for that particular sound. At the same time, if I understand what they are looking for, I can make an instrument that's right for them.

When I make a new instrument, I'm interpreting something that has existed, in a perfect way, for over five hundred years. Each moment has its culture, taste, style and way of doing things. You can tell if an instrument is one or two centuries old, you can even tell if a copy of a Stradivarius was made one or two centuries ago: they are very different. If you want to understand how the violin was interpreted over the centuries, you should go to the Violin Museum in Cremona, where the instruments that win the International Triennial Violin Making Competition are exhibited. You can see how the style, the interpretation, has changed: each instrument is completely different from the other, and this in the space of only 40 years!

The same thing happens in music. Every year there are new interpretations of Beethoven's concertos, because although the music is always the same, every time and place has a different perception, perspective, culture, expectations, taste. That's why we make new instruments, because our time in history needs to express itself, even in violin-making.

Originality

There are two aspects that we have to consider: the way in which you work (the approach and execution) and the result. I was trained in the tradition of the Cremonese school and I still use this method. Although today I make instruments that look very different from the ones made by my teacher Bissolotti, you can still tell that I was trained in Cremona. The way in which violins are made in Cremona has also changed in the new millennium, mainly because of outside influences. That's why I say that perhaps I'm "more Cremonese than the Cremonese".

It's possible to make very nice models of Stradivari violins in the French way: in the final product, only a few details will reveal that it isn't done in the Cremonese way. You could argue that this makes no difference, but I would disagree, because when you follow a certain approach, the results you obtain derive directly from that approach, both in the sound and in the aspect. Instead, if you follow a different method, you will have to do things that will make you achieve the result, but not in the same "automatic" way. That's why I always try to follow the Cremonese method, which is the same as that used by Amati, Stradivari and Guarneri, because it gives you a better result. In this sense, I don't break the rules; I simply adapt the execution to a different idea. In the same way, I don't take any risks because I know what I'm doing.

Although we work with classical models, and the violin has been a violin for five hundred years, each instrument becomes our personal instrument. Unless you are making a copy of an old instrument, when you make your personal instruments you do it in a particular style, you

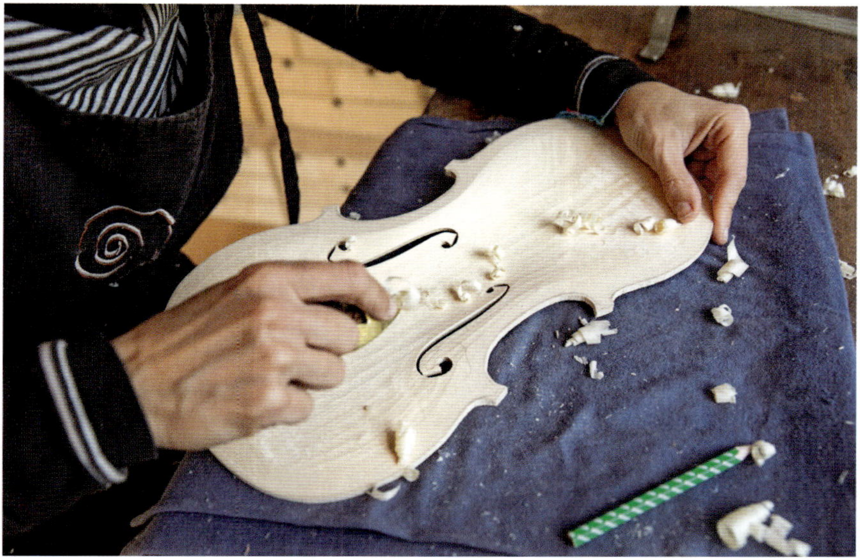

are inspired by a classical model, but you don't copy. Stradivari himself made violins that are very similar but each one is unique.

Talent

I believe that if you train a lot you can achieve a good level of manual skill. It happens also when you play an instrument; you can become a good violin player just because you practise a lot. But I think that it's much easier if you are gifted, it definitely shortens the road. Also, if you aren't gifted you may become a good luthier, but I don't think you will ever reach any peak. In the end, if you aren't talented, the rest is really useless, even the passion.

The master violin-makers I've met are all also excellent artisans, with incredible manual skills. I've never seen anyone work like the Bissolottis (father and son), both of whom were my tutors. And certainly their instruments have an aura.

Territory

Like so many other branches of art and science that were born in Italy during the Renaissance, violin-making is essentially Italian, and although exceptional schools developed in other parts of Europe, they all stemmed from the same root. Cremona has become one of the most important centres thanks to the legacies of Antonio Stradivari, Guarneri del Gesù and Nicola Amati and his family. I think that to make a good instrument, you also have to understand the culture, the music, the language, but also the climate, the social life and the religion (we mustn't forget that the Catholic Church has been one of the greatest "clients" for art and culture), all of which have determined the evolution of violin-making.

After Stradivari, violin-making went into severe decline in Cremona, and by the mid-1750s there was only one luthier left in the whole town. This means that all the know-how shared and transmitted by the violin-makers in Cremona simply disappeared and was forgotten. Nobody knows why. After that, London and Paris developed as great violin-making centres, while Cremona had to wait another 200 years before it could re-establish itself.

Tonewood is our main raw material. It's easy to make mistakes when you aren't experienced, and I certainly did in the beginning. Maple wood (which grows in Bosnia) is used for the back and sides of the instrument, while spruce (available across the Alps) is used for the sound boards. I make the final choice after an expert I trust does the pre-selection for me. The way in which the wood is seasoned, a process that takes at least three to five years, is also very important. Even when you do all of this right, there will always be a certain degree of unpredictability: you could make a good instrument from bad wood, thanks to your skill, or you could make a bad instrument from good wood, just because you made a mistake.

Take the great masters of the past: Guarneri del Gesù used beautiful wood, but not seasoned, very fresh. Stradivari used different types of maple, even of low quality, and his instruments were always beautiful. It can be a tough call!

Tradition and innovation

Violin-making originated five centuries ago. The violin as we know it today was born around the same time, when musicians and composers, realizing that it was best suited to their needs, preferred it to other similar stringed instruments, which rapidly went extinct.

In violin-making, the apprenticeship is fundamental, both in school and in the workshop. There is no manual talent that's specific to violin-making, but a certain degree of aptitude is always necessary as in any other craft. You also have to work swiftly and fluidly, because if it takes too long, you run the risk of falling out of context and losing yourself.

I have never invented a way of working that was totally new, but I have taken inspiration from other violin-makers – as well as carpenters and artisans working in other disciplines – for details and solutions that I thought were better and more appropriate.

Scientific and technological advances help our knowledge of how a violin works: they give us new insights into an instrument, they allow us to see things that our eyes can't perceive, like how an instrument vibrates. But they aren't really useful in traditional violin-making because, in the end, we select the wood with the sole aid of our senses and our experience.

Training

When I was a teenager, the youth orchestra of my home town went on a concert trip to Wales, where we visited a violin-making school. This experience planted a little seed inside me. A few years later, after graduating, I realized that violin-making represented the perfect combination of all my interests: my love of music (I started playing the cello at the age of nine), my desire to study abroad, possibly in Italy, and my natural vocation for manual work.

I was accepted by the International Violin Making School in Cremona, where I studied for four years with Maestro Vincenzo Bissolotti. I received my diploma in 1993, and the same year I won first place for sound quality at the International Violin Making Competition in Prague. I then spent four years training and working in a violin atelier in Zurich and seven years in Vienna, where I dedicated myself exclusively to the restoration of antique instruments. This was a fantastic experience, because it enabled me to cultivate both a keen sensitivity and a deep respect for the craft. Also, as I'm a perfectionist, this was the ideal way for me to build up the necessary confidence to make my own instruments. In 2005 I moved back to Zurich with my family and opened my own workshop. In 2011 I won third prize at the Henryk Wieniawski Violin Making Competition in Poznań, and in 2012 the first prize for viola at the Antonio Stradivari International Triennial Competition in Cremona.

You never finish learning, so I always try to take the courses and seminars that I think will make me enhance my skills and knowledge of wood. These are also important opportunities to meet other luthiers with whom I can share information and experiences.

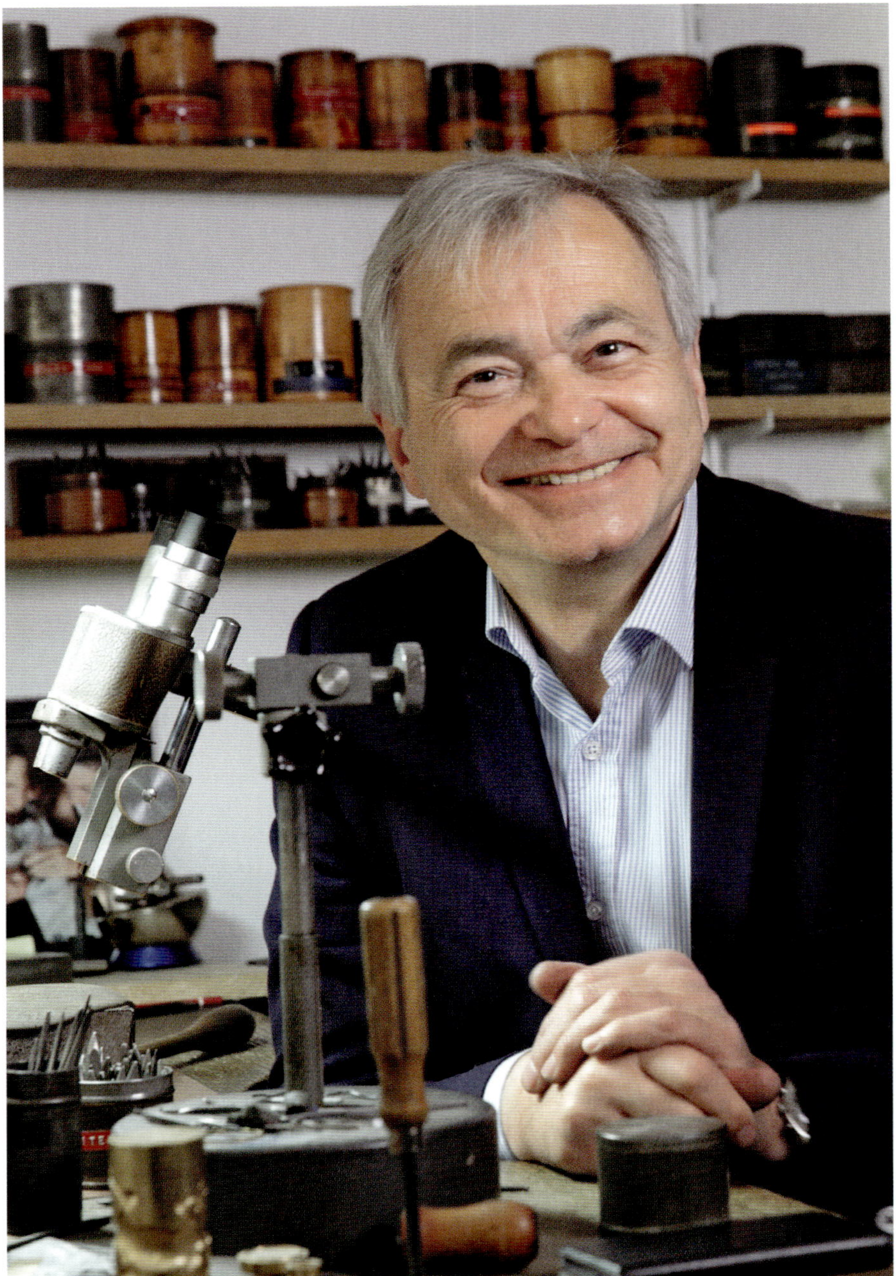

7. GÉRARD DESQUAND, METAL ENGRAVER

The son and grandson of metal engravers, Gérard Desquand has followed in their footsteps to become one of France's few remaining heraldic engravers. Born in Paris in 1951, he attended the École Estienne in Paris, where he subsequently taught for many years. He graduated in 1970 with a Diplôme des Métiers d'Art in engraving and went on to open his own workshop two years later. Desquand started out doing intaglio printing and embossing for luxury packaging before choosing to devote his time exclusively to heraldic engraving. In 1979 he was given the title of Meilleur Ouvrier de France and was named Maître d'art *in 2006. He was president of the Institut National des Métiers d'Art (INMA) from 2013 to 2016.*

Desquand's work, which involves engraving heraldic symbols on rings and seals, is sought after by jewellers and the major fashion houses, as well as by private clients for whom he develops bespoke designs signifying their membership of a group or their family history. For special occasions, he also reinterprets antique cylinder seals, engraved with written characters or figurative scenes. He prefers to work in metal but is also happy to explore other materials such as porcelain, which he uses for its transparency and fragility. He owns a substantial library, from which he draws inspiration for his creations.

Both my father and my grandfather were metal engravers. Apart from the six-month training stint I did with my father, we never worked together, nor did we ever engrave the same kinds of things. I never regretted my choice, and I am grateful to him for having induced me to reflect on the human and social condition and on the pleasure of doing this *métier d'art*. I have been engraving for 50 years now, and it still gives me the same joy: the joy of making and of knowing that I have evolved and that things continue.

In my workshop, I am transmitting my knowledge and skills to an apprentice, Sarah, who was one of my former students at the École Estienne, where I have taught for a long time. She has acquired a solid background in other areas of metal engraving and she is currently also studying the history and meaning of this craft. She will take over from me in time.

To perpetuate this craft, and ensure our survival, even artisans like us, who are very tied to tradition, must find new ways to communicate. I think that all the younger artisans understand this new reality. In the modern world, all serial production is delocalized and the large workshops of the past, with the *maîtres* and the *petit maîtres* and the apprentices, no longer exist. This means that the "secret of the *maître d'art*" has disappeared. It's difficult for people of my generation, who have been trained in a vertical way; today the younger generations look for horizontal training. This is how the new *métiers d'art* will develop, and I believe that today we are turning a new page in this history.

Authenticity

I think that "authentic" is what we call *justesse* in French: nothing more and nothing less than it takes. The right time, the right gesture, the right emotion… Everything that's true, authentic, is also "right". I believe that the secret isn't to freeze anything. Montaigne said that it's good to "limer sa cervelle", meaning to rub and polish our brains against that of others. He was talking of the young and of the intellectual exchange that's necessary for the world to evolve.

There is an emotional relationship between the person who makes an object and the person who uses it, and in the *métiers d'art*, this human relationship is fundamental. Heraldic engraving isn't the luxury goods industry, which churns out products to feed an enormous market. This is a small club and I know that if other engravers look at my work, they will immediately understand that I made it. This is enough for me. If I had had commercial ambitions, I would have probably created an object with a "brand", which is what the masses are looking for.

Competence

Competence is when we respond in the right way to the task that we're facing. I don't think competence is equal to excellence: I think it's the basis of excellence.

Competence in relations with clients, suppliers, the media is very important for the *métiers d'art*. And then, of course, you must be competent in running your business. In the past, it was rather common for artisans to be content with working just enough to earn the money they needed to pay the bills and survive. But the world has changed. You have to be responsible and aware of the fact that if you go out at night, you won't work well the following day.

Craftsmanship

I would say that two thirds of craftsmanship is a *savoir-faire du geste*, a manual know-how and skill. Even the part that's mechanical is always performed with the hands, as in the craft of a *guillocheur*, who performs a very specific kind of decorative engraving.

When we speak of *règles de l'art* we mean the ethics of the trade, which apply to two aspects: the "rules" linked to the skills and the "rules" bound up with the relationship with the clients (the honesty of giving them something made according to the *règles de l'art*) and with your colleagues. In fact, to be a member of the Grand Ateliers de France you have to achieve perfection both in your craft and in human relationships, which goes beyond mere technique but is indispensable if you want to maintain the excellence of your trade. As for the techniques, they must be consistent with what you have learnt and what you are making. It isn't something that has been written down in a manual: you need to reflect each time in order to adapt the "rule" to whatever you are doing in that circumstance. In this way, the craft keeps evolving and stays up to date. If the craft doesn't move, it remains stuck in the past, which is where it comes from, but what we do today is for the future. If, for example, there is a problem with a specific *métier*, we must change it, adapt it. I have a friend, Fanny Boucher, who does heliography. It's a wonderful printing technique and she is the only one in France who still masters it. Even though the market for that product has disappeared, she wanted to preserve the technique and she thought of adapting it to leather, thus moving the technique into home decoration. In this way, she succeeded in giving new life to the craft, and her workshop could progress. I know *maîtres d'art* who have preserved the know-how but have stopped working altogether, because they weren't able to expand their horizons.

Creativity

I think artisans need to break free from a culture of submission and subvert the preconception that they aren't creative by definition. There is no need for an artisan to be artistic, because it's the creative attitude that makes the difference and it's one of the artisan's fundamental skills. For this reason, if artisan creativity isn't protected, they will end up being consumed by the luxury goods industry. Today, the industry no longer dares to create and it turns to the *artisans d'art* (creative craftspeople) to do the research and experimentation; they are the only ones who are still free to create, since they don't have a boss or administrative boundaries. I believe that this is one of the meanings of "excellence": the freedom to create. The young are creative because they are used to working together and they don't ask themselves if they are artists, craftspeople or designers. They don't care. They make things and they leave it to the world to judge.

My creativity comes from my emotions. I am not creative as a person who has to respond to the demands of the market: my ambition is to communicate a message and to preserve, through the authenticity of the engraver's craft, its original function. Although every engraving I make is a creation and a unique piece, I am only implementing the rules of a *savoir-faire* based on a heritage of tradition, I am not creating something the way an artist does.

In the crafts, technique and creation are inextricably linked: a creation can only come to life through the technique. It means that without the technique, you can't do anything. When you have to learn and assimilate the technique, it can be difficult and make you suffer, both in mind and body. Then, when it becomes easy, and you don't suffer any more, perhaps you lose the impression that it can also be creative.

When I know where I'm going because I am guided by the codes and rules and my path is set, this is being an artisan. The intention makes the difference and perhaps this is what distinguishes art from craft.

Interpretation

I believe that the function of interpretation is to capture and convey an emotion, like a musician interpreting a musical composition.

When I engrave my cylinder seals, like the one I dedicated to the history of writing, I preserve the memory of an object – the printing seal – that originated a thousand years before Christ, and I give it new life: I unearth it and place it in today's reality. In this sense, it isn't a creation but the interpretation of an ancient means of communication for modern times. Because the contemporary world has lost itself and must rediscover its roots, it needs to know where it comes from. Writing evolves according to the tools that are used, and in turn the shape and form of these tools change according to the way in which they are used. The cylinder seal I dedicated to Noah's Ark is rather a homage to the species, an ecological engraving for the continuation of nature. It's also called "the master and the student" because for things to continue there has to be someone who teaches and someone who learns. The *métiers d'art* play an important role in an economy of energy, renewal and preservation of the planet: they show us how to go back to a different kind of relationship, like the concept of the "slow city". It's history for the future: an interpretation of history that keeps it fresh and up to date.

Originality

Since 1991, I have focused exclusively on heraldry, the only person in France to do so; for other engravers, heraldry is just one of the things they do. This enabled me to make quicker and better progress and that's why my work is always original and recognizable. What I am relaying to Sarah is that she needs also to find her own originality. She mustn't do as I have done but must find her own way to engrave the wolf, the fox, the dog… which will have to be, nonetheless, perfect. I suppose that what makes an object original, among similar objects, is the emotion you put into it, which in turn is reflected in the reaction of the person who looks at the object.

There are rules that ask to be broken and changed. I'm thinking of

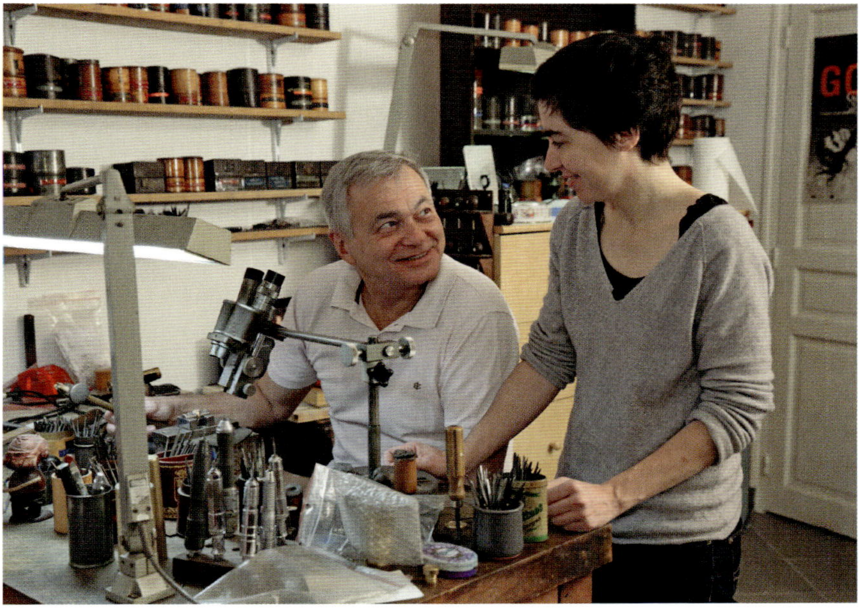

all the rules that stop you from building the future – all the rules that will cause the death of a *savoir-faire*, such as those of the market and of competition. Artisans, manufacturers and designers are responsible for this. Very often, the rules of the market have taken precedence over the rules of the art: a designer who has to create a new product thinks only in terms of the product and not in terms of preserving a heritage of know-how. Our responsibility is to preserve the *savoir-faire* even by doing other things with it.

For sure, the only rules that can't be broken are the rules of quality and of professional ethics, because these are the rules on which the *métiers d'art* depend for their survival.

Talent

I have trouble with words like talent and genius. Talent is always a mix of things, of which manual skill is only one component. You can't be creative if you don't open a book, if you don't go to an exhibition, if you don't travel or look at what other people are doing.

There is a great deal of tactile, sensorial perception involved in engraving. We work in a miniature world with tools that are made of hard metal, and I suppose that in this craft the talent is also to transmit the intensity of emotion in the work of the hand, certainly more than in wood or in stone. It can be a talent, but it takes years to master.

Territory

This type of metal engraving is essentially French, and the few remaining engravers are scattered across the country, from Paris to Lyon and Bordeaux. If you're looking for heraldic metal engraving that's exceptionally well executed, you'll find it here in France. For heraldic engraving in stone, on the other hand, you would have to go to Germany, in the area around Idar-Oberstein, or Italy, because no one in France is still doing it. The history of heraldic engraving is strongly tied to the days before the French Revolution, when the coat of arms wasn't just a prerogative of noble families, but also of artisans, tradespeople, knights and warriors.

Tradition and innovation

Engraving originated in Mesopotamia, where they used stone and clay. Heraldic art, of which heraldic engraving is a very small and specialized part, developed in the Middle Ages. Today, there are no more than ten heraldic engravers still working in France. The transmission of this skill can only be done one to one, because what is taught in school is a global technique that applies to many different types of engraving.

The basic tools of heraldic engraving are the metal punches, and the richness and depth of this craft lie in the thousands of punches that each artisan uses. These tools are impossible to produce today; it would be too expensive and time-consuming. When an engraver retires or dies, we try to reclaim that person's tools. I have bought many myself over the years.

Our craft is very traditional and the manual skills are always the same. Innovations such as 3D printing are quite useless in heraldic engraving, although other artisans have certainly benefited from this new technology, because they can save a lot of time in the planning phases of objects that are very complicated.

In heraldic engraving, the small scale actually preserves the *savoir-faire*. Technically it's possible to do it with laser technology, but a machine can't imitate all the infinitesimal movements of the hand, nor can it replicate the process of what I call "formal synthesis", which is the downsizing of a drawing through a series of passages that require thought and that can't be mechanically reproduced. This level of execution can only be performed by engravers who have a history and who know the evolution of this craft. We engrave a wolf, a fox, a dog in the space of just 3mm. In these 3mm, the wolf, the fox, the dog are perfectly recognizable. When clients come to us, this is what they are looking for.

The machines I use here are the ones I built myself with the help of some friends working in the aerospace industry. In this way, I managed to mix mechanical work with manual work. I use them only for work that would be a waste of time to do by hand. I prefer to devote that time to my research.

Creative crafts today can only survive if they engage in exchanges with other disciplines. This is a global world and you can't close yourself off, because everything works together. In the old days, the crafts were divided into guilds. Today, the *métiers d'art* cross over all the time and spill out even into distant worlds such as the automobile industry, for example when the leather seats of a luxury car are sewn by hand. This means that with the same *métier d'art* you can work both in the car industry and in fashion. To achieve this, we need the new generations.

Training

When I turned 15, my father gave me the freedom to decide what I wanted to do with my life. I thought my future would be in sport, but when I realized that he was happy working as an engraver, I made up my mind to follow him and go to the École Estienne (the municipal professional school of book arts and industries founded in Paris in 1887), where my grandfather had also studied. I obtained a Diplôme des Métiers d'Art in 1970, and went on to train with my father for six months. Every week he would give me an assignment that he appraised at the end like a real *maître* would have done (whereas a *maître d'apprentissage* would have overseen every step of the way). This meant that I had to take all the risk by myself. In fact, the quickest apprenticeship is the one where you have to do the thinking yourself and learn from your own mistakes. However, you never really finish learning, whatever your profession.

The turning point for me came when I realized the true meaning of engraving and its function in society. It was in 1990. I had been engraving for 20 years and was doing it well, but, until then, it was enough for me to know that the client was happy and that I could earn my living. You can spend a whole lifetime without knowing why you are doing something! From the moment I grasped that the meaning of engraving is the transmission of history, of an image, of an idea, the more I advanced and the more I understood my task as an engraver. Today I value the "gesture" more than the "decoration". I believe this also applies to life: as you grow older, you look for the essential and you don't waste time with things that aren't important.

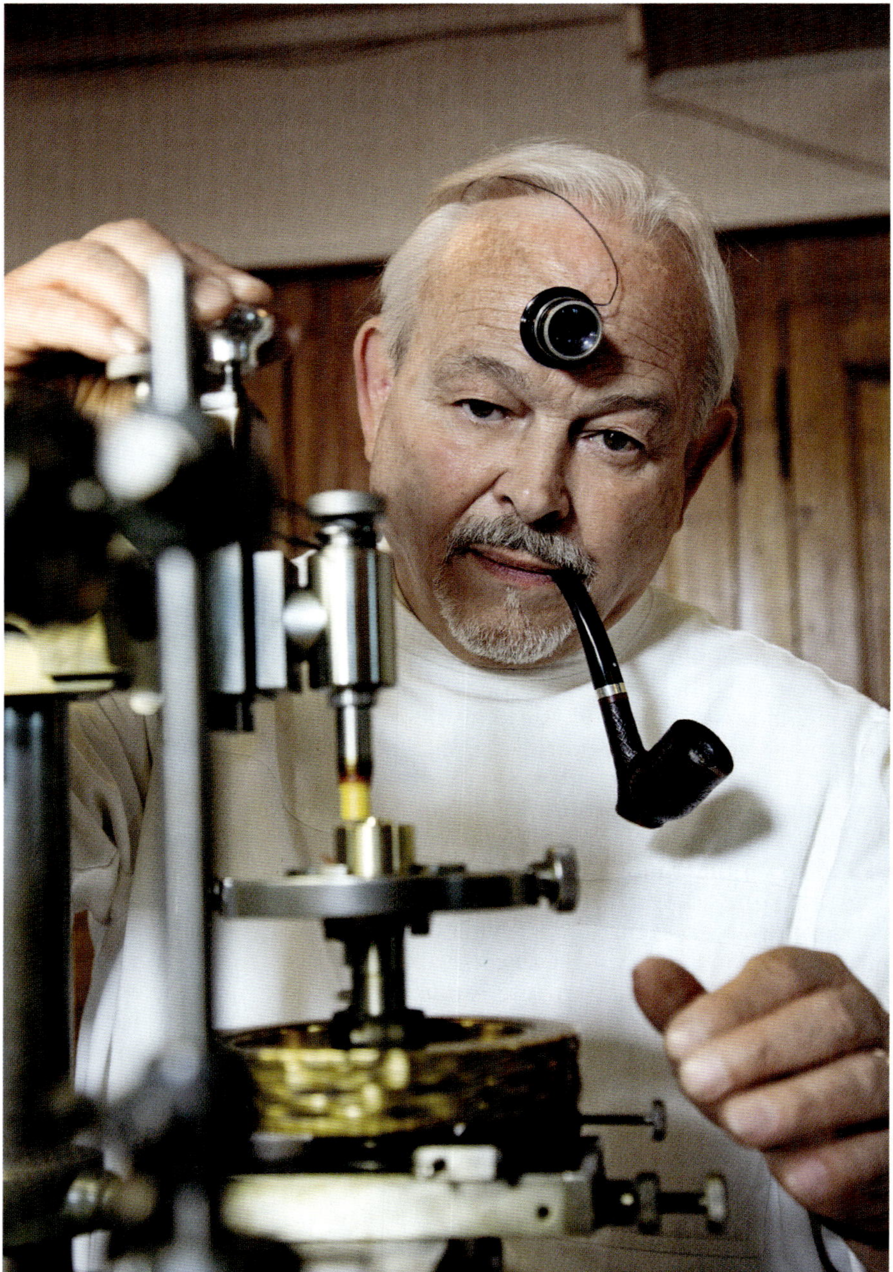

8. PHILIPPE DUFOUR, INDEPENDENT WATCHMAKER

Philippe Dufour hails from the Vallée de Joux (Switzerland), an area of the Jura mountains with a centuries-old tradition of watchmaking. It is no surprise, therefore, that he chose to follow this profession, like his grandfather before him, although he claims that he initially had other ambitions and that it was by chance that he ended up at the watchmaking school in Le Sentier. On completing his studies, he joined Jaeger-LeCoultre, where he sought to broaden his horizons by working in customer and after-sales service, first in Germany and then in the United Kingdom. In the early 1970s, he moved to the Caribbean to manage the local plant of a Swiss watch company. On his return to Switzerland in 1978, after brief stints at Gerald Genta and Audemars Piguet, Dufour decided to strike out on his own, basing himself in the Vallée de Joux. He first took to restoring antique watches, a discipline he considers to provide the best of educations, not only in how watch mechanisms are made but also in problem-solving and the art of finishing.

In keeping with the time-honoured tradition of master watchmakers, Dufour designs and produces personally every element of his watches, which, with their sophisticated complications, can take more than a year to make and are sought after by collectors the world over.

My father was a stonecutter who worked his whole life in a factory that made components for watches. My grandfather was a watchmaker (he had also gone to the watchmaking school in Le Sentier), and he worked for Jaeger-LeCoultre until past the age of 70. He gave me his watchmaker's *layette* (cabinet) when he retired, since I was the only one of his five grandchildren who had followed in his footsteps. It was a great honour for me and I still use his tools. But I became a watchmaker by chance: when I turned 15, my parents told me that they couldn't afford for me to study outside the Vallée de Joux, which didn't leave me much choice in terms of professions. I didn't manage to get into the mechanics school because of my terrible maths, so I ended up at the watchmaking school instead.

My daughter is a watchmaker too. She is talented and we worked together for some years. Today she repairs perpetual movements for Patek Philippe.

I have a friend who retired from Audemars Piguet after 40 years. He comes to my atelier every morning and I teach him the way I work, which differs from how he worked while he was employed. Our goal, as soon as we are ready, is to train a young watchmaker in the old way.

Authenticity

A feature that's much sought-after today is traceability. There are people willing to pay more for something if they know where it comes from.

That's why I insist on putting the hand back at the centre of everything. All the products that are made today, whether good or bad, are anonymous. They are identified by a brand. I think that the artisan should sign the movement if they made it; it's an added value for the watch and, ultimately, for the brand, especially in this day and age, when all the work is fragmented. The market is changing and the industry doesn't seem to have realized it yet. They rely on the testimonials of the famous to sell their watches, without understanding that their companies produce exceptional things, and that they don't need celebrities to promote them but the people who make them!

Competence

When I set up my independent atelier, it was a real moment of madness. You have to erase some words from your vocabulary, like weekends, holidays and retirement, and focus on patience, determination and perfectionism. My leitmotif is to question myself every day and never to be content with where I've got, but to push myself one step further all the time.

Competence involves other aspects of work. For this reason I tell young people that they need to know other languages, such as English or Mandarin, which are the languages of the future in a market that's hungry for the history and competence we can offer.

Craftsmanship

If we consider only the functionality of a watch, then the modern machines are fine. But what makes watchmaking special is the finish, the aesthetics, and this can only be achieved by hand, because the machine leaves unattractive traces. I consider each movement as a painting, and each watch, even if it's of the same model, has its own character, when it's done by hand: what I do on Monday morning or on Friday night will never be identical.

Therefore, a watch that's "made by the book" is made without short cuts. Likewise, the clients enjoy the pleasure of winding a watch. In an experience that involves touch, sight and hearing, they rediscover a relationship that was lost with the quartz and automatic movement. If you don't take care of your watch every day, it "dies". Even for the watch's ticking I use a classic frequency, which is very relaxing. A Japanese client, who bought one of my Simplicity watches many years ago, told me that it gives him happiness. This is the humanity that you have to put into a watch.

I am developing a project with Greubel Forsey called "Naissance d'une Montre – Le Garde Temps". We have entrusted a young watchmaking teacher, Michel Boulanger, with the role of learning the traditional watchmaking techniques before they are permanently lost. Over four years he created an entirely hand-made timepiece. His tourbillon watch was presented at the 2015 Salon International de la Haute Horlogerie in Geneva. The watch will be auctioned in Hong Kong in spring 2016 and the funds will be used to sustain the project to make a total of 11 pieces. The people who buy these watches will take part in the preservation and transmission of this *savoir-faire*.

Consumers are becoming more and more educated; they are curious and have a lot of knowledge. They get their information from magazines, from internet sites and from the many extraordinary forums that can explain, even to a non-expert, that if you look at a watch that has been finished and polished by hand, there will be a play of light that's visible even without a magnifying glass.

Creativity

In watchmaking, functionality is the most important thing. A watch isn't a picture that you hang on the wall; it has to work in different climates or positions, in water or in the absence of gravity. But you can be creative in the shape of the movements, and I am inspired by the culture in which I grew up, and the movements that were made in the Vallée de Joux between 1900 and 1920. When I created the Simplicity, I remembered that this type of movement was subject to very little wear and that all the proportions were very well balanced. I created the world's first wristwatch with both a minute repeater and *grande et petite sonnerie* complications. It took me two and a half years to make one, which I presented at Basel in 1992. In 1996 I presented the Duality, my first double escapement wristwatch.

Interpretation

Although I created my own complications, and was innovative in adapting them to a bracelet watch, I never invented anything new, something that I could patent. I developed my own design interpreting the many movements that I have seen and restored in my life. In making them, I always tried to respect the codes of fine workmanship: functional yet beautiful. Even what you don't see must be beautiful, so that if someone repairs the watch one day, that person will discover this beauty. This to me is the meaning of interpretation, and it has nothing to do with making a watch designed by someone else, because it wouldn't be a "Philippe Dufour" watch to begin with.

Originality

When I made my Simplicity, I "selfishly" made a watch that I liked. But its originality remains within the classicism of watchmaking. I was inspired by the 1950s and 60s because I like that period very much. It's an original watch also in the sense that it's made in small quantities. If you make 100,000 pieces of a watch like the Simplicity each year, it ceases to be original, because you see it all over the place. People today want to be exclusive; they don't want to go to a dinner and see ten people wearing the same watch.

I am not interested in working with strange and unusual materials. It's all right for fashion to make extravagant things, because that's what is expected of them, but it isn't so for us. There's no evidence that new materials are better than the traditional ones.

Talent

I don't think we are necessarily born with a talent. In watchmaking, the eye is more important than the hand. A certain manual aptitude helps, but the most important quality is curiosity. I remember that my brother and I were once given some toy cars that were made so that they never fell off the table: I played with them for three days, and on the fourth I took them apart to see how they worked.

There are some young people who never ask a question, who aren't willing to make sacrifices. But in the world of independent watchmaking, you are the only person on board so you have to have all the qualities it takes to survive and fulfil yourself. You also need to have some dreams. I always say that life is too easy in Switzerland; you don't have to break your back to survive and this doesn't give the young any motivation.

There are some exceptions, of course! Like the young talents sponsored by the Académie Horlogère des Créateurs Indépendants, established in 1985 and of which I am a member. This institution is keeping independent watchmaking alive by supporting young watchmakers in building independent businesses and exhibiting their work at the Baselworld trade fair.

Territory

Watchmaking started relatively late in the Vallée de Joux. It arrived from Geneva in the 18th century, together with the Protestants who were being persecuted in France. The people of the Vallée de Joux learnt to make extraordinary watches even though they weren't big travellers or dealers. They were extremely ingenious and had an exceptional culture. Religion, too, played an important role in this process. The valley was totally cut off from the rest of the world in winter, and little by little entire families of mountain people, young and old, started to

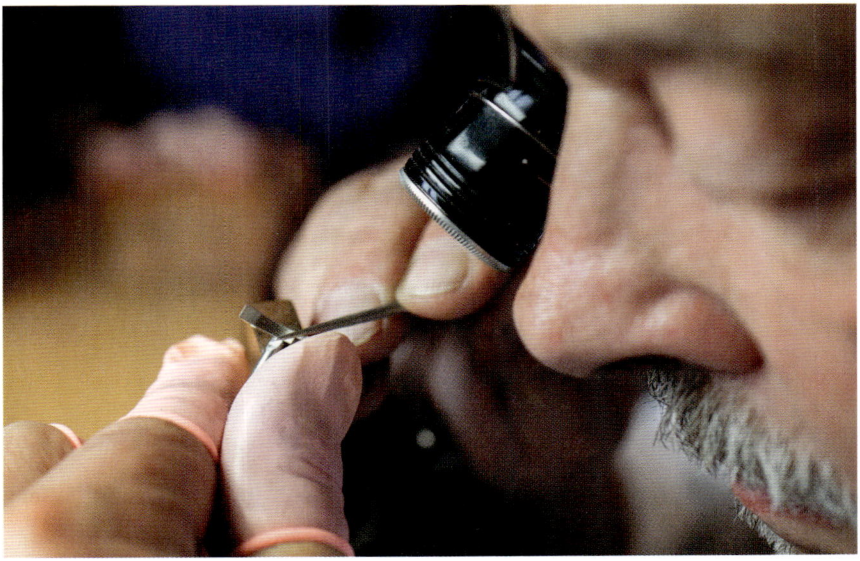

get involved in watchmaking. Seven out of ten of the complications of the 18th and 19th centuries were made here and then sent to Geneva, England or Germany to be mounted in the cases. The Patek Philippe Henry Graves Supercomplication, for instance, was one of the most complicated mechanical watches ever made, with 18 complications in the same watch, and it was all made here in 1933. This example is indicative of the resourcefulness and productivity of this valley.

The Vallée de Joux still lives off its history, which stems from a long tradition of quality. But the trend today is to take in hundreds of workers from neighbouring valleys in France. I think we have to stop relying just on our reputation and begin to cultivate it, so that it may continue to grow and improve.

Tradition and innovation

Today, watchmaking is a highly fragmented process, and only a handful of artisans can make a watch from beginning to end. Traditionally, the students completed their training in the Swiss watchmaking schools with a "montre école", a pocket watch with a complication designed and made entirely by themselves. Can you believe that in 1924 a student managed to make two of these? It was an incredible feat if you consider that nowadays they can't make even a simple mechanism. This is because manual work is "intellectualized": the students study from books as if they were to become white-collar workers, ignoring the fact that watchmakers work with their hands! This is such a terrible waste of human potential; I am sure there are plenty of gifted young people who could make magnificent things with their hands.

I have a very different idea of what training should be: I start from the principle that watchmaking should be taught as an art, and that the students should be introduced to the history, the *savoir-faire*, the tools, the old workmanship and the new technologies. There are some skills in watchmaking, like the *pivotage*, which aren't taught in school simply because they are no longer used in factories. But it's as if a piano virtuoso didn't practise scales daily! Each trade has its "scales", and you can't play if you don't learn all the fundamentals and practise every day. With every generation we lose something of this art, and with every economic crisis we lose a bit more. My dream is to set up a private international watchmaking school reserved for trained watchmakers, where they could spend two or three years doing a master's that would enable them to make their own *montre école*.

At the same time, I always say that we have to live in our time. We can't expect a big factory to do without modern advances. Machines enable us to work better and faster. But the machines are the same the world over; what we have a duty to do here, in the Vallée de Joux, is to provide the added value of creativity and workmanship, knowledge and history, so that a watch isn't top of the range only because it's expensive.

In my work, I haven't invented anything new, but I have updated certain techniques that my grandfather and other old craftspeople used in the past. I don't use any modern technology apart from the computer, which I taught myself to use as far back as 1989. However, I still draw in two dimensions, because the third dimension is in my head.

Training

I studied to become a *horloger-rhabilleur*, a watchmaker-repairer, at the watchmaking school of Le Sentier in the Vallée de Joux. This very important institution, established in 1901, was set up and run jointly by the regional authorities and the local watch manufacturers. In the 1980s it became a State vocational education and training school, and the curriculum has since evolved in tandem with the needs of the modern watch industry.

When I finished school in 1967, I joined Jaeger-LeCoultre on the condition that I be allowed to get some experience abroad. I was sent first to Frankfurt to get familiar with customer service. This was very interesting, because when you are making a watch you don't consider that someone will wear it and face problems that you hadn't even imagined. Then I went to the UK, where I reorganized Jaeger-LeCoultre's after-sales service. In the early 1970s I moved to the US Virgin Islands, where

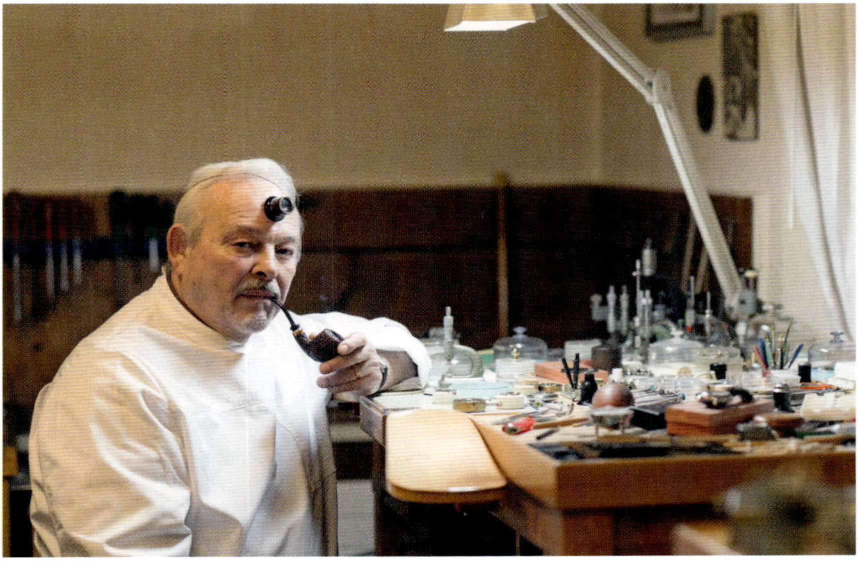

I ran the local plant of a Swiss watch company. It was very common for manufacturers to open factories in these tax havens. On the island of St. Croix alone there were 14 watch factories. We made 3,000 movements a week, under strict Swiss quality standards.

All these experiences abroad opened my horizons: if you always stay in the same place, you end up thinking that what you know is the only truth. When I came back to Switzerland in 1978, the crisis in the watch industry had already started and circumstances brought me, quite unexpectedly, to turn independent and open my own atelier. I spent five years restoring collectors' watches, immersing myself in the wonderful creations of the great watchmakers of the past. I suppose it took me at least 20 years to reach the point where I could confidently invent my own complications. You never stop learning, throughout your entire life, and you discover new things every day. This is the greatness of watchmaking.

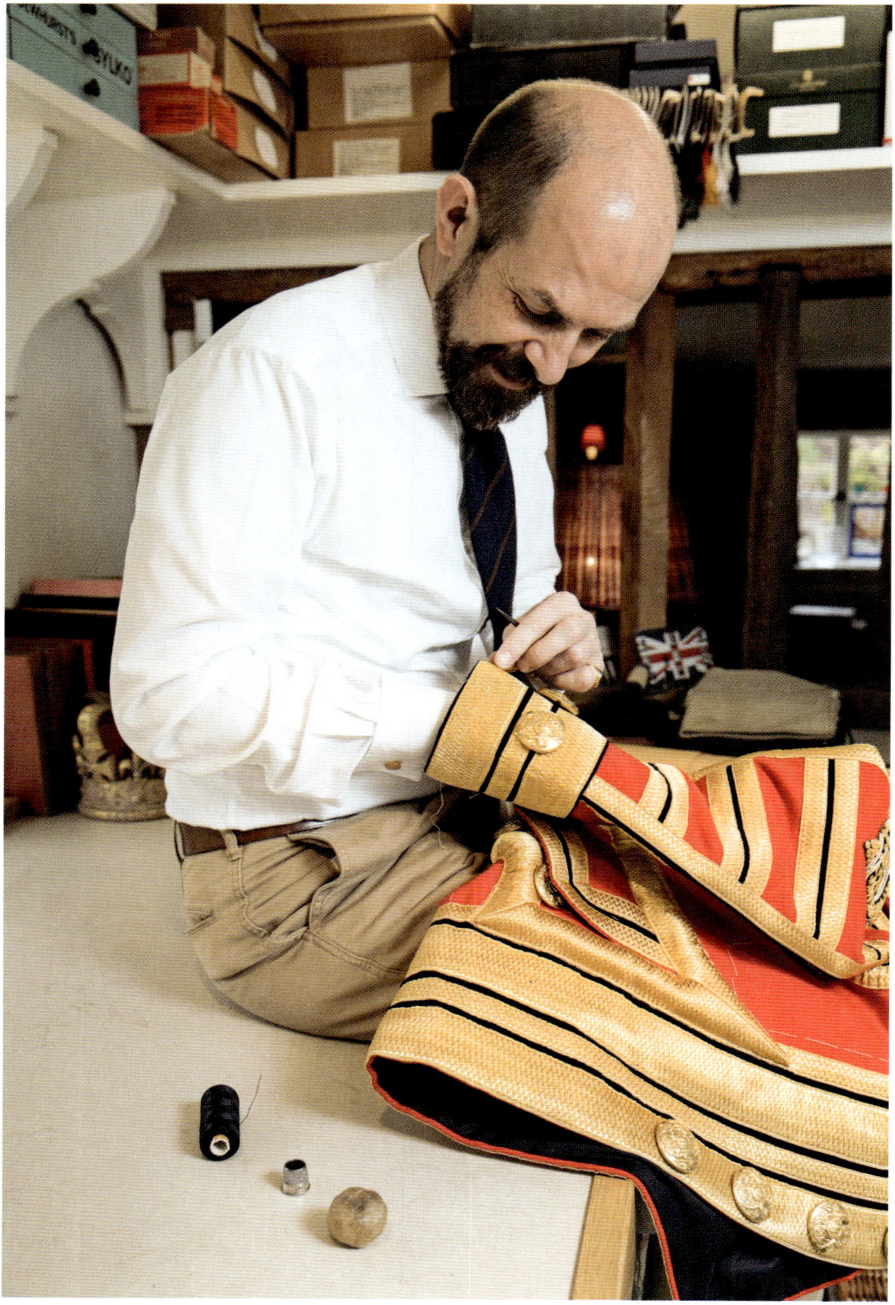

9. KEITH LEVETT, CEREMONIAL AND LIVERY TAILOR

Keith Levett knew from a very early age what he wanted to with his life and has never faltered from this path. Born in 1973, he learned to sew at his grandmother's knee and later developed a fascination with flag design and the evolution of military and ceremonial dress, two interests which stood him in good stead when, in 1989, aged 17, he was interviewed for an apprenticeship at Henry Poole & Co, one of the oldest tailors on London's Savile Row. Levett was placed under the tutelage of two master coat makers, who taught him to set a very high standard for his work.

Within four years, Levett had mastered the art of tailoring and, whilst learning to cut, took over the making of state liveries and other ceremonial work connected with Poole's Royal Warrant, a position he occupies to this day, as the last dedicated livery tailor remaining on Savile Row. At Poole's the complex gold braid work on the livery garments is entirely hand-stitched, requiring some 32,500 stitches alone on the decorative elements of each coat and waistcoat. The time and painstaking effort involved are evidence of Levett's extraordinary love and passion for his craft. He is a master tailor and a director of Henry Poole & Co, as well as being a freeman of the Merchant Taylors' Company in the City of London.

Tailoring had run in my family for generations, although the tradition had stopped at one of my great grandparents. My maternal grandmother used to sew a lot and I grew up listening to the whir of the flywheel turning as she treadled on her old Singer, while I would sit at her feet playing with the scraps of material. It sparked from there. From my grandfather's side I believe I took my extreme perfectionism: I will have it my way or not at all. I don't think I make the best work in the world but I make it to a standard that will justify the cost, and my ambition is to ensure that that standard is maintained.

When I came into the trade, there were many middle-aged and elderly master artisans of whom, having an inquiring mind, I would ask all sorts of questions, but they were very reluctant to share. I am not jealous of what I do; I've done it well enough and I've nothing to prove. If you don't give something back, if you don't teach people to perpetuate the craft, it's going to die or get watered down. I am currently training a young man who did his apprenticeship with one of the best coat-makers we have. He puts his head to what he does, and if he has the stamina he will succeed. We are very alike in many ways; it will be an interesting journey.

Authenticity

Part of the mystique of tailoring is in the fact that perfection doesn't mean standardized: while two suits may be alike, each one is done individually, and your eyes almost see that there is a difference even if you can't quite tell what it is. This is what gives tailoring its beauty and, I suppose, what also gives it its authenticity.

The best of the tailoring craft is located here, in Savile Row. There is an osmosis, a culture of brilliance, of excellence, a pitch of craftsmanship which is taught and surrounds every one of the apprentices who are trained on Savile Row.

If you come to Savile Row, you are buying something that has taken anywhere between 60 to 100 hours of an artisan's time to make. That someone has spent five to seven years learning to do what they do, as opposed to someone on a production line who has had one week's tuition learning to do one very specific thing. That's what gives the garment its character and what the craft is all about.

Competence

The tailors that don't cut, and therefore don't see clients, have to be competent with the garment in front of them. But if you are a cutter, you have to know something about the making of the garments, and the best cutters are the ones who have gone through a tailoring apprenticeship first, because they understand the consequence of what they are cutting. The good cutter must make the client feel at ease, assessing his personality and working out the best way to interact with him.

For a company like Poole's, competence must go beyond the skills of the actual craft. We certainly have current clients whose great-grandfathers were also our clients. In a throw-away society, it's amazing how they crave good English tailoring. But still, we have to go and chase the trade these days, and we do. We do trunk shows and fittings on the East and West Coasts of America and in continental Europe six times a year. Savile Row can't rest on its laurels and wait for people to come to us.

Craftsmanship

When Her Majesty had her Diamond Jubilee, the Royal Mews approached us and showed us some liveries that were too small to go on modern bodies. They had been cut in our cutting room in 1875 and they were still in use in 2002 (for the Queen's Golden Jubilee) but they had finally decided to replace them. They gave one lot to a tailor outside London and the rest came back to us. We replaced like for like, right down to the last stitch. It took me around nine months, because the process begins and ends with one person: I take the order, take the measurements, cut the patterns, fit the garments twice, make them and apply all the braid. Then I do the finishing works (linings, button holes, etc.), I press them, sew the buttons on, and deliver them back to the Palace.

Henry Poole created Savile Row as we know it today. At the height of his business, he had 300 sewing tailors and 14 cutters and that made it easily the biggest tailoring company in the world, with 43 Royal Warrants (no other company, across any sphere of endeavour, had accrued so many distinctions). His was the biggest tailors in the world, the most fashionable in Europe, and what he did had a ripple effect on the rest of the trade. So when it comes to his Royal Warrant, Angus Cundey, our chairman and descendant of Henry Poole, considers it the most important thing that he possesses. We have never lost it and, hopefully, never will. He is prepared to subsidize the State livery that we do so that we make it to the standard that we always have, regardless of what the Royal Household is prepared to pay. The decision about how it's made and the amount of work that goes into it is mine, and he supports that wholeheartedly. It has to do with continuity and about keeping Poole's where it should be, which is absolutely at the top. The other thing that dictates the standard is knowledge, not just of the art of tailoring itself (and it's an art, since it hasn't yet been reduced to the level of an exact science) but of the history and evolution of these garments.

It's very difficult to quantify the standard that goes into a suit that's made "by the book". If you go to a dozen companies on Savile Row, they will all give you a different answer. You have to look at the skin tone of the person you are dressing, and secondarily his personality and how he moves. This is very important, because you can make beautiful clothes from beautiful cloth which you don't sell because they don't go with the face. The quality of the cloth and the cut are the most obvious indicators of perfectly tailored clothes. The fine hand-stitching is also a giveaway. I suppose that a "work of art" is something that looks as if it were made effortlessly, which doesn't look contrived or overworked. Then if it comes from a tailor in Savile Row, it has to look West End and apparently timeless.

Even if you try on a suit that hasn't been made for you, you will know it has been tailored because it just feels different. But if it has been cut for you, it's like an embrace.

Creativity

If you have had a Savile Row education, you can do anything. People like Alexander McQueen, who was trained by Andersen & Sheppard and Gieves & Hawkes, went on to do some amazingly creative things. But I think it's very difficult to be truly original in our trade. One of the first things I was told when I first came here was that there is nothing new under the sun. Everything that's done in tailoring today has been done a century or more before. Pleat-fronted trousers come from the Cossack pants of the 1820s. The peak lapel on the coat is a reinvention of the collar of the same period. Things evolve, but they also go in cycles. Also, the tailoring techniques have remained the same, but many materials have changed, and we are using cloth that's much lighter in weight, nearly half of what it was before the Second World War. So sometimes you have to have a more creative approach because the materials and the techniques simply won't behave in the way you want them to.

Interpretation

The customer has the idea of what he is looking for and it's up to the cutter to look at the figure and decide how to do it. Then the tailor has to understand not just the fabric but also what the cutter has in mind. So there is a double interpretation there. The work that the cutter and the tailor do together requires a great deal of creative intelligence, which in tailoring terms is the ability to visualize what is in your mind's eye and then execute that from start to finish, moulding the original idea and the cloth.

One of the things that makes you a good craftsperson is the ability to take all that you know, shake it around and put it together almost like a jigsaw, redefining it. This is something that can't be done mechanically, with a formula.

The client ultimately looks for the distillation of centuries of tradition and learning that are still relevant today and that's going to make him look sharp without looking dandified, look well dressed without standing out. And because he knows he is imperfect, he is looking for something that is going to emphasize his best features and put into soft focus those which are less flattering. He is also looking for a standard of service which he isn't going to get in the modern world, and which you can almost consider to be part of the craft.

Originality

For the ceremonial stuff, I am a copyist, a train that runs on track. You subconsciously tweak things, because every generation has also cut livery to the edicts of the day. You have to evolve things very subtly and make them balance well with a slightly different silhouette, which has naturally changed since Victorian times. At the same time, in order to preserve and be faithful to the historical look, the livery mustn't appear as if it has been cut today.

The same applies to tailoring. Savile Row is timeless, Savile Row is never fashion. I suppose the real skill of being original, in both senses of the term, lies in the fact that it has to be timeless and yet it must acknowledge the movement of fashion and style. It must remain relevant, otherwise it would fossilize and that would be the end of it. The trick is to be true to Savile Row and true to the craft at the same time, and to create things that have a serviceable life, which for a tailored suit can be between 20 and 30 years on average. So, stylistically a suit has to be classical enough for people to want to wear it for that long.

Talent

Without talent you are nothing, you're an automaton. When we select our apprentices we only pick those who learn quickly and have the gift of foresight, which means thinking one stage ahead of what they are being taught. This is the talent we look for.

Talent in tailoring is the ability to visualize something on the figure, on the person with that face tone. Talent is about being able to see something in your head formed fully and be able to execute it, or induce others to execute it the way you see it. Talent is about making it look effortless. Like a swan gliding smoothly on the water, while it paddles away underneath.

Territory

They used to say that you had to have very deep pockets to have your wardrobe made on Savile Row. But to be able to send your household staff to be dressed on Savile Row showed real status. The most prolific of our customers spent far more on liveries than they ever did on themselves. A good part of Henry Poole's reputation was built on his livery trade. In the 1870s it became so vast that he had to lease separate premises – on top of the five that he already owned on Savile Row – where 50 to 70 artisans worked to make anything from the pantry jackets for the house boy right up to magnificent state liveries that were worn in the days when horse and carriage were still in use. The uniforms were made of jacket, waistcoat, breeches and garters (stockings and shoes, like the wigs and the hats, are made elsewhere), which were richly embellished. The white metal braids were in 90 per cent silver and the gold braids were between 3 to 9 per cent gold, which made them incredibly expensive (about 50 metres of braid go on just one uniform). Today, we use 2.5 per cent gold braids that are woven to order for the Royal Household and Mews.

Whether for tailoring or livery clothes, the raw materials are fundamental and, historically, their provenance depended on where the best suppliers were: velvet from Genoa, gold lace from Lyon, Merino wool first from Spain and then Australia, the best worsted materials were woven in Huddersfield and so on. From the late 19th and into the 20th century, Savile Row was the epicentre of the golden mile of tailoring: all the industries that serviced the tailoring trade (button-makers, gold lacemakers and embroiderers, cloth merchants, boot-makers, shirt-makers, hosiers, dye-sinkers…) were all close at hand and you could produce anything from scratch in just 24 hours.

Tradition and innovation

When I came into the trade, I learnt very quickly that a Savile Row suit whispers to you, it never screams. In a well-dressed man, you don't really notice a lot of details, but the silhouette must be immaculate even when the clothes are quite well worn. That's the secret of good tailoring. The reason the tailoring craft is much the same as it was at the turn of the 20th century is that it's still the best way to make suits. We have a fairly rigorous apprenticeship plan. Out of our 45 tailors and cutters, three to four are apprentices. If they are really good, we expect to get them through in about four to five and a half years. But at the end of that, you learn only when you are out by yourself so, in the strictest sense, seven years are the standard. We do take people from specialist colleges, but I learnt more in one month in Poole's workshops than I did in one year at the London College of Fashion on day release. I had a brilliant teacher but we moved at the rate of the slowest person in the class. At Poole's, I was the slowest person in the room so I learnt both speed and accuracy: there is no point in being taught to make beautiful clothes if you can't make them quickly.

For the ceremonial garments, I always say that half of the job is knowing why you are making what you are making and why it's important to maintain standards, the other is executing. At the height of the Empire there were dozens of workshops producing beautiful liveries, all competing to get the best of the trade, so the standard went through the roof. Being fossilized pieces of ritualistic costume, they have to be made as in their heyday, otherwise it becomes theatre costume, which is something we definitely don't do at Poole's, appointed Livery Tailor in 1869. What I produce today is made to the same standard as in the 1920s and of much the same cut. We only work with the best velvet that comes from Italy, we use only heavy silk satin for the lining, which is quilted for warmth and to give structure, the braids are all hand made in gold or silver, and the accessories are cut-steel buttons. On top of that, we only sew by hand. That's the difference between doing it cheaply and doing it properly. It's very difficult to be innovative when you're in the context of ceremonial garments. I had to relearn something that hadn't been done for over 50 years. So in this sense I was able to chart my own path, following my instinct, and because I had been taught in a certain way, I brought that into what I was doing.

In 200 years we have been touched by technology on very few occasions: in the 1890s, when we allowed in the sewing machine (but only for basic things and the lining, and only if invisible); the introduction of the synthetic fibres that we use for the lining; and the arrival of the computer, which we use only to record orders.

Training

By the time I was 14, I had decided fairly conclusively that I wanted to go into tailoring. The job was waiting for me before I had even left school, because we had a very good career's officer who had connections in Savile Row, and the chairman of Henry Poole & Co was interviewing prospective apprentices. I remember that while he was taking me round the cutting rooms I paused in front of a cabinet full of State liveries. He asked me if I knew what they were, and in fact I did, because I had developed a keen interest in uniforms from the age of seven. This little incident persuaded him to hire me.

The Royal Mews was beginning to think about replacing some of the State liveries, which were becoming too old. The last had been made in 1937, none were made new for the Coronation in 1953 and only one piece had been made for the Silver Jubilee in 1977. This meant that none of the tailors who had done that kind of work before the Second World War were still alive: the whole craft was dead and it had to be relearnt. I began my regular apprenticeship in 1989 under two master coat-makers who were both in their late sixties. Then I did some military tailoring with another company, where they taught me a little bit about the materials and how they behaved and the discipline required, but nothing about the aesthetics nor the specific techniques required by livery garments.

Halfway through my apprenticeship, I had to start doing the State orders with no one who could tell me how to do it and no book to consult. Thank goodness I was able to get access to a dozen of the old pieces and see what was good in each. The first coat I did is still in service in Buckingham Palace and still looks good and well made. I was doing them at the rate of one or two a year for about five years before I thought I had cracked it. But even then, you always strive to improve, to make a piece better and neater.

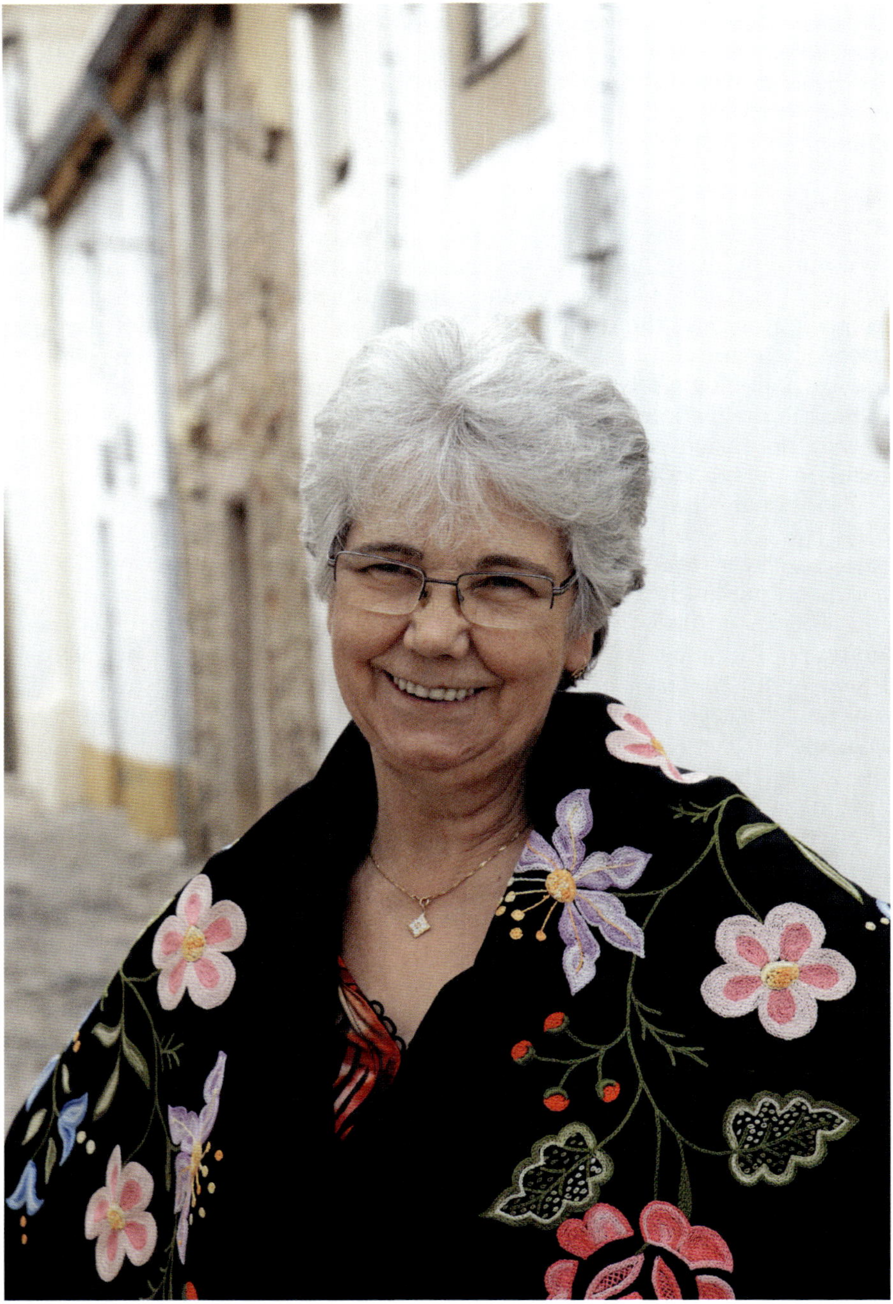

10. DINIS PEREIRA, WOOL FELT EMBROIDERER

Dinis Pereira comes from an area of Portugal famous for its embroideries. Born in 1943 in Nisa, a small village north of Alentejo, she discovered a talent for sewing at a young age. Entirely self-taught, she took up the local speciality of wool felt embroidery at the age of 20. Ten years later, she broke new ground by opening her own studio, employing several young women whom she taught the trade and some of whom still work for her today.

Pereira has represented Nisa's crafts on numerous occasions all over Portugal and Spain and at fairs and events related to Portuguese crafts. In recent years, she was invited to participate in an innovative project by the acclaimed Portuguese artist Joana Vasconcelos, producing embroideries for her art installations and exhibitions. The collaboration has not only given the work of the women of Nisa worldwide exposure but also enabled Pereira to branch out and create new designs and patterns for her work, while remaining true to the traditions of her territory and her people.

In the past, women used to embroider at home and girls were naturally encouraged to learn from a very early age. My mother made bobbin lace, another of Nisa's specialities, but she never really taught me.

Some 30 years ago I started to receive big orders for wool felt embroideries from my two biggest clients: a woman who had a Portuguese handicrafts shop in the United States and a man in Coimbra who did business with Italy. I was also supplying the shop of another Portuguese woman, who used to sell embroidered bed covers and blankets by instalments, since these products were obviously incredibly expensive. In this way, more people could afford to buy them and there came a point when I was receiving orders for ten bedcovers a week. At the peak of the business I had more than 20 people working for me. All this died out around 2009–2010, because the market for this kind of product no longer exists.

Around that time, I met Joana Vasconcelos and started to collaborate on her artworks and installations. Although the pieces I make for her are very different from the traditional blankets and local costumes, I still have the opportunity to develop this work with other women in Nisa. The number varies according to the urgency and volume of the work, but it can involve as many as 15 embroiderers. The sad thing is, however, that although I occasionally teach the technique to other women, nobody from the younger generations is interested in learning it any more.

Authenticity

To be authentic is to know that what I do is well made and genuine. Whenever I use a pattern, I know that it possesses the authenticity to be there. On top of this, I know that the new patterns I've created over the years, however diverse and original, are the photograph of all the patterns that were traditionally done in the past, that they represent something that belongs to this land. They aren't the same, but they are identical.

When I use a geometric design, for example, it isn't "authentic" in the strictest sense, because the patterns of Nisa are always floral, but it can be authentic in a different way. In fact, even making totally different designs has given me pride, because in doing so I have evolved. This is their value for me: they come from the same origin.

Even the embroideries I make for Vasconcelos's works talk about Nisa and about my people and my land. I also cooperate on another project, making embroideries for a small collection of bags, and on those products my name always appears as the artisan who made them.

Competence

Obviously, if you don't have the skill, you don't have the competence, and that takes years of training. But in order to be competent, you need also to take responsibility for what you are doing and for doing it well. If you make something well, your competence is above everything; if you don't, then the competence is lost together with the value of the work you are doing, and you could go as far as losing your own identity. When you are an artisan, you are competent when you dedicate yourself to what you like to do and you always continue to experiment, to find new ideas and solutions. If you aren't competent, you might as well be doing something else, and not waste your time.

Craftsmanship

I believe that for something to be "masterly executed" it has to possess three basic features. First, the pattern must respond to certain criteria, which are both technical and artistic. Some patterns simply don't work because it's impossible to sew and cut them out, or because the outcome isn't graceful, the balance of full and empty spaces simply isn't right. Second, it takes a lot of skill to work with the sewing machine. Third, you have to be very agile in cutting the felt around the stitches to create the pattern: for it to be perfect, the felt must be cut very close to the stitching and always at the same distance.

This technique can only be done by hand, piece by piece. You can't put it together and do it with a machine, because the machine can't stitch and cut the pattern; it has to be done manually. I suppose you could glue it on, instead of stitching it, but then it would be something completely different, and it would lose all of its charm and beauty.

Creativity

I think it's impossible to know what creativity is, because even if you change and evolve, you always go back to the origins. Even when I make new drawings for Vasconcelos, things that are more "creative", I don't lose touch with the traditions. I've developed a few projects with young designers who come here from schools: they tried to move away from the flowers because they wanted to innovate. But in the end, it's something you don't want to see! I help them to understand that it doesn't make sense, that all the drawings we make here have to do with nature, and if they don't, they aren't as beautiful.

Interpretation

When I work with Joana Vasconcelos, I have to interpret an idea that's in her head and that's part of a bigger picture that involves other crafts and techniques. It isn't always easy, but it's a challenge to which I adapt very easily, and the whole process is very smooth and natural. With her, we have pushed the traditions that are tied to this land to a different level without, however, betraying any part of the heritage that they represent. This, I believe, is the true meaning of interpretation.

Originality

Every artisan develops an individual style that's always recognizable. The patterns that are traditionally from Nisa are all based on flowers: carnations, tulips, chrysanthemums and so on. What I've done is put more detail and sophistication into these original patterns, creating designs that are finer and more difficult to execute. But the original and its evolution are always linked: every time I embroider flowers the drawing evolves, but I always go back to the original elements; it's impossible to run away. The only time you move away from the origins is when you embroider a pattern that's either modern, like a geometric pattern, or not with flowers.

I don't know if I'd be able to break the rules. Sometimes I stray, but not completely; I always go back! That's because even if I change the design and make it modern, for example, I always follow the traditional techniques.

Talent

If you are talented, you have everything. If you are talented, you can find the way to get where you want to get to. Creative talent is the most important of all, because it's what makes things progress, grow, break new ground, whereas manual skills can always be taught.

I can tell if a person is talented in this craft just by looking at the way they draw, because the pattern is fundamental in this technique. With my experience, I can make something become beautiful even if it isn't perfect, and I can correct embroideries that haven't been well executed. But this is just the "talent" that comes with experience: what is crucial is the pattern, the drawing, which is the basis of the finished product.

Territory
Nisa is famous for its very particular and precious types of embroidery, a heritage that's collected and exhibited in the Museum of Embroidery and Pottery, which has its seat in one of the traditional houses of Nisa. Apart from wool felt, the other specialities are bobbin lace, *alinhavado* (drawn thread work), needlepoint and long-stitch embroidery, cutwork embroidery and loom-made quilts.

These techniques were used by the girls and women to make their trousseaus, but since it took years to make just a bedspread or a tablecloth, the tradition gradually died out. When I was in my early 20s, one of the school inspectors decided to create an archive of all the beautiful and fine works that were made in Nisa, and an embroidery school was set up at the *Casa do Povo*, the People's House, where the traditional techniques started to be taught again. Until only 20 years ago, at least 200 embroiderers were still active in the area. Originally, all the wool felt that we used came from the Serra da Estrela, a mountainous region north of Nisa, where there were dozens of wool mills. Now most of the felt factories have closed down, and since it's very expensive to use the best quality wool felt, many people use acrylic felt in just black with another colour, not the big variety of colours that I have the opportunity to use when I work with Vasconcelos.

This technique can only be done with felt; nothing else will work. The design emerges when the top layer is cut out and the contours aren't hemmed. This means that the wool fibres of the fabric have to be pressed in a very compact way, or the fabric comes apart.

Each woman draws her own patterns, and in the old days they used whatever paper was in the house. I still have a number of the original designs, some of which are more than a hundred years old. I have boxes full of patterns that I've designed over the years. Sometimes the older people of Nisa give me their little treasure troves of old drawings, which I preserve together with mine.

Tradition and innovation
The technique of wool felt embroidery is very old and it has never changed, not even after the sewing machine was introduced and people had enough money to buy one. In fact, I believe that if there were new and more advanced ways of doing it, I'd probably be the first to use them! But I never even had a computer, and I still draw all the patterns myself, by hand.

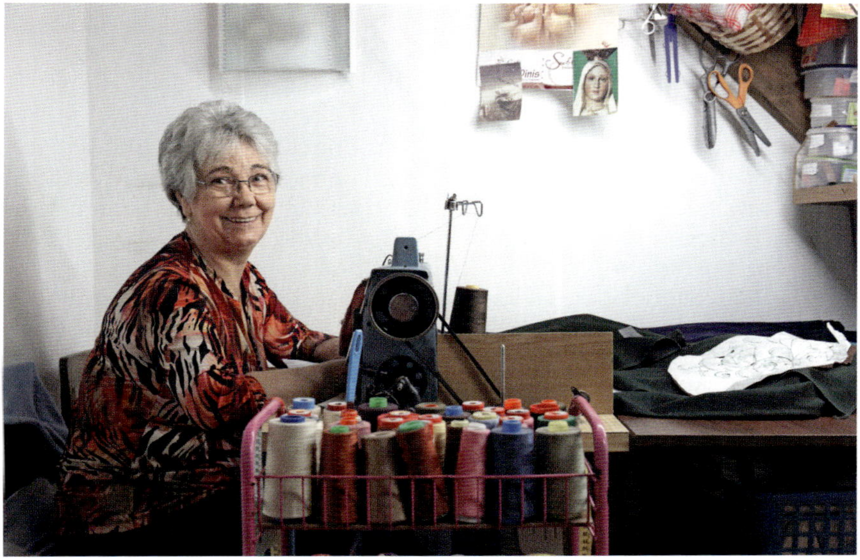

This type of embroidery is made with two overlapping layers of wool felt cloth, normally in contrasting colours, onto which the design, which is drawn on paper, is positioned with pins and then sewn along the lines of the pattern. Once the pattern is sewn, the paper is removed and the top layer of felt is cut off along the stitching until the drawing emerges. The remaining paper is patiently taken out from under the stitches with a pair of small tweezers. It's an expensive technique because it's very time-consuming and because two metres of fabric are used for every metre of the final product. We normally use the discarded cloth to make smaller things like purses, potholders, coasters, pincushions and so on.

I believe that my greatest innovation is in the patterns, which I've developed and changed in my own style. Although they are always inspired by flowers and nature, in the tradition of Nisa, my designs are more sophisticated and intricate, far more demanding in terms of time and attention to detail.

The second innovation, and probably the most significant, was brought about through my cooperation with Joana Vasconcelos. Before, our work went into a store and from there into the customers' homes, but it is now exhibited in places where everyone can see it. It's the best thing that could happen to Nisa, and it makes me sad that I am almost the only one who has benefited. The other artisans weren't open enough to accept that the purpose of our work should be so far removed from the original and traditional use and because they don't want to have to work under the pressure of a deadline.

Training

In my day, compulsory education was only up to the age of ten and after that the poorer children were sent to work as domestic helpers. Our family was so poor that my mother didn't even have enough money to buy us handkerchiefs, so if my brother and I had a cold, we would blow our noses in a piece of cotton cloth that our mother simply cut in two. I remember that I was so ashamed to show how poor we were that I hemmed this piece of cloth myself, to make it look better. I was probably not older than six or seven. I suppose that's when I discovered a natural inclination to make things more beautiful.

In the evenings I would sit by my mother's side as she was busy sewing or darning and I would ask her to give me a piece of cloth to play with. When I was 12, I went to work in the home of a lady who taught me how to cross-stitch. I still have those early embroideries. At 14 I returned to my parents' home, where I sewed men's trousers, aprons and other simple things, which I would sell to earn a little money. I also embroidered the typical Nisa shawls and blankets, which have coloured flower decorations on a white or black background.

I started to make wool felt embroideries when I was about 20, and I opened my first atelier at the age of 30. I was mostly self-taught, apart from occasional advice from other women in Nisa, and I honestly can't remember any particular moment when I realized I had mastered this craft. I believe it just came naturally. I became aware that I was pretty good at it and I soon began to create my own designs and to distance myself from what everyone else was making. I knew that this was what I wanted to do in life and I was also very determined to set up my own business, which was unheard of in those days.

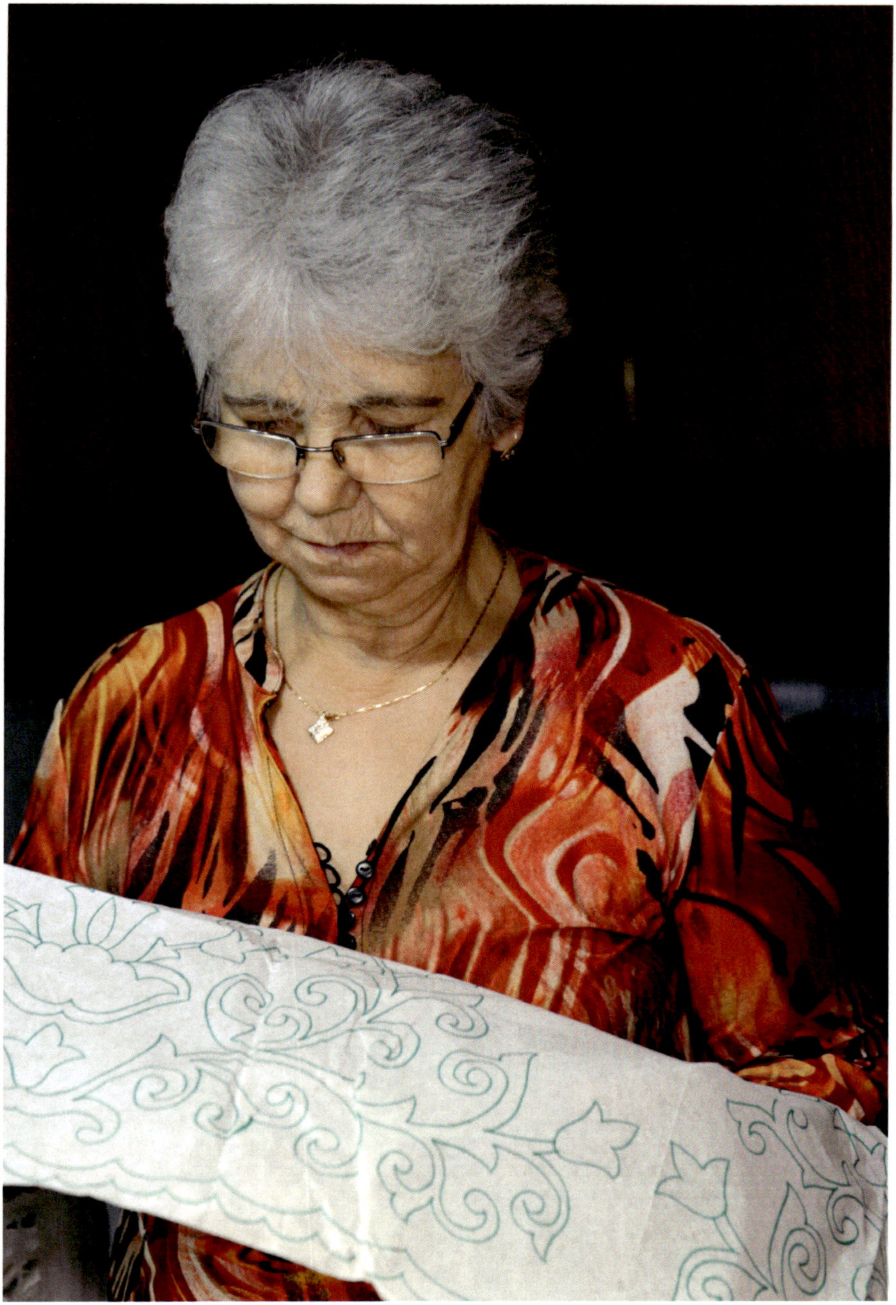

BIBLIOGRAPHY

Agins, Teri, *The End of Fashion: How Marketing Changed the Clothing Business Forever* (New York: Harper, 1999).

AIP – Associazione Italiana della Produzione, *Reti d'impresa oltre i distretti* (Milan: Casa Editrice Il Sole 24 Ore, 2008).

Ajello, Anna Maria, and Saul Meghnagi (eds), *La competenza tra flessibilità e specializzazione: Il lavoro in contesti sociali e produttivi diversi* (Milan: Franco Angeli, 2008).

Alighieri, Dante, *The Divine Comedy: Purgatory*, translated by Henry Wadsworth Longfellow (London: George Routledge & Sons, 1867).

Ambrosini, Maurizio (ed.), *Un futuro da formare: verso un nuovo sistema di formazione professionale: tendenze, valutazioni e proposte* (Brescia: Editrice la Scuola, 2000).

Are, Mario, *L'oggetto del diritto di autore* (Milan: Giuffrè, 1963).

Arendt, Hannah, *Rahel Varnhagen: The Life of a Jewess* (Baltimore: Johns Hopkins University Press, 1997).

Argan, Giulio Carlo, "La storia dell'arte", *Storia dell'arte*, No. 1–2 (1969).

Arrigone, Carlo, and Luigi Campagner, *La scuola dei talenti* (Milan: Odon, 2007).

Arrow, Kenneth J., "The Economic Implications of Learning by Doing", in *Collected Papers of Kenneth J. Arrow, Volume 5: Production and Capital* (Cambridge, MA: Harvard University Press, 1985).

Auerbach, Jeffrey A., *The Great Exhibition of 1851: A Nation on Display* (London: Yale University Press, 1999).

Barenboim, Daniel, and Edward W. Said, *Parallels and Paradoxes: Explorations in Music and Society* (London: Bloomsbury, 2004).

Bassano, Clara, *I distretti orafi italiani: Tipicità degli assetti territoriali e ruolo della comunicazione* (Naples: Edizioni Scientifiche Italiane, 2008).

Battaglia, Salvatore, *Grande Dizionario della lingua italiana* (Turin: UTET, 1966, reprinted 2004).

Battisti, Carlo, and Giovanni Alessio, *Dizionario etimologico italiano* (Florence: Barbèra, 1975).

Baudrillard, Jean, *Le système des objets* (Paris: Gallimard, 1968).

Bauer, Riccardo, *La Società Umanitaria: Fondazione P.M. Loria Milano, 1893–1963* (Milan: Società Umanitaria, 1964).

Becker, Howard S., *Art Worlds* (Berkeley and Los Angeles: University of California Press, 1982).

Bellini, Mario, "Between Styling and Design", in Tonino Paris, Carla Farina and Carlo Martino (eds), *Made in Italy: Il design degli italiani=Italians' Design* (Rome: Rdesignpress, 2005).

Benini, Romano, *Saper fare: Il modello artigiano e le radici dello stile italiano* (Rome: Donzelli, 2010).

Benjamin, Walter, "On Language as Such and on the Language of Man", in *Selected Writings, Vol. 1: 1913–1926*, edited by Marcus Bullock and Michael W. Jennings (Cambridge, MA: The Belknap Press of Harvard University Press, 1996).

Bertola, Paola, and Giovanni Conti (eds), *La Moda e il Design: Il trasferimento di conoscenza al servizio dell'innovazione* (Milan: POLI.design, 2007).

Betti, Emilio, *Teoria generale della interpretazione* (Milan: Giuffrè, 1990).

BIC Lazio – Business Innovation Centre Lazio, "Artigianato artistico: arte con qualcosa in più", *BIC Notes: Quaderno trimestrale su creazione di impresa e sviluppo locale*, No. 2 (2011).

Biscaro, Gerolamo, "La scuola dei quattro martiri coronati presso il Duomo di Milano", *Archivio Storico Lombardo: Giornale della Società storica lombarda* 20, No. 39 (1913).

Bodino, Giampiero, "Parte tutto da un'idea", *Mestieri d'Arte*, No. 4 (December 2011).

Bonaccorsi, Andrea, "La valutazione di Bertoldo", *Il Mulino*, No. 2 (May 2013).

Bordone, Renato, David Kusman and Winfried Reichert, *Dal banco dei pegni all'alta finanza: Lombardi e mercanti-banchieri fra Paesi Bassi e Inghilterra nel Trecento* (Asti: Comune di Asti, 2007).

Borgato, Renata, Ferruccio Capelli and Andrea Ceriani, *Nuovo Rinascimento: Idee per la formazione* (Milan: Franco Angeli, 2010).

Bovone, Laura, and Emanuela Mora, *Saperi e mestieri dell'industria culturale* (Milan: Franco Angeli, 2003).

Branzi, Andrea, "Milano distretto per l'innovazione", *Impresa & Stato*, No. 62 (2003).

Branzi, Andrea, *Ritratti e autoritratti di design* (Venice: Marsilio, 2010).

Branzi, Andrea, and Silvana Annicchiarico (eds), *Che Cosa è il Design Italiano? Le sette ossessioni/What is Italian Design? The seven obsessions*, translated by B. McGilvray and J. Venerella (Milan: Mondadori Electa, 2008).

Braudel, Fernand, *Le Modèle italien* (Paris: Flammarion, 2008).

Brivio, Ernesto, *Le vetrate del Duomo di Milano: Un itinerario di fede e di luce* (Milan: Cassa di Risparmio delle Province Lombarde, 1973).

Bucci, Ampelio, Vanni Codeluppi and Mauro Ferraresi, *Il Made in Italy: Natura, settori e problemi* (Rome: Carocci, 2011).

Buss, Chiara, *Seta, oro, cremisi: Segreti e tecnologia alla corte dei Visconti e degli Sforza* (Cinisello Balsamo: Silvana Editoriale, 2009).

Campagna, Luigia Mirella, and Attilio Pasetto, "Artigianato e piccole imprese: Strategie di innovazione e di esportazione nel mercato globale", *Quaderni di ricerca sull'artigianato: Rivista di Economia, Cultura e Ricerca sociale dell'Associazione Artigiani e Piccole Imprese Mestre CGIA*, No. 58 (2nd quarter 2011).

Cantù, Cesare, *Grande illustrazione del Lombardo-Veneto* (Milan: Corona e Caimi Editori, 1858–1861).

Cappellieri, Alba, *Moda e Design: Il progetto dell'eccellenza* (Milan: Franco Angeli, 2007).

Carcano, Luana, *Maestri del mare: La nautica italiana, una storia di eccellenza* (Venice: Marsilio, 2011).

Carcano, Luana, Antonio Catalani and Paola Varacca Capello, *Il gioiello italiano ad una svolta: Dalla crisi alla costruzione di nuove opportunità* (Milan: Franco Angeli, 2005).

Carini, Alessandra, "Il cuore della meccanica tra via Emilia e il West", in *Affari e Finanza*, supplement of *La Repubblica* (19 May 2008).

Castelfranchi Vegas, Liana (ed.), *Arti minori* (Milan: Jaca Book, 2000).

Castro, Maurizio, "Il settore orafo tra innovazione e tradizione", in Alba Cappellieri (ed.), *Gioiello italiano contemporaneo: Tecniche e materiali tra arte e design* (Milan: Skira, 2008).

Cattaneo, Carlo, "Milano sotto gli Sforza: Principio della Signoria di Spagna", in Antonio Zoncada (ed.), *I fasti delle lettere in Italia nel corrente secolo additati alla studiosa gioventù dal professore Antonio Zoncada: Prose* (Milan: Giacomo Gnocchi, 1853).

Cattaneo, Enrico, *Il contributo delle corporazioni nella costruzione del Duomo* (Milan: Nuove Edizioni Duomo, 1979).

Cavalli, Alberto, "Tradizione e innovazione", in Paolo Colombo (ed.), *A regola d'arte: Attualità e prospettive dei mestieri d'arte in Lombardia e Canton Ticino* (Milan: Vita e Pensiero, 2005).

Cavalli, Alberto, "Vmeste s Beatrice", *Kak Potratit*, No. 12 (December 2009).

Cavalli, Alberto, "Cerez' ser'dze", *Kak Potratit*, No. 2 (February 2011).

Celaschi, Flaviano, "Osare pensare il design del lusso", in Flaviano Celaschi, Alba Cappellieri and Alessandra Vasile (eds), *Lusso versus Design: Italian design, beni culturali e luxury system – Alto di gamma & cultura di progetto* (Milan: Franco Angeli, 2007).

Cellini, Benvenuto, *The Life of Benvenuto Cellini*, translated into English by John Addington Symonds, 3rd edition (New York: Horace Liveright, 1932), https://archive.org/stream/lifeofbenvenutocoocell#page/n3/mode/2up.

Censis – Centro Studi Investimenti Sociali, "Il ciclo lungo della ristrutturazione", *IV Rapporto Osservatorio Nazionale Distretti Italiani* (2013), www.osservatoriodistretti.org/sites/default/files/IV-rapporto-osservatorio-distretti.pdf.

Checchi, Daniele, "Valutazione: c'è un medicinale adatto?", *Il Mulino*, No. 466 (February 2013).

Cheng, François, *The Way of Beauty: Five Meditations for Spiritual Transformation* (Rochester: Inner Traditions, 2009).

Chinea, Eleuterio, *Dalle antiche Botteghe d'Arti e Mestieri alle prime Scuole Industriali e Commerciali in Lombardia* (Milan: Prem. Tip. San Giuseppe, 1933).

Chiostrini Mannini, Anna, *Il bello dell'utile: Ceramiche Ginori e Richard Ginori dal 1750 al 1950* (Florence: Polistampa, 2001).

Colbert, Jean Baptiste, *The political testament of M. Jean Baptist Colbert, minister and Secretary of State wherein is contain'd all that hath pass'd under the reign of Lewis the XIV unto the year 1684: with remarks upon the government of the kingdom of France*, translated from French by William Granville (London: Printed for R. Bentley, 1695).

Cologni, Franco (ed.) *A regola d'arte: Attualità e prospettive dei mestieri d'arte in Lombardia e Canton Ticino* (Milan: Vita e Pensiero, 2005).

Cologni, Franco, "La mente creativa, la mano intelligente: il 'codice' Cellini", in Paolo Colombo (ed.), *La Grande Europa dei mestieri d'arte: L'artigianato artistico d'eccellenza nei Paesi dell'Unione Europea* (Milan: Vita e Pensiero, 2007).

Cologni, Franco, "Revers", *Monsieur*, No. 78 (June 2009).

Cologni, Franco, “La scuola dello stile”, *AD*, No. 342 (November 2009).

Cologni, Franco, “Onore al merito”, *AD*, No. 342 (November 2009).

Cologni, Franco, “Revers”, *Monsieur*, No. 92 (November 2010).

Cologni, Franco, “Revers”, *Monsieur*, No. 95 (February 2011).

Cologni, Franco, *Le Esposizioni Universali: I mestieri d'arte sulla scena del mondo (1851–2010)* (Venice: Marsilio, 2012).

Cologni, Franco, “È solo la passione a dare senso al lavoro”, *Mestieri d'Arte & Design*, No. 7 (April 2013).

Cologni, Franco, and Alberto Cavalli, “Dall'etica all'estetica”, *AD*, No. 366 (November 2011).

Colombo, Paolo, (ed.) *Genio e materia: Contributi per una definizione del mestiere d'arte* (Milan: Vita e Pensiero, 2000).

Colombo, Paolo, Alberto Cavalli and Gioachino Lanotte (eds), *Mestieri d'arte e Made in Italy: Giacimenti culturali da riscoprire* (Venice: Marsilio, 2009).

Colombo, Paolo, Alberto Cavalli and Emanuela Mora, *Artefici di bellezza: Mestieri d'arte nella moda italiana* (Venice: Marsilio, 2013).

Cordaro, Michele, “La storia dell'arte nella concezione di Argan”, in *Annali dell'Associazione Bianchi Bandinelli* (founded by Giulio Carlo Argan), No. 12 (Rome: Graffiti, 2002).

Corradi, Fiammetta (ed.), *Alla ricerca dell'eccellenza: Le politiche per l'eccellenza nell'istruzione superiore in quattro Paesi europei* (Milan: Edizioni Universitarie di Lettere Economia Diritto, 2009).

Corriere della Sera, *Manifesto per il Talento* (2012), www.corriere.it/economia/speciali/2012/manifesto-del-talento/index.shtml.

Courtilz de Sandras, Gatien, and Jean-Baptiste Colbert, *Testament politique de Messire Jean-Baptiste Colbert, ministre et secrétaire d'Etat, où l'on voit tout ce qui s'est passé sous le règne de Louis le Grand jusqu'en l'année 1684, avec des remarques sur le gouvernement du royaume* (The Hague: Henry van Bulderen, 1694).

Cunaccia, Cesare, “La costante dell'effimero”, in *Italian Style, 1945–2007: La sfida italiana*, edited by AD – Architectural Digest Italia (Milan: Condé Nast, 2007).

Cunaccia, Cesare, and Vittoria Filippi Gabardi, *The Whispered Directory of Craftsmanship: A Contemporary Guide to the Italian Handmaking Ability*, Vols 1 and 2 (Milan: Mondadori Electa, 2010–2011).

D'Alembert, Le Rond Jean Baptiste, “Preliminary Discourse”, in *The Encyclopedia of Diderot & d'Alembert Collaborative Translation Project*, translated by Richard N. Schwab and Walter E. Rex (Ann Arbor: Michigan Publishing, University of Michigan Library, 2009), http://hdl.handle.net/2027/spo.did2222.0001.083. Originally published as “Discours préliminaire”. *Encyclopédie ou Dictionnaire raisonné des sciences, des arts et des métiers,* Vol. 1 (Paris: 1751).

Dal Falco, Federica, “Puzzle”, in Tonino Paris, Carla Farina and Carlo Martini (eds), *Made in Italy: Il Design degli italiani* (Rome: Rdesignpress, 2005).

Dardanello, Ferruccio, “Premessa”, in *L'Italia che verrà: Industria culturale, made in Italy e territori*, I Quaderni di Symbola (Unioncamere and Symbola Fondazione per la Qualità Italiane, 2011), www.symbola.net/assets/files/Ricerca%20Industrie%20culturali_1326723510.pdf.

De Balzac, Honoré, *Trattato della vita elegante* (Pisa: ETS, 1998), first published in French in 1830 as *Traité de la vie élégante*.

De Fusco, Renato, "Il Paese degli elettrodomestici. Anni 50: il boom, iniziano i consumi di massa", *L'Europeo*, Special issue of *Triennale Design Museum* (2007).
De Fusco, Renato, *Made in Italy: Storia del design italiano* (Milan: Laterza, 2007).
De la Riva, Bonvesin, *Le meraviglie di Milano*, translated from Latin by Giuseppe Pontiggia (Milan: Bompiani, 2010).
De Masi, Domenico, *Il futuro del lavoro* (Milan: Rizzoli, 2003).
De Michelis, Cesare, "Dopo la modernità, l'emozionante ricerca della regola del Talento", in *La regola del talento: Mestieri d'arte e Scuole italiane di eccellenza* (Venice: Marsilio, 2014).
De Sanctis, Vittorio M., *Il carattere creativo delle opere dell'ingegno* (Milan: Giuffrè, 1971).
De Santillana, Giorgio, and Hertha von Dechend, *Hamlet's Mill: An Essay Investigating the Origins of Human Knowledge and its Transmission through Myth* (Jaffrey: David R. Godine Publisher, 1977).
De Sole, Domenico, "Gucci e i mestieri d'arte". In Paolo Colombo (ed.), *Genio e Materia: Contributi per una definizione del mestiere d'arte* (Milan: Vita e Pensiero, 2000).
De Vecchi, Pierluigi, and Elda Cerchiari, *Arte nel tempo: Dal Gotico Internazionale alla Maniera Moderna* (Milan: Bompiani, 1996).
Delisle, Jean-Michel, "Giornate Europee, i mestieri d'arte entrano in scena", *Mestieri d'Arte & Design*, No. 7 (April 2013).
Delmarcel, Guy (ed.), *Gli Arazzi dei Gonzaga nel Rinascimento* (Milan: Skira, 2010).
Devoto, Giacomo, and Gian Carlo Oli, *Il dizionario della lingua italiana* (Florence: Le Monnier, 2002–2003).
Devoto, Giacomo, and Gian Carlo Oli, *Vocabolario della lingua italiana* (Florence: Le Monnier, 2011).
Di Lucchio, Loredana, "Design: Dall'economia all'ecopatia", in Tonino Paris, Carla Farina, and Carlo Martini (eds), *Made in Italy: Il design degli italiani* (Rome: Rdesignpress, 2005).
Di Vico, Dario, *Piccoli, La pancia del Paese* (Venice: Marsilio, 2010).
Di Vico, Dario, "Le scuole d'arte e i mestieri da salvare", *Corriere della Sera* (6 April 2010).
Diderot, Denis, *Encyclopédie ou Dictionnaire raisonné des sciences, des arts et des métiers* (Paris: Chez Briasson, 1765).
Dizionario di scienze dell'educazione (Rome: LAS, 2008).
Dorfles, Gillo, "Quando perdemmo gli ornamenti: Il design industriale esordisce nel segno del razionalismo", *L'Europeo*, Special issue of *Triennale Design Museum* (2007).
Dorfles, Gillo, "Finalmente è pace tra design e artigianato", *Mestieri d'Arte*, No. 1 (June 2010).

Eco, Umberto, *I limiti dell'interpretazione* (Milan: Bompiani, 1990).
Eco, Umberto, *The Limits of Interpretation* (Bloomington and Indianapolis: Indiana University Press, 1994).
Eco, Umberto (ed.) *History of Beauty* (New York: Rizzoli, 2004).

Fabbrizzi, Fabio, *Opere e progetti di scuola fiorentina, 1968–2008* (Florence: Alinea Editrice, 2009).

Focillon, Henri, *Vie des formes: suivi de Éloge de la main* (Paris: Presses Universitaires de France, 1943).

Focillon, Henri, *The Life of Forms in Art*, 2nd English edition, enlarged (New York: Wittenborn, Schultz, 1948).

Fondazione Aldo Morelato (ed.), *Il mobile significante: Gli oggetti d'arredo e la strumentazione telematica; Giornate Internazionali di Studio Villa Dionisi 2008* (Santarcangelo di Romagna: Maggioli, 2008).

Fondazione Cologni dei Mestieri d'Arte and Fondazione Deutsche Bank Italia, *La regola del talento: Mestieri d'arte e Scuole italiane di eccellenza* (Venice: Marsilio, 2014).

Fontana, Ciro, *L'attività creatrice come oggetto del diritto di autore* (Bergamo: Bolis, 1953).

Forti Grazzini, Nello, *Gli Arazzi dei Mesi Trivulzio: il committente, l'iconografia* (Milan: Cordani, 1992).

Foucault, Michel, *The Order of Things: An archaeology of the human sciences* (New York: Vintage Books, 1994).

Furlanis, Giuseppe, "Design e artigianato", in Maria Pilar Lebole (ed.), *L'Arte del Fare e il Fare Arte: Lezioni, approfondimenti e confronti sull'artigianato artistico fra tradizione e innovazione* (Florence: Edifir, 2004).

Gandolfi, Giuseppe, *Sviluppare il potenziale nelle professioni, nel lavoro, nello studio, nello sport… Approcci, metodi, applicazioni* (Milan: Franco Angeli, 2009).

Gardner, John W., *Excellence: Can We Be Equal and Excellent Too?* (New York: Harper & Brothers Publishers, 1961).

Garroni, Emilio, *Creatività* (Macerata: Quodlibet, 2010).

Genovesi, Emilio, "Officina Italia", in Giovanni Lanzone and Francesco Morace (eds), *Il talento dell'impresa: L'impronta rinascimentale in dieci aziende italiane* (Milan: Nomos, 2010).

Gheno, Stefano, *La formazione generativa: Un nuovo approccio all'apprendimento e al benessere delle persone e delle organizzazioni* (Milan: Franco Angeli, 2010).

Gioia, Melchiorre, *Opere minori*, Vol. 14 (Lugano: G. Ruggia, 1835).

Giordani Aragno, Bonizza, "Italian Fashion", in Charlotte Seeling (ed.), *Fashion: The Century of the Designer, 1900–1999* (Cologne: Könemann Verlagsgesellschaft mbH, 2000).

Givone, Sergio, "Socrate e il calzolaio", in Stefania Ricci (ed.), *Il calzolaio prodigioso: Fiabe e leggende di scarpe e calzolai* (Milan: Skira, 2013).

Gobbi, Linda, "L'Impronta Rinascimentale dalla prima persona singolare alla prima persona plurale", in Giovanni Lanzone and Francesco Morace (eds), *Il talento dell'impresa: L'impronta rinascimentale in dieci aziende italiane* (Milan: Nomos, 2010).

Goruppi, Tiziana, "Introduzione", in Honoré de Balzac, *Trattato della vita elegante* (Pisa: ETS, 1998).

Goubert, Pierre, and Daniel Roche, *L'Ancien Régime, Volume secondo: Cultura e Società* (Milan: Jaca Book, 1987), pp. 321–322. First published in French as *Les Français et l'Ancien Régime, Tome 2: Culture et société* (Paris: A. Colin, 1984).

Grianti, Chiara, "Anarchico e felice", *Business People* (16 May 2008), www.businesspeople.it/People/Cover-Story/Anarchico-e-felice_2593.

Hegel, Georg Wilhelm Friedrich, *Aesthetics: Lectures on Fine Art*, translated by T.M. Knox (Oxford: Oxford University Press, 1975).

Iannuzzi, Fabio, "Arte e artigianato: Lineamenti di una storia dei mestieri d'arte", in Paolo Colombo (ed.), *Genio e materia: contributi per una definizione del mestiere d'arte* (Milan: Vita e Pensiero, 2000).
Intiglietta, Antonio (ed.), *Nelle mani dell'artigiano* (Milan: Guerini e Associati, 2007).
Iuzzolino, Giovanni, *Rilevanza delle agglomerazioni industriali in Italia nel confronto internazionale* www.osservatoriodistretti.org/sites/default/files/distretti-2012-cap-3.pdf.

Kuik, Onnu, Ståle Navrud and David W. Pearce, "Benefit Estimation and Environmental Decision-making", in Ståle Navrud (ed.), *Pricing the European Environment* (Oslo: Scandinavian University Press, 1992).

La Pietra, Ugo, "Design e Artigianato", *Artigianato tra arte e design*, No. 70 (July–September 2008).
La Pietra, Ugo, "Dov'è l'Artigianato?", *Artigianato tra arte e design*, No. 75 (September–November 2009)
La Pietra, Ugo, "In difesa di una vera cultura del fare", *Mestieri d'Arte*, No. 1 (June 2010).
La Pietra, Ugo, "Auto-produzione (da non confondersi con autopromozione)", *Mestieri d'Arte & Design*, No. 5 (April 2011).
Lacroix, Christian, "Préface", in Amandine Maziers and Johanna de Tessières (eds), *L'oeil et la main: Les artisans de la haute couture* (Paris: Éditions du Collectionneur, 2005).
Lai, Franco (ed.), *Fare e saper fare: I saperi locali in una prospettiva antropologica* (Cagliari: Cuec, 2004).
Lanzone, Giovanni, and Francesco Morace (eds), *Il talento dell'impresa: L'impronta rinascimentale in dieci aziende italiane* (Milan: Nomos, 2010).
Le Corbusier, *L'art décoratif d'aujourd'hui* (Paris: Crès et Cie, 1925).
Levi Pisetzky, Rosita, *Il costume e la moda nella società italiana* (Turin: Einaudi, 1985).
Lipovetsky, Gilles, and Elyette Roux, *Le luxe éternel. De l'âge du sacré au temps des marques* (Paris: Gallimard, 2003).
Lucibello, Sabrina, "Tutto è design?", in Tonino Paris, Carla Farina and Carlo Martini (eds), *Made in Italy: Il Design degli italiani* (Rome: Rdesignpress, 2005).

Malaguzzi Valeri, Francesco, *La corte di Ludovico il Moro: la vita privata e l'arte a Milano nella seconda metà del quattrocento* (Milan: Hoepli, 1913).
Malossi, Giannino, with Carola Traverso and Emanuela di Pasqua, "Pomeriggi alla meta-industria", in Marco Richetti and Enrico Cietta (eds), *Il valore della moda: Industria e servizi in un settore guidato dall'innovazione* (Milan: Mondadori, 2006).
Mancinelli, Antonio, Flaminio Gualdoni and Omar Calabrese (eds), *Corneliani* (Bologna: FMR, 2008).
Marzano, Michela, "'Pubblica o muori': quel nuovo sistema che spegne il sapere", *Repubblica* (17 February 2013).
Mathiot, Pascal, *Passaggi singolari: Saggio sulla trasmissione dei saperi* (Milan: Vita e Pensiero, 2003).
Mazzanti, Massimiliano, *Metodi e strumenti di analisi per la valutazione economica del patrimonio culturale* (Milan: Franco Angeli, 2011).
Mazzucotelli Salice, Silvia, and Isabella Medicina, *Maestri del fare: Indagine socio-economica sulla domanda di mestieri d'arte a Milano* (Venice: Marsilio, 2012).

Medici, Giuseppe, "Editorial", *Affari esteri*, No. 1 (1969).

Melegati, Luca, *Le porcellane europee al Castello Sforzesco* (Milan: Civiche Raccolte d'Arte Applicata, 1999).

Messina, Marina, "Questi sono capi d'opera", *Mestieri d'Arte & Design*, No. 5 (April 2012).

Meucci, Renato. *Strumentaio: il costruttore di strumenti musicali nella tradizione occidentale* (Venice: Marsilio, 2008).

Micelli, Stefano, *Futuro artigiano* (Venice: Marsilio, 2011).

Michelsons, Angelo (ed.), *L'artigianato in Europa e in Italia* (Turin: Osservatorio dell'Artigianato della Regione Piemonte, 2003).

Minetti, Maria Giulia, *Il Mobile batte la Moda* (13 April 2008), www.lastampa.it/2008/04/13/societa/il-mobile-batte-la-moda-dwFugNPoAsbzAUT5VWEcqK/pagina.html.

Mocchetti, Ettore, *Il mobile significante: Gli oggetti d'arredo e la strumentazione telematica. Giornate Internazionali di Studio Villa Dionisi 2008* (Santarcangelo di Romagna: Maggioli, 2008).

Morace, Francesco, and Giovanni Lanzone, *Verità e bellezza: Una scommessa per il futuro dell'Italia* (Milan: Nomos, 2010).

Mori, Giovanna, *La collezione dei vetri artistici* (Milan: Civiche Raccolte d'Arte Applicata, 1996).

Morini, Enrica, *Storia della moda. XVIII–XX secolo* (Milan: Skira, 2006).

Morone, Piergiuseppe, *Conoscenza, nuove disuguaglianze e tecnologia dell'informazione* (Soveria Mannelli: Rubbettino, 2004).

Mukerji, Chandra, *Territorial Ambitions and the Gardens of Versailles* (Cambridge: Cambridge University Press, 1997).

Nebbia, Ugo, *La scultura nel Duomo di Milano* (Milan: Amministrazione della Fabbrica del Duomo, 1907).

Nii, Rie, "20th Century – Second Half", in Akiko Fukai (ed.), *Fashion: The Collection of the Kyoto Costume Institute: A History from the 18th to the 20th Century* (Los Angeles: Taschen, 2002).

Nocentini, Alberto, *L'Etimologico: Vocabolario della lingua italiana* (Milan: Mondadori Education S.p.A., 2010).

Nove, Aldo, *Milano non è Milano* (Bari: Laterza, 2004).

Ornaghi, Lorenzo, "Per la definizione del mestiere d'arte", in Paolo Colombo (ed.), *Genio e Materia: Contributi per una definizione del mestiere d'arte* (Milan: Vita e Pensiero, 2000).

Orsi Landini, Roberta, "La Sala Bianca", in Guido Vergani (ed.), *La Sala Bianca: Nascita della moda italiana* (Milan: Electa, 1992).

Pambianco, Carlo, with Luca Testoni, *I signori dello stile: Rivoluzione e successo della moda italiana nel mondo* (Milan: Sperling & Kupfer, 2008).

Pansera, Anty, and Maria Teresa Chirico, *1923–1930, Monza, verso l'unità delle arti: oggetti d'eccezione dalle esposizioni internazionali di arti decorative* (Cinisello Balsamo: Silvana, 2004).

Pasqualotto, Giangiorgio, "Avanguardia e tradizione tra Oriente e Occidente", in Luigi Bonotto, Roberto Melchiori and Tiziano Santi (eds), *Fatticità dell'arte: il fare artistico tra etica e tecnica* (Rome: Derive Approdi, 2001).

Pedroni, Marco, and Lucia Ruggerone, "La moda nelle discipline sociali", in Paola

Bertola and Giovanni Conti (eds), *La moda e il design: Il trasferimento di conoscenza a servizio dell'innovazione* (Milan: POLI.design, 2007).

Pedroni, Marco, and Paolo Volonté (eds), *La Creatività nelle professioni: Atti del convegno (Bolzano, 14 febbraio 2007)* (Bolzano: Bozen-Bolzano University Press, 2007).

Pevsner, Nikolaus, *Pioneers of the Modern Movement: From William Morris to Walter Gropius* (London: Faber & Faber, 1936).

Pirina, Caterina, "Le vetrate del Duomo di Milano dai Visconti agli Sforza", in *Corpus Vitrearum Medii Aevi*, Italia IV, La Lombardia, Vol. 1 (Milan: Provincia, 1973).

Piva, Paolo (ed.), *L'arte medievale nel contesto (300–1300): funzioni, iconografia, tecniche* (Milan: Jaca Book, 2006).

Pollini, Gabriele, "Appartenenza socio-territoriale e identità personale tra localismo, nazionalismo e cosmopolitismo", in Ilaria Riccioni (ed.), *Comunicazione, cultura, territorio: Contributi della sociologia contemporanea. Atti del convegno 30–31 maggio 2008, Libera Università di Bolzano* (Milan-Udine: Mimesis, 2008).

Pons Alain (ed.), *Enciclopedia o dizionario ragionato delle scienze, delle arti e dei mestieri, 1751–1772* (Milan: Feltrinelli, 1966).

Prellezo, José Manuel, Carlo Nanni and Guglielmo Malizia (eds), *Dizionario di scienze dell'educazione* (Rome: Libreria Ateneo Salesiano, 2008).

Realacci, Ermete, "Premessa", in *L'Italia che verrà. Industria culturale, made in Italy e territori*, I Quaderni de Symbola (Unioncamere and Symbola Fondazione per la Qualità Italiane, 2011), www.symbola.net/assets/files/Ricerca%20Industrie%20 culturali_1326723510.pdf.

Ricca, Manfredi and Robins, Rebecca, *Meta-luxury: Brands and the Culture of Excellence* (New York: Palgrave MacMillan, 2012).

Ricciardi, Antonio, "Le PMI localizzate nei Distretti industriali: vantaggi competitivi, evoluzione organizzativa, prospettive future", *Quaderni di ricerca sull'artigianato: Rivista di Economia, Cultura e Ricerca sociale dell'Associazione Artigiani e Piccole Imprese Mestre CGIA*, No. 54 (1/2010), www.quaderniartigianato.com/wp-content/ uploads/2011/05/4_A.Ricciardi-Le-PMI-localizzate-nei-distretti_N°54.pdf.

Rizzini, Marialuisa, "Penelope ha fatto il suo tempo'? Dilettantismo e professionalità nei lavori femminili a Milano tra Otto e Novecento", in *Arti Nobili a Milano, 1815–1915* (Milan: Electa, 1994).

Roncaccioli, Angela, *Aspetti caratteristici e lineamenti evolutivi dell'artigianato urbano: Il caso di Verona* (Padua: CEDAM, 1991).

Rullani, Enzo, "Dopo Taylor: il nuovo rapporto tra conoscenza e produzione", in Andrea Ranieri (ed.), *Il sapere e il lavoro* (Milan: Franco Angeli, 2008).

Sacco, Pier Luigi (ed.), *Il sistema delle Industrie Culturali e Creative in Lombardia: elementi per un nuovo modello di competitività territoriale* (Milan: Fondazione Università IULM, 2011).

Salsano, Emanuele, *Lineamenti di sviluppo locale: I distretti industriali* (Naples: Liguori, 2002).

Santoni Rugiu, Antonio, *Il braccio e la mente: Un millennio di educazione divaricata* (Scandicci: La Nuova Italia, 1995).

Sassu, Antonio (ed.), *Saperi locali in Sardegna: Tradizione e innovazione nell'attività economica* (Cagliari: Cuec, 2004).

Schmutzler, Robert, *Art Nouveau* (New York: H.N. Abrams, 1962).

Schwartz, Gilson, *Iconomics: Challenges for Theory and Policy* (São Paulo: City of Knowledge Research Group, Dept. of Film, Radio and TV, School of Communication and Arts, University of São Paolo, Brazil, 2009), www.oecd.org/site/progresskorea/43699825.pdf.
Sennett, Richard, *The Craftsman* (New Haven: Yale University Press, 2008).
Shell, Janice, "Scultori in bottega", in Mauro Natale (ed.), *Scultura lombarda del Rinascimento: I monumenti Borromeo* (Turin: Allemandi, 1997).
"La Signoria dei Visconti (1310–1392)", in *Storia di Milano*, Vol. 5 (Milan: Fondazione Treccani degli Alfieri per la Storia di Milano, 1955).
Simmel, Georg, "Fashion", *The American Journal of Sociology*, Vol. 62 No. 6 (May 1957), pp. 541–58. Originally published in *International Quarterly*, No. X (October 1904), pp. 130–55.
Siniscalchi, Valeria, "Saperi, economia e territorio nella costruzione di un prodotto tipico: i 'tourtons' delle Hautes-Alpes (Francia)", in Franco Lai (ed.), *Fare e saper fare: I saperi locali in una prospettiva antropologica* (Cagliari: Cuec, 2004).

Tenti, Gianluca, "La bottega delle meraviglie ci salverà", *Mestieri d'Arte & Design*, No. 7 (April 2013).
Thomas, Dana, *Deluxe: How Luxury Lost Its Luster* (London: Penguin Books, 2008).
Traini, Clelia, *Orgoglio italiano: Made in Italy. Innovazione e tecnologia* (N.p.: SEA, 2006).
Treccani, Giovanni, *Dizionario Enciclopedico Italiano* (Rome: Istituto Poligrafico dello Stato, 1970).

Unioncamere Lombardia, Ufficio studi e informazione economica per lo sviluppo locale (ed.), *Dossier Artigianato* (April 2010), www.unioncamerelombardia.it/images/File/OE%20-%20Dossier/DOSSIER%20ARTIGIANATO_aprile2010.pdf.
Urbani, Giovanni, *Intorno al restauro* (Milan: Skira, 2000).

Vacca, Federica, *Design sul filo della tradizione* (Bologna: Pitagora, 2013).
Vasari, Giorgio, *Lives of the Most Eminent Painters, Sculptors and Architects*, translated by Gaston du C. de Vere (New York: Modern Library, 2006), www.gutenberg.org/files/25326/25326-h/25326-h.htm.
Vercelloni, Matteo, *Breve storia del design italiano* (Rome: Carocci, 2008).
Vico, Giambattista, *Selected Writings*, edited and translated by Leon Pompa (Cambridge: Cambridge University Press, 1982).
Villa, Virginia (ed.), *Costruttori di armonie: La liuteria, dalla materia al gesto* (Venice: Marsilio, 2012). Published in conjunction with the exhibition of the same name, held at the Milan Auditorium Fondazione Cariplo (5 December 2012–5 May 2013).
Vitiello, Giuseppe, "Oggetto, percezione e astrazione in fisica", in Fabrizio Desideri and Giovanni Matteucci (eds), *Dall'oggetto estetico all'oggetto artistico* (Florence: Firenze University Press, 2006).
Vitta, Maurizio, "Storia di una tradizione", in Ugo La Pietra (ed.), *Ad Arte: Tradizione e innovazione nell'Artigianato Artistico Lombardo* (Milan: Cestec, 2004).

Wright, Frank Lloyd, *A Testament* (New York: Horizon Press, 1957).

Zingarelli, Nicola, *Vocabolario della lingua italiana* (Bologna: Zanichelli, 2010).
Zoppè, Leandro, *Arti e mestieri in Lombardia: 2000 anni di vita artigiana* (Cinisello Balsamo: Credito Artigiano, 1992).

ACKNOWLEDGEMENTS

The authors wish to thank everyone involved in the research who made this publication possible:

Carlo Amadori, artist, international event organizer and creator of initiatives, including the Salone dell'Arte del Restauro e della Conservazione dei Beni Culturali ed Ambientali in Ferrara.

Ettore Bocchia, master chef at Villa Serbelloni and founder of Italian molecular cuisine.

Gisella Capponi, Director of Rome's Istituto Superiore per la Conservazione ed il Restauro (ISCR), with Lidia Rissotto, former director of the ISCR Scuola di Alta Formazione e Studio, and Anna Maria Marcone, director of the ISCR Laboratori di Restauro.

Marco Ciurcina, information technology legal expert, Studiolegale.it.

Jean-Michel Delisle, former President of the Institut National des Métiers d'Art, Paris.

Cesare Fumagalli, Secretary General of Confartigianato Imprese.

Mariapia Garavaglia, President of the Fondazione Manlio e Maria Letizia Germozzi Onlus.

Ugo La Pietra, artist and designer, lecturer in applied arts, historian, creator and organizer of exhibitions and cultural events, and creative director of the *Mestieri d'Arte & Design* magazine.

Isabella Medicina, researcher.

Stefano Micelli, professor of business economics at Università Ca' Foscari, Venice.

Anty Pansera, applied arts historian and critic, President of the D-come Design Association and former President of the Istituto Superiore per le Industrie Artistiche (ISIA), Faenza.

Pat Reynolds, administrator, Heritage Crafts Association, York.

Juan-Carlos Torres, former CEO, Vacheron Constantin.

Virginia Villa, Director General of the Violin Museum, Cremona.

Verena Zahn, secretary of the head of the Legal Department, Zentralverband des Deutschen Handwerks (ZDH), Berlin.

The Japanese Ministry of Economy, Trade, and Industry (METI), via the METI Public Relations Office, Tokyo.

We would like to thank the master artisans who gave their time generously and affectionately to this research. Their contribution, which this publication includes, is an authentic and valuable expression of the finest artistic crafts.

We further extend our thanks to Barbara Geary Truan and Elizabeth Coleman of the Michelangelo Foundation for Creativity and Craftsmanship and to Alessandra de Nitto, Federica Cavriana and Francesca Sammartino of the Cologni Foundation for the Métiers d'Art.

Our gratitude goes also to Alba Cappellieri, Sandra Jaeschke, Paola Locati, Aviva Obst, Kitty Oliveira for their invaluable assistance.

A very special thank you to Joana Vasconcelos.

Photo credits

Carlo Andreacchio with his son Massimiliano: © Emanuele Zamponi
Ludovic Avenel: TBertelsen / © MichelangeloFoundation2016
José Luis Bazán: SPozzoli / © MichelangeloFoundation2016
Sophie Beale: TBertelsen / © MichelangeloFoundation2016
Marc-Jens Biegel: TBertelsen / © MichelangeloFoundation2016
Renata Casartelli: SPozzoli / © MichelangeloFoundation2016
Caterina Crepax: SPozzoli / © MichelangeloFoundation2016
Elena Dal Cortivo: TBertelsen / © MichelangeloFoundation2016
Elke Dannenberg: TBertelsen / © MichelangeloFoundation2016
Ulrike Dederer: TBertelsen / © MichelangeloFoundation2016
Gérard Desquand: SPozzoli / © MichelangeloFoundation2016
Philippe Dufour: courtesy of Philippe Dufour
Alessandro Rametta and Andrea Capriotti of La Fucina di Efesto: TBertelsen / © MichelangeloFoundation2016
Pierluigi Ghianda: © Emanuele Zamponi
Pino Grasso with his daughter Raffaella: TBertelsen / © MichelangeloFoundation2016
Keith Levett: TBertelsen / © MichelangeloFoundation2016
Eugenio Monti Colla: © Susanna Pozzoli
Gio Batta Morassi: © italia-sumisura.it – Dario Garofalo
Dinis Pereira: SPozzoli / © MichelangeloFoundation2016
Lorenzo Rossi: © italia-sumisura.it – Dario Garofalo
Gabriella Sacchi: © italia-sumisura.it – Dario Garofalo
Filippo Villa: © Peter Elovich

Repro
Studio Pointer s.r.l., Mogliano Veneto (Treviso)

Printed by
L.E.G.O. s.p.a., Vicenza
for Marsilio Editori® s.p.a. in Venice

EDITION	YEAR
10 9 8 7 6 5 4 3 2 1	2017 2018 2019 2020 2021